Remedies

Remedies

THE CITY
LAW SCHOOL
CITY, UNIVERSITY OF LONDON
—— EST 1894 ——

Authors

Julie Browne, Associate Professor of Law, The City Law School
Nigel Duncan, Professor Emeritus of Legal Education, The City Law School
David Emmet, Barrister, former Reader, The City Law School
Peter Hungerford-Welch, Barrister, Professor of Law & Associate Dean,
The City Law School
Nikki Walsh, Solicitor, Senior Lecturer & Associate Dean, The City Law School

Editor

David Emmet, Barrister, former Reader, The City Law School

Series Editor

Julie Browne, Associate Professor of Law, The City Law School

OXFORD
UNIVERSITY PRESS

OXFORD
UNIVERSITY PRESS

Great Clarendon Street, Oxford, OX2 6DP,
United Kingdom

Oxford University Press is a department of the University of Oxford.
It furthers the University's objective of excellence in research, scholarship,
and education by publishing worldwide. Oxford is a registered trade mark of
Oxford University Press in the UK and in certain other countries

© City University London 2022

The moral rights of the authors have been asserted

Eighteenth edition 2016
Nineteenth edition 2018
Twentieth edition 2020

Public sector information reproduced under Open Government Licence v3.0
(http://www.nationalarchives.gov.uk/doc/open-government-licence/open-government-licence.htm)

Published in the United States of America by Oxford University Press
198 Madison Avenue, New York, NY 10016, United States of America

British Library Cataloguing in Publication Data
Data available

Library of Congress Control Number: 2022934448

ISBN 978–0–19–285796–5

Printed and bound in the UK by
TJ Books Limited

FOREWORD

These manuals have been written by a combination of practitioners and members of staff of the City Law School (formerly the Inns of Court School of Law), and are designed primarily to support training on the Bar course, wherever it is taught. They provide an extremely useful resource to assist in acquiring the skills and knowledge that practising barristers need.

This series of manuals exemplifies the practical and professional approach that is central to Bar training. I congratulate the authors on the excellent standard of these manuals, and I am grateful to Oxford University Press for their ongoing and enthusiastic support.

Professor Andrew Stockley
Dean
The City Law School
City, University of London
2022

GUIDE TO USING THIS BOOK

This Manual is designed to serve a practical purpose, rather than to be a legal textbook on Remedies. It is intended to be a first point of reference, not a complete work on the relevant law. It provides a bird's-eye view of the relevant law, enabling the reader to research more deeply in suitable practitioner works.

The approach taken is a problem-solving one. It is assumed the reader has a problem to answer, and wants to know:

- what remedy is available;
- the circumstances in which it is available; and
- what must be established in order to be granted that remedy.

The reader will then find a starting point, and an outline of the basic principles, which they can use to help them direct their fuller research.

It is also written to a considerable extent in a way which will enable the reader to use it as a 'how to' guide. There are many examples, and a chapter of exercises. You are strongly advised to tackle the exercises, as they illustrate how the principles explained actually work in practice.

This Manual will be of use not only studying for the Bar on the Bar Professional Training Course, but also in pupillage and early practice.

OUTLINE CONTENTS

DETAILED CONTENTS

TABLE OF CASES

TABLE OF LEGISLATION

TABLE OF RULES AND REGULATIONS

Introduction

1.1 Role and context of remedies

It is usually in the first months of practice that barristers come face to face with the realities of dealing with the problems and objectives of clients. Armed with a considerable amount of textbook law, practitioners soon discover that the task of finding a resolution or remedy to a specific problem demands additional skills: a knowledge of the range of major remedies, the ability to recognise which remedy can be sought in any situation and the likelihood of success of a particular remedy, how to choose between alternative remedies, and an understanding of how to calculate damages.

For most students, academic training has focused on substantive law: researching, classifying, and analysing legal arguments. Such analysis has a central role in the barrister's work. However, to the client, it is of secondary importance. The client's crucial and primary question for you, as legal adviser, will be what solution the law offers to the client's problem; that is, what is the remedy? It is not uncommon to hear former students say that they simply had not appreciated the importance of knowing how to go about *solving* a problem; that is, what damages to claim, whether or not to seek an injunction, and how to find appropriate remedies in an unfamiliar area of law.

The term 'remedy' is wide-ranging and can include any positive solution to a client's problem. The Civil Procedure Rules 1998 (CPR) use the term 'remedy' rather than 'relief', for example permitting a party to apply for a remedy from sanctions previously ordered by the court. As an adviser, you will wish to take an overview of all possible remedies, including routes which do not involve court intervention, such as self-help remedies, exhausting internal complaints procedures, or filing complaints with agencies such as the Equality and Human Rights Commission. This Manual focuses on remedies which a court can give, the most common being (a) a money award of damages; and (b) orders that defendants refrain from certain acts or restore the position the claimant was in before the cause of the claim arose. Though the study of remedies involves both substantive law principles and rules of procedure and enforcement, it does not lie squarely in either of these areas. Substantive law is decided by the court and answers the question, 'Is the defendant liable?' Procedural rules govern the issue, 'How can that liability be enforced?' The law of remedies falls between them, overlapping but distinct. Having determined that the defendant is liable, it answers the question, 'What remedy will the law permit?'

1.2 Classifying remedies

While not all of the wide range of available remedies fit into set categories, most will fall into general areas and it is helpful to start with an understanding of these:

(a) *Compensatory remedies*. These compensate the claimant for losses suffered. The most common compensatory remedy is damages; that is, a sum of money to put the claimant in as good a position as before the harm and recognition of loss. If a defendant fails to satisfy a judgment ordering payment of damages, there are various methods of enforcement available against the defendant's assets and wages (see Sime, *A Practical Approach to Civil Procedure*, 24th edn, Oxford University Press, 2021, Chapter 48). A winning claimant will normally be awarded costs and, although these compensate for costs expended, they are not deemed to be part of the damages award.

(b) *Coercive remedies.* These aim to prevent harm from occurring or re-occurring. The most common preventative remedy is an injunction, which is an order by the court that the defendant does or refrains from doing a certain act to prevent harm occurring. An injunction, by itself, normally does not involve compensation to the claimant. In addition to injunctions, courts have a variety of specialised orders, for example an order for specific performance of a contract, which requires the defendant to perform contractual obligations. Failure to obey a court order is contempt of court, for which the court may order payment of a fine and/or a period of imprisonment and/or sequestration of assets.

(c) *Declaratory remedies.* These interpret documents such as wills and contracts, and resolve disputes about the parties' rights. The most common is the declaration. In one sense, a declaration can be a preventative remedy in that it will resolve uncertainty about the parties' rights or legal ownership before either side has taken steps based on an (erroneous) view of the matter. In another sense, these types of remedies can be seen as indirectly 'coercive' in that a declaration puts the parties on notice of the legal interpretation of the matter. If either side subsequently acts contrary to that interpretation, the courts are likely to award compensation to the injured party and possibly an injunction preventing further acts.

(d) *Exemplary or punitive remedies.* These aim to punish the offending party for deliberate or particularly grave wrongful acts. The most common is an order requiring a defendant to pay a sum of money as exemplary or punitive damages. This remedy is distinct as it does not 'compensate' in the sense of restoring the claimant's position. Nor is it coercive in the sense of requiring the defendant to do or refrain from doing an act. Rather, it is to penalise the defendant through civil rather than criminal litigation, and is often done to send a clear message of the court's view of particular conduct.

Remedies can also be categorised as either legal or equitable. Damages are the most common legal remedy. The most frequently used equitable remedies are injunctions and specific performance, although the list is extensive and includes *quantum meruit*, rescission, rectification, constructive trust, subrogation, contribution, and receivership. Traditionally there were separate courts of law and equity, each providing their own specific type of remedies. Although the merger of modern courts diffused the distinction, it remains important in at least one respect: a claimant will often be denied an equitable remedy if the legal remedy (e.g. an award of monetary damages) would be adequate (see **7.2.2**, **8.5.2**, and **8.7.2.2**).

1.3 Further sources of information

The course manuals on specialist areas of law will assist with an in-depth study of remedies relevant to those areas. A list of practitioners' works on specific subjects can also be found in Chapter 9 of the **Opinion Writing and Case Preparation** manual. Increasingly, texts are appearing in electronic form which may also be helpful. The following practitioner texts are of particular interest:

Burrows, A., *Remedies for Torts, Breach of Contract, and Equitable Wrongs*, 4th edn, Oxford University Press, 2019.

McGregor, H., *McGregor on Damages*, 21st edn, Sweet & Maxwell, 2021.

Mitchell, C., Mitchell, P., and Watterson, S., *Goff and Jones: The Law of Unjust Enrichment*, 9th edn, Sweet & Maxwell, 2016.

Multiple authors, *Kemp & Kemp: Quantum of Damages*, looseleaf, Sweet & Maxwell, 2021.

Who to sue?

2.1 Introduction

When considering the remedies available to your client, it is important to consider the client's legal status and that of the person the remedy is sought from. This involves an awareness of the different types of legal persons and the limits on some persons' legal capability and liability.

2.2 Legal personality

2.2.1 General

Where the claimant and defendant are individuals acting on their own behalf, you will need to consider whether they are treated differently before the law. For example, there are limits placed on the legal capacity of minors and of persons suffering from mental disorder.

The claimant or defendant may be a group of people acting together, for example a business which wishes to sue a supplier for breach of contract or a sports club seeking damages for the negligence of builders. You will need to determine precisely who the legal persons are for whom you are acting and against whom you are seeking a remedy. The three principal legal forms which the group may take are: a trust, a corporation, and an unincorporated association. These different forms may be used for a variety of purposes; from running a business to a local social club.

Once you have determined the legal status of the claimant and defendant, you need to consider what, if any, limits are placed on the capacity of such legal persons and who can bind the group (i.e. how do the rules of agency apply to this type of legal status?).

2.2.2 Trusts

When dealing with a problem which involves a trust, you need to ensure that you are clear on the distinct roles of the settlor, trustees, and beneficiaries. The legal ownership of any property is vested in the trustees, who are under a duty to hold it for the benefit of the beneficiaries. Thus, for example, when acting for the trust, you will need to ensure that whatever action is being proposed is within the trustees' power both in equity and under the specific terms of the trust.

2.2.3 Corporations

A corporation is a legal person separate from its members. A corporation may be formed: (a) by Royal Charter, for example the BBC; (b) by statute, for example local authorities; or (c) under the Companies Acts as a private or public company. You will need to ensure that you are clear which individual(s) have the legal authority to act on behalf of the corporation.

2.2.4   Unincorporated associations

Unincorporated associations have no legal personality separate from their members. The principal legal effect is that one member may be liable for the acts of another member. The three main types of such associations are: (a) trade unions and employers' associations; (b) clubs (where the difference between a proprietary and a members' club is important); and (c) partnerships. You will need to ensure that you know what type of unincorporated association you are dealing with and who has the authority to act for it.

2.3   Business associations

Although the different forms of legal person may be used for a variety of reasons (for example, a club may incorporate as a limited company), the main use of incorporation is to trade. It is important to understand the different legal forms used to trade: (a) sole trader (an individual who sets up in business and trades in their own name); (b) partnership (persons carrying on a business in common with a view of profit); and (c) a company (a corporation created by registration under the Companies Act 2006 (CA 2006)).

2.3.1   Formation

2.3.1.1   Sole traders

No formalities are required to set up as a sole trader and the personality of the 'trader' is indistinguishable in law from that of the individual. The debts of the business are the liability of the sole trader personally and without limit. For accounting purposes, however, the sole trader will distinguish between assets 'owned' by the business and personal assets.

2.3.1.2   Partnerships

No formalities are required to form a partnership. It will exist if it satisfies the definition in s. 1(1) of the Partnership Act 1890 (PA 1890), namely 'the relation which subsists between persons carrying on a business in common with a view of profit' (companies are expressly excluded by s. 1(2)). There are few restrictions on the formation of partnerships, although the business must be lawful.

The Limited Liability Partnerships Act 2000 created another form of legal entity known as a limited liability partnership. Forming such a partnership requires similar formalities to those needed to form a company (see **2.3.1.3**); that is, registration with the Registrar of Companies and filing of certain documents with the Registrar. As with a company, the liability of the partnership itself will be unlimited and the liability of the individual partners will be limited to an obligation to contribute to the assets on the winding up of the partnership to the extent set out in the Act. The 2000 Act specifically provides that the law relating to partnerships does not apply to a limited liability partnership, and that the law relating to companies on relevant matters such as registration, insolvency, and winding up is applicable to such partnerships. These entities are more like companies than partnerships. Although the limitation on partners' liability is attractive, the price paid is disclosure of information about the partnership, including financial matters.

2.3.1.3   Companies

A company can only be formed by complying with the formalities set out in the CA 2006, which requires certain documents including the articles of association (the constitutional document) to be filed with the Registrar of Companies, who will issue a certificate of incorporation, enter the company in the register of companies, and open a file for the company at Companies House.

A company exists as a legal person distinct from its members from the date in the certificate of incorporation. The principal effect of this is that the company alone is liable for its debts. While the company has unlimited liability for its debts (i.e. can be liquidated to obtain assets to pay creditors), the members are not liable for the debts of the company, and their liability to contribute to the company's assets, to enable it to pay its creditors, may be limited by share or guarantee.

Companies can be categorised on the following basis:

(a) The liability of members to contribute to assist the company to pay its debts:

    (i) company limited by shares—members' liability to contribute (at any time) is limited to the nominal value and any premium on shares (mostly used for trading purposes);

    (ii) company limited by guarantee—members' liability to contribute (on liquidation only) is limited to the amount of guarantee given (mostly used for non-trading organisations, e.g. educational institutions);

    (iii) unlimited company—members' liability to contribute (on liquidation only) is unlimited (rare).

(b) The ability to offer its securities (shares and debentures) to the public:

    (i) public company—the name must end with the words 'Public Limited Company' (or 'plc');

    (ii) private company—any other company. Unless it is an unlimited company, the name of a private company must end with the word 'Limited' (or 'Ltd'). All unlimited companies and companies limited by guarantee must be private. Some guarantee companies (particularly charities) are exempt from the requirement that the name must end with the word 'Limited'.

A group of companies exists where one company controls one or more other companies, either through voting rights of members or determining the composition of the board of directors. The holding (controlling) company is (usually) the principal shareholder of the subsidiary (controlled) company. The law, for most purposes, treats the various companies in the group as distinct legal persons with liability only for their own debts.

2.3.2 Internal management and control of the association

2.3.2.1 Sole traders

A sole trader is free to employ others and whatever 'say' is given to others in the running of the organisation is a matter between them; the law has no impact here, save to provide contractual remedies if appropriate.

2.3.2.2 Partnerships

The term 'partner' is usually used to describe an 'equity' partner (i.e. one with full rights). Other types of partners usually have very limited, if any, 'partnership' rights, for example 'sleeping' partners (who take no active part in management) or 'salaried' partners (usually 'in fact' employees).

The equity partners own the firm (i.e. have invested their own capital) and manage the business (i.e. have the right to attend meetings and participate in the decision-making process of running the business). The rights of the partners should be set out in a partnership agreement. However, the PA 1890 implies terms into any partnership insofar as they are not inconsistent with what has been agreed. Section 24 contains most of these provisions, which include the right to take part in the management of the partnership business and to have access to the books, and that differences may be decided by simple majority of the partners (except a change in the nature of the business, and introduction or expulsion of a partner, all of which require unanimity). Section 24 is subject to agreement to the contrary, express or implied (except expulsion of a partner, which must be express), and s. 19 provides that the rights and duties of partners may be varied by consent of all the partners, express or inferred by conduct.

Sections 28–30 of the PA 1890 require partners to act in good faith towards one another, for example to give full information and account for benefits derived from the firm. Although not expressly stated in the PA 1890, partners have a duty to act within their actual authority.

2.3.2.3   Companies

A company as a legal person must make decisions, but this must be done by the individuals controlling it. It is necessary to determine what decisions are decisions of the company and not just of the individuals. The members, as owners, make decisions collectively by voting in general meetings (on most matters a simple majority is sufficient but some decisions, mostly those which relate to the company's constitution, require a 75 per cent majority). Such decisions will be decisions of the company. The CA 2006 requires certain formalities for such meetings which are much more stringent for public than private companies. Decisions made without following the proper procedures can be challenged as irregular and invalid.

It is impractical for members to have general meetings to make all the decisions necessary to run the business. Much of the decision-making power is therefore delegated to the directors, who must also act collectively through decisions at board meetings unless the power to sub-delegate has been given. There are thus two decision-making organs of the company—the general meeting and the board. As a general rule, once members have delegated their decision-making powers to the board, they cannot simultaneously exercise the delegated powers. In most public companies, the members and directors will not be the same people, and ownership (which is with the members) is therefore separated from the management powers (which are with the directors). This can cause problems where there is disagreement about the manner in which the business should be conducted. Small private companies are more likely to have a few members who are also directors of the company (i.e. the same people own and control the business).

The law on the powers of directors is contained in the CA 2006, ss. 171–177 and 182. These duties include:

- acting in accordance with the company's constitution;
- promoting the success of the company;
- exercising independent judgement;
- exercising reasonable care, skill, and diligence;
- avoiding conflicts of interest;
- not accepting benefits from third parties; and
- declaring any interest in transactions or arrangements with the company.

Members' rights are contained in the articles of association, which are deemed to be a contract by CA 2006, s. 33. The articles usually have detailed provisions about calling meetings, appointing and removing directors, powers of directors, and paying dividends, etc. A company limited by shares can adopt a model form of articles set out in a statutory instrument.

Where directors act wrongfully or some other person commits a wrong against the company, it is the company which must sue (*Foss v Harbottle* [1843] 2 Hare 461). The power to institute proceedings is usually delegated to the directors. If the directors refuse, the members may be permitted to take collective action on behalf of the company but will have to do this collectively (i.e. a majority of the members will have to agree to initiate action and follow the proper rules, usually by calling a meeting of members and putting the matter to a vote, to make the decision valid). While this option appears attractive, it has been disapproved in some cases; see, for example, *Breckland Group Holdings Ltd v London and Suffolk Properties Ltd* [1989] BCLC 100. A simple majority of members can always dismiss directors with whom they disagree. Only in very rare circumstances can an individual member bring an action on behalf of the company.

The Companies Act 2006, s. 994 affords some protection to members by enabling them to petition the court for an order where the company's affairs are conducted in a manner which is unfairly prejudicial to them. In addition, the Department for Business, Energy and Industrial Strategy has the power to investigate a company in a variety of circumstances.

2.3.3   Contractual capacity and agency rules

2.3.3.1   General agency rules

Where one person (the agent) negotiates a contract on behalf of another (the principal), there are two matters you should check to determine who is bound by the contract.

The authority of the agent

An agent's *actual* authority is that which is agreed between the agent and the principal. This can be *express actual authority* (that is, expressly agreed), or *implied actual authority* (that is, impliedly given by the principal). Implied authority can include authority to do everything necessarily and ordinarily incidental to the carrying out of the activity expressly authorised (sometimes called *incidental authority*), to do whatever an agent in that trade, profession, or business would usually have the authority to do (called *usual authority*), or to act in accordance with reasonable customs and usages of the places where they act (called *customary authority*).

An agent's *apparent* (sometimes also called *ostensible*) authority is the authority as it appears to others based on the principle that third parties are entitled to assume that an agent has the authority it appears to, or would normally have because of their position. Generally, an agent's actual and apparent authority are the same. However, an agent's apparent authority may be greater than their actual authority, for example where restrictions have been placed on their authority (perhaps a car salesman whose authority is limited to contracts of a certain relatively low value), but the principal has not notified third parties of these restrictions. The agent's actual authority may exceed their apparent authority, for example where the principal specifically gives the agent more authority than an agent in their position would usually have, but third parties are unaware of this.

Whatever the agent's actual authority, the principal will generally be bound by contracts which come within the agent's apparent authority. However, even where the principal is bound by the contract, if an agent has acted outside their actual authority, the principal will have an action against the agent for breach of the agency agreement.

Disclosed/undisclosed principal

Usually, an agent discloses to the third party that they are acting as an agent for a principal. The contract is between the principal and the third party. The general rule is that the agent is not liable on the contract, nor can they enforce it. There are exceptions to this, for example where, by custom or trade, the agent is liable or where the agent in signing accepts personal liability.

Where an agent does not disclose that they are acting on behalf of someone else, the agent can sue and be sued on the contract, as the agent appeared to be the contracting party. The undisclosed principal can usually intervene and claim against the third party, provided the terms of the contract are not inconsistent with such intervention.

2.3.3.2 Sole traders

The contractual capacity of a sole trader is determined by the general rules for contractual capacity of the individual in the law of contract.

General agency rules will apply to acts of employees, and the sole trader will be personally liable for torts and breaches of contract committed in the course of business. The assets available to satisfy judgment debts will be the personal and business assets of the trader.

2.3.3.3 Partnerships

As with sole traders, there is no limit on the contractual capacity of partners except the general rules of contract law.

Normal agency rules apply to partnerships and are codified in the PA 1890, ss. 5–18. Each partner is both agent and part of the principal. Acts of individual partners carrying on the business of the partnership in the usual way will bind all the partners unless the partner is acting outside their authority and the third party is aware of this, or is not aware of dealing with a partner (s. 5). Case law has established that all partners will have usual authority to buy and sell goods and pay debts, give receipts, and draw cheques, but that the 'usual' authority of partners in trading partnerships is wider than non-trading partnerships (e.g. professional partnerships), and includes borrowing money. Where limits are placed on a partner's authority, the firm will still be bound unless the third party has notice of the limitation (ss. 5 and 8). Section 6 deals specifically with acts done and instruments executed in the firm's name and s. 7 with pledging the firm's credit.

Tortious liability is covered by ss. 10 and 11. Section 10 makes the firm liable for loss or damage caused in the ordinary course of business or with the authority of co-partners. Under s. 11 the firm is liable to make good the loss suffered from misapplication of money or property received by a partner within their apparent authority or by the firm in the course of business.

The combined effect of ss. 14, 17, and 36 on the liability of incoming and outgoing partners is that partners are not liable for acts done before or after the time they were partners unless they have been held out to be partners outside this period (s. 14), for example by having their names on the letterhead as partners or by failing to give proper notice of retirement from the partnership under s. 36. They remain liable for debts and obligations incurred while a partner even after their retirement (unless discharged by agreement of all the parties).

Although a partnership enjoys no separate legal status, Civil Procedure Rules (CPR), PD 7A, para 5A.3 requires a partnership to sue and be sued in the name of the firm rather than the individual partners (see *Drafting* manual, para 5.3).

2.3.3.4 Business names

Whether acting for or against a business association, it is important to get the legal name correct. This will not be difficult where the business name is the legal name of the person running it: in the case of sole traders and partners, their surnames and, in the case of a company, its corporate name. However, the business may use a 'trade' name (i.e. not the legal name of the person running it). In these circumstances, the CA 2006 requires disclosure of the legal name on correspondence, at business premises, etc.

2.3.4 Cessation of business: termination of association

2.3.4.1 Sole traders

Sole traders may cease trading at any time for any reason. If there are business debts on cessation, they will remain personally liable for them.

2.3.4.2 Partnerships

Section 32 of the PA 1890 provides that a partnership formed for a fixed term will end at the expiration of the term and a partnership at will (i.e. without a fixed term) may be ended by any partner giving notice to the others of intention to dissolve, the partnership being dissolved from the date in the notice. Section 32 is subject to agreement to the contrary, for example that dissolution may occur only by mutual agreement of all the partners, in which case a single partner cannot terminate by notice. The court does have power to order dissolution on one of the grounds in PA 1890, s. 35, which include a partner being in wilful or persistent breach of the partnership agreement. Resort will be made to this provision only where the partners have no power to dissolve or cannot reach agreement to dissolve.

2.3.4.3 Companies

A company ceases to exist when its name is removed from the register of companies. It may be liquidated voluntarily by the members passing a resolution. The court may order the company to be liquidated if one of the grounds set out in the Insolvency Act 1986, s. 122 is proved. These grounds include that it would be 'just and equitable' to do so.

2.3.4.4 Insolvency

Where an individual becomes insolvent (i.e. unable to pay their debts), creditors may institute bankruptcy proceedings. All the individual's assets, subject to a few exceptions such as essential living items, vest in the trustee in bankruptcy. These assets include all causes of action held by the individual except personal claims, such as a right to sue for defamation. Where a company becomes insolvent, any creditor may petition to have the company put into liquidation. All the company's assets then vest in the liquidator, including any causes of action held by the company. Both the trustee in bankruptcy and the liquidator have a duty to use the assets to pay the creditors according to the rules under the Insolvency Act 1986.

Liability for breach of contract

3.1 Introduction

Although this Manual is primarily about remedies, we cannot easily discuss remedies for breach of contract without reminding ourselves of what needs to be established in order to create liability for breach of contract. There can be no remedy for breach if there is no liability in the first place.

Although everyone training for the Bar will have studied the law of contract at the academic stage, you are unlikely to have done so in a practical way, that is in a way that is geared to solving disputes, in other words litigation. So this chapter does not aim to give a comprehensive overview of the law of contract. Instead, we will go through the essential ingredients that must be established before there can be liability in damages for breach of contract, and the various factors that can prevent or limit liability. Liability for other remedies, such as specific performance and injunction, will be covered in later chapters.

Any practitioner dealing with a claim for breach of contract needs to be familiar with these ingredients. They are relevant not just in the context of remedies, but more broadly. You will be applying them whenever you write an opinion or draft a statement of case in a claim for breach of contract.

3.2 Ingredients of a claim for damages for breach of contract

There are effectively six requirements that must be satisfied before liability can be established in a contract case:

(1) The existence of an enforceable contract

(2) That the contract contains the relevant term(s), that is the term(s) alleged to have been breached

(3) A breach of the contract

(4) That the claimant has suffered loss or damage

(5) That the loss was caused by the breach

(6) That the loss was not too remote

We shall work through these requirements in the following sections, with some useful expansions and diversions.

3.2.1 The existence of the contract

We will take this fairly briefly, as it should be familiar ground to all who have studied contract law in the past. There are basically five requirements for a contract to exist:

(1) There must be an agreement

(2) There must be an intention to be legally bound

(3) It must be an agreement between the claimant and the defendant

(4) One of the parties must make a promise

(5) The other party must provide consideration

3.2.1.1   Agreement—certainty

The essence of a contract is that the parties must be in agreement with each other. If they are not of the same mind, and have different understandings of what they are actually agreeing to, there can be no contract. It follows that there needs to be certainty as to the subject matter of the contract and as to its major terms. If it is not possible to identify what goods are being sold, or what services are to be provided, or what a party must do in order to perform the contract, it is unenforceable and so not binding. But this doesn't stop the parties coming to an understanding of what the precise subject matter is and so turning the uncertain agreement into an enforceable one.

3.2.1.2   Agreement—offer and acceptance

One of the first things we learn is that agreement is reached when one party accepts another's unconditional offer. This is almost always true, but we need to remember that agreement can be reached by implication, without a formal offer and acceptance. Analysing the process of offer and acceptance is a useful way of establishing whether, and if so when, agreement has actually been reached. If there has been a series of offers and counter-offers during the negotiation process, this is the moment at which the terms of the contract become settled and binding. But the essence of the contract is agreement, not acceptance of an offer as such.

Distinguish an offer from an 'invitation to treat', or an advertisement. An offer involves an intention to be bound on the part of the offeror and a belief in the genuineness of the offer on the part of the offeree. An invitation to treat invites the recipient to make an offer.

Once it has been made, an offer remains open until the offeror communicates that they are withdrawing that offer or the offeree rejects it. Of course the offeror can stipulate that the offer remains open only for a limited time, or until the occurrence of a specific event. If it has not been accepted by then, it lapses, and any purported acceptance by the offeree becomes a new offer, which the original offeror can accept or reject.

Acceptance must be communicated to the offeror. A party cannot tacitly accept the offer by remaining silent and doing nothing. However, an offer can be accepted implicitly, or by conduct. If, for example, the offeree acts as if they were bound by the contract, or starts to perform their obligations under it, they may be presumed to have accepted the offer. The offeror can also stipulate a method of acceptance, for example in writing. A purported oral acceptance will then probably not be valid. But silence or inaction cannot be prescribed as a method of accepting. The offeror cannot say 'if you do not respond you will be deemed to have accepted'.

Acceptance of an offer must also be unqualified. If the offeree attaches any conditions or qualifications to their acceptance, they have made a counter-offer. They may alternatively expressly reject the original offer and make a counter-offer. The counter-offer then remains open until the other party gives an unequivocal acceptance, or it is withdrawn. In the case of complicated continuing negotiations it is a question of fact whether and if so when agreement was reached. The whole correspondence must be looked at.

3.2.1.3   Intention to be bound by contract

This requirement is often referred to as the intention to create legal relations. There is no contract if the parties did not intend to enter into a binding legal contract. There are many occasions in life on which two parties may agree on something without intending that agreement to have legal consequences. We can identify three main situations:

(a) It was a purely social or domestic agreement. Everyday agreements between friends and family are obviously not intended to be legally binding. Agreements to split the cost of a meal in a restaurant, or share the cost of petrol on a journey, almost certainly cannot be enforced, even when the parties have a business relationship. Similarly an arrangement that one member of a household will be solely responsible for cleaning while the other takes on all the gardening. But it is not impossible in rare circumstances that an agreement of this nature could become binding a contract.

(b) The agreement was 'subject to contract'. This is a necessity when commercial businesses are negotiating a complex contract. The negotiations may continue over a long period, and certain aspects of the contract may be finalised while other aspects are still being negotiated. The parties do not intend any of the contract to become binding until they have everything completely agreed, and (usually) set down in writing. Their intention not to be bound until then can almost certainly be inferred from all the circumstances, even if they do not expressly say that they are negotiating subject to contract, or their draft agreement is not headed 'draft'. Furthermore if the parties have been expressly negotiating subject to contract, only a formal written contract or clear factual evidence that they were no longer negotiating subject to contract will be sufficient to create a binding agreement (*Joanne Properties Ltd v Moneything Capital Ltd* [2020] All ER (D) 44 (Dec)).

The parties may on the other hand be held to have entered into a contract where they intended to make a formal written agreement but never in fact did so (*Harvey Shopfitters Ltd v ADI Ltd* [2004] 2 All ER 982). And if a contract has not yet been formally concluded, but the parties start to perform it as if it had been concluded, that may be evidence that they intend to be bound.

(c) The agreement was a conditional agreement, and the condition was not fulfilled. This needs slightly closer examination.

3.2.1.4 Conditional agreements

The parties may intend their agreement to take effect only if a certain condition is satisfied, or a certain event occurs. The contract is binding if the condition is fulfilled, but ceases to be binding if it isn't. But we need to distinguish the situations where the condition is something outside the control of either party and where one party has it within their power to bring the condition about.

Let us take an example of an agreement by which a dealer A agrees to sell a car to a customer B for £5,000 depending on the fulfilment of one of the following conditions:

(a) If the government abolishes road tax. If road tax is abolished the contract becomes binding; if not, both parties are relieved from their obligation.

(b) If B passes her driving test. Again, the contract is binding if B passes, but not if she fails. But what if B does not take a driving test? It may be implied in these circumstances that B has an obligation not to prevent the condition being fulfilled, that she is in beach of that obligation and that therefore the main obligation should be enforced.

(c) If B arranges to have the car inspected by an independent mechanic and she is satisfied by the mechanic's report. Clearly there is no problem if B is satisfied. But what if she says she isn't? There are some conflicting authorities on this situation, but it is clearly arguable that B has the right to withdraw from the agreement.

But an otherwise valid conditional agreement is always binding subject to the condition, so a party cannot lawfully repudiate the contract before it is known whether the condition will be fulfilled or not.

3.2.1.5 It is a contract between the claimant and the defendant?

This is such an obvious requirement that it hardly needs mentioning, but it can sometimes be overlooked when drafting a statement of case for breach of contract. A claimant cannot under normal circumstances establish the liability of a defendant for breach of contract if they were not both parties to the contract. But see **3.2.1.6** to **3.2.1.9**.

3.2.1.6   Privity

The starting point is the well-known doctrine of privity. The doctrine is essentially simple: only the parties to a contract may sue on it. However, there are exceptions. In particular there are ways round a lack of privity in the law of trusts and when a duty of care is owed in tort, but we will not discuss those here.

There is also the Contracts (Rights of Third Parties) Act 1999. If the contract expressly provides for a third party to enforce a term, or if the term purports to confer a benefit on a third party, the third party may enforce that term, subject to various conditions designed to ensure that they are not in any better position than they would have been had they been a party to the contract. The third party must be expressly identified in the contract by name, description, or as a member of a class.

The term does not purport to confer a benefit on the third party if on the proper construction of the contract the parties did not intend it to be enforceable by the third party. There is therefore a rebuttable presumption in favour of the third party having such a right, and the burden of proof is on the party seeking to show that the parties did not so intend (*Nisshin Shipping Co Ltd v Cleaves & Co Ltd* [2004] 1 All ER (Comm) 481).

3.2.1.7   Agency

However, the person who actually acted in the formation of the contract may have been acting as an agent, and the contract will be between the principal and the third party. There is more detail on this principle in **2.3.3.1**.

An agent may have actual or apparent authority to enter into the contract. In either case the principal can be bound. Actual authority may be express or implied. Implied authority can arise by virtue of:

(a) the relationship between principal and agent. For example, husband and wife, a company and its officers;

(b) custom—the custom of a trade or market, or previous dealings between the principal and agent;

(c) an implied extension of express authority—authority given for one transaction must impliedly cover another linked transaction.

Apparent authority can also give rise to a binding contract between principal and third party if the principal expressly or (more usually) impliedly represents to the third party that the agent is authorised to act as their agent and the third party relies on that representation.

If an agent was unauthorised and had no apparent authority, the principal can still be bound by a contract with a third party if they subsequently ratify the agent's act before the time for the performance of the contract has arrived. The effect is retrospective.

Once the agency has been shown to exist, the general rule is that the principal can both sue and be sued on the contract, whether they were a disclosed or undisclosed principal.

3.2.1.8   Assignment

A third party may be able to sue on a contract to which they were not a party if the benefit of the contract has been validly assigned to them. Generally speaking this benefit will be a debt or specified sum.

A legal right to a debt or thing in action can be assigned under s. 136(1) of the Law of Property Act 1925. No consideration is required. It must be done in writing and with written notice to the debtor. If so, the assignee can sue the debtor for the sum due.

A contractual right can also be assigned in equity. There are two ways in which this can happen: the assignor informs the assignee of the assignment; or the assignor instructs the debtor to discharge the debt by paying the assignee. The assignment should be in writing; but there does not need to be written notice to the debtor. Whether there needs to be consideration is a complex issue in determining rights as between assignor and assignee; but it is irrelevant to the debtor, whose obligation cannot be wiped out.

Generally speaking the burden, as opposed to the benefit, of a contractual obligation cannot be assigned without the consent of the other party. So a party cannot without consent assign its obligation to provide goods, services, or payment to someone else. When consent is given and the burden is assigned, this is called 'novation'.

3.2.1.9   Death and bankruptcy

When a party to a contract dies, their contractual liabilities and rights pass to their personal representatives, who may sue or be sued.

When a party to a contract is declared bankrupt, most of their contractual liabilities and rights, with some exceptions, pass to the trustee in bankruptcy, who may sue or be sued.

3.2.1.10   Promise and consideration

It is the essence of a contract that it is a bargain made between two (or more) parties, each of whom takes on some obligation or warrants something to be true. In essence therefore each party is making a promise. But it is often said that one party makes a promise, while the other provides consideration. This makes sense where one party agrees to provide goods or services while the other agrees to pay for them. The promise to pay is then the consideration. But sometimes the contractual bargain can be made without the payment of money. In such a case there must still be valuable consideration for the promise, but this may be in the form of providing a valuable benefit, or accepting a detriment (for example forbearance to sue, in consideration of the settlement of a claim).

The consideration need not be comparable in value to the value of the promise, or even adequate consideration for it. It is enough that there is consideration. This is the vital requirement for a binding contract. Without it the agreement is one-sided only and unenforceable.

The consideration must move from one of the parties, not a third party, and the consideration must not be a benefit granted or money paid in the past: it must be some new benefit given in exchange for the present promise.

This requirement is of most significance where the parties agree to rescind or vary the contract after it has been concluded. An agreement to rescind will only be valid if both parties give up their rights under the contract. A variation will not give rise to a binding agreement if only one party benefits. A promise to accept part-payment of a debt in full settlement of it is not normally binding.

3.2.2   The contract contains the relevant term(s)

The relevant terms are those which are alleged to have been breached by the defendant, or which entitle the claimant to the remedy they seek. There can be no liability for breach if they were not terms of the contract in the first place. They are the terms which will need to be pleaded.

3.2.2.1   What are the terms of the contract?

When parties find themselves in a contractual dispute, it is inevitable that the dispute turns primarily on whether the defendant is in breach of contract. But sometimes that will depend on whether the relevant term was part of the contract at all. (And sometimes it will depend on the meaning of the term, but the principles relating to the construction of contracts are beyond the scope of this Manual.)

If the contract is written down, there is a rebuttable presumption that it contains the whole of the contract. However, while this presumption may be hard to rebut in the context of high-value commercial litigation, it is much more easily rebutted in less specialised circumstances. Contracts may be contained in several documents or emails, in which case the court will consider the intention of the parties in deciding what they actually agreed. The guidelines of offer and acceptance (see **3.2.1.2**) may be helpful.

It is also not uncommon for a contract to be concluded partly in writing and partly orally, particularly in everyday transactions, and if there is clear evidence (sometimes known as extrinsic evidence) of what was agreed by the parties outside any written terms, this can be admitted to establish the true intention of the parties, and the terms of their contract. Extrinsic evidence is also admissible to show that the contract was entered into in reliance on a misrepresentation, or in consideration of a collateral contract or warranty.

If there is an 'entire agreement' clause, which is almost invariably the case in commercial contracts, it is probably effective to exclude extrinsic evidence of other terms, and of any collateral agreement or warranty, but arguably not extrinsic evidence of a misrepresentation that is not a term of the contract.

3.2.2.2   Standard terms and conditions

There is a well-known process sometimes referred to as a 'battle of the forms'. A makes an offer, enclosing A's standard terms and conditions. B purports to accept, subject to B's standard terms and conditions. This is of course a counter-offer. A then makes another counter-offer on A's standard terms. And so on. Each party is trying to ensure that the contract is finally agreed on their own terms. Eventually a compromise is reached and it is somewhat unclear whose standard terms are incorporated.

A party to a contract cannot be bound by standard terms and conditions of which they are unaware. It follows that standard terms provided only after the conclusion of a contract are not part of it, unless the other party was made aware of them beforehand.

3.2.2.3   Express terms

Express terms are those which the court finds as a fact were agreed orally between the parties, and those which were stated in writing. In theory they are express because the exact wording is known. But some oral terms will be accepted as express terms if the gist is clear, even if they cannot be transcribed into precise words. In the end, so long as a term can be shown by evidence to be a term agreed by the parties, it doesn't really matter much whether it is express or implied.

The law categorises terms into three types: conditions, warranties, and intermediate or innominate terms. It will be convenient to look at what these are and their different effects before dealing with implied terms (though implied terms too can come into any of these three categories).

3.2.2.4   Conditions

A condition is a term which is fundamental to the contract, or goes to the root of it, so that if breached, the innocent party is basically deprived of the benefit of the contract.

If a condition is breached, the innocent party has the right to treat the contract as having come to an end, and is no longer obliged to fulfil their obligations under it. This is so regardless of whether the breach is serious or minor. They may also claim damages for any loss they have suffered.

They may alternatively elect to affirm the contract, so treating both parties as still bound. They may still claim damages and insist that the defaulting party remedy the breach. But sometimes the facts are such that the innocent party has no choice but to treat the contract as over because the defaulting party will simply be unable to perform, or the breach is incapable of remedy.

If the parties designate a term as a 'condition' it almost certainly is a condition. If the parties expressly agree that breach of a term will allow the innocent party to treat the contract as at an end, it is likewise a condition. But it may also be a condition if not so described, or if there is no express provision for termination in the event of its breach, if it is sufficiently fundamental, even if it is called a 'warranty'. It is a matter of interpretation.

Another way of making a term a condition is to describe it as 'of the essence' of the contract. This is most common in relation to time. The presumption, unless the parties stipulate otherwise, is that a requirement as to time (either time of performance or time of payment) is not a fundamental term.

3.2.2.5 Warranties

A warranty is a lesser term, which does not nullify the benefit of the contract if breached. The innocent party may claim damages, but may not terminate the agreement, no matter how serious the breach.

A term is not necessarily a warranty just because it is described as such. Since the development of intermediate terms, probably very few terms these days are warranties.

3.2.2.6 Intermediate terms

An intermediate (or innominate) term is a term which may operate as a condition or a warranty, depending on the seriousness of the breach. A term which may be breached in either a serious or minor way, and is not described as a condition, is probably an intermediate term.

If an intermediate term is breached it is necessary to look at the nature of the breach and its effect to determine what happens. If the breach is fundamental or very serious, the innocent party may claim to be discharged from the contract as if the term were a condition. If the breach is minor, they may only claim damages, as if the term were a warranty.

3.2.2.7 Implied terms

Implied terms are any others which are not express. The extrinsic evidence rule does not apply. Most contracts contain implied terms. However, as a general rule express terms will always prevail over implied terms. A term can only be implied into a contract if it is not inconsistent with the express terms.

There are basically four ways that a term can be implied into the contract:

- By law (statute or common law)
- By custom
- By the previous course of dealings between the parties
- By fact.

3.2.2.8 Terms implied by law

The most important statutory implied terms are in contracts involving the sale of goods and the supply of services.

The Sale of Goods Act 1979 is concerned exclusively with contracts for the sale of goods. Under this Act (as amended by the Sale and Supply of Goods Act 1994) the following terms (among others) are to be implied:

(a) There is an implied condition that the seller will have the right to sell the goods at the time of sale (s. 12).

(b) Where the seller sells in the course of their business, there is an implied condition that the goods will be of satisfactory quality (s. 14(1)).

(c) Where the seller sells in the course of their business, there is an implied condition that the goods will be reasonably fit for any purpose which the buyer makes known to the seller (s. 14(3)).

(d) Where the seller sells goods by reference to a description, there is an implied condition that the goods will conform to the description (s. 13).

Note that these terms are all stated to be conditions, so breach will entitle a buyer to reject the goods. However, where there is a breach of the terms mentioned in (b) and (c) and it is so slight that it would be unreasonable to reject the goods, the breach may be treated as a breach of warranty.

However, the Sale of Goods Act 1979 no longer applies to consumer contracts, meaning those where the contract is between a trader and a consumer. These contracts are now governed by the Consumer Rights Act 2015. All the terms mentioned in (a) to (d) are also imported into consumer contracts for the sale or supply of goods (see ss. 9, 10, 11, and 17). However, they are not described as conditions, merely as terms. This is because the remedies available to a consumer are expressly set out in the Act, along with the circumstances in which they are available. There are still circumstances in which the consumer may reject the goods and treat the contract as at an end, so giving them similar rights as under the Sale of Goods Act.

The Sale of Goods Act 1979 also expressly states that a stipulation as to time of payment is not 'of the essence' (and therefore a condition) unless a contrary intention appears. Whether a stipulation as to time of delivery is of the essence depends on the terms of the contract, but remember there is a presumption against. If there is no provision for time of payment, common law will imply 'on delivery'. This rule is unaffected by the Consumer Rights Act 2015.

If the price, or a mechanism for determining the price, is not stipulated, there is no term implied by the Act, but common law will imply 'a reasonable price'.

The Supply of Goods and Services Act 1982 (as amended by the Sale and Supply of Goods Act 1994) is primarily concerned with contracts for the supply of services, but such contracts often involve also the supply of goods (e.g. a contract to supply and install a fitted kitchen), and in fact can apply to contracts which involve the transfer of goods even where there are no services supplied. Under this Act the following terms (among others) are to be implied:

(a) There is an implied condition that the transferor will have the right to transfer the goods (s. 2).

(b) Where the transferor transfers goods in the course of their business, there is an implied condition that the goods will be of satisfactory quality (s. 4(2)).

(c) Where the transferor transfers goods in the course of their business, there is an implied condition that the goods will be reasonably fit for any purpose which the transferee makes known to the transferor (s. 4(4) and (5)).

(d) Where there is a contract for the supply of a service and the supplier acts in the course of a business, there is an implied term that the supplier will carry out the service with reasonable care and skill (s. 13).

Note that the terms identified in (a) to (c) are stated to be conditions. However, the term in (d) is not a condition, it is an intermediate term.

The Supply of Goods and Services Act 1982 no longer applies to consumer contracts, which are again now governed by the Consumer Rights Act 2015. All the terms identified in (a) to (d) appear in this Act (see ss. 9, 10, 17, and 49), and the remedies and their availability are also set out, so the terms are all referred to as terms, not as conditions.

Where a contract for the supply of a service in the course of a business is silent as to time of performance, the Act inserts an implied term that it will be carried out within a reasonable time. The same is true of the Consumer Rights At 2015. If there is no provision for time of payment, common law will imply 'within a reasonable time'.

If the price, or a mechanism for determining the price, of the service is not stipulated, both Acts insert an implied term that the person liable will pay a reasonable charge.

3.2.2.9   Terms implied by custom

A term may also be implied by the custom of a particular trade or local market, provided it is not inconsistent with the express terms of the contract. The custom must be clear, well established, well known and reasonable.

3.2.2.10   Terms implied from previous dealings

If the parties have habitually contracted on the same terms, or in relation to very similar subject matter, and previous contracts have contained certain terms which are missing from the contract under consideration, they may be implied into it. For example if A and B have always previously contracted on A's standard terms, but those terms are not expressly incorporated into the contract, it may well be implied that the parties intended them to be.

But as usual, that will only be if they are not in contradiction to the express terms. So if, for example, after many contracts on A's standard terms, A and B expressly refer in this contract to B's standard terms, they clearly did not intend to incorporate A's.

3.2.2.11   Terms implied by fact

A term may be implied on the facts of the case. The idea is not to impose on the parties anything they did not intend or mean, but to add into the contract anything that they must have intended or meant if only they had thought about it. There are two tests used.

The 'officious bystander' test derives from *Shirlaw v Southern Foundries (1926) Ltd* [1939] 2 KB 206 at 227, where the judge suggested that a term can be implied if it is so obvious that if, while the parties were making their agreement, some officious bystander had intervened and suggested some new express term, both parties would have turned to him and said testily 'Yes of course!'.

The 'business efficacy test' derives from *Luxor (Eastbourne) Ltd v Cooper* [1941] AC 108 at 137. A term can be implied if it is necessary to give business efficacy to the transaction, so that it can take effect as the parties must have intended. The key word is 'necessary'. Necessary means that the contract would lack commercial or practical coherence without it. The implied term must go no further than is necessary to give effect to the express intention of the parties.

In almost any case, these two tests should produce the same result. But the Supreme Court has given a thorough review of the circumstances in which a term will be implied into a contract, and the conditions necessary, in *Marks & Spencer plc v BNP Paribas Securities Services Trust Co (Jersey) Ltd* [2016] 4 All ER 441. This should now be regarded as the leading case, but essentially it upholds the tests explained here.

3.2.3   The defendant has breached the contract

3.2.3.1   What is a breach?

Inevitably there can be no liability for breach of contract without a breach. It must of course be the defendant as opposed to anyone else who is in breach. A defendant may be in breach of contract in one of five ways:

(a) By doing something they promised not to

(b) By failing to do something they promised to do

(c) A state of affairs subsists which is contrary to that promised

(d) They made a representation of fact which was false

(e) They took some action which prevented them performing the contract

But essentially all of these involve a failure to fulfil a promise, meaning that there has been a failure to perform the contract. Liability for damages therefore arises when there has been a failure to perform, without lawful excuse, one or more of the obligations (whether a conditions, a warranty, or an intermediate term) contained in a contract. A failure to perform in this sense includes a refusal to perform, defective performance, delayed performance, and action taken which prevents performance.

Liability for breach of contract is strict, unless the term breached did not impose an absolute obligation, for example an obligation to use reasonable care and skill, or reasonable endeavours.

But not every failure to perform amounts to a breach of contract. The contract may contain terms which deal with that situation and prescribe an agreed resolution (for example a force majeure clause). The parties may agree otherwise in order to preserve their ongoing relationship. The contract may be frustrated.

Also, one party's obligation to perform may depend on the other party's performance. One party may be contractually bound to perform fully before the other party is under any obligation to perform at all. Where the parties' obligations are concurrent, each party's right to the other's performance depends on being able to show that they are ready, willing, and able to perform. If they demonstrate that they are not, the other party may not be obliged to perform. This is known as an anticipatory breach.

3.2.3.2   What is the effect of a breach?

The question that arises quite frequently is whether a breach of contract by the defendant not only entitles the claimant to a remedy in damages, but also brings the contract to an end.

This depends in varying circumstances on the term which has been breached, the nature of the breach, or the choice made by the claimant.

As explained in **3.2.2.4**, **3.2.2.5**, and **3.3.3.6**, breach of a condition entitles the claimant to make a choice either to affirm the contract or treat it as at an end, while breach of a warranty allows them a claim for damages only, with the contract subsisting. The effect of breach of an intermediate term depends on the seriousness of the breach. The emphasis in practice is very much on the nature of the breach rather than the nature of the term. A 'fundamental breach' entitles the claimant to bring the contract to an end. It is most unlikely that breach of a condition (a fundamental term) is not also a fundamental breach.

A fundamental breach by the defendant may also be described as a repudiation of the contract, or a repudiatory breach. A repudiation can be express, or implied reasonably from the circumstances, which must show either an intention to renounce the obligations under the contract or an absolute refusal to perform. A repudiatory breach is one which 'goes to the root of the contract' or deprives the defendant of substantially the whole benefit they were hoping to obtain by performing their remaining obligations (see *Hongkong Fir Shipping Co Ltd v Kawasaki Kisen Kaisha* [1962] 2 QB 26). This can happen where the claimant genuinely seeks to fulfil their obligations, but it becomes clear that they are not doing so in the promised manner, or that they are in fact unable to do so with the result that performance has become an impossibility. The defendant may also be in fundamental and therefore repudiatory breach if there is a series of breaches, none of which is fundamental in itself, but which are fundamental in their cumulative effect. However, a repudiation does require a deliberate intention, not an accidental oversight or a misreading of the situation (*Eminence Property Developments Ltd v Heaney* [2010] All ER (D) 193 (Oct)).

Repudiation can take place at any point before the defendant has fully performed their obligations under the contract. It may be an anticipatory breach, before the time for performance falls due, because the defendant expressly renounces the contract or shows that they will be unable to perform it; or it may occur whilst the contract remains only partly performed. However, the doctrine of part performance provides that where the defendant has substantially performed but not completed performance of their contractual obligations, the claimant cannot treat the contract as having come to an end, even if the breach is fundamental, but is limited to a claim for damages.

3.2.3.3   Affirmation or acceptance

So, in response to what seems to be a fundamental breach by the defendant, the claimant has a choice. They can either affirm the contract or accept the repudiation. In some case law the latter is described as 'rescinding' the contract, but this term is misleading and should be avoided. Rescission is a remedy for misrepresentation and it is not the same thing as accepting a fundamental breach.

If the claimant chooses to affirm, the contract remains alive, and the defendant remains obliged to complete the performance as originally agreed, whilst the claimant can seek damages to compensate for any loss they have suffered. There will, however, be occasions when this choice is not in reality open to the claimant, as the continuation of the contract is simply an impossibility.

Alternatively the claimant can choose to (or sometimes has no choice but to) accept the repudiation and treat the contract as having come to an end. This acceptance must be clear and unequivocal. It must be communicated expressly to the defendant, or the claimant's subsequent conduct must be such as to send a clear and unequivocal message. The effect is then that the defendant is relieved from any further performance under the contract, but remains fully liable to the claimant in damages. The claimant is also discharged from performing any subsequent obligations, but not obligations which came into existence before the wrongful repudiation (*Hurst v Bryk* [2000] 2 All ER 193).

The choice is all or nothing. The claimant cannot accept the defendant's repudiation in respect of one obligation, but still require them to perform another obligation. The choice is also final, so all future contractual obligations are terminated and the defendant cannot take advantage of their repudiation by relying on any of the terms in the contract (see *Briggs v Oates* [1991] 1 WLR 407).

However, the claimant must choose carefully if there is any doubt about the seriousness of the defendant's breach. If the claimant purports to accept a repudiation by the defendant, and a court later decides that they were not entitled to do so, it is then the claimant who has repudiated the contract. In the case of an anticipatory repudiatory breach, if the claimant has terminated the contract before the time for completion of performance, the court must look at the position at the date of that termination. Whether there was or was not a fundamental breach at that date involves looking at the benefit the claimant hoped to gain from the contract and the extent to which they had been deprived of it, or a substantial part of it, at that date, taking account (among other things) of the extent to which the breach was remediable (*Ampurius Nu Homes Holdings Ltd v Telford Homes (Creekside) Ltd* [2013] 4 All ER 377).

Parties can of course agree to avoid the normal consequences of the common law. Their contract may provide expressly for the circumstances in which it will be terminated or not in the event of a breach, or what efforts must be made to remedy a breach before any further consequences follow.

3.2.4 The claimant has suffered loss or damage

Although a breach of contract may be established, there can be no effective liability for that breach unless it has caused the claimant loss or damage. Technically loss and damage are not the same thing: loss means financial loss, but damage is a broader concept of harm, for example injury to the person, or loss of reputation. However, damage can be given a value in terms of money when it comes to the assessment of damages. Most claims for breach of contract are in reality for loss, but in pleadings the term 'loss and damage' is almost invariably used, alleging both have been suffered by the claimant.

What loss or damage can be proved is a matter of evidence. The general rule is that the claimant must prove both the fact of damage and its amount, although where it is clear that a loss has been caused, difficulty in actually assessing that loss will not bar relief. There is usually no difficulty in proving loss, but problems can arise when the loss claimed is speculative. The claimant will almost certainly have entered into the contract with the objective of making a profit, but they may have been willing to take the risk of a loss. The test is whether the claimant can show that they would have made a profit on the balance of probabilities. Once it can be shown that the claimant would probably have made a profit, the loss is established and the court must quantify it as best it can. However, the more speculative it is, the lower the award of damages will be: damages awards are conservative in these circumstances. Similar issues arise where the breach of contract is alleged to have caused the claimant loss of business.

There is a possible exception to the normal balance of probabilities test where the loss depends upon a large number of contingencies, but can still be shown to exist. If the claimant can show they had a chance of receiving a benefit, and that the breach of contract has caused them to lose that chance, they can recover damages for the loss of the chance even where the chance was less than a probability (see *Chaplin v Hicks* [1911] 2 KB 786).

There is no more to be said about this ingredient here. The chief consideration when it comes to loss and damage is the quantification of it, in other words the assessment of damages, which is dealt with in **Chapter 5**.

3.2.5 The loss and damage was caused by the breach

There can be no liability for loss unless there is a causative link between the breach and the loss. Put simply, the breach must have caused the loss. In the majority of cases this is so straightforward and obvious that it scarcely needs thinking about. But, strictly speaking, the test is essentially the 'but for' test—the claimant must be able to prove that but for the defendant's breach of contract there would have been no loss (see *Banque Bruxelles Lambert SA v Eagle Star Insurance Co Ltd* [1995] QB 375). This has to be established on the balance of probabilities.

But this test may not always be quite enough by itself. The breach must be the effective or dominant cause of loss rather than providing merely an opportunity to sustain loss. It is for the court to exercise common sense in assessing whether a breach was the cause or merely the occasion for the loss (see *Galoo Ltd v Bright Grahame Murray* [1994] 1 WLR 1360).

Difficulties can arise when there are multiple or competing causes of the loss. Provided the 'but for' test is satisfied it does not matter if there is also another concurrent cause of the loss. Where the breach is one of a number of causes of the loss, and all have had an equal impact in causing that loss, the breach will be taken to have caused the loss (see *Monarch SS v Karishamns* [1949] AC 196). Where the breach partly causes the loss and the loss is otherwise due to the actions of a third party, liability for breach will arise if the acts of that party were contemplated by the defendant (see *De La Bere v Pearson Ltd* [1908] 1 KB 48; *Beoco Ltd v Alfa Laval Co Ltd* [1994] 3 WLR 1179).

3.2.6   The loss was not too remote

It may seem surprising that we are considering this topic as an essential requirement that must be satisfied in order to establish lability for breach of contract. After all, an allegation that the loss suffered by the claimant was too remote to be recovered is one that will be raised by the defendant. But once the issue is raised, the burden of proof is on the claimant to show that their loss is recoverable loss. So lack of remoteness is in fact an essential ingredient in establishing liability.

Not all loss that has been caused by a breach of contract will be recoverable. It must not be too 'remote' from the breach. The basic test for remoteness in contract, first laid down in *Hadley v Baxendale* [1854] 9 Ex 341, is whether the loss suffered is 'such as may fairly and reasonably be considered either arising naturally, i.e., according to the usual course of things, from such breach of contract itself, or such as may reasonably be supposed to have been in the contemplation of both parties, at the time they made the contract, as the probable result of the breach of it'.

Although there are two limbs to this test, they are not mutually exclusive. Each is based on what might reasonably be contemplated as a result of the breach (see *Jackson v Royal Bank of Scotland plc* [2005] 2 All ER 71, where the House of Lords reaffirmed the *Hadley v Baxendale* test). Nevertheless the two limbs can be applied separately: it is enough that either one is satisfied for the loss to be recoverable.

The first limb is often quoted as referring to loss that is a 'natural and probable consequence' of the breach. It is probably very close to the idea of reasonable foreseeability, and causes little difficulty in practice. The test can be applied largely by common sense, and does not require any specific evidence to establish it, other than evidence of how the loss was caused.

The second limb has been considered further in cases such as *Victoria Laundry (Windsor) Ltd v Newman Industries Ltd* [1949] 2 KB 528 and *The Heron II* [1969] 1 AC 350. It is now clear that the loss must have been contemplated by the parties at the time of the contract as a likely, rather than a probable, result of the breach. In *The Heron II* the phrases 'not unlikely', 'a real danger', and 'a serious possibility' were all used. This limb is subjective: it depends on what the parties could reasonably have foreseen, not what the reasonable person could foresee. This will depend in many cases on the actual knowledge of the parties, and specific evidence may be required as to what that knowledge was, typically the defendant's knowledge of the claimant's business and circumstances. In the light of that special knowledge what the parties can reasonably be supposed to have contemplated may be considerably wider than what is reasonably foreseeable in the objective sense.

It is not necessary that the parties should have contemplated the precise damage suffered or the precise causation of it, or the precise quantum of it. It is enough that the type of damage was within their contemplation. The degree of likelihood of the loss flowing from the breach that is required is not easy to define. It is probable that a higher degree of likelihood is required in contract than in tort: *H Parsons (Livestock) Ltd v Uttley, Ingham & Co Ltd* [1978] QB 791.

In a radical departure, the majority of the House of Lords in *Transfield Shipping Inc v Mercator Shipping Inc (The Achilleas)* [2008] 4 All ER 159 approached the question of remoteness more from the point of view of what damage the parties had assumed responsibility for. They took the view that a loss that was beyond what the parties could reasonably have foreseen, and on a true construction of the contract could be taken to have assumed responsibility for, was of a different kind and too remote to be recovered under the first limb of *Hadley v Baxendale*. The net result was the same as would have been reached applying the conventional test, but the case gives rise to the question of whether a new approach might develop.

When there is co-extensive liability for breach of contract and negligence, the correct test for remoteness is the contractual, not the tortious, test (*Wellesley Partners LLP v Withers LLP* [2015] EWCA Civ 1146).

3.3 What can defeat or limit the claim?

3.3.1 The claimant has repudiated the contract

It is not uncommon when the parties are in a contractual dispute that each accuses the other of being in breach of the contract. The defendant may allege that the claimant is in fundamental breach and has therefore repudiated the contract, and that therefore the defendant is discharged from their obligations and is not in breach by failing to perform them. Exactly the same principles apply in reverse as when the claimant has accepted a repudiation by the defendant. See **3.2.3.2** and **3.2.3.3**.

3.3.2 The defendant has lawfully rescinded the contract

The claimant's claim will fail if the defendant is not in fact in breach at all, but has lawfully rescinded the contract, or is entitled to rescind it, on the basis that they entered into it in reliance on a misrepresentation by the claimant. There is more on this in **Chapter 6**.

3.3.3 Reliance on an exclusion or limitation clause

3.3.3.1 Incorporation of exclusion or limitation clauses

An exclusion clause in a contract seeks to exclude a party's liability for any loss or damage in certain defined circumstances; a limitation clause is one which limits such liability either generally, to certain types of loss, or to a specified sum. Such clauses are very common in contracts, and the defendant may well wish to rely on one to defeat or limit the claimant's claim.

The first issue in relation to an exclusion clause is whether the clause has been incorporated into the contract. It cannot be incorporated if the claimant is unaware of it. The defendant cannot hide it in the small print. There are three ways in which such a clause can be validly incorporated:

(a) Because it is in the main body of a written contract which the claimant has signed. This will be more or less conclusive.

(b) Because it is contained or referred to in a document intended to have contractual effect and the defendant has expressly brought it to A's notice before or at the time of contracting, or taken reasonable steps to do so. What steps are reasonable is a question of fact. The more unusual or unexpected the clause, the more notice is required.

(c) Because there has been a long and consistent course of dealing between the claimant and the defendant and the clause has always been part of their previous contracts.

3.3.3.2 Interpretation of exclusion or limitation clauses

If the clause is found to be a part of the contract, the court will then have to examine the clause to see whether it operates in the circumstances which have occurred and covers the loss or damage which has been suffered. There is a common law rule, known as the *contra proferentem* rule, which requires an exclusion clause to be strictly construed against the person seeking to rely on it. The rule also applies, though less strictly, to limitation clauses.

Such clauses, if intended to exclude liability for negligence, must do so expressly (almost certainly by using the word 'negligence') or be capable of no other interpretation.

Otherwise, whether a clause is effective depends on the actual breach and the true construction of the contract. The more serious the breach, the less likely it is that the parties intended an exclusion clause to apply: *Photo Production Ltd v Securicor Transport Ltd* [1980] AC 827. A party cannot rely on an exclusion clause in the event of their own repudiation or fundamental breach unless the parties clearly intended the clause to apply in these circumstances. In order for it to do so, it needs to be drafted in very clear and unequivocal terms. And even if the parties' intention is clear, the clause may still be held unreasonable under the Unfair Contract Terms Act 1977 or unfair under the Consumer Rights Act 2015.

3.3.3.3   The Unfair Contract Terms Act 1977

However, the Unfair Contract Terms Act 1977 (UCTA) imposes restrictions on the effectiveness of some exclusion and limitation clauses in business contracts (in other words all contracts other than consumer contracts). The main restrictions are as follows:

(a) A contract term or notice cannot exclude or limit liability for personal injury or death resulting from negligence (s. 2(1)). Negligence means breach of any contractual obligation or common law duty to take reasonable care or exercise reasonable skill, or breach of the common duty of care under the Occupiers' Liability Act 1957.

(b) A term or notice can otherwise only exclude or restrict liability for negligence if it satisfies the reasonableness test (s. 2(2)).

(c) In a contract on standard terms an exclusion or limitation clause must satisfy the reasonableness test (s. 3).

(d) A term cannot exclude or restrict liability for breach of the implied term as to title under s. 12 of the Sale of Goods Act 1979 (s. 6(1)).

(e) A term cannot exclude or restrict liability for breach of the implied terms as to satisfactory quality or fitness for purpose under s. 14 of the Sale of Goods Act 1979, or correspondence with description under s. 13 of that Act unless it satisfies the reasonableness test (s. 6(2)).

The reasonableness test is set out in s. 11 of UCTA, with additional guidelines in Sch. 2. The essential test is whether the term was a fair and reasonable one to be included in all the circumstances, but there are many specific matters to be taken into consideration where relevant. The burden of proving reasonableness rests with the party seeking to rely on the clause.

3.3.3.4   The Consumer Rights Act 2015

UCTA no longer applies to consumer contracts. These are now governed by the Consumer Rights Act 2015. This Act goes a long way beyond UCTA, and introduces a new code applicable to contracts between a trader and a consumer. It applies to contracts for the sale, hire, and transfer of goods, for the supply of digital content, and for the supply of services to a consumer. The main restrictions are as follows:

(a) A trader cannot by a term or consumer notice exclude or restrict liability for death or personal injury resulting from negligence (s. 65(1)). Negligence is defined in the same way as in UCTA.

(b) A term which excludes or restricts liability for breach of any of the following statutory terms is not binding on a consumer (s. 31):

- The term as to title (s. 17)

- The term as to goods being of satisfactory quality (s. 9)

- The term as to goods being fit for a particular purpose (s. 10)

- The term as to goods conforming to a description (s. 11).

(c) And most importantly, any other term or consumer notice which is unfair is not binding on a consumer (s. 62). A term or notice is unfair if, contrary to the requirement of good faith, it causes a significant imbalance in the parties' rights and obligations under the contract to the detriment of the consumer. Section 63 and Sch. 2 then go on to provide a non-exhaustive list of terms which may be regarded as unfair.

(d) A trader must ensure that any written contract term or consumer notice is transparent, meaning that it must be expressed in plain and intelligible language and be legible (s. 68).

(e) If a term in a consumer contract or notice could have different meanings, the meaning that is most favourable to the consumer is to prevail (s. 69).

3.3.4 Force majeure clauses

Many contracts contain what is known as a force majeure clause. This is not a precise legal term but it describes a clause by which the parties agree that one or both of them will be excused in whole or part from performance, or entitled to suspend or delay performance, in the event of some specified occurrence beyond their control. The rules on incorporation and interpretation are similar to the rules for exemption clauses (see **3.3.3.1** and **3.3.3.2**). If what would otherwise be a breach of contract comes within the force majeure clause, it can be excused and there will be no liability.

It is for the party relying on a force majeure clause to prove that it applies. They will usually need to show four things:

(a) that the event specified has occurred;

(b) that they have been prevented, hindered, or delayed from performing their obligation by that event;

(c) that their non-performance was due to circumstances beyond their control; and

(d) that there were no reasonable steps that they could have taken to avoid or mitigate the event or its consequences.

It is unclear whether a party can rely on a force majeure clause when the event specified was one which was reasonably foreseeable at the time of the contract and could have been provided for. It may be difficult to argue that they should be allowed to do so. However, there is no absolute rule that they cannot. Unless the contract expressly states the contrary, a force majeure clause will not be construed to cover an event brought about by a party's negligence or wilful default. Beyond these rules the scope of a force majeure clause will depend on its construction. 'Prevented' requires performance to be physically or legally impossible. 'Hindered' or 'delayed' require something less.

The Unfair Contract Terms Act 1977 and the Consumer Rights Act 2015 are capable of applying to force majeure clauses where appropriate.

3.3.5 Expiry of limitation period

The can be no liability if the claim is time-barred, because the limitation period has expired. The limitation period in contract is six years, or 12 years if the contract was by deed. However, there are many exceptions, including:

(a) The limitation period for a personal injury claim is prima facie three years. This will be dealt with more fully under liability in tort (**Chapter 4**), but it applies just as much where injury is caused by a breach of contract.

(b) The limitation period for a claim for recovery of rent or mortgage interest is six years even if the lease or mortgage was by deed.

Time starts to run from when the cause of action accrues, which in contract is the date of breach.

3.3.6   Accord and satisfaction

This is old-fashioned terminology for a contract which settles a dispute arising out of another contract. The parties to the original contract have agreed to rescind it for consideration (usually the payment of money and/or forbearance to sue). In such a case no claim can be maintained on the original contract; a new claim will have to be commenced for breach of the settlement accord.

3.3.7   Failure to mitigate

The claimant has a duty to mitigate their loss. This does not mean that they are required to minimise their loss at all costs, rather that they must take all reasonable steps to do so. If the claimant fails to do what they could reasonably have done to minimise their loss, damages will be assessed on the basis of what the loss would have been had the claimant taken those reasonable steps. Any reasonable expense incurred in order to be able to mitigate may be recovered as damages. Indeed, if it was reasonable for the claimant to incur that expense in an attempt to mitigate, it will be recoverable even if, in fact, no mitigation is achieved. No remoteness test is applied to the reasonable cost of mitigation.

The claimant is also under a duty not to do anything unreasonable subsequent to the damage which might exacerbate it, and not to incur any unreasonable expense which increases the extent of their loss (see *Payzu Ltd v Saunders* [1919] 2 KB 581 and *Banco de Portugal v Waterlow and Sons Ltd* [1932] AC 452). If the claimant does so, damages will be assessed on the basis of what the loss would have been had they not taken that action or incurred that expense. However, a claimant is not deemed to have the benefit of hindsight: the test is simply whether it was reasonable for the claimant to have behaved as they did at the time.

Where the effect of the mitigating act is to wipe out the loss from the breach, according to *British Westinghouse Co v Underground Electric Railways Co of London* [1912] AC 673, the claimant will be entitled to nominal damages only. If the claimant actually makes a profit out of mitigating, they are not obliged to set that gain off against other claims against the defendant.

When dealing with mitigation the courts apply the test of what is reasonable subjectively; that is, the question is whether it was reasonable for this claimant in all the circumstances to have behaved as they did, not whether a reasonable person would have behaved in that way.

The burden of proof is on the defendant to show that the claimant has failed to take reasonable steps to mitigate, not on the claimant to show that they have done so. Any suggestion that the claimant should have to show their actions or decisions were reasonable is probably bad law (see *Geest plc v Lansiquot* [2003] 1 All ER 383).

3.3.8   The claimant's poverty

It has been held that loss which results purely from the claimant's own poverty is irrecoverable (see *Owners of Dredger Liesbosch v Owners of Steamship Edison* [1933] AC 449). However, it would seem that if the claimant's poverty prevents them from mitigating the loss, this will not affect the claim for damages (see *Perry v Sidney Phillips and Son* [1982] 1 WLR 1297 and *Alcoa Minerals of Jamaica v Broderick* [2000] 3 WLR 23). It has also been held by the House of Lords in *Lagden v O'Connor* [2004] 1 All ER 277 that if a claimant incurs a greater loss as a result of their poverty than they would have done if they had been able to afford to mitigate, that greater loss is recoverable. It is now highly arguable that the principle of *The Liesbosch* is no longer good law.

3.3.9 Contributory negligence

The question can sometimes arise whether contributory negligence by the claimant can be a partial defence to a claim for breach of contract. The answer is generally that it cannot. There are three classes of case in which the issue can arise:

(a) Those where liability arises both in contract and tort co-extensively, in which case the Law Reform (Contributory Negligence) Act 1945 applies and damages will be reduced to take account of any contributory negligence on the part of the claimant (see *Forsikringsaktieselskapet Vesta v Butcher* [1989] AC 852). Co-extensive liability is dealt with more fully in **Chapter 4**.

(b) Those where the breach of contract does not amount to a tort as well, in which case the 1945 Act does not apply and any contributory negligence on the part of the claimant can be disregarded (see *Lambert v Lewis* [1982] AC 225).

(c) Those where there is both strict liability in contract and co-extensive liability in contract and tort. In such a case there can be no defence of contributory negligence (*Barclays Bank plc v Fairclough Building Ltd* [1995] 1 All ER 289).

4

Liability in tort

4.1 Introduction

4.1.1 The aim of this chapter

There are a great many torts, but to go into the elements of all of them is beyond the scope of this chapter. Some involve the performance of some deliberate act calculated or likely to cause harm to the claimant, for example assault and battery, conversion, defamation. Others are torts of strict liability, for example *Rylands v Fletcher* liability, product liability. Interference with goods is dealt with in **Chapter 9**. But the most common torts involve the breach of some duty owed by the defendant to the claimant, for example negligence, occupiers' liability, and breach of statutory duty. These are the ones we will deal with in this chapter, with only passing references to other torts.

As with breach of contract in **Chapter 3**, we cannot sensibly write about damages for negligence without first considering the basic principles of liability in negligence. This chapter is also of particular importance because it may be some years since you studied this subject, and unlike the law of contract this is a fast-moving area of law, with many relevant new cases being reported every year. So this chapter is intended to be both a reminder and an update to your knowledge in this area.

However, this chapter does not aim to give a comprehensive statement of the law of negligence or provide details of all the latest cases—you will need to look these up for yourself. Instead we will go through the essential ingredients that must be established before there can be liability in negligence, and the various factors that can prevent or limit liability, with an overview of recent case law in the relevant sections.

4.1.2 The scope of this chapter

As well as the tort or negligence, we shall also look at the related torts of occupiers' liability and breach of statutory duty. These are three torts whose practical significance is so great that we need to reintroduce them to you from a practitioner's point of view. We will also consider the situation when there is concurrent liability in contract and negligence.

The commonest by far of all tortious claims is the action for damages for personal injury. Such claims will almost always be founded on negligence, occupiers' liability, or breach of statutory duty. Although you will have studied these at the academic stage, you are likely to have done so in a rather academic way, and some practical notes on these three important causes of action now follow.

4.2 Negligence

4.2.1 Ingredients of the tort of negligence

There are effectively five requirements that must be satisfied before liability can be established in negligence:

(1) That the defendant owed the claimant a duty of care

(2) That the defendant was in breach of that duty (i.e. negligent)

(3) That the claimant suffered loss and damage

(4) That the damage was caused by the defendant's negligence

(5) That the damage was not too remote

As well as these ingredients, in many cases the court is concerned with the question of quantum, that is, the extent of the damage recoverable in financial terms. Assessment of damages is dealt with in later chapters. However, it must be realised that in negligence, far more than in contract, it is not always easy to draw a line between what is an issue of liability and what is a matter of damages.

4.2.2 The practitioner's view of negligence

At the academic stage you will largely have been concerned with the duty situation, the principles of reasonable foreseeability, etc. The practitioner is largely concerned with breach of duty, that is, negligence. The situations in which a duty of care is owed by one person to another are on the whole so well established that in practice it is unusual for an issue to arise as to duty. It is only in the comparatively rare cases where there is no clear authority on whether a duty is owed, or a claimant seeks to establish a new duty situation, that a court will be concerned with this aspect of the tort. A general practitioner is, however, concerned almost every day with the question of whether someone has been negligent or not.

4.2.3 The defendant owed the claimant a duty of care

4.2.3.1 The basic requirements

Various attempts have been made over the years to define the circumstances in which a duty of care is owed by one person to another. The classic approach is that laid down in *Caparo Industries plc v Dickman* [1990] 2 AC 605; namely that there are three conditions to be satisfied:

(a) A relationship of 'proximity' or 'neighbourhood' between the claimant and the defendant.

(b) It is reasonably foreseeable that negligence by the defendant could cause loss and damage to the claimant

(c) It is fair, just, and reasonable that a duty of care should be imposed.

How this test is applied varies from one type of case to another. It is only by reference to particular types of case that one can deduce precisely what duty is owed (as opposed to whether it is owed). This test will guide the court when it is considering new duty situations. It is of little help to parties and their legal advisers when considering liability in a particular case. Regard needs to be had to previous cases where duty situations, and their limits, have been established.

However, more recently the Supreme Court has stated consistently that this is not the only approach: there cannot be a single test. Instead the court should adopt an approach based on precedent, and on the development of the law incrementally and by analogy with established authorities. When a question arises as to whether a duty should be created in a previously undecided situation, the court should look for the closest analogies, and exercise its judgement. It is this exercise of judgement that involves consideration of what is fair, just, and reasonable in all the circumstances (*Robinson v Chief Constable of West Yorkshire Police* [2018] 2 All ER 1041; see also *James-Bowen v Metropolitan Police Commissioner* [2018] 4 All ER 1007). But this exercise is unnecessary when a case falls within an established duty situation: *Darnley v Croydon Health Services NHS Trust* [2019] 1 All ER 27.

These cases explain rather than alter the law laid down in *Caparo v Dickman*, which therefore still has some relevance.

4.2.3.2 The relationship of proximity

Whether the relationship exists depends partly on the factual relationship of the parties and partly on reasonable foreseeability. The proximity may be physical, circumstantial, or to do with the conduct and intention of the parties towards each other.

Where the defendant's act has caused physical injury to the claimant or done physical damage to the claimant's property, there is automatically sufficient proximity for a duty of care to arise.

The assumption of responsibility by the defendant towards the claimant, particularly in the context of professional services, may give rise to a relationship of proximity, or even be enough in its own right to establish a duty of care. See **4.2.5.1**.

The existence of a contract between the parties may either tend to evidence the existence of a duty or tend to preclude a separate duty in tort. See **4.6** to find out more about concurrent liability in contract and tort.

4.2.3.3 Reasonable foreseeability

This is strictly speaking a question of fact, but the situations in which it has been held to be reasonably foreseeable that negligence could cause harm to the claimant are often so well established that it becomes a matter of law. Once a duty situation has been established, it is of no particular significance any longer.

Whether the potential harm is reasonably foreseeable depends on what the reasonable person in the defendant's situation might be expected to foresee, not what the defendant actually foresaw.

Where the defendant is a child, the test is what a reasonable child, not adult, in the defendant's situation would foresee—*Mullin v Richards* [1998] 1 All ER 920.

4.2.3.4 Fair, just, and reasonable

Whenever it is claimed that a duty of care should exist in a situation where none has previously been imposed, the court must consider this third requirement, but adopting the incremental approach summarised here. There are circumstances in which the courts are obliged to consider whether a duty of care is owed. They may hold that no duty is owed, in spite of the other two requirements being satisfied, if it would not be fair, just, and reasonable to impose a duty.

4.2.3.5 Negligent misstatement

The requirements for the existence of a duty of care in cases of negligent misstatement are in principle the same, but a little different in their application. The relationship between the parties must be more than proximate, it must be 'special': *Hedley Byrne & Co Ltd v Heller & Partners Ltd* [1964] AC 465. This can arise with or without the existence of a contract, but it is not created simply by the existence of a contract. It must be reasonably foreseeable that the claimant would rely on the defendant's statement. This is probably all that is required in the case of a specific statement made to a specific claimant. The defendant may have had some special knowledge rendering it reasonably foreseeable. In the case of a general statement made to sections of the public as a whole, reasonable foreseeability that the claimant would rely on the statement is insufficient (*Caparo Industries plc v Dickman* [1990] 2 AC 605)—rather an actual intention on the part of the defendant is required: *Possfund Custodian Trustee Ltd v Diamond* [1996] 2 All ER 774.

It must be reasonable for the claimant to rely on the statement. This probably goes both to the special relationship and to reasonable foreseeability. In *NRAM Ltd v Steel [2018] 3 All ER 81* the Supreme Court held that it was not reasonable for the claimant to rely on a representation about a fact wholly within their own knowledge.

Henderson v Merrett Syndicates Ltd [1994] AC 145 suggests that liability is based on an assumption of responsibility by the defendant and that there should be a common approach to negligent statements, advice, and professional services.

4.2.3.6 Who can have a duty imposed on them?

In *Chandler v Cape plc* [2012] 3 All ER 640, it was held that in certain circumstances a duty could be imposed on the parent company of the company that had actually committed the tort.

4.2.4   Common duty situations in practice

Particularly common and important duty of care situations in practice are:

(a) The duty owed by users of the highway to other users and to those beside the highway.

(b) The duty owed by manufacturers of products to users or consumers of these products. This has now largely been superseded by product liability under Pt I of the Consumer Protection Act 1987.

(c) The duty owed by professional persons to their clients: such duties are usually contractual as well as tortious, but may arise in tort alone, particularly in cases of clinical negligence.

(d) The duty owed by builders (and others responsible for safety in buildings) to owners and occupiers of buildings. Specific cases have severely restricted the scope of these duties (see *D & F Estates Ltd v Church Commissioners* [1989] AC 177 and *Murphy v Brentwood District Council* [1991] 1 AC 398, in which the House of Lords held that *Anns v Merton London Borough Council* [1978] AC 728 was wrongly decided).

(e) The duty owed by employers to their employees. Frequently known as the three-fold duty laid down by *Wilson's and Clyde Coal Co Ltd v English* [1938] AC 57, it is strictly a single duty, but for practical purposes it is a duty with five identifiable limbs:

    (i)   to provide a safe place of work,

    (ii) to provide a safe system of work,

    (iii) to provide effective supervision,

    (iv) to provide proper plant and materials,

    (v)   to provide competent staff.

The duty arises both in tort and contract, but for practical purposes it can be treated as a tortious duty. It is a duty of reasonable care, not an absolute duty, but the standard of care expected can be surprisingly high on occasions. The duty is non-delegable: that is to say, no one can discharge it but the employer, who cannot avoid liability by appointing someone else to discharge it.

4.2.5   Other duty situations

4.2.5.1   Assumption of responsibility

The courts have developed the doctrine of 'assumption of responsibility' in determining whether a duty of care is owed and the scope of such a duty. The leading case is *Henderson v Merrett Syndicates Ltd* [1994] AC 145. Other recent cases showing the application of the doctrine are: *Williams v Natural Life Health Foods Ltd* [1998] 2 All ER 577; *Costello v Chief Constable of the Northumbria Police* [1999] 1 All ER 550; *Leach v Chief Constable of Gloucestershire Constabulary* [1999] 1 All ER 215; *Watson v British Board of Boxing Control* [2001] 2 WLR 1256; *Lennon v Metropolitan Police Commissioner* [2004] 2 All ER 266; and *Morcom v Biddick* [2014] All ER (D) 248 (Feb).

It is not the case that a builder who enters into a contract with a house purchaser automatically assumes responsibility so as to give rise to a concurrent duty in tort: *Robinson v PE Jones (Contractors) Ltd* [2012] QB 44. This may be the beginning of a retreat from widespread concurrent liability in contract and tort.

4.2.5.2   Statutory bodies

An important issue is whether a duty of care can be owed by a statutory body which acts negligently in the discharge of its statutory functions. The leading cases are *X v Bedfordshire County Council* [1995] 3 All ER 353 and *Stovin v Wise* [1996] 3 All ER 801. Other cases involving public authorities are: *Gorringe v Calderdale Metropolitan Borough Council* [2004] 2 All ER 326; *Carty v Croydon LBC* [2005] 2 All ER 517; *Neil Martin Ltd v Revenue and Customs Commissioners* [2006] All ER (D) 137 (Revenue and Customs owe no duty of care to a taxpayer); *Jain v Trent Strategic*

Health Authority [2009] 1 All ER 957; *Connor v Surrey County Council* [2011] QB 429; *Sumner v Colborne* [2018] 3 All ER 1049; and *N v Poole Borough Council* [2019] 4 All ER 481. Other cases involving emergency services are: *Capital and Counties plc v Hampshire CC* [1997] 2 All ER 865; *OLL Ltd v Secretary of State for Transport* [1997] 3 All ER 897; *Kent v Griffiths* [2000] 2 All ER 474; *Bailey v HSS Alarms Ltd* The Times, 20 June 2000; and *HXA v Surrey County Council; YXA v Wolverhampton City Council* [2021] EWHC 2974 (QB), [2021] All ER (D) 43 (Nov) where it was held that a local authority owed no duty of care to protect children from abuse by their parents.

4.2.5.3   The police

Several attempts have been made to establish a duty of care owed by the police to a victim or witness to a crime. There is no general rule that there is such a duty: *Brooks v Metropolitan Police Commissioner* [2005] 2 All ER 489 and *Michael v Chief Constable of South Wales* [2015] 2 All ER 635. However, there is also no general rule that there is no such duty: *Robinson v Chief Constable of West Yorkshire Police* [2018] 2 All ER 1041. The distinction seems to be whether the danger of injury to a member of the public was one which the police themselves created, in which case a duty will be owed, or one which they did not themselves create, in which case no duty will arise. There may, however, be liability under the Human Rights Act 1998: *Van Colle v Chief Constable of Hertfordshire Police; Smith v Chief Constable of Sussex Police* [2008] 3 All ER 977. The police may also owe a duty of care to an undercover informer, though not in respect of economic loss (*Informer v Chief Constable* [2012] 3 All ER 601).

4.2.5.4   Nervous shock

The scope of the duty with regard to causing nervous shock in someone other than the primary victim was established in *Alcock v Chief Constable of South Yorkshire Police* [1992] 1 AC 310. The scope of the duty was extended in *Walters v North Glamorgan NHS Trust* [2002] All ER (D) 65 (Mar). In *P and another v Royal Wolverhampton NHS Trust* [2020] EWHC 1415 (QB) it was held that a duty may be owed where the nervous shock is caused by an event occurring some time after the negligent act or omission.

4.2.5.5   Solicitors' liability

The leading case on the duty owed by solicitors drafting a will to potential beneficiaries is *White v Jones* [1995] 2 AC 207. Other cases are: *Carr-Glynn v Frearsons* [1998] 4 All ER 225 and *Gibbons v Nelsons* The Times, 21 April 2000. An analogous situation arises in respect of pensions: *Gorham v British Telecom* [2000] 4 All ER 867. However, no duty of care is owed to an executor claiming on behalf of a beneficiary: *Chappell v Somers & Blake* [2003] 3 All ER 1076.

4.2.5.6   Clinical negligence

The question of when and to what extent a medical practitioner should inform a patient of the risks inherent in a procedure so that they can give informed consent has been fully considered by the Supreme Court in *Montgomery v Lanarkshire Health Board* [2015] 2 All ER 1031. A doctor has a duty to take reasonable care to ensure that the patient is informed about any material risks involved in the recommended treatment, and of any reasonable alternative treatments. The test of materiality is whether, in the circumstances, a reasonable person in the same position as the patient would be likely to regard a particular risk as significant, or the doctor is or should reasonably be aware that the patient would be likely to attach significance to it. The doctor is entitled to withhold from the patient information as to a risk if they reasonably consider that its disclosure would be seriously detrimental to the patient's health. The 'therapeutic exception' is, however, a limited exception to the general principle, and does not allow doctors to prevent their patients from taking an informed decision.

The Court of Appeal held in *Webster v Burton Hospitals NHS Foundation Trust* [2017] EWCA Civ 62 that the *Montgomery* decision meant that the *Bolam* test (*Bolam v Friern Hospital Management Committee* [1957] 2 All ER 118) was no longer the correct test in informed consent cases.

4.2.5.7   Other relevant cases

Other important recent cases concerned with the circumstances in which a duty of care will be owed, its nature, and its scope are: *Customs and Excise Commissioners v Barclays Bank plc* [2006] 4 All ER 256 (a bank does not owe a duty of care to a claimant in whose favour a freezing order has been granted); *Calvert v William Hill Credit Ltd* [2009] Ch 330 (no duty of care owed by a bookmaker to a problem gambler to prevent him gambling, where he would probably have ruined himself with another bookmaker in any event); *Orchard v Lee* [2009] ELR 178 (the duty and standard of care to be expected of children playing children's games); *Mitchell v Glasgow City Council* [2009] 3 All ER 205 (no duty of care owed by council to family of tenant killed by another tenant whose threatening behaviour the council was aware of and was taking action to prevent); *Everett v Comojo (UK) Ltd* [2012] 1 WLR 150 (the management of a nightclub held liable to a guest for an injury caused by a criminal assault by another guest); *McKie v Swindon College* [2011] IRLR 575 (duty owed by ex-employer not to give false information to the ex-employee's current employer, even though not given in a formal reference); *Scullion v Royal Bank of Scotland plc (t/a Colleys)* [2011] 1 WLR 3212 (no duty of care owed by mortgage lender's valuer to purchaser of buy-to-let property—*Smith v Eric S Bush* [1990] 1 AC 831 distinguished); *Smith v Ministry of Defence* [2013] 4 All ER 794 (there is no blanket immunity against claims by members of the armed forces injured on active military service); *Sebry v Companies House* [2015] 4 All ER 681 (the Registrar of Companies owes a duty to a company not to wrongly register a winding-up order against it which should have been registered to another company); and *James-Bowen v Metropolitan Police Commissioner* [2018] 4 All ER 1007 (an employer owes no duty to their employees to conduct litigation in a manner which protects them from economic or reputational harm).

4.2.5.8   Non-delegable duties

In *Woodland v Essex County Council* [2014] 1 All ER 482, the Supreme Court has revived the concept of non-delegable duties. Where there is a non-delegable duty of care the defendant can be held liable for the negligent acts of those for whom it would not normally be vicariously liable. The duty may exist either because the defendant has assumed that duty, or because it is fair, just, and reasonable to impose it.

However, a non-delegable duty may not exist, even where vicarious liability does: see, for example, *Armes v Nottinghamshire CC* [2018] 1 All ER 1.

4.2.6   Vicarious liability

4.2.6.1   As between an employer and an employee

In practice the majority of tortious actions are probably founded on vicarious rather than direct liability. Generally speaking a defendant will be vicariously liable for the tortious acts of their employees or agents, but not independent contractors. Vicarious liability for the act of an independent contractor will only arise where the defendant's duty was non-delegable and/or absolute. Vicarious liability for the acts of an employee or agent arises if the employee was acting in the course of their employment. If the employee was at their place of work during working hours, it is very difficult to show that they were not. Their act must be 'so divergent from the employment as to be plainly alien to and wholly distinguishable from the employment' (*Harrison v Michelin Tyre Co Ltd* [1985] 1 All ER 918).

Nowadays it is very rare for an employee or agent to be outside the scope of their employment. The test in *Harrison v Michelin Tyre Co Ltd* is very difficult to satisfy. Particular difficulties arise where the employee has committed a crime or some other wholly unauthorised act while employed by the defendant. The test to be applied in such cases was considered by the House of Lords in *Lister v Hesley Hall Ltd* [2001] 2 All ER 769 and applied in *Mattis v Pollock* [2004] 4 All ER 85, *Gravil v Carroll* [2008] All ER (D) 234 (Jun), *Maga v Trustees of the Birmingham Archdiocese of the Roman Catholic Church* [2010] 1 WLR 1441, and again by the Supreme Court in *Mohamud v WM Morrison Supermarkets plc* [2017] 1 All ER 15.

The test is essentially whether there is a sufficiently close connection between the position in which the wrongdoer is employed and the wrongful conduct to justify a finding of vicarious liability as a matter of justice. Applying this test in *Weddall v Barchester Healthcare Ltd; Wallbank v Wallbank Fox Designs Ltd* [2012] EWCA Civ 25, the Court of Appeal reached opposite conclusions in two very similar cases involving the employer's liability for a criminal assault by one employee on another. The same test had to be applied in *Bellman v Northampton Recruitment Ltd* [2019] 1 All ER 1133, another case of assault. In *Majrowski v Guy's and St Thomas' NHS Trust* [2006] 4 All ER 395, the House of Lords held an employer vicariously liable for harassment by one employee against another.

In a very different case, *Various Claimants v WM Morrison Supermarket plc* [2020] 4 All ER 1, the defendant was held not to be vicariously liable for a criminal data breach by a rogue employee, thereby breaching the privacy and confidentiality of its other employees, the claimants. The Supreme Court in that case took the opportunity to review the authorities, including those mentioned, and to examine closely the limits of the 'close connection' test. These cases were recently applied in *Chell v Tarmac Cement Limited* [2022] All ER (D) 21 (Jan).

The principles to be applied where considering the liability of innocent partners in a firm for the fraudulent acts of another partner are exactly the same (*Dubai Aluminium Co Ltd v Salaam* [2003] 1 All ER 97).

4.2.6.2   Outside the relationship of employer and employee

We were reminded in *E v English Province of Our Lady of Charity* [2012] 4 All ER 1152 and *Various Claimants v Catholic Child Welfare Society and others* [2013] 1 All ER 670 that vicarious liability can arise out of relationships other than that of employer and employee. Applying that case, the Supreme Court held in *Cox v Ministry of Justice* [2017] 1 All ER 1 that the prison service was vicariously liable for the negligent act of a prisoner; and in *Armes v Nottinghamshire County Council* [2018] 1 All ER 1 that a local authority was vicariously liable for the acts of foster parents towards a child in their care. However, in *Brayshaw v Partners of Aspley Surgery* [2019] 2 All ER 997 it was held that a doctors' surgery could not be vicariously liable for the acts of a locum which went beyond recognised medical practice. It should also be noted that in *Barclays Bank v Various Claimants* [2020] 4 All ER 19, the Supreme Court ruled that these cases had not replaced the fundamental rule that an employer cannot be vicariously liable for the acts of an independent contractor, whose relationship is not akin to that of an employee.

4.2.6.3   Vicarious liability between contractors

It was held in *Viasystems (Tyneside) Ltd v Thermal Transfer (Northern) Ltd* [2005] 4 All ER 1181 that it is possible for more than one employer to be vicariously liable for the acts of the same individual workman. It is also well established that an employee of one company can become in effect the servant of another if the first company lends the employee's services to the second company and the second company has a sufficient degree of control over the way the services are to be performed (*Mersey Docks and Harbour Board v Coggins & Griffith (Liverpool) Ltd* [1947] AC 1). The Court of Appeal in *Biffa Waste Services Ltd v Maschinenfabrik Ernst Hese GmbH* [2009] QB 725 held that the right or duty of a contractor to supervise the workmen of a subcontractor did not give them sufficient control to trigger this principle. The court went on to hold that the principle under which a person hiring an independent contractor was liable for the contractor's negligence in carrying out any extra-hazardous activity should be severely restricted and applied only to activities which were exceptionally dangerous whatever precautions were taken.

4.2.7   The defendant was negligent

Whether the defendant was negligent, in other words in breach of the duty of care, is a question of fact and evidence, but in most cases is the only live issue.

4.2.7.1   Standard of care

However, whether a defendant is negligent depends on the standard of care expected of them. This is whatever is reasonable in the circumstances. What is reasonable in the circumstances is to be judged objectively. A body which sets itself very high standards of safety or establishes a policy will not be negligent merely because it fails to match up to those standards or fulfil that policy: *Esdale v Dover District Council* [2010] EWCA Civ 409.

What is reasonable in the circumstances will, however, depend on the level of skill and expertise professed by the defendant: *Whitehouse v Jordan* [1981] 1 WLR 246. So if a professional person claims to be an expert, or a specialist, to have some special skill or to have a great deal of experience, the standard of care they are obliged to provide is that of someone having that expertise, specialism, or skill or experience; and that will also be true if they have overstated their capabilities.

In a case of professional negligence, an error of judgement is not of itself negligence. The professional defendant is probably protected if they have acted in accordance with received professional opinion, even if there is other professional opinion against them: *Bolam v Friern Hospital Management Committee* [1957] 1 WLR 582. However, it may be possible to show that professional opinion is illogical and unreasonable: *Bolitho v City & Hackney HA* [1997] 4 All ER 771.

A practitioner of alternative medicine is to be judged by the standards appropriate to their art, not by the standards expected of an orthodox medical practitioner; but it may be considered appropriate for an alternative medical practitioner to have some awareness of orthodox medicine: *Shakoor v Situ* [2000] 4 All ER 181.

By s. 1 of the Compensation Act 2006, a court considering a claim in negligence may have regard to whether a requirement on a defendant to take certain steps might deter people from undertaking or participating in a desirable activity. The aim is to try to halt in certain instances the deterrent effect of potential liability.

4.2.7.2   *Res ipsa loquitur*

The principle of *res ipsa loquitur* is frequently pleaded, but rarely successful or even relevant. It raises a presumption of negligence on the defendant's part in certain circumstances, in the absence of any evidence of negligence. It is always preferable to prove negligence by evidence rather than rely on *res ipsa loquitur*. It is therefore very much a last resort for a claimant who is unable to prove negligence by any other means.

The presumption arises if three conditions are satisfied:

(a)   what happened is something that would not normally happen without negligence;

(b)   the thing that caused the damage was under the sole control of the defendant; and

(c)   there is no evidence as to how or why the accident took place;

There is then a presumption that the accident was caused by the defendant's negligence which it is for the defendant to rebut.

4.2.7.3   Joint tortfeasors

In *Fish & Fish Ltd v Sea Shepherd UK* [2015] AC 1229 the Supreme Court has clarified the law on common design. In order to be liable with a principal tortfeasor a defendant must be proved to have combined with the principal tortfeasor to commit the tort; and that requires proof that the defendant acted in pursuance of a common design and in a way which furthered the commission of the tort by the principal tortfeasor.

4.3.7.4   Compensation Act 2006

Two significant principles have been established.

(i)   By s 1 of the 2006 Act:

A court considering a claim in negligence or breach of statutory duty may, in determining whether the defendant should have taken particular steps to meet a standard of care (whether by taking precautions against a risk or otherwise), have regard to whether a requirement to take those steps might—

(a)   *prevent a desirable activity from being undertaken at all, to a particular extent or in a particular way, or*

(b)   *discourage persons from undertaking functions in connection with a desirable activity.*

The section is entitled 'Deterrent effect of potential liability' which explains the purpose of the provision. There has been concern that fear of litigation, and the demands of insurers, have tended to produce a defensive attitude to the conduct of public affairs, particularly by local authorities and schools, and s. 1 seeks to reverse this trend.

Section 1 largely reinforces the decision of the House of Lords in *Tomlinson v Congleton BC* [2003] 3 All ER 1122, where it was held that the social value of an activity is a factor to be taken account of in deciding the extent of any duty of care. This principle was recently applied in *Humphrey v Aegis Defence Services Ltd* [2017] 2 All ER 235.

(ii) By s. 2 of the 2006 Act:

> *An apology, an offer of treatment or other redress, shall not of itself amount to an admission of negligence or breach of statutory duty.*

This is intended to put paid to the possibility that saying 'Sorry' after an accident, or behaving in a considerate manner to the victim of an accident (e.g. offering a lift to someone whose vehicle has been damaged), could be taken as an admission of liability.

4.2.7.5   Claimants taking obvious risks

In line with the Compensation Act 2006, there is a growing trend in case law against finding a defendant liable to a claimant who has been injured in circumstances where the claimant voluntarily undertook an activity involving a risk which was plainly obvious, even if the defendant could in theory have done more to help the claimant avoid it: see, for example, *Poppleton v Trustees of the Portsmouth Youth Activity Committee* [2009] All ER (D) 150 (Jun), *Vaughan v Ministry of Defence* [2015] All ER (D) 207 (May), and the cases referred to in **4.3** under occupiers' liability.

4.2.7.6   Social Action, Responsibility and Heroism Act 2015

Under this Act there are three matters to be taken into account in deciding whether someone has been negligent:

(i)   whether the defendant was acting for the benefit of society or any of its members (s. 2);

(ii) whether the defendant demonstrated a predominantly responsible approach towards protecting the safety of others (s. 3); and

(iii) whether the defendant was acting heroically by intervening in an emergency to assist an individual in danger (s. 4).

As lawyers have pointed out, this Act adds nothing to the pre-existing law: these three matters would always be relevant to the reasonableness of a defendant's actions in any event.

4.2.8   The claimant has suffered loss and damage

4.2.8.1   Proving loss and damage

The claimant must establish loss and damage in order to recover damages. The claimant does not, however, have to establish the extent of their loss, so long as they can prove it does exist: the court will then assess the damage as best it can. Difficulty of assessment is no bar to recovery. On this principle damages can be recovered for loss of a chance or opportunity.

4.2.8.2   Pure economic loss

There may, however, be some limitation in law as to the type of loss in respect of which damages can be recovered. The primary example is pure economic loss in negligence. Although the House of Lords ruled in *Junior Books Ltd v Veitchi & Co Ltd* [1983] 1 AC 520 that there is no fundamental rule that pure economic loss is not recoverable, consistent lines of case law show that such loss is in most cases not recoverable in negligence (e.g. *Leigh & Sillavan Ltd v Aliakmon Shipping Co Ltd* [1986] AC 785; *Peabody Donation Fund v Sir Lindsay Parkinson & Co Ltd* [1985] AC 210). Even damage that at first sight appears to be damage to property may in fact be deemed pure economic loss (*D & F Estates Ltd v Church Commissioners* [1989] AC 177;

Murphy v Brentwood District Council [1991] 1 AC 398). The major exception is economic loss resulting from negligent misstatement or negligent professional advice (*Hedley Byrne & Co Ltd v Heller and Partners Ltd* [1964] AC 465; *Caparo Industries plc v Dickman* [1990] 2 AC 605; *Henderson v Merrett Syndicates Ltd* [1994] AC 145).

Nevertheless, it should not be thought that economic loss is not generally recoverable in tort as a whole. Many torts result solely or primarily in pure economic loss to the claimant: misrepresentation, deceit, procuring breach of contract, conspiracy, slander of title, slander of goods, conversion, breach of copyright, and infringement of patent. In all these cases damages for pure economic loss may be recovered.

4.2.8.3 Consequential economic loss

It is, however, long established that economic loss is recoverable when it is immediately consequent on recoverable physical damage done to the claimant (see *Spartan Steel & Alloys Ltd v Martin* [1973] QB 27). It must be immediately consequent; and the property damaged must be the claimant's, not a third party's. It has now been held that the claimant may be the beneficial as well as the legal owner of the property, and it does not matter that the beneficial owner is not themselves in possession of the property (*Shell UK Ltd v Total UK Ltd* [2010] 3 All ER 793). As will be seen in **Chapter 10**, economic loss consequent on physical injury in personal injury claims is also recoverable.

4.2.8.4 Other exceptions

There are isolated cases where liability for economic loss has been held to exist on the facts of the case. These are probably difficult to follow and depend on the exceptional proximity of the parties. E.g.:

(a) *The Greystoke Castle* [1947] AC 265

(b) *Caltex Oil (Australia) Pty v The Dredge Willemstad* (1976) 136 CLR 529—an Australian case much cited but not yet followed in this country

(c) *Junior Books Ltd v Veitchi Co Ltd* [1983] 1 AC 520.

4.2.8.5 Condition falling short of injury

In *Rothwell v Chemical & Insulating Co Ltd ('the Pleural Plaques Litigation')* [2007] 4 All ER 1047, the House of Lords held that the existence of a condition, which does not cause injury in itself, but merely evidences the possibility of injury in the future, is not damage capable of giving rise to liability in tort, even when combined with anxiety about the risk of injury. However, this case was distinguished by the Supreme Court in *Dryden v Johnson Matthey plc* [2018] 3All ER 755 where the latent condition was already causing the claimants some form of loss.

4.2.9 The loss was caused by the defendant's negligence

4.2.9.1 The basic rule

The claimant must show causation—that the tortious act caused their injury, loss, or damage. It need not have been the sole cause. It is usual to apply the 'but for' test: the claimant must show that *but for* the defendant's tortious act they would not have suffered the injury or loss. This must be shown on the balance of probabilities. If the claimant would probably not have suffered the loss, or would probably have received a benefit but for the defendant's negligence, then they can recover that loss even if it was not a certainty. It may be sufficient in some circumstances to show that the tortious act increased the likelihood of damage occurring (*McGhee v National Coal Board* [1973] 1 WLR 1), but it must still have caused the injury on the balance of probabilities (*Kay v Ayrshire and Arran Health Board* [1987] 2 All ER 417). If a claimant would probably have suffered damage in any event, there is no claim where the defendant's negligence has increased the likelihood of damage or deprived them of their chance of avoiding it: *Hotson v East Berkshire Area Health Authority* [1987] AC 750; *Gregg v Scott* [2005] 4 All ER 812.

4.2.9.2 Exceptions

However, the 'but for' test will not be rigidly applied where the claimant can show that one or both of two defendants caused them damage, but is unable to show that either of them did so on the balance of probabilities. In such circumstances it is enough to show that either of them made a material contribution to the claimant's damage by materially increasing the risk of such damage (*Fairchild v Glenhaven Funeral Services Ltd* [2002] 3 All ER 305, followed in *Barker v Saint-Gobain Pipelines plc* [2005] 3 All ER 661). This principle was expressly held to apply in mesothelioma cases in *Sienkiewicz v Greif (UK) Ltd* [2011] AC 229.

But note that the *Fairchild* principle does not apply in ordinary cases where the 'but for' test can be simply applied (*Hull v Sanderson* [2008] All ER (D) 39 (Nov)). If there are two material causes of the injury, one tortious and the other non-tortious, the 'but for' test should be applied to the tortious cause, and if satisfied, liability will be established (*Bailey v Ministry of Defence* [2009] 1 WLR 1052). It was also stated by the judge in that case that there is no special rule in medical negligence cases.

In cases of personal injury where the claimant has suffered mesothelioma as a result of exposure to asbestos, and there are several defendants potentially liable under the principle of *Fairchild*, but no evidence as to the extent to which each has exposed the claimant to risk, a special rule has been laid down by s. 3 of the Compensation Act 2006. In such cases the potential defendants are jointly and severally liable, and each may therefore be liable for the whole of the claimant's loss, irrespective that some of the loss may have been caused by the claimant themselves during a period of self-employment or by employers who are not liable in negligence. This section was enacted to reverse the decision of the House of Lords in *Barker v Corus (UK) Ltd* [2006] 3 All ER 785.

Another exception to the strict rule on causation was allowed by the House of Lords in *Chester v Afshar* [2004] 4 All ER 587. It was held that where a surgeon negligently failed to warn a patient of the risk of damage inherent in an operation, and the patient underwent the operation, and the risk materialised, the patient did not have to show that if properly advised she would not have had the operation, only that she would not have had it on the day she did. The court recognised that it was departing from the principles of the law on causation, but held that this departure was justified in the interests of justice. In the circumstances, this must therefore be seen as only a very narrow and specific exception to the rule.

4.2.9.3 Supervening events

Causation may be broken by a supervening act or event, in which case the claimant's claim will fail. The supervening act may come between the defendant's tortious act and damage, in which case the chain of causation may be broken altogether, but whether it is broken is a question of fact and degree. If the supervening act was reasonably foreseeable and/or made little difference to the chain of events, the chain is probably not broken. In *Corr v IBC Vehicles Ltd* [2008] 2 All ER 943, the House of Lords held that it was a question of fairness. The deceased in that case, having been injured as a result of the defendant's negligence, developed a psychiatric illness which made him suicidal, and he did eventually commit suicide. It was held that the chain of causation was not broken, because the suicide could not be regarded as an intentional act, and it was reasonably foreseeable because the duty of care owed by the defendant to the deceased embraced psychological as well as physical injury, and suicide was a common manifestation of depression. If, on the other hand, the supervening event was not reasonably foreseeable and was a wholly new event, the chain of causation may be broken even if the 'but for' test is still satisfied. If the supervening act was one which the defendant had a duty to prevent, then the chain of causation is not broken (*Reeves v Metropolitan Police Commissioner* [1999] 3 All ER 897).

Alternatively, the supervening event may occur after the claimant has suffered damage, and its effect is to add to the claimant's damage. In such circumstances the question is whether the second event was natural, in which case causation is broken (*Jobling v Associated Dairies Ltd* [1982] AC 794), or whether it was a tortious act, in which case causation is not broken (*Baker v Willoughby* [1970] AC 467). The principle of *Baker v Willoughby*, that the second tortfeasor should be liable only for the additional harm caused to a claimant who had already been injured by the first tortfeasor, was upheld in *Murrell v Healy* [2001] 4 All ER 345, where the court had to consider what loss of earnings would have flowed from the first accident even though it had been superseded by the second accident which caused a complete loss of earnings. *Baker v Willoughby* was also followed in *Wright v Cambridge Medical Group* [2013] QB 312, where it was held that a doctor who negligently failed to refer a patient to hospital could not escape liability entirely when the hospital was then itself negligent, so causing the claimant much greater harm, on the basis that the subsequent harm would have occurred in any event even if the doctor had not been negligent.

Where the supervening event was brought on by a second tortious act, but was such that it might well have resulted in due course from the first tortious act, the second tortfeasor will not be fully liable for the consequences of the event; rather, a discount should be made (*Heil v Rankin* The Times, 20 June 2000).

4.2.9.4   Subsequent events

The question of whether an original tortfeasor can be liable for additional injury caused by a subsequent event has arisen twice recently. In *Spencer v Wincanton Holdings Ltd* [2009] All ER (D) 194 (Dec), the claimant, having suffered a leg injury as a result of the defendant's negligence, suffered a further injury some time later, a partial cause of which was the fact that he was disabled by the original injury, even though another partial cause was his own unwise and risky behaviour. It was held that the defendant could be liable for the subsequent injury. It is a question of fact whether the later injury has in substance been brought about by the original injury or by the claimant's own act. Here the judge had rightly held that the original tortfeasor remained liable, though there was a substantial finding of contributory negligence. In *Dalling v RJ Heale & Co* [2011] All ER (D) 54 (Apr) the claimant had been injured by the defendant's admitted negligence. One consequence of the injury was that he took to heavy drinking, and as a result of this, fell over while drunk, so sustaining a bad head injury. Again, it was held that the defendant could be liable for the head injury, though again subject to a very substantial discount for contributory negligence.

For an example of how the law deals with a case where several of these rules come together at the same time, see *Ellis v Environment Agency* [2008] All ER (D) 163 (Oct). In that case the claimant: (1) had a pre-existing degenerative back condition, (2) suffered an accident at work which was the defendant's fault, causing a back injury, (3) suffered an accident at work which was not the defendant's fault, causing a leg injury, and (4) suffered an accident at home causing a serious leg injury, which was caused in part by the original back injury. The court applied the 'but for' test strictly, and allowed the claimant to recover in full for the injury resulting from the third accident, based on the defendant's negligence on the occasion of the first accident, making no deduction for any causative effect which the middle injury may have had. The pre-existing condition was relevant only to the claim for loss of future earnings.

4.2.9.5   *Novus actus interveniens*

This well-known maxim refers to the situation that arises when there is a chain of causation which leads from the defendant's negligence to the claimant's loss and damage, but it is so lengthy, or indirect, or unforeseeable that the chain is held to be broken, and the real cause of the loss and damage is a *novus actus interveniens* (a new intervening act), so that the defendant cannot be held liable for it. It may be an event over which neither party had control, an act by a third party, or even the claimant's own act.

In the recent case of *Clay v TUI UK Ltd* [2018] 4 All ER 672 the Court of Appeal gave the following guidance as to the test to be applied. Determining whether there had been a *novus actus interveniens* requires a judgement to be made as to whether, on the particular facts, the sole effective cause of the loss, damage, or injury suffered was the *novus actus interveniens*, rather than the prior wrongdoing, and that the wrongdoing, whilst it might still be a 'but for' cause and, therefore, a cause in fact, had been eclipsed so that it was not an effective or contributory cause in law. Where the line was to be drawn was not capable of precise definition. However, various considerations might commonly be relevant. In a case involving intervening conduct, they might include: (i) the extent to which the conduct had been reasonably foreseeable—in general, the more foreseeable it was, the less likely it was to be a *novus actus interveniens*; (ii) the degree of unreasonableness of the conduct—in general, the more un-reasonable the conduct, the more likely it was to be a *novus actus interveniens* and a number of cases had stressed the need for a high degree of unreasonableness; and (iii) the extent to which it had been voluntary and independent conduct—in general, the more deliberate the act, the more informed it was and the greater the free choice involved, the more likely it was to be a *novus actus interveniens*.

4.2.9.6 Loss of a chance

As in contract (see **3.2.4**), the court may also depart from the strict application of the 'but for' test and the requirement to prove loss on the balance of probabilities by allowing damages to be recovered for the loss of a chance. Sometimes the loss depends upon a contingency, but can still be shown to exist. If the claimant can show they had a chance of receiving a benefit or not suffering a detriment (as opposed to a speculative chance), and that the defendant's negligence has caused them to lose that chance, they can recover damages for the loss of the chance even where the chance was less than a probability (see *Allied Maples Group Ltd v Simmons & Simmons* [1995] 4 All ER 907, followed recently in *Perry v Raleys Solicitors* [2019] 2 All ER 937).

An odd result of this rule is that a claimant who sues their solicitors for causing their claim against a third party to fail does not have to show the claim would have succeeded, only that it had a chance of success. They can recover damages against the solicitors, even if they would probably not have recovered damages from the original defendant.

The burden of proof is on the claimant to show what real or substantial chance they would have had. But if they find it more difficult to do this because of the defendant's negligence, that difficulty should not be held against them, and they may recover even the full value of the benefit they have lost the chance of obtaining: *Sharif v Garrett & Co* [2002] 3 All ER 195.

4.2.10 The loss was not too remote

It may seem surprising that we are considering this topic as an essential requirement that must be satisfied in order to establish lability for negligence. After all, an allegation that the loss suffered by the claimant was too remote to be recovered is one that will be raised by the defendant. But once the issue is raised, the burden of proof is on the claimant to show that their loss is recoverable loss. So lack of remoteness is in fact an essential ingredient in establishing liability.

Broadly speaking, the test for remoteness in tort is reasonable foreseeability: it must have been reasonably foreseeable that the damage suffered by the claimant might result from the defendant's act (*The Wagon Mound (No 1)* [1961] AC 388). With what degree of likelihood is not entirely clear, but the cases tend to suggest only a slight degree of likelihood is required in tort (*The Wagon Mound (No 2)* [1967] 1 AC 617), with rather more likelihood in contract (e.g. *H Parsons (Livestock) Ltd v Uttley Ingham & Co Ltd* [1978] QB 791).

It is not necessary that the precise damage suffered should have been foreseeable; the broad type of damage will suffice. Personal injury is generally regarded as a broad type of damage in itself. It is not necessary that the damage should have come about in precisely the foreseeable manner. It is not necessary that the actual seriousness or quantum of damage should have been foreseeable. For example, in *Corr v IBC Vehicles Ltd* [2008] 2 All ER 943 it was held that where depression is a foreseeable consequence of the injury, so too is the suicide of the victim. On the other hand, in *Hadlow v Peterborough City Council* [2011] All ER (D) 193 (Oct), a teacher was left alone in a room with three pupils known to have a tendency to violence. This was a clear breach of duty. However, the teacher was injured not by the pupils, but when she fell over a chair as she attempted to leave to fetch another person to join her in the room. This was held to be an unforeseeable consequence of the defendant's negligence.

The test must be separately applied to all heads of loss. It does not follow that because the primary loss is foreseeable, all consequential loss is also.

Reasonable foreseeability appears to be the correct test for all torts, except torts of strict liability and deceit (see **6.4.3**).

When there is co-extensive liability for breach of contract and negligence, the correct test for remoteness is the contractual, not the tortious, test (*Wellesley Partners LLP v Withers LLP* [2015] EWCA Civ 1146).

4.2.11 Scope of duty cases

There is a particular problem which arises in some cases where the court is faced with an issue that cannot easily fall into the category of being one of duty, assumption of responsibility, causation, remoteness, or measure of damages. As a result of the defendant's negligent misstatement or advice, which the claimant has followed, the claimant finds they are in a situation where other events have come into play which have resulted in a greater loss than it would be just to make the defendant responsible for. The problem is that the events would have occurred in any event, but the claimant would not have suffered the consequences of them if they had not followed the defendant's advice. So in theory the 'but for' test is satisfied, and the events may be reasonably foreseeable, but they are not in any way the result of the defendant's negligence. The court's solution in these cases is to apply the 'scope of duty' test, and consider how far the duty of care extended, or what responsibility the defendant assumed and limit the loss recoverable to what was within the scope of that duty. The leading case is *South Australia Asset Management Corp v York Montague Ltd* [1996] 3 All ER 365 (generally referred to as *SAAMCO*) and applied in *Hughes-Holland v BPE Solicitors* [2017] 3 All ER 969, *Meadows v Khan* [2019] 2 All ER 607, *Manchester Building Society v Grant Thornton UK LLP* [2021] 4 All ER 1, and *AssetCo plc v Grant Thornton UK LLP* [2021] 3 All ER 517.

4.3 Occupiers' liability

4.3.1 The statutory duties

The liability of occupiers to visitors and non-visitors is statutory. The liability to lawful visitors is laid down by the Occupiers' Liability Act 1957 (OLA 1957), which imposes a duty of care similar in standard and scope to the common law duty of care. Liability to non-visitors or trespassers is governed by the Occupiers' Liability Act 1984 (OLA 1984), which imposes no general duty but lays down the circumstances in which a duty will arise, and then defines a duty of a lower standard and narrower scope than that owed to lawful visitors.

4.3.2 Lawful visitors—OLA 1957

Liability under the OLA 1957 is based on negligence, that is, breach of a duty of reasonable care. The statutory guidelines and defences included within the Act equate occupiers' liability with common law negligence to a considerable extent. Although the Act covers the relationship of employer and employee, it is not usually appropriate in such circumstances. Where the occupier is the employer of the visitor, a claim will usually be brought in negligence or for breach of statutory duty rather than under the OLA 1957. Where the occupier is the visitor's landlord, liability can only be under the Defective Premises Act 1972, where the same principle of reasonable care will apply (see, for example, *Drysdale v Hedges* [2012] All ER (D) 345 (Jul)).

An occupier owes a duty to take reasonable care to see that the visitor is safe. The standard is to be measured objectively, not by reference to standards set by the occupier for itself. So a local authority which failed to match up to a policy that went beyond what a reasonable occupier would do could not be found liable: *Esdale v Dover District Council* [2010] EWCA Civ 409. What amount of care is reasonable is a matter of balancing the seriousness of the risk with what is reasonably foreseeable. In several recent cases the courts have found against a claimant on the ground that the risk of injury, or at least the seriousness of it, was not reasonably foreseeable to the extent that precautions should have been taken: see *Grimes v Hawkins* [2011] EWHC 2004 (QB), *Cockbill v Riley* [2013] All ER (D) 05 (Apr), *West Sussex County Council v Pierce* [2013] All ER (D) 166 (Oct), and *Richards v London Borough of Bromley* [2013] All ER (D) 184 (Nov).

By s. 2(5) OLA 1957, the common duty of care does not impose on an occupier any obligation to a visitor in respect of risks willingly accepted as theirs by the visitor. But the fact that the visitor has taken a conscious decision to run an obvious risk does not of itself absolve the occupier of liability where the risk of serious injury was also foreseeable by the occupier: *White Lion Hotel v James* [2021] All ER (D) 61 (Jan).

4.3.3 Trespassers—OLA 1984

Liability under the Occupiers' Liability Act 1984 is very difficult to establish. The danger must be due to the state of the premises, not the claimant's activity on the premises: *Keown v Coventry Healthcare NHS Trust* [2006] 1 WLR 953. In essence, a claim is only likely to succeed where the danger is not one which the claimant can appreciate, but of which the defendant is aware. As a result, while child trespassers may occasionally succeed in claims under the 1984 Act, adults will almost always fail, unless there is some hidden trap—see, for example, *Donoghue v Folkestone Properties Ltd* [2003] 3 All ER 1101. The decision of the Court of Appeal in *Tomlinson v Congleton BC*, which somewhat surprisingly allowed a claim by an adult trespasser in respect of a perfectly obvious risk, was subsequently overruled by the House of Lords (both decisions are reported at [2003] 3 All ER 1122).

Tomlinson was applied and extended in *Evans v Kosmar Villa Holidays plc* [2008] 1 All ER 530. The rule that there is no duty to protect people against obvious risks (unless they do not have an informed choice or lack capacity) applies equally where a duty would otherwise arise under a contract or under OLA 1957.

4.4 Breach of statutory duty

4.4.1 The end of civil liability for breach of statutory duty

Before reading further, it is important to note that by virtue of s. 69 of the Enterprise and Regulatory Reform Act 2013 civil liability for breach of statutory duty, either under an Act or under health and safety regulations made by statutory instrument, has been abolished, unless new regulations are made allowing such liability. This affects causes of action arising after 1 October 2013, so only claims commenced before that date can succeed on the basis of breach of statutory duty (unless the Limitation Act is disapplied or the claimant relies on a date of knowledge to start time running).

However, the statutory duties themselves have not been abolished, so breaches of statutory duty may still be used as evidence of negligence and pleaded as such.

4.4.2 Introduction

A great many injuries are suffered by people in the course of their work. In most cases of industrial injury, a claim is likely to allege breach of a statute or statutory regulation as evidence of negligence.

Statutory duties are to be found covering more or less any workplace, work situation, or industrial process that you can think of. They are laid down by statute (e.g. the Factories Act 1961) or by statutory instrument (e.g. the Workplace (Health, Safety and Welfare) Regulations 1992). Most older statutes and regulations have been replaced by new regulations based on European directives.

The relevant directives and statutory provisions are gathered together in the major reference work *Redgrave's Health and Safety,* 9th edn by M Ford, J Clarke, and A Smart (LexisNexis Butterworths, 2016) where you will find not only frequently relevant provisions such as the Lifting Operations and Lifting Equipment Regulations 1998 and the Work at Height Regulations 2005, but also such obscure delights as the Equipment and Protective Systems

Intended for Use in Potentially Explosive Atmospheres Regulations 1996, the Justification of Practices Involving Ionising Radiation Regulations 2004, and the High-activity Sealed Radioactive Sources and Orphan Sources Regulations 2005.

The duties laid down by statute are unlike common law duties. They are not general, but highly specific. They do not, for the most part, involve any principles of negligence or reasonable foreseeability. Three broad types of duty can be identified.

4.4.3 Absolute duties

Many duties are absolute. They require that something 'shall be done' without further qualification. They are very strictly construed, and breach of an absolute duty will give rise to liability even where there is no fault on the part of the defendant. So, for example, it is no defence that compliance with a duty would mean the defendant could not operate machinery at all (*John Summers & Sons Ltd v Frost* [1955] AC 740), or that all the evidence showed that the accident which in fact happened was an impossibility (*Galashiels Gas Co Ltd v O'Donnell* [1949] AC 275). However, the courts may construe duties as less than absolute in order to avoid unintended liabilities—see *Fytche v Wincanton Logistics plc* [2004] 4 All ER 221 (HL).

Although there is no direct liability for breach of statutory duty, breach of an absolute duty can still evidence negligence.

4.4.4 Duties of reasonable care

Such duties require persons to act with reasonable care; the standard of care is similar to the common law standard, and a reasonable foreseeability test will be applied. In such cases the word 'reasonably' usually appears in the statute: for example a duty to prevent something happening 'so far as is reasonably practicable'; a duty to 'take such steps as are reasonable in all the circumstances to ensure that' something does or does not happen. However, even when the regulation uses the words 'reasonably foreseeable', it does not follow that the common law concept of reasonable foreseeability is to be applied. The regulation must be interpreted in the light of its context, including the relevant European directive: *Hide v Steeplechase Co (Cheltenham) Ltd* [2014] 1 All ER 405.

4.4.5 Hybrid duties

These are duties which are less than absolute, but which require more than reasonable care: for example, a duty to 'take such steps as may be necessary to prevent . . .'; or to 'take all appropriate precautions'. There is no single test for breach of such duties. The standard of care required is a question of the interpretation of each individual statutory section or regulation. Words which tend to indicate a hybrid duty are words such as: adequate, secure, appropriate, sufficient, necessary, practicable. As with absolute duties, breach of a hybrid duty can still evidence negligence.

4.4.6 To establish liability

There are as many as seven conditions to be satisfied before a claimant can succeed in establishing negligence through a breach of statutory duty:

(a) That the legislation applies. The statutes or regulations are not of general application. For example, the Workplace (Health, Safety and Welfare) Regulations 1992 (SI 1992/3004) only apply to workplaces as defined in reg. 2. It may well be that the defendant has done something prohibited by the regulations, but if it was not done in a workplace, there will be no liability. Always check the application of the statute or regulations. This will usually be found in the legislation itself.

(b) That the duty is imposed upon the defendant or upon someone for whom the defendant is vicariously liable. Somewhere in the statute or regulations will be a provision stating upon whom the duties are imposed. Different duties are imposed on different people: for example, under the Railway Safety (Miscellaneous Provisions) Regulations 1997 (SI 1997/553), some duties are imposed upon Network Rail, others upon train operators, and yet others on employers contracted to work on the railway. Always make sure you are suing the right person.

(c) That the duty is owed to the claimant. The statute or regulations may state to whom a duty is owed, or it may be a matter of construction. The duty will usually be owed to the person(s) whose safety the legislation is intended to protect. Others may be injured by a breach of statutory duty, but will be unable to claim (e.g. *Hartley v Mayoh & Co* [1954] 1 QB 383).

(d) That the defendant is in breach of duty. This sounds obvious, but it may need careful examination of the facts and the legislation. Regulations are specific, not general. The defendant is only in breach if they have done exactly what they are forbidden to do; conversely they will be in breach unless they have done *exactly* what is required. Note that where a regulation requires a defendant to do something so far as is 'practicable' or 'reasonably practicable' the claimant need not show that it was practicable or reasonably practicable, only that it was not done. It is for the defendant to show that it was not practicable or reasonably practicable. See, for example, *Larner v British Steel plc* [1993] 4 All ER 102.

(e) That the claimant has suffered damage. This must usually amount to personal injury or death. There are few, if any, statutory duties giving rise to liability for damage to property.

(f) That the damage is of the kind the statute was intended to prevent. There is no liability if the damage is of a different kind from that which was contemplated (*Gorris v Scott* (1874) LR 9 Ex 125). But the damage need not have been caused in the precise manner anticipated.

(g) That the breach of statutory duty caused the damage. Causation is obviously an essential requirement.

4.4.7 Work equipment

Whether a defendant is in breach of a statutory duty will depend frequently on the construction of the regulation or statute. One term that needs to be considered quite frequently is 'work equipment'. There are two recent House of Lords' cases on the meaning of 'work equipment': *Spencer-Franks v Kellogg Brown & Root Ltd* [2009] 1 All ER 269 and *Smith v Northamptonshire County Council* [2009] 4 All ER 557.

4.5 What can defeat or limit the claim?

The matters discussed in this section are capable of affecting liability for negligence, occupiers' liability under the OLA 1957, or a breach of statutory duty used as a foundation for a claim in negligence.

4.5.1 The defence of *volenti non fit injuria*

This is not frequently raised and not easy to establish. For example, in *Corr v IBC Vehicles Ltd* [2008] 2 All ER 943, it was held that suicide by a victim of personal injury, although plainly a deliberate act, was not a voluntary act because it arose from the depression he suffered as a result of his injury. For an example of a successful defence of *volenti*, see *Morris v Murray* [1991] 2 QB 6 and *Geary v JD Wetherspoon plc* [2011] All ER (D) 97 (Jun). The defence cannot be relied upon where the defendant has a duty to protect the claimant against themselves (*Reeves v Metropolitan Police Commissioner* [1999] 3 All ER 897).

4.5.2 Contributory negligence

4.5.2.1 Statutory basis

The power of the court to reduce damages to take account of the claimant's contributory negligence derives from the Law Reform (Contributory Negligence) Act 1945, s. 1(1), which reads:

> *Where any person suffers damage as a result partly of his own fault and partly of the fault of any other person or persons, a claim in respect of that damage shall not be defeated by reason of the fault of the person suffering the damage, but the damages recoverable in respect thereof shall be reduced to such extent as the court thinks just and equitable having regard to the claimant's share in the responsibility for the damage.*

'Fault' is defined in s. 4 as:

> *negligence, breach of statutory duty, or other act or omission which gives rise to a liability in tort or would, apart from this Act, give rise to the defence of contributory negligence.*

Contributory negligence is therefore a partial defence, and accordingly a factor which reduces damages where the claim is made in tort. It is, however, not applicable to all torts: excluded are deceit (see **7.4**), conversion (Torts (Interference with Goods) Act 1977, s. 11), and assault and battery (*Co-operative Group (CWS) Ltd v Pritchard* [2012] 1 All ER 205). Contributory negligence is for the defendant to raise and prove. Once established, the court is obliged to apportion responsibility in some way.

4.5.2.2 Apportionment of responsibility

How apportionment is to be made is entirely within the court's discretion and depends on the facts of each case. The court will take into account not only negligence by the claimant, which was a partial cause of the accident, but also negligence which was a partial cause of the injury, or which exacerbated the injury (such as failure to wear a seat belt). So, for example, an extremely drunk claimant who allowed himself to be driven by a drunk driver was held to be contributorily negligent with regard to his injuries suffered in an accident caused by the drunk driver (*Campbell v Advantage Insurance Co Ltd* [2021] EWCA Civ 1698). It is not just the extent to which the claimant caused their own injury that is relevant, but the extent to which they are blameworthy. Two claimants, both injured in the same accident and both guilty of the same omission, may not necessarily have to bear the same degree of responsibility for their own injury. The more culpable the defendant, the less responsibility on the claimant's part. The party whose act is the greater cause of the injury may not be the party who is most blameworthy: causation and blameworthiness must be balanced: see *Jackson v Murray* [2015] 2 All ER 805.

What is being measured is the extent to which the claimant is responsible for their own damage as opposed to anyone else. So if, for example, the claimant and two companions lawfully enter the defendant's premises, where the claimant is injured as a result of negligence attributable partly to the defendant, partly to their own companions, and partly to themselves, it is nonsense to say contributory negligence cannot be more than 25% simply because three other people are involved. Contributory negligence may be 50% or more. In *Fitzgerald v Lane* [1989] AC 328 the judge found the claimant and two defendants in a road accident 'all three equally at fault', and assessed damages on the basis of one-third contributory negligence. The House of Lords held that the judge's finding of fact meant that contributory negligence was 50% as against each defendant.

Where there is some contributory negligence but for which the accident would not have occurred, but it is too remote in time, place, and circumstance to have been a potent cause of the injury suffered, it may be disregarded (*St George v Home Office* [2008] 4 All ER 1039).

4.5.2.3 The form of assessment

Contributory negligence is always assessed as a percentage or fraction and is a round number, for example 20%, 25% (one-quarter), one-third, 40%, one-half, etc. The normal minimum is 10%—anything below that is likely to be ignored by the court.

4.5.3   Apportionment of liability

4.5.3.1   Apportionment between two defendants

Where a court has found two defendants to be liable to the claimant, or when the defendant has successfully claimed a contribution from a third party, a decision has to be made as to what proportion of the claimant's damages each should pay.

It must be remembered, however, that liability in tort is joint and several. So if the court holds two defendants equally liable, either of them is liable for 100% of the claimant's loss and will have to pay the full amount if the other cannot (see *Barker v Saint-Gobain Pipelines plc* [2005] 3 All ER 661). But if both defendants are able to pay, the court will apportion damages as it sees fit, considering the different degrees of fault, blameworthiness, and causation. If there is more than one claimant, apportionment may be different in respect of each claimant (see, e.g., *Wright v Lodge* [1993] 4 All ER 299).

4.5.3.2   Apportionment between two defendants and a claimant

Care needs to be taken in the apportionment of liability between defendants when there has also been a finding of contributory negligence by the claimant. The proportion of contributory negligence must be dealt with first, and only then is apportionment made between the defendants. That is why the net result in *Fitzgerald v Lane* [1989] AC 328 (see **4.5.2.2**) was that the claimant had to bear 50% of his loss himself, and each defendant was liable for 25%.

If a court holds the claimant 10% to blame and apportions liability two-thirds to the first defendant and one-third to the second defendant, the first defendant will pay 60% of the claimant's loss (i.e. two-thirds of 90%) and the second defendant will pay 30%.

If a court holds the claimant 20% to blame and the second defendant 25% to blame, the second defendant will pay 20% of the claimant's loss (i.e. one-quarter of 80%). Similarly if a court orders a third party to make a 25% contribution.

Sometimes a court apportions liability between the parties in such a way as to produce a total of 100%. If, for example, the court holds the claimant 10% to blame, the defendant 50%, and the third party 40%, the claimant will recover 90% of their loss from the defendant, who will then receive a contribution of four-ninths from the third party.

4.5.3.3   Apportionment between two causes

Where the claimant's injury is the result of more than one cause, and they claim against a defendant who can be shown to be liable for some, but not all, of that injury, then the court must make an apportionment, attempting to assess what proportion of the claimant's injury the defendant can be said to be responsible for. This may be a difficult task, but it must be undertaken as best it can (*Holtby v Brigham & Cowan (Hull) Ltd* [2000] 3 All ER 421).

4.5.4   The defence of *ex turpi causa non oritur actio*

The House of Lords and the Supreme Court have strongly reinforced the principle that a claimant cannot bring a claim for damages for loss arising from their own criminal act. In *Gray v Thames Trains Ltd* [2009] 4 All ER 81 the House of Lords held that the victim of a railway accident who went on to kill someone as a result of his post-traumatic stress disorder was unable to recover damages for his loss of liberty and earnings from the company responsible for the accident. *Gray* was upheld and applied by a seven-judge Supreme Court in *Henderson v Dorset Healthcare University NHS Foundation Trust* [2021] 2 All ER 257, a case where a paranoid schizophrenic woman stabbed her mother to death. In *Stone & Rolls Ltd v Moore Stephens (a firm)* [2009] 4 All ER 431 the liquidator of a company which had defrauded a bank was unable to recover damages from the company's auditors who had negligently failed to detect the fraud. Another example is *Joyce v O'Brien* [2013] EWCA Civ 546, where the claimant was injured by the dangerous driving of his partner in crime as they made their getaway from a burglary. However, the principle does not apply when the criminal act is not the cause of the injury or loss: *Delaney v Pickett* [2012] 1 WLR 2149. The rationale behind the doctrine has recently been considered by the Supreme Court in *Les Laboratoires Servier v Apotex Inc* [2015] 1 All ER 671, which held that it is a matter of public policy rather than a defence, and that it is limited to criminal and quasi-criminal acts; it cannot extend to torts. In *Hewison v Meridian Shipping PTE* [2002] EWCA Civ 1821 the claimant's claim for loss of future earnings in a personal injury claim was dismissed because the earnings would have derived from a job he had obtained by a criminal deception.

4.5.5 Reliance on an exclusion notice

Such a defence will rarely if ever succeed as the Unfair Contract Terms Act 1977 (UCTA) will almost certainly apply. The Act covers notices as well as contract terms. The following restrictions apply:

(a) A defendant cannot by a contract term or notice exclude liability in negligence for death or personal injury (s. 2(1)). Negligence means breach of any contractual obligation or common law duty to take reasonable care or exercise reasonable skill, or breach of the common duty of care under the Occupiers' Liability Act 1957.

(b) A term or notice can otherwise only exclude or restrict liability for negligence if it satisfies the reasonableness test (s. 2(2))

(c) A defendant cannot by a term or notice fix the claimant with full knowledge and willing acceptance of a risk (s. 2(3) UCTA).

(d) By ss. 11(3) and 13(1) a notice purporting to disclaim a duty of care (if such a duty would have existed but for the disclaimer) will only be effective if it satisfies the reasonableness test (*Smith v Eric S Bush* [1990] 1 AC 831).

The reasonableness test is set out in s. 11 of UCTA, with additional guidelines in Sch. 2. The essential test is whether the term was a fair and reasonable one to be included in all the circumstances, but there are many specific matters to be taken into consideration where relevant. The burden of proving reasonableness rests with the party seeking to rely on the clause.

4.5.6 Expiry of limitation period

The limitation period in tort is prima facie six years, but three years in the case of a claim for personal injury or death. Time starts to run from when the cause of action accrues, which in negligence is the date of injury or damage. This may be some time later than the negligent act. If the potential damage is merely a contingent liability, which might not arise, no actual damage is sustained until the contingency is fulfilled, which is when time starts to run (*Law Society v Sephton* [2006] 3 All ER 401). Where a claimant has entered into an unprofitable transaction as a result of the defendant's negligent advice, the date of damage is the date the transaction was irrevocably entered into (*Pegasus Management Holdings v Ernst & Young* [2008] EWHC 2720 (Ch)).

However, in a personal injury claim, by s. 14 of the Limitation Act 1980 time may alternatively start to run from the date of knowledge, which is the earliest date on which the claimant knew:

(a) that the injury was significant;

(b) that the injury was attributable to the act or omission alleged to have caused it; and

(c) the identity of the defendant.

Similarly, in a case of latent damage to property or latent economic loss, by s. 14A time may alternatively start to run from the 'starting date', which is the earliest date on which the claimant knew:

(a) that the damage was sufficiently serious to justify commencing proceedings;

(b) that the damage was attributable to the negligence alleged to have caused it; and

(c) the identity of the defendant.

Knowledge does not have to be absolute certainty. It is enough for the claimant to have broad knowledge of the facts on which the complaint is based, combined with knowing as a real possibility that the alleged acts or omissions caused the damage (*Haward v Fawcetts* [2006] 3 All ER 497).

The time allowed is three years from the date of knowledge, but subject to an absolute time bar of 15 years from the date of negligence in any event (s. 14B).

4.5.7   Failure to mitigate

The law and practice relating to failure to mitigate in tort is exactly the same as in contract—see **3.3.7**.

4.6   Concurrent liability in tort and contract

4.6.1   When can concurrent liability arise?

Although we have dealt with liability separately in **Chapter 3** and **Chapter 4** for breach of contract and in negligence, it is wrong to assume that these liabilities are always distinct from each other. They may be liability in both at the same time, particularly in the context of professional services. There are two main circumstances in which there may be concurrent liability in contract and tort:

(a) in a negligence claim; and

(b) in a misrepresentation claim.

Concurrent liability in misrepresentation will be dealt with in **Chapter 6**.

4.6.2   How does concurrent liability arise

4.6.2.1   The contractual obligation

The contractual obligation arises in contracts for the supply of services. In most such contracts, whether for professional or other services, there is an implied term that they will perform the services with reasonable care and skill—s. 13 of the Supply of Goods and Services Act 1982 in the case of a business contract and s. 49 of the Consumer Rights Act 2015 in the case of a consumer contract (see **3.2.2.7**). This is just as true in contracts with professional advisers as in contracts with tradespeople. Since this obligation is implied by law there is no real argument in most cases as to whether it exists. It does not depend on any decision by the court as to whether it is fair, just, and reasonable to impose such an obligation.

Where there is concurrent liability, it is usual therefore to regard the contractual claim as the primary basis for liability.

4.6.2.2   The tortious duty

The tortious duty arises at common law in accordance with common principles—see **4.2.3**. This may be because it is an established duty situation where no consideration is required as to whether the duty should exist, or in accordance with the approaches explained in **4.2.3.1** (*Caparo v Dickman*), **4.2.3.5** (negligent misstatement), and **4.2.5.1** (assumption of responsibility). It is well established that there is no objection in principle to a common law duty of care coming into existence concurrently with a contractual obligation: *Henderson v Merrett Syndicates Ltd* [1994] 3 All ER 506.

It follows that the tortious claim, where it exists, is likely to be regarded as the secondary basis for liability.

4.6.2.3   When does the tortious duty exist?

The duty does not arise merely because the parties are in a contractual relationship. The existence of the contract can operate both ways evidentially. Sometimes the contract evidences an assumption of responsibility. This is likely to be the case particularly as between a professional person and their client. It has long been established that a doctor owes a duty to their patient both in tort and contract (if there is one). It is now likely that the same decision will be reached in most cases involving contracts for professional services.

In fact, the duty is likely to exist in almost every case where there is a contract for the performance of services. Either there is an assumption of responsibility, or the contract fulfils the three-part test: there is a relationship of proximity, reasonable foreseeability, and it is fair, just, and reasonable to impose a duty because it goes no further than the contractual obligation.

Sometimes, however, the contract evidences the fact that the parties chose to define their relationship contractually and speaks against any separate duty in tort: *Greater Nottingham Co-operative Society v Cementation Piling & Foundations Ltd* [1989] 1 QB 71. Where the contract is inconsistent with the assumption of responsibility, then a separate duty of care is excluded—*Henderson v Merrett Syndicates Ltd.*

4.6.2.4   The standard of care

Where there is a concurrent duty of care, it will be identical in standard and scope to the contractual obligation. What is 'reasonable' care and skill for the purposes of the contract depends on the level of skill and expertise professed by the defendant (see **4.2.7.1**). The courts will not impose a higher duty in tort than in contract or vice versa. It follows that if the defendant was negligent when there are concurrent duties, concurrent liability must arise.

4.6.3   **The effect of concurrent liability**

In most cases the fact that there is concurrent liability is of no practical significance. It will not result in any greater or lesser ease of establishing liability or the quantum of damages. The basic measure of loss will be the same. However, there are three situations in which it may make a difference to the outcome of the claim.

4.6.3.1   Limitation

Although the primary limitation period is six years in contract and tort, time starts to run from a different moment. In contract the starting date is the date of breach (i.e. in negligence cases the date of the negligence). In tort the starting date is the date on which damage occurs, which may be years later. There will therefore be cases in which the claimant wishes to argue that there is liability in tort because it may be too late to succeed in contract.

The alternative 'starting date' under s. 14A of the Limitation Act in the case of latent damage only applies to a claim in tort. Again a claimant may need to argue for tortious liability.

4.6.3.2   Contributory negligence

A defendant may wish to argue that there is concurrent liability in tort in order to be able to establish contributory negligence by the claimant. There can be no finding of contributory negligence where the defendant is liable solely in contract—s. 1 of the 1945 Act does not cover such liability, even if the breach of contract was a breach of an obligation to take reasonable care. However, where the defendant is concurrently and co-extensively liable in contract and tort, then damages may be reduced for contributory negligence: *Forsikringsaktieselskapet Vesta v Butcher* [1988] 2 All ER 43. On the other hand, where there is strict liability in contract as well as concurrent liability for negligence, there can be no finding of contributory negligence: *Barclays Bank v Fairclough Building Ltd* [1995] 1 All ER 289. See further **3.3.9**.

4.6.3.3   Remoteness of damage

There is a different test for remoteness in tort and contract—see **3.2.6** and **4.2.10**. Either test can be more beneficial to the claimant on the facts of a particular case. It follows that there may be cases in which a different result may be achieved in tort and contract by the application of a different remoteness test. However, when there is co-extensive liability for breach of contract and negligence, the correct test for remoteness is the contractual, not the tortious test (*Wellesley Partners LLP v Withers LLP* [2015] EWCA Civ 1146). This could lead a claimant to seek to establish liability solely in tort.

5

Damages in contract and tort

5.1 Introduction

In **Chapter 3** we looked at liability for breach of contract, in **Chapter 4** we looked at liability in tort, and in this chapter we consider the question of how damages will be assessed. However it is not always easy to draw a line between what is an issue of liability and what is an issue of damages. It is therefore important to read this chapter in conjunction with **Chapters 3 and 4**. In previous editions of this Manual, we divided damages in contract and tort into separate chapters. But there are many principles relating to the quantification of damages which are applicable both to contractual and tortious liability, which meant there was a considerable amount of overlap and repetition between the two chapters. So, for this edition, we are dealing with damages in tort and contract in a single chapter.

5.2 Basic principles

5.2.1 The right to damages

Where a contract has been breached, the award of damages is the primary remedy. Damages are available as a matter of right. They will be assessed by a court in accordance with the evidence presented to it. Once a claimant has proved that they suffered damage and/or loss, their inability to prove the amount of that loss does not preclude damages being awarded. The court must assess the loss as best it can, however difficult that may be. Inevitably, however, the less evidence there is, and the more speculative the loss, the more restrained the court will be in quantifying it. Even where loss cannot be proved, nominal damages may be claimed, although cases of this type are relatively rare.

5.2.2 The compensatory principle

The underlying principle of the damages award is known as the compensatory principle. The aim is provide full compensation to the claimant for the loss suffered as a result of the wrong and to restore them to the position they would have been in had that wrong not been done. The aim is not to penalise the defendant as such. If restoring the claimant to that position means that the defendant will be left better off than they would have been had they not committed the wrong, then the law does not act to prevent this result—*British Transport Commission v Gourley* [1956] AC 185. It follows from the compensatory principle that the claimant is prima facie entitled to recover not just the loss directly resulting from the wrong, but also their consequential loss, including future loss.

A claimant's 'loss' includes any harm to the person or property of the claimant including any diminution of the claimant's assets caused by the breach. However, in calculating the total 'loss', any benefits which the claimant has enjoyed (or savings made) as a result of the breach must be set off against the loss. The court will not generally award damages which will put the claimant in a better position than they would have been in if the wrong had not occurred, although the practical effect of some damages awards may do just that.

In a few situations the defendant's gain may however be taken into account; for example, where a defendant in the position of a fiduciary is required to account for the profit made by their acts. Compensation for the claimant can also be measured by lost opportunity; for example, where the defendant wrongly uses the claimant's car, the defendant may be required to pay a reasonable rental value for the use of the car for the relevant period, notwithstanding that the claimant would not have used it or otherwise leased it to someone else during the period.

Difficulties and arguments in the assessment of damages almost all derive from the problem of trying to apply the compensatory principle to the facts of a given case, and quite often from a failure to apply it.

5.2.3 The problem with rules

In trying to work out in a particular case what is and is not recoverable in order to fulfil the compensatory principle, courts and practitioners have developed a large number of rules. These rules are usually along the lines of 'where situation A has arisen, the measure of damages shall be the difference between X and Y'. Some of these rules are statutory. For example there are several in Part VI of the Sale of Goods Act 1979. **Table 5.1** sets out some of the most common rules.

The trouble with these rules is that although they often do work, sometimes if followed they fail to achieve what ought to be achieved by the application of the compensatory principle. See, for example, *Bence Graphics International Ltd v Fasson UK Ltd* [1997] 1 All ER 979: the Court of Appeal had to depart from the prima facie rule in s. 53(3) of the Sale of Goods Act.

Difficulties often arise because of the arguments raised by the parties, seeking to maximise or minimise the claimant's loss. These arguments often blind the courts to what ought to be achieved by the application of the compensatory principle. A good recent example is *Tiuta International Ltd v De Villiers Surveyors Ltd* [2018] 2 All ER 203 a case which had to reach the Supreme Court before the correct and obvious answer was reached.

5.2.4 The practical formula

5.2.4.1 The basic formula

Rather than trying to apply rules, apply this practical formula. This almost always works. It enables you to understand decisions of the higher courts and predict what the correct result should be.

The formula is this: remember the objective, which is to put the claimant into a certain hypothetical financial position, and then ask yourself 'what needs to be done to put the claimant into the position they would have been in if . . . ?'

There are basically two '*position ifs*' that can be applied in contract cases (though they have to be slightly adapted in cases of misrepresentation—see **Chapter 6**). These are:

(a) 'the position the claimant would have been in if the contract had been performed'

Or:

(b) 'the position the claimant would have been in if the contract had not been made'.

The *position if* in tort is simple: it is 'the position the claimant would have been in if the tort had not been committed'.

5.2.4.2 The three ingredients

In order to apply this formula to the facts you need to look at three ingredients of the claimant's claim, which together make up all that is prima facie recoverable:

(a) The losses that the claimant has sustained which they would not otherwise have sustained.

(b) The expenditure that the claimant has incurred which they would not otherwise have incurred.

(c) The benefits gained and sums received by the claimant (whether by way of mitigation or not) which they would not otherwise have gained or received.

Table 5.1 **Damages arising from some common breaches of contract**

Type of contract	Where a claim is made against the person who confers the benefit			Where the claim is against the person who receives the benefit
	Non-performance	*Delayed performance*	*Defective performance*	*Non-performance*
Transfer of property or goods	(a) The difference between the cost of buying the same goods in the market and the contract price if it has not been paid. (b) Or, if there is no market, then the loss of user profit.	(a) The difference between the market value at the due date for delivery and the market value at the date of actual delivery. (b) Or, if intended to be used, then the loss of profit which could have been expected from that use.	Where the goods are defective, or are not of contract quality, then the value of the goods in their expected or intended condition less their market value in the defective condition (diminution of value), and, if wanted for use, the loss of user profit. However, if the defect can be cured, then the measure is the cost of cure. Betterment will be ignored.	(a) Where there is a failure to pay or accept the goods, then the difference between the contract price and the selling price on the market. (b) Or, if there is no market, then the loss of user profit suffered.
Contract for a loan	The difference between the contract cost of the loan and the market cost of the loan.	Same as for non-performance.		
Contract for services	The difference between the market cost of the same service and the contract cost, less the contract price if it has not already been paid.	The value of the service if rendered on the due date, less its value on the date when rendered.	Where the value of the property is reduced, then the diminution in the value of that property. However, if reasonable, the cost of cure measure will be awarded instead if the work has been or will be done. If there is no reduction in value, then such consequential losses as arise.	Where there is a failure to accept a service: (a) A failure to supply cargo in a contract of carriage, then the difference between the contract rate and the market rate for carriage. (b) In a wrongful dismissal, the difference between the contract wage and any substitute wage. (c) Where there is a failure to allow work to proceed, then the contract price less the costs saved by not having to carry out the work.

Source: Table compiled from *McGregor on Damages* and Burrows, *Remedies for Torts and Breach of Contract*.

In some situations, (a) and (b) may be virtually indistinguishable from each other, but that does not matter, because essentially, a sum of money calculated as (a) plus (b) minus (c) will always restore the claimant to the position they would have been in if . . . (whichever 'if' is appropriate), subject only to the three barriers of causation, remoteness, and mitigation (see **3.2.5**, **3.2.6**, and **3.3.7** in relation to contract and **4.2.9**, **4.2.10**, and **4.5.7** in relation to tort).

For a good illustration of how this calculation works to achieve the compensatory principle, see *Ng v Ashley King Developments Ltd* [2010] 4 All ER 914. In recovering damages from a purchaser who had failed to complete the purchase of a house, the vendor had to set off the amount of the deposit which they had forfeited, but could also claim the deposit they had lost to the vendor of the property they had hoped to buy.

With regard to (c), benefits gained and sums received need only be taken into account if they have resulted from the defendant's wrongdoing. If the claimant would have *or could have* made those gains in any event they do not need to be deducted—see, for example, *Needler Financial Services Ltd v Taber* [2002] 3 All ER 501.

5.2.5   The *position if* in contract

In a breach of contract case, a claimant, depending on how one looks at it, can be said to have suffered two quite distinct losses. These are commonly referred to as expectation loss and reliance loss.

Expectation loss is forward looking (*Robinson v Harman* (1848) 1 Ex 850), and damages assessed on this basis are intended to put the claimant into the position they would have been in if the contract had been performed. They can therefore recover any benefits they would have received under the contract or from elsewhere as a result of the contract, including loss of profit. Damages for expectation loss are the common law's alternative to specific performance.

Reliance loss is retrospective, and damages assessed on this basis are intended to put the claimant into the position they would have been in if they had never entered into the contract. They cannot therefore recover any of the benefits they would have received under the contract. Damages for reliance loss are the common law's alternative to rescission.

The choice of which basis to use in calculating the claim for damages will depend on the kind of loss which has occurred as a result of the breach, and which method achieves the most advantageous result for the claimant.

5.2.6   The *position if* in negligence

The aim is to put the claimant into the position they would have been in if the tort had not been committed; in negligence therefore, the position they would have been in if there had been no negligence. This is also the correct *position if* in a case of contractual negligence.

The position is best looked at in a common-sense way, without trying too hard to consider whether the test is forward-looking or retrospective. It may actually be either. If there was a tortious act by the defendant which should never have been performed, the *position if* is that which would have prevailed if the defendant had never done anything at all; this is basically retrospective. If however the defendant has done something they were obliged to do but in a negligent manner, the *position if* is that which would have prevailed if the defendant had acted in a competent manner; this is basically forward-looking.

So the *position if* in tort can often involve a subsidiary question of fact: what would the claimant have done if the tort had not been committed? This is particularly so in cases of negligent advice. For example, in a case of a negligent valuation given to a house purchaser by a surveyor, it must be decided whether the claimant would probably not have bought the house, or whether they would have bought it at a lower price. If the claimant would not have bought the house, then the basic measure of damages is the purchase price minus the market value of the house. If they would have bought it at a lower price, then the basic measure is what the claimant paid minus what they would have paid.

5.2.7   The *position if* when there is concurrent liability

Where there is concurrent liability in tort and contract, the *position if* will be the same in each case. The defendant's negligence under a contract is a failure to perform services with reasonable care and skill, so the position if they were not in breach of contract must be the position if they had performed those services competently, not if they had never performed them at all.

5.2.8   Test question

Here is a question to test whether you have understood the material on *position if.* The answer is at the end of this chapter.

In 2019 Charles Clifford decided to start a business taking holiday passengers on pleasure cruises along the south coast of England. He wished to charter a 1930s sea-going paddle steamer, of which there were only two remaining in the UK, both owned by Desmond Steamers Ltd.

Charles instructed Edward Rance, a marine surveyor, to inspect both paddle steamers, and to advise him as to their seaworthiness and as to the number of passengers that could safely be carried at one time. Edward advised him that both were seaworthy, and that the *Aurora* could safely carry 100 passengers and the *Beryl* 200 passengers.

On the basis of this advice, Charles felt that there was a market that would enable him to make profits using either the *Aurora* or the *Beryl*, but decided to charter the *Aurora* for three years, 2019, 2020, and 2021.

In fact, due to new health and safety regulations, of which Edward ought to have been aware, passenger numbers were reduced, and the *Aurora* was licensed to carry only 50 passengers from 2018, and the *Beryl* 100.

Once Charles discovered this, it was too late to charter the *Beryl*, which the owner had chartered to another operator on the Welsh coast. For 2022 the *Beryl* is available again, and Charles has chartered her in place of the *Aurora*.

As a result of being able to carry only 50 passengers rather than 100 for the last three years, Charles's profits are less than he expected, and less than he would have made if he had chartered the *Beryl*. He has made a claim against Edward, who has admitted liability, but is disputing the measure of damages.

Advise Charles whether the correct measure of damages is:

[A] The difference between the profit he has made and the profit he would have made if the *Aurora* had been able to carry 100 passengers.

[B] The difference between the profit he has made and the profit he would have made if he had chartered the *Beryl* and been able to carry 100 passengers.

[C] The difference between the profit he has made and the profit he would have made if he had chartered the *Beryl* and been able to carry 200 passengers.

[D] Whatever amount will restore him to the position he would have been in if he had chartered neither steamer.

5.3   Damages in contract

5.3.1   Expectation loss (or loss of bargain)

Since the aim of someone entering into a contract is to derive some benefit from it, and since the aim of damages is to put them into the position they would have been if they had gained that benefit, in most cases the claim will include a claim for loss of profit. Applying the *position if* test it should not be difficult to work out what profit is recoverable in any given case. The difficulties tend to come over what is not recoverable. The claimant cannot recover what they would have spent in any event. So they cannot get back the contract price: they would have to have paid this in order to make any profit. If they have not yet paid it, the defendant will have a valid counterclaim for it. Nor can the claimant recover any expenditure incurred in the process of performing their side of the bargain.

A good illustration is *St Albans City and District Council v International Computers Ltd* [1996] 4 All ER 481. The defendant supplied the claimant with faulty software which caused the claimant to overstate the number of households in its district. As a result it set its community charge too low, and paid too high a precept to the county council. It was able to recover the second sum but not the first, because it had recouped the loss by setting a higher community charge in the following year.

5.3.2   Reliance loss (or wasted expenditure)

The alternative to claiming expectation loss is to claim reliance loss. The aim is to restore the claimant to the position they would have been in if the contract had never been made. Reliance loss arises where the claimant has expended money in preparation for, or in partial performance of, the contract, which is then wasted as a result of the defendant's repudiatory breach. The *position if* test is also relatively easy to apply in this case. Basically the claimant recovers everything they have spent in connection with the contract minus everything they received as a result of it. If the claimant was providing goods or services, they will recover any expense incurred in order to be able to do so and the value of any goods or services already provided. However, they will be liable to repay the contract price. If the claimant paid the contract price, they can recover that sum plus any consequential losses, but must give credit for the value of any goods or services received.

Pre-contractual expenditure, incurred in contemplation of the contract, can also be recovered, provided it was within the parties' contemplation as likely to be wasted if the contract were breached—*Anglia Television Ltd v Reed* [1972] 1 QB 60.

Common examples of reliance expenses are for collection of goods (where the buyer is required by the contract to collect the goods and after incurring charges the seller repudiates the contract), storage, and transport charges.

Reliance loss will be claimed in cases where expectation loss is too speculative to recover (see, e.g., *McRae v Commonwealth Disposals Commission* [1950] 84 CLR 377; *Anglia Television Ltd v Reed* [1972] 1 QB 60).

5.3.3   Choosing between expectation and reliance loss

Generally the claimant will be permitted to choose the method on which to base their claim: they can elect to recover their expectation loss or their reliance loss—*Cullinane v British Rema Manufacturing Co* [1954] 1 QB 292. The defendant is not entitled to insist that the claimant must pursue one basis over another. Since the claimant would presumably have hoped to make a profit from the contract, or at least expected to be better off in some way after its performance than before, they will naturally usually elect to recover their expectation loss.

However, a claimant will not be permitted to claim damages for a reliance loss where this would compensate them, in effect, for a bad bargain, thereby putting them in a better position than they would have been in had the contract been performed. Where the loss flows from having entered into the contract rather than from its breach, only the lower expectation loss will be recoverable. (See *CCC Films (London) Ltd v Impact Quadrant Films Ltd* [1985] QB 16 and *C & P Haulage v Middleton* [1983] 1 WLR 1461.)

So there will not be many situations in which a claimant will be allowed or prefer to claim their reliance loss. But we can identify the following:

(a) Where the claimant's anticipated profit under the contract was too speculative to be capable of satisfactory proof. In this case their claim for expectation loss will probably fail.

(b) Similarly, if it would be almost impossible to assess the quantum of the expectation loss.

(c) If the benefit which the claimant hoped to derive from the contract was non-pecuniary.

(d) If a claim for reliance loss can be simply and easily agreed, but a claim for expectation loss would lead to lengthy litigation.

A claimant must elect one basis or the other. There is no possibility of 'a bit of both'. This is conceptually unsound because there can only be one *position if*. It is also likely to lead to a degree of double recovery. However, note that some consequential losses may be recoverable on either basis.

5.3.4   Restitution (unjust enrichment)

There is a third basis for calculating loss in contract. That is where the claimant, in performing their obligations under the contract, has conferred a benefit on the defendant and wishes to claim back the benefit (or the value) given. For example, where the claimant has paid in advance for a product which is not delivered, they are entitled to the return of the money paid. The 'loss' to the claimant is measured by reference to the amount of benefit (including the reasonable value of services) given to the defendant, rather than focusing on the amount of the claimant's loss, although in some cases this may be the same amount. In breach of contract cases, actions based on a claim for restitution may be for *quantum meruit*, and where there has been a total failure of consideration (failure to perform), the action will be for the recovery of money had and received.

The effect of a restitutionary claim is to restore both parties to the position they would have been in if the contract had never been made. This differs from the expectation basis, which is meant to put the claimant in the position they would have been in if the contract had been performed. It also differs from the reliance basis in that a restitution claim assumes that no contract had been made, but the party in breach may be left in a worse position. Damages for breach of contract which are awarded purely for restitutionary loss have been rare (see *Wrotham Park Estate Co Ltd v Parkside Homes Ltd* [1974] 1 WLR 798). It is important to bear in mind that claims for restitution are not limited to cases of breach of contract and are frequently part of claims for other equitable remedies (see later in this chapter and **Chapter 14**).

A claim in restitution will only be permitted if the breach is a serious one which amounts to a total failure of consideration. If this is proved, restitution may be claimed even if the result is to leave the claimant in a better position than they would have been in if the contract had been performed. This is a complex area and you are advised to consult specialist texts on contract law.

The various bases may also be combined within one claim provided the losses are not duplicated, allowing the claimant to recover twice for the same loss. It is possible to have a situation where the claimant paid in advance for a product, and incurred installation expenses. After installation the product was found to be defective. The claimant may recover the money paid for the product (in restitution) and the costs of installation (incurred in reliance). If expected profits were also lost as a result of the breach, the net (not the gross) profits could be recovered as well.

Where a contract entitles the defendant to perform in a number of alternative ways, then it will be assumed that the defendant would have chosen to perform in the way most advantageous to them and damages will be assessed on that basis.

5.4   Damages in tort

The mode of assessing damages varies greatly according to the tort, the nature of the loss, etc. Without considering each tort separately, one can nevertheless identify certain types of damage and consider how they are quantified in general terms:

- Personal injury
- Economic loss consequent on injury or death
- Economic loss
- Damage to property
- Interference with property
- Other kinds of personal non-financial damage.

Most torts are capable of giving rise to several of these different types of damage all at once. There may be some special rules as to how each type of damage is to be quantified in respect of the particular tort that has caused it: reference should be made to specialist textbooks, for example *Clerk and Lindsell on Torts*; *McGregor on Damages*.

Personal injury and economic loss consequent on injury and death are dealt with in **Chapters 10** and **11**. This chapter will concentrate on the remaining four types of damage, which are recoverable both in contract and tort

5.5 Economic loss

5.5.1 What is economic loss?

Economic loss is any loss which in essence is measurable as a sum of money even if only with difficulty. It can therefore be quantified on an arithmetical basis. It may consist of a loss in the sense that the claimant has lost some money or something of value; or it may consist of a loss of income or profit where the claimant has not gained something that they expected; or it may be economic loss consequent on physical damage. Where there is an element of future loss, a degree of informed speculation may be required. The law relating to personal injury has developed some approaches to this, and these are explained in **Chapter 10**. It may also be necessary for a court to quantify a chance in order to award damages for lost opportunity.

5.5.2 Profit or income?

Argument can sometimes arise over whether a claimant is entitled to lost income or profit. Apply the *position if* test. Profit is income minus expenditure, so the answer depends on whether the claimant has or has not incurred the expenditure.

Example: D's breach of contract or negligence deprives C of the use of his ice-cream van for two weeks, and so C cannot sell any ice-cream for that period. He has two days' stock of ice-cream in hand, which melts and is lost. He has five days' stock on order which it is too late to cancel and which he must pay for, but which he hopes to resell to another van-owner. He has not yet ordered any stock for the second week. C can in due course recover:

(a) Loss of income for the first two days.

(b) Loss of income for the next five days, but less any re-sale price (mitigation).

(c) Loss of profit for the next seven days. A claim for loss of income would over-compensate C, because he does not incur the cost of the ice-cream.

5.5.3 Quantifying loss of profit

A claim for loss of profit will arise in cases where the business use of the goods or service contracted for is lost or delayed as a result of the breach of contract. A claimant can recover both for the loss of the promised contractual performance and the loss of profit resulting from not being able to put the performance to use. For example, if the claimant purchases a car for business from the defendant and the defendant cancels at the last minute, the claimant has lost the benefit of the car itself, but has also lost the chance to use it in their business until they can secure another car, that is, a loss of profit.

Where there is no difference between the market price and the contract price, a claim for loss of profit will succeed only if it can be established that there was a market—that is, that the supply of the goods or services in question outstripped the demand for them—otherwise only nominal damages will be available (see *WL Thompson Ltd v Robinson (Gunmakers) Ltd* [1955] Ch 177; *Lazenby Garages Ltd v Wright* [1976] 1 WLR 459). Whether or not there is an available market depends upon whether there is an available buyer who is prepared to pay a fair price on that day. Where there is only a hypothetical sale, there is an available market only where, on the relevant day, there were sufficient possible traders in touch with each other to evidence a market in which the goods could have been sold (see *Shearson Lehman Hutton Inc v Maclaine Watson & Co Ltd (No 2)* [1990] 3 All ER 723).

Where there has been an inadequate repair causing an explosion, and thereby loss of profit, that loss of profit cannot be claimed because the further damage arises from another cause. Damages will then be limited to the replacement of the defective equipment and to the loss of profit while the repair is being affected.

5.5.4   Savings and gains

The third stage of the *position if* test involves deducting any savings and gains the claimant has made as a result of the defendant's breach of contract. If any benefit accrues to the claimant as a result of the breach, this must be taken into account. If the claimant saves the cost of performance as a result of the breach, this saving must also be deducted from the overall award, as will any sums of money earned from new employment in a claim for wrongful dismissal.

Benefits gained and sums received need only be taken into account if they have resulted from the defendant's wrongdoing. If the claimant would have *or could have* made those gains in any event they do not need to be deducted—see, for example, *Needler Financial Services Ltd v Taber* [2002] 3 All ER 501.

However, it is not enough to require a deduction that the claimant is able to make a greater profit once the breach has occurred than it would have been able to if there had been no breach. In *Fulton Shipping Inc of Panama v Globalia Business Travel SAU* [2018] 1 All ER 45, the claimants chartered a vessel to the defendants, who in repudiatory breach terminated the charterparty two years early and redelivered the vessel to the claimants. The claimants claimed their loss of profit over those two years, to which they were plainly entitled, and sold the vessel to a third party. It emerged that the sale price of the vessel was substantially greater than its value would have been two years later, and the defendants argued that the claimants should give credit for that difference. The Supreme Court held not. A benefit arising from a breach of contract needs to be deducted only if it was caused by the breach, or if it was a gain through an act of mitigation. Here it was not the breach of contract that had caused the claimants to sell the vessel; they could in fact have done that at any time during the term of the charterparty. Nor was it an act of mitigation.

5.5.5   Recovery of sums paid to another by way of settlement

It is not a rule of law that a person (A) who has settled a claim against them by B and seeks to recover the sum paid as damages from a third party (C) must prove that they were or would have been liable to B. The question is whether the payment and the amount of the payment were reasonable. If the settlement is reasonable, then it is likely to have been reasonably foreseeable that A would make the payment by way of settlement to B, and there is no reason why A cannot recover it from C. If it is unreasonable, then not only is payment unforeseeable, but the chain of causation is broken, and so A cannot recover the sum from C for both those reasons. If it is reasonable for A to make settlement with B, but the amount paid is not reasonable, then the amount paid is not foreseeable, and is not the correct measure of loss in A's claim against C. See *John F Hunt Demolition Ltd v ASME Engineering Ltd* [2008] 1 All ER 180.

5.5.6   Loss of a chance

Damages for loss of a chance are recoverable in contract—see **3.2.4**. Where such damages are recoverable, essentially they are quantified in accordance with the chance. So if the claimant has lost a 25% chance of gaining a benefit which would have been worth £10,000, damages will be assessed at £2,500. However, it is rare that the odds can be established precisely, or the benefit valued precisely, so do not expect an arithmetical assessment in every case. The court may assess damages more broadly. The court may award up to the full value of the benefit lost, valued at the time it was lost.

5.5.7 Staff time

It is frequently the case that the defendant's breach of contract has caused the claimant's employees to expend a considerable amount of time dealing with the situation brought about by the defendant's act in order to mitigate loss or carry out repairs or otherwise. Whether the wages of those employees are recoverable as damages must depend on the facts of the case. It is largely a matter of proving the existence of any loss.

If the employees have been paid overtime, or part-time staff have been taken on in order to cope, then there is clearly a measurable loss. If the employees have simply worked harder or longer for no extra pay, and have not been thereby prevented from doing other work which would have resulted in a profit, then probably no loss can be established. But in practice that is not usually the case. If every hour spent on rectifying the consequences of the defendant's breach is an hour that sooner or later will not be applied to other profit-making activity, then it may be possible to establish a loss.

Strictly speaking the loss is the profit that would have been made elsewhere, but it may be most easily measured by reference to the value of the employees' work per hour. This is likely to be the case for managers and directors. However, it is almost impossible to prove the loss accurately by evidence. In practice therefore there is a convention that provided it can be established that there has been disruption to the business in order to mitigate the loss, there will be no need to show additional expenditure or loss of profit—the court will simply accept the loss as measured by the hourly value of the employees' work. And even this may be calculated in a rough and ready way.

If the claimant maintains a 'repairs department' whose sole purpose is to rectify damage done by negligent third parties, then there is a good argument for claiming a share of the entire cost of running that department.

5.6 Damage to property

5.6.1 Two methods of assessing damages

When the claimant has suffered economic loss or personal injury, there is really only one way of calculating the amount required to achieve the correct *position if* and no issue arises. But where the damage claimed is in respect of property, the destruction or loss of it, or damage to it, there are broadly speaking two ways of achieving the *position if*:

(a) By looking to the value of the property, and awarding the claimant the value of property lost or destroyed, or the diminution in value of property damaged ('difference in value').

(b) By looking to reinstatement of the property, and awarding the claimant the cost of replacing property lost or destroyed, or repairing property damaged ('cost of cure').

Which of these two measures is appropriate is based on the facts of the case and on common sense. It is a matter for the court's discretion, not simply of the claimant's choice. Before a claimant can recover reinstatement cost (usually the greater sum) they must as a minimum show that they genuinely intend to carry out the reinstatement and that it is reasonable to do so. What is reasonable cannot be looked at without also considering the claimant's duty to mitigate.

It is worth noting that in *Coles v Hetherton* [2014] 3 All ER 377 the Court of Appeal held that when it comes to damaged motor vehicles the two modes are actually the same thing: the correct measure of damages is diminution in value, but the reasonable cost of repair can generally be taken as representing that diminution in value. More than anything else the value of the vehicle will be the deciding factor: a court will award, or an insurance company will pay, whichever is the lesser of the cost of repairing a damaged motor vehicle or its value just before it was damaged.

5.6.2   Making the choice

A helpful way to look at it is to ask 'What is the claimant's true loss? Is it that they have been deprived of their property; or that its sale value has been reduced; or is it that they have been put to expense?' The answer will depend on what is reasonable, what is practicable, and sometimes simple common sense. Nobody has any difficulty with the idea that in the case of a damaged motor vehicle, damages will be whichever is the lesser of the cost of repair, or the value prior to the accident.

A claimant cannot normally get new for old. So a claimant whose five-year-old car is written off cannot get the cost of a new one. However, where there is no second-hand market replacement cost may be what is required to compensate the claimant. For example a claimant whose building has burned down may well recover the cost of rebuilding. But where property is irreplaceable damages may have to be on a diminution in value basis.

Where property is kept for its value (e.g. a painting), damages will usually be limited to its value. Where property is kept for use (e.g. a ship), the claimant may well be able to recover its replacement cost (*Owners of Dredger Liesbosch v Owners of Steamship Edison* [1933] AC 449). However, a claimant whose working crane was destroyed was able to recover its resale value, not the cost of obtaining a replacement crane (*Southampton Container Terminals Ltd v Hansa Schiffahrts GmbH* [2001] 2 Lloyd's Rep 275). Where a chattel is merely damaged the choice may be three-way—cost of repairs, diminution in value, or cost of replacement less residual value. In such a case, particularly where the chattel is a ship, the decision depends on what is reasonable.

5.6.3   Example cases

The leading case is *Ruxley Electronics and Construction Ltd v Forsyth* [1996] 1 AC 344. The claimant had built a swimming pool for the defendant but had not built it to the agreed depth. The lack of depth did not diminish the value of the defendant's property and he genuinely intended to increase the depth if awarded the funds to do so. It was held that it was not reasonable, and he recovered damages for loss of amenity only.

In *Radford v De Froberville* [1977] 1 WLR 1262 a contract for the sale of land required a wall to be built separating the land sold from that belonging to the claimant. In a claim for damages for breach of contract the claimant was held entitled to receive the cost of building the wall as compensation from the defendant because the claimant genuinely wanted the work done and convinced the court that the money would be used for that purpose, even though the land had not been diminished in value by the failure to carry out the contractual obligation.

In *Tito v Waddell (No 2)* [1977] Ch 106 a mining company had agreed to replant land after it had been mined and had then failed to do so. It was held, in an action for damages seeking the cost of replanting, that the claimants could not succeed since there was no evidence that they intended to use the money to carry out the contractual obligation. Instead, damages were assessed on the basis of the diminution in the value of the land—a much smaller sum of money.

5.6.4   Profit-earning property

Goods and buildings which produce an income for the claimant need special care. If the claimant recovers the cost of repairing a damaged building or chattel, they can also recover as consequential loss the income lost as a result of the damage. If they recover the value of a chattel or building lost or destroyed, they can only recover lost income to the extent that the profit-earning potential is not already included in the value. Care must be taken to avoid double recovery (see *Dominion Mosaics & Tile Co Ltd v Trafalgar Trucking Co Ltd* [1990] 2 All ER 246). The market value of a ship or a racehorse, for example, is likely to include its earning capacity. However, a claimant who can prove fixed future engagements may be able to recover the profit lost on these as well as market value at the date of destruction.

5.6.5   Consequential economic loss

Consequential economic loss can also usually be recovered. Where property is destroyed the claimant may recover damages for loss of its use until it is replaced: where it is damaged the claimant may recover damages for loss of its use while it is being repaired. This may include the cost of hiring an alternative, so long as this is reasonable, but only to the extent that it is reasonable. For example, while it is generally accepted that a claimant who uses their car for business may claim the cost of hiring another car while their own car is being repaired, a claimant who incurred a hire charge of £6,596.50 when the profit he lost through not being able to use his car for two weeks was £423 was unable to recover the hire charge (*Hussain v EUI Ltd* [2019] All ER (D) 76 (Oct)).

Care must be taken where the chattel is a profit-earning chattel (e.g. a ship available for charter). If damages are awarded on a cost of repair or replacement basis, then an additional sum can be recovered for loss of profit in the interim. But if damages are assessed on the basis of its market value at the date of destruction, this value would include its profit-earning potential and so damages cannot be awarded for loss of profit as well (though there have been cases where damages in respect of loss of profit on fixed future engagements have been recovered). If a profit-earning building is destroyed, similar care must be taken to avoid double recovery (see *Dominion Mosaics and Tile Co Ltd v Trafalgar Trucking Co Ltd* [1990] 2 All ER 246).

5.6.6 Negligent valuation of property

Where a claim for negligent performance of a contract is made against a surveyor, the rule is that the correct measure of damages is normally diminution of value.

In cases of negligent survey reports, on the basis of which the claimant has bought property at a price above what they would have paid if the report were correct, the measure of damages is normally diminution in value, not cost of cure. However, this is not an absolute and invariable rule and will not be followed if its application would manifestly not do justice in the case (see *Hipkins v Jack Cotton Partnership* [1989] 2 EGLR 157). The claimant can recover the difference between the price they paid and the actual value of the property, but not the cost of rectifying the defects, even if they have reasonably carried out those repairs (*Watts v Morrow* [1991] 1 WLR 1421). If the surveyor had not been negligent, they would have identified the defects and given a correct valuation. In these circumstances the claimant would have bought at a lower price and then incurred this expenditure in any event. Even if they would not have bought the house if properly advised of its value, they cannot recover this cost, because it has not been caused by the surveyor's negligence.

There may, however, be consequential losses recoverable: in particular the cost to the claimant of cancelling the purchase, including in an appropriate case the cost of renting alternative accommodation—*Patel v Hooper & Jackson* [1999] 1 All ER 992.

Where a finance company lends money on the basis of a negligent valuation of the property, it is entitled to recover, as part of the measure of damages, interest at a proper rate of interest but not necessarily the rate provided by the loan. (See *Swingcastle Ltd v Alastair Gibson* [1991] 2 AC 223.)

Similarly a valuer who negligently overvalues property causing a mortgage lender to make an advance it would not otherwise have made is liable for any loss caused by the overvaluation itself, but not loss resulting from any fall in property prices. There is no causative link between such loss and the valuer's negligence: *South Australia Asset Management Corp v York Montague Ltd* [1996] 3 All ER 365.

5.7 Interference with property

5.7.1 Goods

Loss caused by interference with goods arises particularly in cases of conversion and trespass. If the claimant has been permanently deprived of goods, damages will be assessed on the same alternative bases as if they were destroyed: the claimant may either recover the value of the goods lost or the cost of replacing them, whichever is reasonable. They may also recover consequential damages for loss of use. If the deprivation is temporary, damages are likely to be simply for loss of use. The rules of mitigation may well require the claimant to replace lost goods within a reasonable time in order to minimise loss. However, the claimant will probably not be required to do so if they cannot afford to: see *Lagden v O'Connor* [2004] 1 All ER 277 and **3.3.8**.

5.7.2 Land

Where the case involves trespass to land, damages are recoverable without proof of loss. If the claimant can show financial loss deriving from the loss of use of their land, damages are likely to be assessed on that basis. Otherwise they may be assessed on the basis of what would have been a fair rent for the land (*Swordheath Properties Ltd v Tabet* [1979] 1 WLR 285) or a fair sum for granting an easement (*Bracewell v Appleby* [1975] Ch 408). Where a nuisance has caused loss of enjoyment of land, damages are likely to be assessed on a loss of amenity basis. If the nuisance cannot be stopped by injunction, damages in lieu may well be quantified on a diminution in value basis.

5.8 Time of assessment

5.8.1 Rule

The original strict rule was that damages should be assessed at the date the cause of action accrues, which is the date of breach in contract or the date of damage in tort, or at the date of loss if this is not immediate. The effect of this rule was that the value of any benefit lost, or the cost of any reinstatement work, would be assessed as at the date the damage occurred, even if it had changed in value since.

However, this is no longer an absolute rule—*Johnson v Agnew* [1980] AC 367. Even before this case the courts had been very willing to regard the rule as flexible. The original rule fails to take account of the problems caused by inflation and the consequent variability of the cost of goods and services, or of the changing value of money. There is also in any event the potentially conflicting rule that the court should take into account in assessment all relevant events between the date of accrual and the date of assessment. So the strict rule is now often ignored where it would 'give rise to injustice, and the court has power to fix such other date as may be appropriate in the circumstances' (*Johnson v Agnew*). The *position if* principle basically requires damages to be valued at the date of assessment except insofar as any alteration in value between the date of accrual and the date of assessment has been caused by extraneous factors or the claimant's failure to mitigate.

Strictly speaking, damages are to be assessed at the date when damage occurs. This will frequently, but not necessarily, be the same as the date when the cause of action arose. However, courts are also bound to take account of all events which occur prior to trial, which would tend to suggest that damages should be valued as at the date of trial. This latter approach is adopted in cases of personal injury and death. In cases of damage to property and economic loss the courts seem to adopt a more discretionary and flexible approach. The same result was achieved in *Alcoa Minerals of Jamaica v Broderick*.

5.8.2 Discretion

The effective date is therefore a matter of the court's discretion. It is actually highly unlikely that damages will be valued literally at the date of accrual. Any evidence of the cost of restoring the claimant to the *position if* will be based on the date the cost was ascertained. It is hardly reasonable to expect a claimant to rectify damage instantly in every case. The appropriate date also needs to be considered in conjunction with the claimant's duty to mitigate. It would be contrary to the mitigation principle to value damages at a date earlier than that on which the claimant could reasonably have been expected to rectify the damage.

In the case of an anticipatory breach of contract, where the claimant has the option to accept the defendant's repudiation, the relevant date will prima facie be the date of breach if the claimant accepts the repudiation, because the duty to mitigate arises immediately, but the date on which performance was due if the claimant affirms the contract.

In *Ageas (UK) Ltd v Kwik-Fit (GB) Ltd and another* [2014] All ER (D) 60 (Jul) the court restated the principle that the normal date for assessment of damages is the date of breach, and that departure from that rule could only be justified if it was necessary to give effect to the over-riding compensatory principle. But the judge also reiterated that there are circumstances where future events should be taken into account in order to do justice. The case involved the sale of a company, and the question arose as to what the value of the company was at the date of the breach. The value depended on a future contingency, so the issue was whether the value should be taken with or without the benefit of hindsight as to the outcome of that contingency. The court held that in this case hindsight should be allowed, giving particular weight to how the parties had allocated risk in the contract. The contract said that the buyer should receive the benefit if the contingency had a favourable outcome, and it should not be deprived of that benefit.

5.8.3 Fraud

But where the claimant has been induced by fraud to buy shares which have since increased in value, the loss should be measured by reference to the value of the shares at the date of purchase rather than at the date of assessment. The original strict rule should not be departed from to the benefit of a fraudulent defendant: *Great Future International Ltd v Sealand Housing Corporation* (The Times, 17 December 2002).

5.8.4 Personal injury

Note that the original rule has effectively been abandoned altogether in personal injury cases, where the relevant date is the date of assessment.

5.8.5 Damage to property

In the case of repairs to property, damages should be assessed as at the date on which it is reasonable to expect the claimant to undertake the repairs: *Dodd Properties (Kent) Ltd v Canterbury City Council* [1980] 1 All ER 928. This may be as late as the date of trial or assessment: *Alcoa Minerals v Broderick* [2000] 3 WLR 23. The court may have regard to the fact that a claimant may be unable to carry out the repairs until such time as they have established liability and are awarded damages, in which case date of trial will necessarily be the appropriate date: *Perry v Sidney Phillips & Son* [1982] 3 All ER 705.

5.8.6 Loss of goods or services

In the case of goods or services, where damages are calculated by reference to market price, the damages payable may be more or less than would have been payable at the date when the breach occurred. Where alternative goods are readily available on the market or alternative service providers readily available, and the claimant has the funds to acquire them, then prima facie damages will be valued at the date of loss, but this is not an absolute rule. The original rule may be justified because the claimant is required to act reasonably and to mitigate by going to the market to replace the goods or services as soon as is possible after the breach (see *C Sharpe & Co Ltd v Nosawa* [1917] 2 KB 814).

But where the price of the contract has already been paid, and it may not be reasonable to expect the claimant to replace the goods or services by going to the market, since they may not have the money to do so, damages will be quantified by reference to the market value at the time of assessment. And where it appears probable that the defendant may make good their default, then damages will be assessed at the time when that probability ceases. So the effective rule is that damages will be assessed as at the date on which it was reasonable to expect the claimant to replace the goods.

In tort, the date of assessment is also within the court's discretion. The general rule, reaffirmed in *BBMB Finance (Hong Kong) Ltd v Eda Holdings Ltd* [1990] 1 WLR 409, is that the value of goods lost is to be assessed at the date of loss or conversion. However, the rule is not absolute, and in other cases, particularly where damages are being awarded under the Torts (Interference with Goods) Act 1977, s. 3, as an alternative to return of the goods, a later date may be appropriate (*IBL Ltd v Coussens* [1991] 2 All ER 133).

5.8.7   Sale of land

Damages for breach of a contract for the sale of land will be based on the value of the land at the date of assessment: *Wroth v Tyler* [1974] Ch 74; *Johnson v Agnew. Johnson v Agnew* was followed in *Hooper v Oates* [2013] 3 All ER 211. There, a purchaser failed to complete the purchase of a house, the sellers accepted his repudiation, and attempted to find another buyer. After three years (during which it was let) the sellers gave up their attempt to sell the house and moved back in. The question arose whether damages should be assessed at the date of the breach, or at a later date which more accurately reflected the sellers' loss, the market value of the house having fallen significantly in the meantime. It was held that the later date was appropriate, since the diminution in value would have been suffered by the buyer rather than the sellers if he had completed the purchase. The position would have been the opposite if the sellers had made no attempt to sell the house immediately after the initial breach, as they would then have been in breach of the duty to mitigate.

Equally, a buyer of land is entitled to seek specific performance of the contract of sale and, if damages are awarded instead of specific performance, those damages will be assessed at the date of judgment, rather than at the date of breach (see *Wroth v Tyler* [1974] Ch 30).

5.8.8   Supervening event

Where, after breach, an event occurs which has a material effect on the amount of loss that the claimant has suffered, that supervening event cannot be ignored. This is particularly so where the event was a contingency that was, or could have been, anticipated by the parties to the contract, since, if the event had not occurred, the damages would have had to be assessed with reference to the chance of its occurring: see for example in *Golden Strait Corp v Nippon Yusen Kubishika Kaisha* [2007] 3 All ER 1. In that case a charterparty was repudiated but would have come to an end anyway on the outbreak of the Gulf War two years later, it was held that damages must be limited to the period up to the time the war started.

5.8.9   Foreign currency

In cases where foreign currency liability arises, the sum in sterling to be paid is the applicable rate for exchange on the date of payment (see *Miliangos v George Frank (Textiles) Ltd* [1976] AC 443).

In *The Folias* [1979] AC 685 and *Attorney-General of the Republic of Ghana v Texaco Overseas Tankships Ltd* [1994] 1 Lloyd's Rep 473 it was held that if the contract discloses no intention as to the currency in which damages for breach are to be payable, they should be calculated in the currency in which the claimants incurred the loss.

5.9   Other types of loss

5.9.1   Loss of reputation

5.9.1.1   Contract

The general rule is that damages cannot be awarded in contract for loss of reputation caused by wrongful dismissal or because a wrongful dismissal may make it more difficult to find alternative employment (see *Addis v Gramophone Co Ltd* [1909] AC 488, more recently affirmed in *Malik v BCCI* [1995] 3 All ER 545). However, in cases where the obtaining of publicity is the main purpose of the contract, damages for the lost chance of enhancing reputation will be recoverable (breach of actors' contracts; breach of advertising contracts). Equally, dishonouring a trader's cheque in breach of contract will entitle the trader to damages for lost reputation and, where goods or services are provided directly to the claimant's customers but are not of contract quality, again, damages for lost reputation can be recovered.

There is also no difficulty in recovering damages for loss of reputation in contract where the loss can be shown to be a financial loss, provided it is not too remote. For example, loss of goodwill, loss of income, loss of future profits, loss of business opportunity, and loss of financial status can all be recovered in damages, which will be assessed as economic loss in the usual way, making the best assessment possible in the light of the evidence.

5.9.1.2   Tort

Damages for loss of reputation may be substantial in cases of defamation. In most other cases the loss of reputation may well be treated as future economic loss and assessed accordingly.

5.9.2   Distress, disappointment, and inconvenience

5.9.2.1   Contract

The general rule is that damages for distress are not available in an action for breach of contract. However, there has been some slackening in the strictness of this rule where 'the contract which has been broken was itself a contract to provide peace of mind or freedom from distress': *Bliss v South East Thames RHA* [1985] IRLR 308. The most common examples of this exception are the spoilt holiday cases: *Jarvis v Swan's Tours* [1973] QB 233; *Jackson v Horizon Holidays* [1975] 1 WLR 1468. There is a comprehensive examination of the quantification of damages for distress and disappointment in spoilt holiday cases in *Milner v Carnival plc* [2010] 3 All ER 701.

The result is that in contracts entered into for purposes of enjoyment, damages will be available for disappointment, and in contracts entered into to avoid distress or to gain peace of mind, damages will be available for the failure to prevent that distress (see *Heywood v Wellers* [1976] QB 446). The scope of this exception was extended by the House of Lords in *Farley v Skinner* [2001] 4 All ER 801. It is not necessary that the very purpose of the contract should have been to provide pleasure, relaxation, or peace of mind; it is sufficient that this was a major or important part of the contract. However, damages under this head should be restrained and modest. The House of Lords regarded £10,000 (current value about £17,000) as right on the upper limit. Where the damages are for injury to feelings, the appropriate range is £500 to £25,000 (*Chief Constable of West Yorkshire v Vento* [2003] IRLR 102) (current value about £800 to £41,000).

Applying this principle, it was held in *Hamilton Jones v David & Snape* [2004] 1 All ER 657 that a claimant could recover damages for the distress caused by the loss of the company of her children, where this loss was caused by the negligence of her solicitors, who had been specifically instructed in order to avoid such a loss.

Damages for distress can also be claimed as consequential to physical inconvenience because this is taken to be obviously within the contemplation of the parties at the time of contracting (see *Perry v Sidney Phillips and Son* [1982] 1 WLR 1297). Damages for distress arising out of wrongful dismissal from a contract of employment cannot be recovered (*Addis v Gramophone Co Ltd* [1909] AC 488, reaffirmed by the House of Lords in *Johnson v Unisys Ltd* [2001] 2 All ER 801). No claim for inconvenience or distress can be made by a company (see *Firsteel Cold Rolled Products v Anaco Precision Pressings* The Times, 21 November 1994).

Distinguish mental distress of this kind from suffering, mental illness or nervous shock, for which damages may be recoverable as a personal injury.

Mental distress must also be distinguished from physical inconvenience, for which damages may be recoverable in contract. This is a non-pecuniary loss, probably indistinguishable in reality from loss of amenity. The quantum is wholly within the court's discretion and difficult to predict.

5.9.2.2   Tort

There is no rule that damages for other mental distress are not recoverable in tort, but the circumstances may in fact be quite limited. Mental distress or injury to feelings, which amounts to suffering, is a personal injury and is dealt with under that head. Damages for grief, anguish, upset, worry, or fear which falls short of nervous shock or mental illness are not recoverable: *Hicks v Chief Constable of South Yorkshire* [1992] 2 All ER 65.

However, damages for mental distress may be recoverable when tacked on to damages for some torts, e.g. deceit, false imprisonment, defamation, assault, nuisance; or if they can be categorised as aggravated damages. Mental distress is probably only recoverable in negligence where the distress is directly consequent on physical inconvenience—*Perry v Sidney Phillips & Son* [1982] 1 WLR 1297; or where it is in effect loss of amenity in a case where loss of amenity is recoverable.

Damages for injury to feelings involving mental distress are very similar to damages for pain and suffering and can be assessed in the same way.

Inconvenience and discomfort can result from virtually any tort, and may be recoverable as a separate head where it does not overlap with loss of amenity. Damages for inconvenience and discomfort are likely to amount to a modest sum.

5.9.3   Loss of liberty (in tort)

Damages can be awarded for loss of liberty. Such loss may result from false imprisonment, malicious prosecution, or negligence (see *Meah v McCreamer* [1985] 1 All ER 367). Loss of liberty is also likely to overlap with mental distress and inconvenience, and damages for all three may well be assessed together as a single lump sum.

Such losses are assessed with very little to go on but the judge's own intuitive judgement, and comparison with awards in previous cases (so far as they can be ascertained), in much the same way as pain, suffering, and loss of amenity are assessed in personal injury cases.

5.10   Damages quantified by the parties to a contract

5.10.1   Liquidated damages clauses

Many contracts contain provisions designed to avoid the need for a dispute about damages to arise. This is particularly true of commercial contracts. The parties may provide an assessment of damages for themselves, by determining the amount of any damages to be paid in the event of a given breach, or a formula by which such damages can be determined, and inserting this into the contract. Such a clause is known as a liquidated damages clause, and usually uses that term. It may need to be construed by the court to establish its precise ambit, but provided the contract is still enforceable, such a term can prevail, if it is not held to be unreasonable under the Unfair Contract Terms Act 1977, and a court will award as liquidated damages the sum agreed, rather than damages quantified on the compensatory principle.

However, the court must be satisfied that the sum agreed is liquidated damages rather than an unlawful penalty.

5.10.2   Penalty clauses

Many contracts, again especially commercial contracts, contain penalty clauses. Such a clause stipulates that if a party fails to fulfil an obligation, or is late in performance, they will be liable to pay a penalty. There is nothing wrong in this. If the clause is a genuine attempt to pre-estimate the loss that would arise in the event of breach, or a reasonable incentive to complete work on time it is perfectly valid.

On the other hand it may be an unlawful penalty clause and therefore unenforceable. An unlawful penalty is a sum intended (a) to exceed the true loss and so pressurise and punish the party in breach; or (b) to underestimate the true loss and so let a contract-breaker off lightly. The Supreme Court has recently looked at this question and clarified the law which had stood unchanged for over 100 years. The case is *Cavendish Square Holding BV v Makdessi; Parking Eye Ltd v Beavis* [2016] 2 All ER 519.

The starting point is that an unenforceable penalty clause must be penal in its nature, meaning that its intent is to punish a person who breaches a contract. If the penalty is no more than an adjustment of the price payable under the contract where certain obligations are not fulfilled, it is not a penalty. It follows that it is not a penalty simply because it does not involve a genuine attempt to pre-estimate loss. The true test is whether the clause is a secondary obligation which imposes a detriment on the contract-breaker out of all proportion to any legitimate interest of the innocent party in the enforcement of the primary obligation. In a simple case, there will be no legitimate interest in recovering anything more than straightforward compensation. But there are times when a party has a legitimate interest to protect which justifies a penalty payment beyond mere compensation.

Within this new framework, the old guidelines laid down in *Dunlop Pneumatic Tyre Co Ltd v New Garage and Motor Co Ltd* [1915] AC 79 can still be valid. These are ('penalty' always meaning an unlawful penalty):

(a) The term used is not conclusive. What is called a 'penalty' may be liquidated damages, and what is called 'liquidated damages' may be a penalty.

(b) A penalty is designed to cast fear into the offending party; the essence of liquidated damages is a genuine pre-estimate of loss.

(c) Whether it is a penalty or liquidated damages is a matter of construction, to be judged on the circumstances at the time the contract was made, not at the time of breach.

(d) It is a penalty if it prescribes a sum which is extravagant in comparison with the greatest amount of loss that might actually arise.

(e) It is a penalty if the breach is the non-payment of a sum of money and the amount prescribed is greater than the amount due.

(f) There is a presumption (but no more) that it is a penalty if the clause prescribes a single lump sum payable on the occurrence of several events, some of which will lead to serious, and others trifling, damage.

(g) If the consequences of a breach are such that an accurate pre-estimate is almost impossible, that makes it probable that the sum is a genuine attempt at a pre-estimate.

See also *Philips Hong Kong Ltd v Attorney-General of Hong Kong* (1990) 61 BLR 41.

It was pointed out in *Azimut-Benetti SpA v Healey* [2011] 1 Lloyd's Rep 273 that not all clauses setting amounts payable in default of performance are liquidated damages clauses or penalty clauses. If a clause is not a penalty, but commercially justifiable, it may be enforced even where it is not a genuine pre-estimate of damage.

5.10.3 Accelerated payment of sum due

Sometimes a contract provides that in the event of a breach, all sums payable in future under the contract will immediately fall due. The intention is that such a sum should then be recoverable as a debt rather than as damages.

There is no clear authority on the validity of such terms, but they are likely to be construed as penalties unless they are genuinely attempting a pre-estimate of loss. This is because future sums due under a contract are not debts, so the sum alleged to be due is probably not a pre-estimate of loss. If the effect of payment is that the claimant recovers not only the contract price, but also avoids having to set off their expenditure, or anything they may gain by way of mitigation, then it seems not to be a genuine pre-estimate of loss.

5.11 Other types of damages

5.11.1 Exemplary or punitive damages

5.11.1.1 Tort

Exemplary, or punitive, damages can be awarded in tort in the three situations laid down in *Rookes v Barnard* [1964] AC 1129, and confirmed in *Cassell & Co Ltd v Broome* [1972] AC 1027. These are:

(a) Where there has been oppressive or unconstitutional action by the servants of the government. These can include, for example, civil servants, politicians, local government officers, county councillors, and the police.

(b) Where the defendant's conduct has been calculated to make a profit which may well exceed the compensation payable to the claimant. This is not confined to strictly financial profit, but may include other benefits, for example the eviction of a tenant.

(c) Where such damages are expressly authorised by statute. There do not appear to be any major examples of this.

Exemplary damages are recoverable for trespass, false imprisonment, malicious prosecution, assault, defamation, private nuisance, interference with business, intimidation, misfeasance in public office, and possibly breach of copyright, but not for negligence, public nuisance, breach of statutory duty, or deceit. The view that exemplary damages were strictly limited to those torts for which they had been held recoverable before *Rookes v Barnard* is incorrect (see *Kuddus v Chief Constable of Leicestershire Constabulary* [2001] 3 All ER 193 (which added misfeasance in public office to the list)).

The quantum of exemplary damages, where awarded, is highly arbitrary and within the discretion of the judge or jury. However, the defendant's means must be taken into account.

In *Thompson v Commissioner of Police of the Metropolis* [1997] 2 All ER 762 the House of Lords laid down some ground rules for cases involving misconduct by the police. The judge must give the jury guidance with regard to quantum, and indicate a range for exemplary damages of £5,000 to £50,000.

A good example of the reasoning process that goes into the quantum of an award of exemplary damages can be found in *Ramzan v Brookwide Ltd* [2012] 1 All ER 903.

5.11.1.2 Contract

Exemplary damages are not available for breach of contract claims (see *Addis v Gramophone Co Ltd* [1909] AC 488).

5.11.2 Aggravated damages

5.11.2.1 Tort

Aggravated damages can be awarded in a case of malicious falsehood (see *Khodaparast v Shad* [2000] 1 All ER 545). Such damages go beyond merely compensating the claimant for loss, but include an element of damages for injury to feelings caused by the defendant's conduct and malicious intent.

In cases of assault and similar torts, an award of damages may be made not only in respect of the physical injuries but also in respect of an injury to feelings including the indignity, mental suffering, humiliation, or distress that might be caused by an attack. However, this should be seen as part of the compensatory award, not as aggravated damages, except possibly in a wholly exceptional case (*Richardson v Howie* [2004] EWCA Civ 1127).

5.11.2.2 Contract

Aggravated damages are not available for breach of contract claims.

5.11.3 Damages under the Human Rights Act 1998

This is, not surprisingly, a developing area, but the question of when damages should be awarded for breach of the Human Rights Act 1998 (HRA 1998), and how such damages should be assessed, was considered in some depth by the Court of Appeal in *Anufrijeva v Southwark London BC* [2004] 1 All ER 833, and by the House of Lords in *R (on the application of Greenfield) v Secretary of State for the Home Department* [2005] 2 All ER 240.

Since the European Convention on Human Rights, incorporated into the HRA 1998, has objectives which go beyond merely compensating those whose human rights have been violated, an award of damages is not automatic where there has been a breach of the Act. Indeed in the vast majority of cases, a finding of violation is sufficient recompense in itself. Damages should only be awarded where actual loss has been caused by the breach. Damages should not be assessed by comparison with awards in tortious claims in the English courts, but rather by comparison with awards made by the European Court of Human Rights (ECtHR), which are more modest. Such awards are not precisely calculated, but are assessed on the basis of what is judged to be fair in each individual case. English courts should aim to be neither significantly more nor less generous in their awards than the ECtHR. See also *Van Colle v Chief Constable of Hertfordshire Police* [2007] 3 All ER 122 (reversed by the House of Lords on liability [2008] 3 All ER 977).

In *DSD v Metropolitan Police Commissioner* [2015] 2 All ER 272 the Supreme Court held that damages could be awarded under the Human Rights Act for harm caused by serious investigative failings by the police, even where the police owed no duty of care at common law and would not have been liable in negligence.

5.12 Other matters

5.12.1 Action for an agreed sum

This remedy is available where there is a duty to pay the sum of money agreed and the action providing the right to claim exists. For example, the Sale of Goods Act 1979, s. 49 provides that an action for the price only arises once the property in the goods has passed to the buyer, even though the duty to pay arises as soon as the seller is willing and able to deliver.

If the injured party elects to affirm the contract, they can claim the agreed sum if all that is necessary has been done to make the action available or, arguably, if they can complete doing that which is necessary to make the action available (see *White & Carter (Councils) Ltd v McGregor* [1962] AC 413).

5.12.2 Insurance

It is a long-established principle that the fact that the claimant is insured against their loss and may have received some benefit from their insurance policy is not a matter to be taken into account in assessing damages. The defendant cannot seek to have their liability reduced by the amount received by the claimant from their insurer (*Bradburn v Great Western Railway Co* [1874] LR 10 Exch 1).

It is also the case that, even in a subrogated claim where the insurer brings the claim in the name of the claimant, damages should be assessed on the basis of what would be a reasonable sum to compensate the claimant, not the amount of loss actually suffered by the insurer (*Bee v Jenson* [2007] 4 All ER 791).

5.12.3 Taxation of damages

Account must be taken in the assessment of damages of whether the award of damages will be subject to taxation, and if so, the damages must be such sum as after taxation will leave the claimant in the position they would have been in (after taxation) but for the defendant's wrong.

The issue really only arises in relation to damages awarded for lost earnings by an individual. Damages for lost profit by a business will be taxed in the same way as any profit, so tax is unlikely to need consideration.

The general rule is that where the loss which is compensated for by the payment of damages is loss of income, the tax which would have been paid on that income if earned in the normal way will be deducted from the damages awarded (see *British Transport Commission v Gourley* [1956] AC 185). But this rule applies only if the damages are not themselves subject to taxation. The first £30,000 of damages for loss of income from employment are exempt from tax (s. 403 Income Tax (Earnings and Pensions) Act 2003 (ITEPA)). So if the total sum awarded is no more than £30,000 tax should be deducted under the *Gourley* principle. If the award is £30,000 anything above that amount will be taxed by HMRC. So the *Gourley* principle no longer applies, and the sum awarded should be that sum which, after tax will leave the claimant with the same net sum as they would have been left with had they paid tax on their earnings—*Shove v Downs Surgical plc* [1984] 1 All ER 7.

No tax is payable on damages for personal injury; so damages for lost earnings should be assessed on the basis of net earnings (s. 406 ITEPA). This includes injury to feelings (*Moorthy v HMRC* [2018] 3 All ER 1062).

5.12.4 Interest on damages

We are concerned here with interest on damages. Where the claimant is able to show that as a result of the defendant's breach of contract or negligence they have suffered a loss of interest on their capital, that loss of interest may itself be part of their claim and can be awarded as damages.

The Senior Courts Act 1981 (SCA 1981), s. 35A and the County Courts Act 1984 (CCA 1984), s. 69, give the court discretion to award interest on all or any part of damages for all or any part of the period from the date of the cause of action until the date of payment or judgment. However, the award of interest is prima facie mandatory in cases of personal injury and death, unless there are special reasons why it should not be awarded (s. 35A(2)). Because of this there are particular rules for claims for personal injury (see **10.16**) and fatal accidents (see **11.2.6** and **11.9**).

If the contract itself fixes interest, and is claimed on that basis, the court has no power to fix any different rate. Any claim for interest must be mentioned specifically in the appropriate statement of case.

In other cases, both the rate of interest and the period for which it is awarded are within the court's discretion. However, the discretion to award interest is generally exercised in cases of financial loss; the rate will usually be based on current market rates—the usual maximum being the current Judgments Act 1838 rate. The period will usually be date of loss to date of trial.

For a detailed account of the rules for the awarding of interest, the rates of interest, the period of interest, and the calculation of interest, see **Drafting** manual, section 6.1.

ANSWER TO THE QUESTION IN 5.2.8

The correct answer is **[B]**.

Charles is entitled to be restored to the position he would have been in if Edward had not been negligent.

If Edward had not been negligent,

(a) Charles would not have been able to carry 100 passengers on the *Aurora*—this was forbidden by regulations. So answer [A] is wrong.

(b) Charles would not have been able to carry 200 passengers on the *Beryl* for the same reason. So answer [C] is wrong.

(c) Charles would have been able to charter the *Beryl* and carry 100 passengers. So answer [B] is correct.

(d) Answer [D] is wrong. Edward has nothing to gain by seeking to be restored to the position he would have been in if he had chartered neither steamer. That might have been what he would have done had he decided he would be unable to make a profit on the venture at all. But that is not the case: he did make a profit with the *Aurora*, albeit less than he anticipated. So damages on a reliance loss basis would leave him worse off.

Liability and damages for misrepresentation

6.1 Introduction

The law provides remedies in certain situations where one person has made a false representation to another, who has then acted to their detriment in reliance upon that representation. This will usually, but not invariably, mean that the representee has entered into a contract with the representor. It will also usually, but not invariably, mean that the representee has suffered loss.

Remedies are available at common law, in equity, and by statute. An action may be brought in some circumstances in tort and in other circumstances in contract. The remedies available are damages and rescission. The historical development of the law has resulted in substantial overlap between the actions and remedies available.

6.2 What makes a misrepresentation actionable?

Various conditions must be satisfied to make a misrepresentation actionable:

(a) There must be a statement made by the representor or their agent. The statement may be oral or written, or by conduct and it may be express or implied.

(b) The statement must be a statement of fact, past or present, as opposed to a statement of opinion, intention, or law (but see **6.3.6**). However, it is not always possible to draw a clear dividing line, and what may at first sight appear to be a statement of opinion or intention can sometimes be shown to be a statement of fact. Silence can amount to a representation.

(c) The representation must be made to the representee, directly or indirectly, or to a class of which the representee is a member. This class may be the public at large.

(d) The representee must reasonably have been induced by the representation or reasonably have acted in reliance upon it, believing it to be true. The representation need not be the only inducement. Once this is established, no further element of causation is required (*Downs v Chappell* [1996] 3 All ER 344). The result will usually be that the representee has entered into a contract. A representation is a continuing thing, so that a representation made to an individual who then forms a partnership which enters into a contract can be said to have been relied on by the partnership (*Cramaso LLP v Ogilvie-Grant and others* [2014] 2 All ER 270).

(e) The representor must either have intended the representee to act upon the statement, or at least the facts must be such that they ought to have realised that the representee might do so.

(f) The representation must be false. No more is prima facie required. Whether the misrepresentation was fraudulent, negligent, or innocent affects the cause of action and remedy available.

6.3   The causes of action available

There are six causes of action available with regard to misrepresentation.

6.3.1   Deceit

This is a tortious action, available where the misrepresentation was made fraudulently. The definition of fraud is laid down by *Derry v Peek* (1889) 14 App Cas 337: the defendant must have made the representation knowing it to be false, or not believing it to be true, or with reckless dishonesty, not caring whether it was true or false (see *Thomas Witter Ltd v TBP Industries Ltd* [1996] 2 All ER 573). Provided this mental element is present, and there was an intention that the claimant should rely on the representation, there is no separate requirement that there should be an 'intention to deceive': *Eco3 Capital Ltd v Ludsin Overseas Ltd* [2013] EWCA Civ 139. It is enough that the claimant has acted in reliance upon the representation—no contract is necessary. The claimant does not have to prove as a matter of law that they believed the representation to be true, or that they would not have entered into the contract but for the representation. It is enough that the fraudulent misrepresentation was a material cause of the representee entering into the agreement: *Hayward v Zurich Insurance Co plc* [2016] 4 All ER 441. The burden of proof is on the representee, but if the fraudulent representation was intended to induce them to enter into the contract, there is a strong evidential presumption that it did so (*BV Nederlandse Industrie van Eiprodukten v Rembrandt Enterprises Inc* [2019] 4 All ER 612).

The remedies available are:

- rescission, if the claimant has been induced to enter into a contract;
- damages, if the claimant has suffered loss;
- both rescission and damages, if appropriate.

6.3.2   Statutory misrepresentation

This is a tortious action under the Misrepresentation Act 1967 (MA 1967), s. 2(1), where the misrepresentation was made negligently. The claimant need show only that the representation was false, that they entered into a contract in reliance on it, and that they suffered loss thereby. The burden of proof then shifts onto the defendant to show (if possible) that they reasonably believed the representation to be true, both when it was made and at the time the contract was made. The remedy is damages.

6.3.3   Misrepresentation in equity

This is an action for rescission of the contract, sometimes known as 'innocent' misrepresentation. It is available in all cases where the misrepresentation is less than fraudulent, whether or not the representation has become a term of the contract (MA 1967, s. 1(a)). The claimant need show only that they entered into a contract in reliance on the defendant's misrepresentation. The remedy is rescission, but the court can award damages in lieu of rescission (MA 1967, s. 2(2)).

6.3.4   Breach of contract

This is available as a cause of action where the representation has become a term of the contract. Whether it has done so is a question of fact. Breach of contract is proved by showing the representation to be false. The remedy is damages.

6.3.5   Breach of collateral warranty

This cause of action arises where the representation was of contractual effect, but did not become a term of the contract, usually because the representation was oral, and the contract written. There is then an implied collateral contract: in consideration of the warranty made by the representor, the representee agreed to enter into the main contract. The remedy is damages.

6.3.6 Negligent misstatement

This is a common law action in negligence following *Hedley Byrne & Co Ltd v Heller and Partners Ltd* [1964] AC 465. The claimant must prove the existence of a duty of care, breach of the duty (negligence), and loss. This cause of action will usually arise, but not necessarily so, when there is no contract between the claimant and defendant, though the loss usually flows from a contract between the claimant and a third party.

The scope of negligent misstatement is somewhat wider than negligent misrepresentation and may include not just misstatement of fact, but also the giving of negligent opinions and advice. The remedy is damages.

6.4 Damages

The measure of damages is subject to different principles and is likely to vary according to the cause of action giving rise to the remedy. There is, however, a fundamental distinction between tortious and contractual damages, because, as explained in **5.2.4**, the *position if* is different.

6.4.1 Damages in tort

Tortious damages are designed to put the claimant into the position in which they would have been had the tort not been committed. Where the tortious act is the making of a misrepresentation, then damages are designed to put them in the position they would have been in had the misrepresentation not been made. What that position is is a question of fact, but the courts will usually assume that the claimant would not have entered into the contract, and so damages will put them into the position in which they would have been had the contract never been made.

Broadly speaking, therefore, the claimant can recover the contract price and any consequential loss, but not loss of bargain—the profit they would have made on the contract if the misrepresentation had been true. From the contract price must be deducted the value of any property the claimant has received under the contract. The damages are the difference between what the claimant paid and the value of what they received. That value may often need to be taken as the value now, rather than the value at the time of receipt, because otherwise the claimant may be left enriched or undercompensated (*Naughton v O'Callaghan* [1990] 3 All ER 191). But if the claimant has failed to mitigate by disposing of the assets after discovering the truth, then the relevant figure is the value at the date they should have disposed of them (*Downs v Chappell* [1996] 3 All ER 344).

Where the claimant has been induced by fraud to buy shares which have since increased in value, the loss should be measured by reference to the value of the shares at the date of purchase, rather than at the date of assessment. The original strict rule should not be departed from to the benefit of a fraudulent defendant (*Great Future International Ltd v Sealand Housing Corporation* The Times, 17 December 2002). Where but for the misrepresentation the claimant would still have entered into a contract but at a lower price, the damages are the difference between what was paid and what would have been paid.

6.4.2 Damages in contract

Contractual damages are designed to put the claimant into the position in which they would have been had the contract not been breached. Where the breach of contract consists of the representation being false, then damages are designed to put them into the position in which they would have been had the representation been true.

Broadly speaking, therefore, the claimant can recover damages for loss of bargain and any consequential loss, but not the contract price. Damages for loss of bargain are the difference between what was promised and what was actually received. In many cases, this will result in greater damages than in tort, but not where the contract in fact would have resulted in a bad bargain for the claimant, or where the rules of remoteness would limit contractual damages to a greater extent than tortious damages.

6.4.3 Damages for deceit

These will be assessed on tortious principles (*Doyle v Olby (Ironmongers) Ltd* [1969] 2 QB 158). The damages are therefore designed to compensate the claimant for all loss flowing from the fraudulent representation and to put them into the position they would have been in if the deceit had not been committed, rather than if the representation had been true, so lost profits will not normally be recoverable. However, the claimant can recover damages in respect of the profit they would have made elsewhere had they not been the victim of the deceit (see *East v Maurer* [1991] 2 All ER 733). If, as a result of the deceit, the claimant has entered into a profitable contract with the defendant, but if there had been no fraudulent misrepresentation would have entered into an even more profitable contract, then they can still claim the difference between the profit they would have made and the profit they have in fact made (*Clef Aquitaine v Laporte Materials (Barrow) Ltd* [2000] 3 All ER 493).

However, the remoteness test of reasonable foreseeability does not apply. A claimant is entitled to recover all loss directly flowing from the deceit, including consequential loss, whether or not it was foreseeable. The quantum will be what is required to compensate the claimant for the deceit, even if some part of the loss is loss that might have been sustained even if there had been no deceit (see *Smith New Court Securities Ltd v Scrimgeour Vickers (Asset Management) Ltd* [1996] 4 All ER 769).

In that case the claimant was induced by fraud to purchase Ferranti shares at more than the market price. It subsequently turned out that because of a fraud practised on Ferranti the shares were worth substantially less than their market price on the date of purchase. The claimant claimed the difference between the price paid and the true (unknown) value. The Court of Appeal, applying the 'position if' test simply, held that it could only recover the difference between the price paid and the (incorrect) market value. The House of Lords held that the defendant's fraud had caused the claimant to be locked into possession of shares it would otherwise have been able to dispose of, so that the further loss was caused by the defendant's fraud.

The measure of damages where the deceit has deprived the claimant of their property is the value of the property, not the cost of replacing it (*Smith Kline & French Laboratories Ltd v Long* [1988] 3 All ER 887).

6.4.4 Damages under MA 1967, s. 2(1)

After some initial doubt, it is now clear that these will be assessed on tortious principles, since they are akin to damages for deceit (*André & Cie SA v Michel Blanc et Fils* [1977] 2 Lloyd's Rep 166; *Sharneyford Supplies Ltd v Edge* [1986] Ch 128). It has also been established that damages under s. 2(1) are not subject to a test of reasonable foreseeability, but are recoverable on the same basis as damages for deceit (*Royscot Trust Ltd v Rogerson* [1991] 2 QB 297).

6.4.5 Damages for breach of contract or breach of collateral warranty

These will be assessed according to contractual principles, applying the remoteness rule in contract (*Hadley v Baxendale* (1854) 9 Ex 341; *The Heron II* [1969] 1 AC 350), which, if anything, is somewhat stricter than the rule in tort (*H Parsons (Livestock) Ltd v Uttley Ingham & Co Ltd* [1978] QB 791) (see **3.2.6** and **4.2.10**).

6.4.6 Damages for negligent misstatement

These will be assessed according to tortious principles at common law and will depend on the scope of the duty under *Hedley Byrne & Co Ltd v Heller and Partners Ltd* [1964] AC 465 and the reasonable foreseeability test.

6.4.7 Damages in lieu of rescission under MA 1967, s. 2(2)

Even if a claimant has sought only rescission of a contract (plus perhaps some consequential losses), the court may still decide to award damages in lieu of rescission. This is in the discretion of the court, apparently irrespective of the wishes of either party. The option is available whenever the innocent party could have rescinded the contract at some time after it was made, not only if the remedy remains available at the time of the court's order (*Thomas Witter Ltd v TBP Industries Ltd* [1996] 2 All ER 573).

The measure of damages under s. 2(2) also appears to be within the court's discretion, but on a strict reading of the Act, it seems likely that damages will be simply an alternative to rescission—that is, the tortious measure of what is sufficient to return the claimant to their pre-contractual position—and may not even include any consequential loss, which will have to be recovered, if possible, under s. 2(1) or for breach of contract. There is no sound authority on this issue.

6.5 Contributory negligence

In cases of misrepresentation, the question sometimes arises whether a defendant will be liable if the claimant could, with reasonable diligence, have discovered the falsity of the representation and could reasonably have been expected to do so. In the case of fraudulent misrepresentation, this is no defence (*Standard Chartered Bank v Pakistan National Shipping Corp* [2003] 1 All ER 173). It must follow that the position is the same where a claim is made under MA 1967, s. 2(1), on the basis of *Royscot Trust Ltd v Rogerson* [1991] 2 QB 297.

However, where there is concurrent liability in negligence at common law and under MA 1967, s. 2(1), damages under both heads may be reduced for the claimant's contributory negligence (*Gran Gelato Ltd v Richcliff (Group) Ltd* [1992] Ch 560, applying the same rule as that established for concurrent liability in tort and contract in *Forsikringsaktieselskapet Vesta v Butcher* [1986] 2 All ER 488).

For breach of contract, contributory negligence is no defence. In negligence, at common law, contributory negligence is in principle available as a defence. But it must be remembered that the duty under *Hedley Byrne & Co Ltd v Heller and Partners Ltd* [1964] AC 465 arises only where it was reasonably foreseeable that the claimant would rely on the defendant's statement, and it would be odd in such circumstances to hold that the claimant was at fault in relying upon it: see, for example, *Gran Gelato v Richcliff* above.

6.6 Mitigation

The claimant has a duty to mitigate in the usual way, and all the principles explained in **3.3.7** and **4.2.7** apply.

An interesting exception occurred in *Hussey v Eels* [1990] 2 QB 227. The claimants bought a bungalow from the defendants for £53,250. In pre-sale inquiries, the defendants negligently represented that the building had not been subject to subsidence. This turned out to be untrue, and the cost of repairs was estimated at over £17,000. However, the claimants decided that rather than repair the bungalow, they would seek planning permission to demolish it and build two new bungalows on the site instead. They were granted planning permission and sold the land to a developer for £78,500. They claimed damages from the defendants for diminution in value, i.e. the difference between the price they paid and the true value of the property, a difference that was valued at £17,000, the cost of repairs. The defendants disputed the claim on the basis that the claimants had mitigated their loss out of existence by selling at a profit to the developer. The Court of Appeal held that the profit made on resale was not to be taken into account when assessing damages for the negligent misrepresentation, since the resale was not part of a continuous transaction commencing with the original purchase of the property. The negligence which caused the damage could not therefore be said to be the cause of the profit, and the claimants were entitled to damages on a diminution in value basis.

6.7   Exclusion of liability for misrepresentation

It is difficult to exclude liability for misrepresentation. If the representation has become a term of the contract, any term purporting to exclude or restrict liability is subject to the reasonableness test in s. 11 of the Unfair Contract Terms Act 1977 (UCTA) (s. 3 UCTA). If the representation is non-contractual, any term purporting to exclude or restrict liability is also subject to the reasonableness test (s. 3 Misrepresentation Act 1967, as amended by s. 8 UCTA). Both such terms would almost certainly also be held to be unfair under s. 62 of the Consumer Rights Act 2015.

However s. 3 MA 1967 does not apply to entire agreement clauses. An entire agreement clause may well preclude the existence of any collateral contract or collateral warranty.

Any term by which a party warrants that they have not entered into the contract in reliance on any representation other than those contained within it may well be of no effect. If it is to be of effect, it will have to satisfy the reasonableness test, and it is unlikely to do so if it would prevent liability for negligent misrepresentation, and it will certainly be void if it would prevent liability for fraud.

6.8   Rescission

6.8.1   When is rescission for misrepresentation available?

Rescission is available as a remedy, in principle at least, wherever the representee has been induced by the representation to enter into a contract, even if the representation has become a term of the contract (MA 1967, s. 1(a)). However, rescission, being an equitable remedy, is within the court's discretion, and the court has a further discretion to award damages in lieu of rescission.

6.8.2   The 'right' to rescind

Rescission is not simply a remedy granted by the court. Where a representee has a 'right' to rescind (i.e. the circumstances have arisen in which a court would have the discretion to order rescission), they may do so by giving notice of this to the representor. It may then not be necessary to apply to the court at all, though the court's assistance may be required to enforce rescission.

6.8.3   The effect of rescission

Rescission simply involves putting the parties into the position they were in before the contract was made, with the repayment of the contract price and the return of any property transferred. This is usually only possible if it was a contract involving goods, shares, or land. If it was a contract for services, rescission is only a possible remedy if granted before any services have been performed.

If the contract price has been paid in full or in part, rescission will involve repayment. If the property has changed its value since the date of the contract, a financial adjustment can be made. If the claimant has suffered consequential loss, they may bring a claim for damages in addition to seeking rescission.

6.8.4 Bars to rescission

The court's discretion to order rescission will not be exercised where any of the bars to rescission have arisen. The main bars are:

- where *restitutio in integrum* is no longer possible;
- where the claimant has affirmed the contract;
- where a third party has acquired an interest in the subject matter of the contract;
- where there has been an unreasonable lapse of time.

The bars to rescission are dealt with more fully in **7.3.5**.

Equitable remedies in contract

7.1 Introduction

In contract cases, and in particular for breach of contract, the primary remedy is damages. However, in certain situations there is a range of equitable remedies available, both to remedy a breach of contract and to enforce contractual rights. Injunctions are of particular importance and have a chapter to themselves (**Chapter 8**). Five others are dealt with in this chapter: specific performance, rescission, restitution, rectification, and account of profits. They have certain features in common.

(a) *Equitable remedies are discretionary*. Equitable remedies are not available as of right: they will only be granted in the exercise of the court's discretion in accordance with certain well-established principles.

(b) *Common law remedies must be inadequate*. An equitable remedy will be granted only if damages would not in all the circumstances of the case be an adequate remedy for the claimant.

(c) *The maxims of equity apply*. The famous maxims, 'You must come to equity with clean hands' and 'Equity does not act in vain' are to be taken seriously. The court will not exercise its discretion in favour of a claimant who is also in breach of contract, or grant an injunction which could never be enforced.

7.2 Specific performance

7.2.1 What is specific performance?

Specific performance is an order requiring a party to a contract to perform or complete the performance of their obligations under the contract. The effect of the order is therefore to put the parties into the position they would have been in had the contract been performed, and it is the equitable equivalent of damages in respect of the claimant's expectation loss.

The remedy is discretionary, but the circumstances in which it will or will not be granted are to a considerable extent certain. Rather than attempting to define when specific performance will be granted, the courts have defined the bars to the granting of an order, and tend to approach the exercise of discretion negatively: if there is nothing *against* the making of an order, it will be made. There are numerous possible bars, the most important of which is designed to prevent the common law remedy of damages and the equitable remedy of specific performance overlapping.

7.2.2 Adequacy of damages

7.2.2.1 Basic rule

The first and principal hurdle for a claimant to overcome is to show that *damages would not be an adequate remedy*. In most cases, damages are adequate and so specific performance will not be ordered. In order to show that they are not adequate, the claimant will usually have to demonstrate the uniqueness of the thing contracted for and/or the financial ineffectiveness of damages.

7.2.2.2   Uniqueness

Contracts, broadly speaking, are for the sale of property or the performance of services.

In contracts for the sale of property, the adequacy of damages may well depend on the uniqueness of the thing which the claimant contracted to buy. It may be unique either because there is no other thing in existence like it or because, however ordinary the thing is, the claimant, if awarded damages, would be unable to obtain another thing like it from anywhere else.

Commodities and shares are usually considered not to be unique; they are readily available on the market. So, a contract for the sale of shares will not be specifically enforced (*Cuddee v Rutter* [1720] 1 P Wms 570) because damages would enable the claimant to buy other identical shares. But it would be different if substitute shares were not available (e.g. where the breach deprived a claimant of a majority shareholding) (*Harvela Investments Ltd v Royal Trust Co of Canada (CI) Ltd* [1986] AC 207).

Land, on the other hand, is considered unique, however ordinary a simple house and garden may appear to be, and contracts for the sale of land are routinely enforced by specific performance. This tradition is so deeply rooted that the remedy may be regarded as virtually automatic, unless any of the other bars arises.

Goods and chattels fall somewhere in the middle of the uniqueness spectrum. Ordinary goods are not unique and specific performance will not be granted where substitutes can readily be obtained. But if the goods have some special or rare quality, an order may be granted: however, the courts are reluctant to recognise sentimental value as rendering goods unique. Ordinary goods may become unique if in all the circumstances no substitute can in fact be obtained: in *Sky Petroleum Ltd v VIP Petroleum Ltd* [1974] 1 WLR 576, an order was made requiring the defendants to deliver petrol to the claimants at a time of petrol shortage. Section 52 of the Sale of Goods Act 1979 gives the court a discretion to order specific performance of a contract for the sale of specific or ascertained goods, but does not seem in effect to have made such orders any more common than they would have been at common law.

Contracts for the performance of services are likely to be unique only where there is a personal service involved, in which case they are unlikely to be enforced for other reasons (see **7.2.3.4**). Where the services could be performed by anyone, damages are likely to be an adequate remedy.

7.2.2.3   Financial ineffectiveness

There are various reasons why damages may not provide complete compensation, but the fact that they do not does not necessarily mean that the court will consider them to be an inadequate remedy.

In particular, damages will not usually be deemed an inadequate remedy merely because they would be difficult to assess. Older cases accepted the idea that difficulty in assessment of damages should point towards specific performance being granted, but later cases have shown reluctance on the part of the courts to follow this line. In this respect, courts are more lenient in granting injunctions than specific performance.

The defendant's inability to pay may be a relevant consideration.

Damages may not be adequate where the defendant's obligation is a continuing one, lasting beyond the date of judgment, such that an award of damages now will only compensate the claimant for their loss so far and a further action might be required in the future.

Where damages, if awarded, would be purely nominal, they may be considered to be an inadequate remedy on the ground that specific performance would in such circumstances be the more appropriate remedy (e.g. *Beswick v Beswick* [1968] AC 58).

Although a contract requiring the defendant to pay money will normally not be specifically enforceable, because damages would be an adequate remedy, *Beswick v Beswick* shows that it may be enforceable where payment is to be made to a third party or where the payment is in the form of an annuity or other periodical payment, which is a continuing obligation.

7.2.3 Other bars

7.2.3.1 Contracts requiring supervision

Traditionally, the court would not order specific performance where the enforcement of the order would require the court's constant supervision (e.g. *Ryan v Mutual Tontine Association* [1893] 1 Ch 116). More recent authority suggests that this principle is exaggerated (e.g. *Posner v Scott-Lewis* [1987] Ch 25).

Arguably, the difficulty of supervision is no longer a bar to specific performance, but rather a factor going to the court's discretion (*Tito v Waddell (No 2)* [1977] Ch 106). It may be that the need for supervision—even constant supervision—will not prevent specific performance being granted where it is important to protect the claimant's interest and where it is clear from the contract and/or order what the defendant is required to do.

7.2.3.2 Contract too vague

Specific performance will not be granted where the terms of the contract are so vague that it is impossible for the order to state exactly what the defendant is required to do, or for the defendant to know what should be done to comply with the order, or for the court to say whether the defendant has complied with the order or is in contempt.

7.2.3.3 Building contracts

The court will not normally make an order requiring a builder to erect or complete a building, on three grounds:

- damages would be adequate if another builder could do the work;
- it is likely to be difficult to specify exactly what the builder must do;
- constant supervision may be required.

However, in modern conditions, particularly where the contract is in a detailed form, specific performance may be granted if three conditions are satisfied:

- the work is precisely defined by the contract;
- damages will not adequately compensate the claimant;
- the defendant is in possession of the land on which the building is to be done (*Wolverhampton Corporation v Emmons* [1901] 1 QB 515; *Carpenters Estates v Davies* [1940] Ch 160).

7.2.3.4 Contracts involving personal services

It is well established that the court will not order specific performance of a contract involving personal services or service contracts which are personal in nature. The prime example is the contract of employment. With regard to the employee's services, the rule is now statutory and absolute (Trade Union and Labour Relations (Consolidation) Act 1992, s. 236). In all other circumstances, the rule remains discretionary, but is nevertheless well entrenched. The rule applies not only to contracts of personal service in the strict sense, but also to contracts involving the performance of services of a personal nature.

The greater the personal element involved in the contract, the less likely it is that specific performance will be ordered. However, the rule is not absolute, and the courts are unwilling to make it so (e.g. *CH Giles & Co Ltd v Morris* [1972] 1 WLR 307). Modern conditions of employment may make it possible for an employee to get an order against an employer (*Hill v CA Parsons & Co Ltd* [1972] Ch 305). Where the contract requires the performance of services which are not personal in nature, there is no bar, even if the services are to be performed by a particular individual.

7.2.3.5 Contracts to carry on a business

The court will not normally specifically enforce a contract in such a way as to require a person to carry on a business. This long-standing principle was affirmed by the House of Lords in *Co-operative Insurance Society Ltd v Argyll Stores (Holdings) Ltd* [1997] 3 All ER 297. This will be so even where damages may strictly not be an adequate remedy. The original reason was because such an order would require the constant supervision of the court, but it probably exists now as a principle in its own right, justified on the basis that it is against the public interest to require someone to carry on a business at a loss if a plausible alternative exists.

7.2.3.6   Equity will not act in vain

Specific performance will not be granted where it would be in vain to do so, for example, where once the order was made the defendant could still lawfully terminate the contract at any time (*Sheffield Gas Consumers Co v Harrison* [1853] 17 Beav 294), or where the defendant would be incapable of fulfilling their obligations (*Castle v Wilkinson* [1870] LR 5 Ch App 534).

7.2.3.7   Coming to equity with clean hands

A claimant will not be granted specific performance of a contract unless they have performed all their obligations under the contract hitherto and remain ready and willing to perform any future obligations. This willingness must be pleaded and proved. A claimant who is also in breach of contract will not normally be granted specific performance of it, though this bar may not arise if the breach is trivial (*Dyster v Randall and Sons* [1926] Ch 932). How clean the claimant's hands are is a matter of the court's judgement and goes to its discretion.

7.2.3.8   Delay

There is no statutory limitation period barring claims for specific performance, but unreasonable delay will amount to a bar in equity. This is known as the doctrine of laches, and is again a matter of the court's discretion. How long a delay is unreasonable depends on the facts of the case, but in most circumstances not long is allowed. It was generally thought that one year was the upper limit for most cases, but this may be too strict. A delay of over two years was held not unreasonable in *Lazard Bros v Fairfield Properties* [1977] 121 SJ 893.

7.2.3.9   Want of mutuality

The doctrine of mutuality traditionally required an order for specific performance to be refused against a defendant where the defendant could not have enforced the contract by specific performance against the claimant. However, it is now clear that the doctrine can be waived by the court, which must judge mutuality at the time of judgment as opposed to the time of the contract (*Price v Strange* [1978] Ch 337).

7.2.3.10   Hardship

Specific performance will be refused where it would cause severe hardship to the defendant. This is simply part of the court's overriding discretion to refuse specific performance where it would be unjust to grant it. However, in a case of hardship, the hardship must be severe, not be brought about by the defendant's own acts, and lead to injustice. See, for example, *Patel v Ali* [1984] Ch 283.

7.2.3.11   Contract only partly specifically enforceable

Where the court cannot grant specific performance of the contract as a whole, it will not grant specific performance only of that part of the contract which is specifically enforceable (*Ryan v Mutual Tontine Association* [1893] 1 Ch 116). However, where a contract can be divided into one or more separate agreements, one part of the contract can be specifically enforced while the others are not.

7.2.4   Damages in lieu of specific performance

Damages originally obtainable in lieu of or in addition to specific performance under the Chancery Amendment Act 1858 (also known as Lord Cairns' Act) can now be obtained by virtue of the Senior Courts Act 1981, s. 50. Such damages will be assessed on the same basis as damages at common law (*Johnson v Agnew* [1980] AC 367).

7.3 Rescission

7.3.1 What is rescission?

Rescission is an equitable remedy whereby a contract made between two parties is set aside, and they are restored to the position they would have been in had the contract never been made. The contract is in effect voidable: valid until it is rescinded, and thereafter treated as if it had never taken effect. Rescission is the equitable equivalent of damages in respect of the claimant's reliance loss.

7.3.2 When is rescission available?

There are three main situations in which rescission is available as a remedy:

- misrepresentation;
- undue influence; and
- duress.

Its availability as a remedy for misrepresentation is dealt with in **Chapter 6**. Rescission is the only effective remedy where a contract has been obtained by improper pressure amounting to undue influence.

For many years, it was believed that rescission could sometimes, though rarely, be a remedy for mistake. However, in *Great Peace Shipping Ltd v Tsavliris Salvage (International) Ltd* [2002] 4 All ER 689, it was held that where a contract is valid and enforceable at common law, it cannot be rescinded in equity. Where a contract has been entered into as a result of a mutual mistake, it may in certain circumstances be unenforceable at common law, but then it is void—the remedy of rescission plays no part.

7.3.3 The act of rescission

Rescission is not just a judicial remedy: a party to a contract may rescind it for misrepresentation, mistake, or undue influence by giving notice to the other party, and, if accepted by the other party, the contract will be at an end and there will be no necessity for recourse to the courts. However, a court order either for rescission or to declare the validity of the claimant's act of rescission may be necessary where there is a dispute between the parties, and an order for enforcement may also be required and involve application to the court.

7.3.4 Repudiation distinguished from rescission

Rescission is not to be confused with repudiation of a contract (which is a breach of contract) or with the claimant's right to accept a defendant's repudiatory breach as a discharge from the contract, which is sometimes referred to as 'rescission' (see **3.2.3.3**).

Rescission is not the appropriate remedy where there has been a fundamental or repudiatory breach of contract. The claimant must seek damages, and it is more likely that they will be awarded damages for expectation loss rather than reliance loss—see *Howard-Jones v Tate* [2012] 2 All ER 369.

Where there has been a breach of contract, repudiatory or not, the claimant is entitled to seek damages to put them into the position they would have been in had the contract been performed. Where the claimant seeks rescission, the claimant is asking to be put into the position they would have been in had the contract not been made. This may involve a claim for damages for consequential loss, but there can be no claim for damages in respect of the claimant's expectation loss.

7.3.5 Equitable bars to rescission

Rescission is a discretionary remedy and there are equitable bars that will prevent its being granted. There are four bars in particular.

7.3.5.1   *Restitutio in integrum* is not possible

Restitutio in integrum is the process by which the parties return and recover benefits gained under the contract. The contract will cease to be capable of rescission if the parties can no longer be restored to their original positions. The most likely reason for this is that the subject matter has changed so much that the party who gave it will not get back the same thing that they originally had (e.g. goods have been destroyed or seriously damaged, or business assets have been disposed of). If the subject matter has merely diminished in value, this will not bar rescission, unless the loss is due to the acts of the buyer.

Nevertheless, equity does not require that restitution should be precise. There will be no bar, so long as it can be achieved substantially and fairly, so that a party gets back substantially the same thing they parted with, and the change does not result in injustice. This will be so particularly if a financial adjustment can be made to take account of the alteration of the subject matter (*Erlanger v New Sombrero Phosphate Co* [1878] 3 App Cas 1218). The court will not apply the bar too strictly in cases of undue influence involving a breach of fiduciary relationship (*O'Sullivan v Management Agency and Music Ltd* [1985] QB 428). It has been held at first instance that the impossibility of *restitutio in integrum* is also a bar to rescission for duress at common law (*Halpern v Halpern* [2006] 3 All ER 1139); however, the Court of Appeal (*Halpern v Halpern* [2007] 3 All ER 478) reversed this decision so as to allow the point to remain open.

7.3.5.2   Third party acquiring rights

The right to rescind is lost if an innocent third party has acquired an interest under the contract for value before the claimant seeks to rescind. This is an application of the basic principle that equity will not defeat the bona fide purchaser for value without notice ('equity's darling'). There is, of course, no bar if the third party is a volunteer or the defendant's trustee in bankruptcy.

7.3.5.3   Affirmation

If the claimant, with knowledge of their right to rescind, nevertheless affirms the contract, their right to rescind is waived. A claimant may affirm either expressly, by informing the defendant that they intend to proceed with the contract, or by conduct, for example by continuing to take the benefit of it or by doing something which would suggest an intention not to rescind or seek rescission. However, the claimant can affirm only after they have discovered the truth. This means not only that the claimant must be aware of the facts of which they were previously unaware (e.g. that the defendant's representation was false), but that the claimant must also be aware of their legal rights and their option to rescind (*Peyman v Lanjani* [1985] Ch 457).

Failing to give notice of rescission within a reasonable time after discovering the truth may amount to affirmation. On the other hand, once notice has been given, continuing to perform the contract until trial, where there is no real alternative, does not constitute affirmation.

7.3.5.4   Delay

Delay between discovery of the truth and seeking to rescind may also evidence affirmation. An intention to rescind must always be communicated to the defendant. As a matter of practice, a claimant should be advised to communicate this intention at the earliest moment. If the first notice of rescission is the service of proceedings, there is a good chance the claimant will be held to have affirmed.

Delay between the date of the contract and seeking rescission may, however, amount to a bar in itself, even where there is no question of affirmation. It will never do so in a case of fraud or breach of fiduciary duty, but it may do so in other cases (*Leaf v International Galleries* [1950] 2 KB 86).

7.3.5.5   Damages in lieu of rescission

Damages in lieu of rescission may be recovered for misrepresentation under the Misrepresentation Act 1967, s. 2(2) (see **6.4.7**).

7.4   Quasi-contract—the law of restitution

Quasi-contract is sometimes described as an action for money had and received or unjust enrichment or benefit. This occurs in the following situations.

First, 'where the claimant has been compelled to pay money for which the defendant is liable, [they] may sue the defendant for the money so paid' (*Cheshire, Fifoot and Furmston's Law of Contract*).

The second situation is where money has been paid under a mistake which, had it been true, would have required the payment of the money. It is no longer necessary to distinguish a mistake of fact from a mistake of law (*Kleinwort Benson Ltd v Lincoln City Council* [1998] 4 All ER 513). Accordingly, tax wrongly paid under a mistake of law is recoverable (*Deutsche Morgan Grenfell Group plc v IRC* [2007] 1 All ER 449).

The third situation is where money is paid where there has been a total failure of consideration or where money is paid in pursuance of a void contract. Money paid in pursuance of an illegal contract is rarely recoverable in quasi-contract.

Fourth, where one party is bound to pay a sum of money to another and agrees to pay that money to a third party and has informed that third party of the intention to pay, that party is liable in quasi-contract to make the payment.

Fifth, where a wrongful (tortious) act has been committed against the claimant who, as a consequence, has suffered loss, the claimant may be entitled to recover for the loss in quasi-contract—where action can be brought in tort, the claims are alternatives to each other.

The sixth situation is where a claim to *quantum meruit* for reasonable remuneration for work done or services rendered where no price was fixed or where a new contract has been substituted for the old.

For an interesting analysis, see *Rover International Ltd v Cannon Film Sales Ltd (No 3)* [1989] 3 All ER 423. See also *Lipkin Gorman v Karpnale* [1991] AC 548 for an example of unjust enrichment.

This area is developing rapidly as a method by which redress can be sought. See *DO Ferguson and Associates v Sohl* [1992] 62 BLR 95.

7.5   Rectification

7.5.1   What is rectification?

Rectification is a discretionary equitable remedy for mistake in contract. Where two parties have agreed the terms of a contract, but they are then incorrectly set down in or excluded from a document which purports to contain the full terms of the contract, the court may order the rectification of that document. It is the *writing* that is being put right, not the contract itself.

7.5.2   What is required?

The mistake must be the mistake of both parties. If the mistake is that of one party only, or one party was indifferent as to the detail that the claimant wants rectified, rectification will not be ordered. The exception is where the omission or error is due to the defendant's fraud. If terms are omitted from a document, it will be rectified to include them only if they were expressly agreed by the parties or are customary terms which could be implied in any event. A document which accurately records an oral agreement made by mistake cannot be rectified.

7.5.3   Standard of evidence required

Clear evidence is required before rectification will be ordered; there must be strong and convincing evidence that the document failed accurately to record the intention of the parties. It is most unlikely that rectification will be ordered solely on the claimant's oral evidence.

7.5.4 Bars to rectification

Rectification is barred by delay; where a third party has acquired rights for value; and where judgment has been obtained in an action in which rectification could have been sought, but was not.

7.6 Account of profits

It was established by the decision of the House of Lords in *Attorney-General v Blake* [2000] 4 All ER 385 that there is another equitable remedy available for breach of contract: an account of profits. In an exceptional case, the court is not limited to the remedies of damages, specific performance, and injunction, but may order the defendant to account for all or some of the profits they have made through their breach of contract. The case is likely to be exceptional where the contractual obligation is very close to a fiduciary obligation. The remedy will be granted where the court thinks it just in all the circumstances.

It remains to be seen whether the remedy will be granted in other cases. Although not limited in principle, it may be that the exceptional circumstances required will arise only in cases of the kind in *Blake,* which involved a convicted spy.

8 Injunctions

8.1 Introduction

An injunction is an equitable remedy by which the court makes an order to the defendant telling them to do or not to do a specific act. It is widely available in contract, tort, and family law, subject to certain requirements established by case law.

8.2 Prohibitory and mandatory injunctions

An injunction may be prohibitory or mandatory. A prohibitory injunction forbids the defendant to do something; a mandatory injunction requires the defendant to do something. Whether an injunction is mandatory or prohibitory is strictly speaking a matter of substance, not of the form of words used. So, an order forbidding the defendant from not doing something is 'mandatory'; an order requiring the defendant to stop doing something is 'prohibitory'. The distinction may be significant, because a claimant is supposed to couch a mandatory order in positive terms; but a mandatory order is generally harder to obtain than a prohibitory order. In practice, therefore, the almost invariable tendency is to phrase injunctions prohibitively wherever possible, for example an order forbidding the defendant from allowing a state of affairs to continue.

In contract, a mandatory injunction to stop a breach is very rare, because in most cases it is to all intents and purposes an order of specific performance and will be sought as such. However, there is no such thing as interim specific performance, and in the pre-trial stages of a claim an interim mandatory injunction may occasionally be sought.

8.3 Final and interim injunctions

A final injunction, sometimes known as a perpetual injunction (even if limited in time), is an order made at trial. However, most injunctions are sought as a matter of some urgency: the claimant cannot wait until trial. It may be that the defendant's alleged wrongdoing will cause the claimant irreparable continuing damage pending trial, or the damage will have been done by the time the case comes on for trial. The claimant will then seek an interim injunction, which will last only for a temporary period, until trial at the latest. Such an injunction, in cases of extreme urgency, may be sought without notice to the defendant, but if sought without notice will usually only be granted with permission to the defendant to apply to set it aside or for a short time.

The principles applicable to the grant of interim injunctions are basically procedural rather than equitable and are very different from the principles governing the grant of final injunctions.

8.4   Injunction for breach of contract

8.4.1   Support of contractual rights

An injunction can only be granted in support of a legal or equitable right. If the claimant has no such right which needs protecting or has no *locus standi* to bring the action to protect the legal rights of others, no injunction can be granted. In contract, it is the claimant's contractual rights which are being supported. The claimant must therefore show a valid contract and a breach, or threatened breach, by the defendant.

8.4.2   Actual or threatened breach

Where the breach is actual, it will be relatively easy to prove. An injunction can readily be granted to restrain a continuing breach or to prevent the repetition of a breach. But sometimes the breach is merely threatened and lies in the future. In such circumstances, a *quia timet* injunction may be granted to forbid the apprehended breach, but a high degree of proof is required. The claimant will have to show a high probability of the breach occurring, and the likelihood of substantial damage resulting (*Fletcher v Bealey* [1885] 28 ChD 688; *Attorney-General v Manchester Corporation* [1893] 2 Ch 87).

Take care not to confuse an anticipatory breach (which is actual) with a threatened breach (which is not).

8.4.3   Prevention of breach of a negative stipulation

As explained in **9.2**, injunctions to restrain a breach of contract are almost always prohibitory unless interim. It follows that the need for an injunction arises where the defendant has done, or threatens to do, something they promised in the contract not to do: the injunction will be in support of a negative stipulation in the contract. Such a stipulation will normally be express, but an injunction can be granted to prevent a breach of an implied negative stipulation, provided that it does not amount to specific performance by the back door (see **8.6**). An injunction will not, however, be granted in support of an implied negative stipulation in a contract of employment or personal service (*Mortimer v Beckett* [1920] 1 Ch 571).

8.4.4   When is a final mandatory injunction appropriate?

The only circumstance in which a final mandatory injunction may be appropriate for breach of contract is where it is necessary to undo the effects of a breach by the defendant of a negative promise. For example, the claimant sells the defendant part of their land, and the contract contains a covenant that the defendant will not erect a building on the land which is out of keeping with the houses in the neighbourhood. The defendant builds a Japanese pagoda, and the claimant seeks a mandatory injunction requiring it to be pulled down.

8.4.5   The terms of the injunction

The terms of any injunction for breach of contract must be carefully drawn. The claimant's rights are defined by the contract and so the claimant cannot get an order any wider in scope than that which the contract entitles them to, unless the defendant's acts amount also to a tort or some other wrong.

8.5   The grant of an injunction

8.5.1   In general

Being an equitable remedy, an injunction will only be granted in the discretion of the court, and the usual equitable bars apply. However, the hurdles are not on the whole as difficult to overcome as they are for an order of specific performance. A prohibitory injunction to forbid a breach of an express negative stipulation will normally be granted, the important exception being where this would indirectly amount to specific performance of a contract which would not be specifically enforced in equity (see **8.6**).

8.5.2   Inadequacy of damages

The claimant must, of course, show that damages would not be an adequate remedy, but this is a much lower hurdle where the claimant seeks to prevent the defendant doing something rather than where the claimant requires the defendant to do something: in the case of a prohibitory injunction to restrain a breach of contract, damages are not likely to be considered adequate (*Doherty v Allman* [1878] 3 App Cas 709). However, damages may be adequate where the likely harm would be trivial, and a much stiffer test will be applied where the claimant seeks a mandatory injunction (*Shepherd Homes Ltd v Sandham* [1971] Ch 340). A claimant is entitled to argue that damages would not be an adequate remedy when the contract contains a limitation of liability clause that would result in them not being fully compensated for the breach. It is not a good argument that the limitation on damages was the parties' commercial choice, because the defendant's primary obligation is to fulfil the contract (*AB v CD* [2014] 3 All ER 667).

8.5.3   Other bars

Other bars will prevent the grant of an injunction in the same way as they prevent an order for specific performance:

(a)   *Contract too vague.* An order will not be made if it does not allow the defendant to understand precisely what they may or may not do (see **7.2.3.2**).

(b)   *Equity will not act in vain.* An injunction will not be made if it would have no effect (see **7.2.3.6**).

(c)   *Clean hands.* An injunction will not normally be granted to prevent a breach of contract by the defendant if the claimant is also in breach; and the claimant must show that they are ready and willing to perform all their future obligations (see **7.2.3.7**).

(d)   *Delay.* Delay may lead to an injunction being refused, but this is by no means as serious a bar as it is to specific performance. Where, however, the claimant's delay effectively amounts to acquiescence in the defendant's breach, an injunction may not be granted (e.g. *Sayers v Collyer* [1884] 28 ChD 103) (see **7.2.3.8**).

(e)   *Hardship.* See **7.2.3.10**.

8.6   Back-door specific performance

8.6.1   Ground for refusal of an injunction

An important additional ground for the refusal of an injunction arises where a prohibitory injunction, if granted, would in effect amount to an order for specific performance of the contract, but an order for specific performance would not be made. In other words, a claimant who is not entitled to specific performance cannot get it by the back door of an injunction. Where the injunction would have the same effect as an order for specific performance, the decision whether to grant it will be made on specific performance criteria, for example *Hill v CA Parsons & Co Ltd* [1972] Ch 305; *Sky Petroleum Ltd v VIP Petroleum Ltd* [1974] 1 WLR 576.

8.6.2 Contracts of personal service and back-door specific performance

The issue arises most commonly in cases involving a contract of personal service, which cannot be specifically enforced and so cannot be indirectly enforced by an injunction restraining the defendant from withdrawing their services. However, where there is an express negative stipulation in the contract, typically a restraint of trade clause, this may be enforced by an injunction. So, although the claimant may not be able to compel the defendant to perform services for the claimant, they may be able to prevent the defendant performing services for someone else (*Lumley v Wagner* (1852) 1 De G M & G 604).

However, even an order restraining the defendant from working for someone else may still in effect amount to specific performance if the defendant would have no other means of earning a living. Accordingly, an injunction will not be granted in support of an express negative stipulation in a personal service contract if the end result will be that the defendant is still compelled to work for the claimant (*Rely-a-Bell Burglar and Fire Alarm Co v Eisler* [1926] Ch 609) or is given the stark choice of working for the claimant or being unemployed (*Warner Bros Pictures Inc v Nelson* [1937] 1 KB 209). Some alternative means of earning a living must be open to the defendant before an injunction will be granted. The same principle applies where the contract is one of personal service by the claimant to the defendant (*Page One Records Ltd v Britton* [1968] 1 WLR 157).

If a claimant is prevented by this rule from obtaining an injunction against the person to whom they are contracted, they cannot get round it by instead seeking an injunction to restrain a third party from inducing a breach of the contract (*Warren v Mendy* [1989] 3 All ER 103).

An injunction will never be granted in support of an implied negative stipulation in a contract of personal service.

8.7 Injunctions in tort

8.7.1 Introduction

An injunction can only be granted in support of a legal right. Since a tort is a legal wrong, the claimant has a right to prevent that legal wrong if it has caused, is causing, or will cause them damage or if they have *locus standi* to prevent damage to the public at large. Injunctions are particularly useful in tort to restrain trespass, nuisance, defamation, inducing breach of contract, and all the torts involving intellectual property. Except in cases of trespass and nuisance, interim injunctions are likely to be sufficient.

8.7.2 Prohibitory injunctions

8.7.2.1 The primary remedy

Although, strictly speaking, an injunction can only be granted where damages would not be an adequate remedy, when the claimant seeks to prevent a tort or the infringement of a property right the granting of an injunction is more or less automatic. Injunction has become the primary remedy, and damages in lieu should only be awarded in very exceptional circumstances (see *Watson v Croft Promosport Ltd* [2009] 3 All ER 249 and *HKRUK II (CHC) Ltd v Heaney* [2010] EWHC 2245 (Ch)). Unless the claimant is barred, once their legal right is established an injunction will be granted, unless:

- the injury to the claimant's legal rights is small;
- the injury is assessable in money;
- a small money payment would be adequate compensation; and
- it would be oppressive to the defendant to grant an injunction (*Shelfer v London Electric Lighting Co* [1895] 1 Ch 287; *Kennaway v Thompson* [1981] QB 88).

Where these conditions are made out, damages are likely to be awarded in lieu (*Jaggard v Sawyer* [1995] 1 WLR 269). However, it should not be regarded as significant that the claimant has indicated a willingness to accept partial damages in lieu (*Watson v Croft Promosport Ltd*).

8.7.2.2 Appropriateness of an injunction

An injunction has in effect become a right to which the claimant is entitled unless there are special circumstances (*Pride of Derby and Derbyshire Angling Association Ltd v British Celanese Ltd* [1953] Ch 149). This is because an injunction is so obviously appropriate and because damages will rarely be adequate. Damages can only compensate a claimant for past damage; they will never prevent future recurrence. And if damages are relatively small, a defendant might simply regard them as the price to be paid for the right to commit a tort.

8.7.2.3 Refusal of injunctions

The equitable bars to the granting of an injunction have the same meaning in tort as in contract. Injunctions may be refused where the conditions set out in **8.7.2.1** are satisfied or the claimant is barred in equity by delay, acquiescence, or their own conduct. But in a serious case, injunctions are rarely refused. This is so, even if considerable hardship may be caused to the defendant (*Redland Bricks Ltd v Morris* [1970] AC 652), or if the interest of the public at large is overwhelmingly greater than the private interest of the claimant (*Attorney-General v Birmingham Borough Council* [1858] 4 K & J 528).

8.7.3 Mandatory injunctions

8.7.3.1 Nature

In tort, a mandatory injunction orders the defendant to undo the wrong. It will usually be sought in a case of trespass, to require the defendant to remove something from the claimant's land, or remove from their own land something which causes a nuisance. The leading case is *Redland Bricks Ltd v Morris* [1970] AC 652.

8.7.3.2 Difficulty of obtaining a mandatory injunction

Mandatory injunctions are much harder to obtain than prohibitory injunctions. Their grant is certainly not automatic. Damages in lieu will usually be regarded as the primary remedy, and the adequacy of damages hurdle is not easy to cross.

A mandatory order will not be made where hardship may be caused to the defendant. The bars are similar to those to specific performance or are arguably stricter. A mandatory injunction may be refused not only where serious hardship would be caused to the defendant, but simply where the hardship suffered would on balance be greater than that suffered by the claimant if the order were refused.

8.7.4 *Quia timet* injunctions

Either prohibitory or mandatory *quia timet* injunctions may be granted to restrain a tort, usually nuisance. A high degree of proof is required: the claimant must show, on good evidence, that the tort is highly likely to occur and to occur imminently (*Fletcher v Bealey* [1885] 28 ChD 688; *Attorney-General v Manchester Corporation* [1893] 2 Ch 87).

8.8 Interim injunctions

8.8.1 Jurisdiction

Jurisdiction to grant interim injunctions in the High Court derives from the Senior Courts Act 1981, s. 37.

County court jurisdiction to grant interim injunctions derives from the County Courts Act 1984, s. 38(1), which allows the court to make any order which could be made by the

High Court if the proceedings were in the High Court. See Sime, *A Practical Approach to Civil Procedure*, 24th edn, Oxford University Press, 2021, Chapter 42.

8.8.2   Principles

As stated earlier, the principles applicable to the granting of interim injunctions are largely procedural. A summary of the relevant principles is set out in **8.8.2.1**. A more detailed explanation may be found in Sime, *A Practical Approach to Civil Procedure*, Chapter 42.

8.8.2.1   The *American Cyanamid* guidelines

While the granting of an injunction lies within the discretion of the court, the guidelines applicable to such applications are found in the leading case of *American Cyanamid Co v Ethicon Ltd* [1975] AC 396. Generally, the factors which the court will consider may be approached as a series of steps and the case for an injunction may fall at any point in the sequence:

(a) *Is there a serious question to be tried?* If the answer is 'yes' (and it is often a fairly easy threshold to meet):

(b) *Would damages be an adequate remedy (that is, if the claimant succeeds at trial), would they be adequately compensated by a (monetary) award?* If damages would be inadequate:

(c) *If the defendant succeeded at trial (that is, they demonstrated a right to do the act(s) which the claimant sought to enjoin), would they be adequately compensated by the claimant's undertaking as to damages?*

(d) *Where does the balance of convenience lie?* The factors which the court will take into consideration and the weight attached to each will vary with each case.

(e) Where factors appear to be evenly balanced, the court will consider preserving the status quo. This means the state of affairs immediately before the issue of the claim form, unless the claimant has delayed, in which case the status quo will be that existing immediately before the application. See *Garden Cottage Foods Ltd v Milk Marketing Board* [1984] AC 130 (HL).

In some established areas, the *American Cyanamid* approach is not strictly adhered to in determining whether to grant the injunction. Various factors may be of more or less importance, depending on the nature of the dispute or third parties who may be affected by the granting of the injunction. Some of these areas are industrial disputes, defamation cases, actions against public authorities (where the public interest is an important factor in determining the balance of convenience), and covenants in restraint of trade.

8.8.2.2   Where granting an interim injunction would dispose of the action

It is important to distinguish between injunctions intended to be temporary in nature (that is, effective until later trial) and those which would, in effect, dispose of the dispute because there are no further issues between the parties which need to be determined at a later trial. If this is the case, the *American Cyanamid* guidelines on the balance of convenience are not applied. Rather, it is appropriate for the court to consider the degree of likelihood that the claimant would have succeeded in establishing their right to an injunction at a trial on the merits. An injunction will only be granted if the claimant's case is overwhelming. See Sime, *A Practical Approach to Civil Procedure*, Chapter 42, and *Cayne v Global Natural Resources plc* [1984] 1 All ER 225 (CA).

8.8.3   Interim mandatory injunctions

In *R (San Marco London Ltd) v Her Majesty's Revenue & Customs* [2013] EWHC 3218 (Admin) the Administrative Court reviewed the principles applicable to the grant of interim mandatory injunctions. Effectively, the court needs to have in mind the following considerations: first, that the overriding consideration is to attempt to find the course that will provide the least risk of injustice; second, that an order requiring a party to take some positive step may well carry a greater risk of injustice if it turns out to have been wrongly made; third, that it is legitimate where a mandatory injunction is sought to consider whether the court has a high degree of assurance that the claimant will be able to establish the right at trial; finally, that even where the court did not feel that high degree of assurance, it might still be right to grant a mandatory injunction where the risk of injustice if the injunction is refused outweighs the risk of injustice if it is granted.

8.8.4 Procedure

Applications for interim injunctions are governed by the Civil Procedure Rules (CPR), Pts 23 and 25. An application must be made by application notice, supported by written evidence, usually in the form of a witness statement. This evidence should set out the facts on which the applicant relies. Under normal circumstances, the application notice should be served not less than three clear days before the hearing. However, in urgent cases applications can be made without notice, even before the issue of a claim form. In these circumstances, an injunction can be made without the respondent being heard. However, the order made will only last until a return date, when there will be a further hearing.

A more detailed explanation of the relevant procedure will be found in Sime, *A Practical Approach to Civil Procedure*, Chapter 42, and a more detailed explanation of the relevant documents will be found in the **Drafting** manual, Chapter 19.

Bailment and interference with goods

9.1 Definition

We can define bailment as being the delivery of goods on an express or implied condition that they must be restored by the bailee to the bailor (or dealt with according to the bailor's directions) as soon as the purpose for which they are bailed has elapsed or has been performed.

Bailment is an area of law which combines elements of property law in addition to those of contract and tort.

9.2 When does bailment arise?

Bailment arises whenever one person (the bailee) is voluntarily in possession of goods belonging to another person (the bailor).

Although bailment is usually created by a contract, this does not necessarily have to be the case, as the legal relationship of bailor and bailee can arise independently of any contractual agreement.

The element common to all types of bailment is the imposition of an *obligation*. This arises when the bailee takes goods into their possession and thereby assumes responsibility for the safe keeping of those goods.

For bailment to arise, the actual or constructive possession of the goods must be relinquished by:

- the owner of the goods; or
- the bailor, or
- an agent who is duly authorised for the purpose,

to the bailee, who then either keeps the goods or performs some act with them.

Every bailee has a common law duty to take reasonable care of the bailor's goods and not to convert them to their own use (*Morris v CW Martin and Sons Ltd* [1966] 1 QB 716). The standard of care to be applied is the standard demanded by the circumstances of each particular bailment.

The concept of what are 'goods' capable of being bailed was recently extended to include human sperm preserved for possible future use: *Yearworth v North Bristol NHS Trust* [2009] 2 All ER 986.

9.3 Classification

Bailment has in the past been categorised in many ways, with fine distinctions between them. However, for present purposes, there are two basic types: gratuitous bailment and bailment for reward.

9.3.1 Gratuitous bailment

Gratuitous bailment arises when a chattel is deposited with the bailee, who simply retains it until its return is demanded. Because the bailee does not receive any reward for their services, neither party acquires any rights or assumes any obligations until there is actual delivery and acceptance of the chattel. It is only then that the bailee becomes obliged to carry out their promise.

This category includes situations where property is lent to another for a specific purpose, without charge.

EXAMPLES

(a) Joe asks Fred, as an unpaid favour, to look after his sound system for him whilst he goes on holiday. Fred agrees. If Fred was to change his mind at any time prior to receiving the system, there is nothing that Joe can do about it. However, once Fred accepts delivery of the goods, he is bound to look after them, and to return them to Joe upon demand.

(b) Joe lends Fred his sound system to use at his birthday party. Fred is entitled to use it for that purpose only, and then is obliged to return it.

9.3.2 Bailment for reward

Bailment for reward covers situations where a chattel is pawned or pledged as security for a loan or the performance of an obligation, or where goods are hired for reward.

EXAMPLES

(a) Anna borrows £100 from Tim, to be repaid in six months' time together with 10 per cent interest. She leaves her watch with Tim as security. Tim is the bailee of the watch.

(b) Sue hires a motor mower from Gardenhire Ltd, for seven days, at a cost of £20. She becomes a bailee of the mower.

9.3.3 Termination of bailment

Bailment will usually terminate at the end of the period agreed between the parties. At the conclusion of the bailment, the bailor has the right to immediate possession of the goods. When this arises will depend on the circumstances of the individual case, or on the terms of the contract if there is one.

9.4 Torts (Interference with Goods) Act 1977

Bailment, and the remedies available in respect of breach by bailor or bailee as well as the rights of third parties, are governed by the Torts (Interference with Goods) Act 1977, which basically protects the right to possession of and title to the goods.

Apart from a new tort of statutory conversion under s. 2(2), the 1977 Act did not create any new torts and so previous case law regarding pre-existing torts is still relevant.

9.4.1 Causes of claim

Section 1 of the 1977 Act defines the torts for which a defendant may be liable if they wrongfully interfere with a claimant's chattels or goods. These are:

- conversion (s. 1(a));
- trespass (s. 1(b));
- negligence (so far as it results in damage to goods or to an interest in goods) (s. 1(c));
- any other tort so far as it results in damage to goods (s. 1(d)).

These subdivisions are not mutually exclusive: conduct by a particular defendant may fall into one or more of these categories.

Conversion is the most common tort, and the main textbooks should be consulted for detailed guidance on this complex subject. However, some of the basic principles are set out in **9.4.2**.

9.4.2 Conversion

9.4.2.1 Definition

Anyone who, without authority, takes possession of another person's goods, with the intention of asserting some right or dominion over them, is prima facie guilty of a conversion, provided that there is an intention on the part of the person so dealing with them to assert a right inconsistent with the rights of the owner. This can include (but is by no means limited to) wrongfully taking or parting with possession of goods, wrongfully retaining them, denying the title of the person entitled to possession, or, when acting as a bailee, so neglecting them that they are destroyed or totally lost. More particular examples are set out in **9.4.2.3**.

The general rule is that the right to bring a claim for conversion belongs to the person who can prove that they had, at the time of the conversion, either actual possession or the immediate right to possess the goods.

The injury suffered by the claimant in such a case is twofold:

- an injury to the claimant's right to possession;
- an injury to the claimant's title in the goods.

9.4.2.2 An alternative definition

Conversion is a deliberate act of dealing by a defendant with a chattel in a manner inconsistent with the claimant's right which deprives the claimant of the use and possession of the chattel. One exception to the proposition that conversion is a deliberate act is contained in s. 2(2) of the 1977 Act, namely, where a bailee is in breach of their duty to the bailor and thereby allows the goods to become lost or destroyed.

9.4.2.3 Conduct amounting to conversion

For liability to be established in conversion, it is sufficient that the conduct of the defendant is inconsistent with the rights of the claimant. It follows that a whole range of acts can amount to conversion, from total abrogation of the claimant's rights in the goods to lesser conduct which may or may not amount to deprivation of the claimant's rights in the goods, depending upon the particular circumstances.

The following are the most common situations when conversion may arise:

(a) *Conversion by wrongful taking*. Peter wrongfully takes a watch belonging to Mary. Peter's intention must be either to deny Mary's rights or to assert a right which is inconsistent with her ownership. In the latter case, the assertion of the right need not be that of full ownership: it is sufficient if assertion of the right is inconsistent with Mary's true entitlement.

(b) *Conversion by transfer*. This occurs when the defendant purports to give the claimant's goods to a third party along with some right over the goods which actually belongs to the claimant. To extend this example, Peter gives Mary's watch to Antonia as a present.

(c) *Conversion by wrongful sale*. This occurs when property is wrongfully sold so that the property and the title to it are passed to a third party, irrespective of whether or not the goods are actually delivered to the buyer. Thus, if Peter sells Mary's watch to William, who buys it in good faith, Peter is guilty of conversion.

(d) *Conversion by detention*. There must be detention of the goods which is adverse to the rights of the true owner. A demand by the claimant and a refusal by the defendant must be shown. If Mary lends Peter her watch, but he thereafter refuses to return it when asked, Peter has committed an act of conversion.

(e) *Conversion by destruction*. Conversion will occur when the chattel is dealt with in such a manner that its original identity is destroyed. The destruction must be wilful. If Peter accidentally drops and treads on Mary's watch, no act of conversion is committed. If, however, he deliberately throws it into the river, the tort has been committed.

(f) *Conversion by loss*. Loss of someone else's chattel may amount to an abuse of possession (and therefore to conversion) if it is other than purely accidental.

(g) *Conversion by denial of right*. This can be considered to be a residual category embracing activities which do not fall into any of these categories. This form of conversion occurs when a defendant deals with goods in a manner which amounts to denial of the true title. However, even absolute denial of title is not per se sufficient to amount to conversion, because there must in addition be some further dealing with the goods; in other words, some positive conduct on the part of the defendant, such as actively barring the claimant access to their goods whilst also repudiating the claimant's right to their goods.

The essential element in conversion is dealing with the goods in a manner which is altogether inconsistent with the title of the true owner. Therefore, a defendant may be liable for conversion of goods notwithstanding the fact that they have never been in possession of them or physically handled them. However, the categories of conversion are not closed, and in many cases, it will be a matter of judicial discretion whether to treat the act as sufficiently inconsistent with the true owner's rights for a conversion to have taken place.

9.4.3   Subject matter of conversion

By s. 14(1) of the 1977 Act:

> . . . *unless the context otherwise requires* . . . *'goods' includes all chattels personal other than things in action and money.*

The definition does not purport to be exhaustive or all-embracing.

It is generally considered that the exclusion of money is limited to money in the sense of currency, so that valuable or antique coins can be converted (*Moss v Hancock* [1899] 2 QB 111).

9.4.4   Who may bring a claim for conversion and against whom?

9.4.4.1   Claimant

The right to bring a claim for conversion belongs to the person who is able to establish that at the time of conversion they either had:

- actual possession of the goods; or
- the immediate right to possess the goods.

It is doubtful whether an equitable right is sufficient to ground a claim in conversion (*The Future Express* [1993] 2 Lloyd's Rep 542).

9.4.4.2   Defendants

(a) *The immediate tortfeasor*. This should be self-explanatory.

(b) *Agents*. In order for an agent to be liable in conversion, it is necessary to consider the agent's actual or constructive knowledge of the true ownership of the goods. This is a detailed area of law, beyond the scope of this chapter.

9.4.5   More than one claimant

The policy behind the 1977 Act is that a claimant should only recover their own actual loss and no more, and that multiplicity of actions should be avoided.

9.4.5.1   Double liability

Section 7(1) defines the scope of double liability, which may arise where:

(a) two or more rights of claim for wrongful interference are founded on a possessory title (s. 7(1)(a)); or

(b) the measure of damages in a claim for wrongful interference founded on a proprietary title is or includes the entire value of the goods, although the interest is one of two or more interests in the goods (s. 7(1)(b)).

Section 7(2) provides that where there are two or more claimants in the same claim against one defendant, the relief granted will be such as to avoid double liability of the defendant towards the claimants.

Section 7(3) provides that if there are two claimants, but only one claimant is a party to the claim and that claimant receives more than they would have if s. 7(2) applied, then that claimant must account to any other person having a claim for that excess.

Section 7(4) protects a defendant who overpays in the event of double liability by permitting a defendant to recover overpayment from a claimant to the extent that that claimant has been unjustly enriched by the overpayment. Therefore, if a bailor and bailee both have the right to sue for conversion, they cannot both exercise such rights and thereby obtain double recovery from a defendant. Either bailor or bailee may sue, and whoever is the first person to obtain damages will conclude the case (*Nicolls v Bastard* [1825–42] All ER Rep 429 at p. 430). The successful claimant must then account to the other party for the proportion of damages representing their interest in the goods.

9.4.5.2 Competing rights to the goods

Section 8(1) of the 1977 Act permits a defendant to plead by way of a defence to the claimant's claim that a third party has title to the goods which is equal to, or superior to, that of the claimant.

9.4.5.3 Co-owners

If two or more people own a chattel, then one co-owner cannot bring a claim against another co-owner for interference with their right to possession because each co-owner has a right to possession which is lawful. However, if one co-owner goes further and performs an act which could only be permitted if they alone had exclusive possession of the goods, then a claim by the other co-owner or co-owners will be permitted. Such a claim is only allowed if there has been 'a destruction of the particular chattel or something equivalent to it' (s. 10(1)).

Section 10(1) of the 1977 Act affirms the well-established proposition that one co-owner cannot maintain an action against another co-owner.

9.4.6 Forms of remedy

9.4.6.1 Nature of the remedy

The appropriate remedy is often prescribed by the state of the goods. If the goods have been destroyed or disposed of, then the claimant's remedy will be confined to judgment for a sum of money. However, if the goods are still in the possession or control of the defendant, then the remedies available to an aggrieved claimant are somewhat wider.

9.4.6.2 Available remedies

Where the goods are in the possession or control of the defendant, s. 3(1) of the 1977 Act provides the following remedies:

(a) an order for specific delivery of the goods and payment of any consequential damages (s. 3(2)(a));

(b) an order for delivery of the goods, but also giving the defendant the option of paying damages by reference to the value of the goods in addition to payment of any consequential damages (s. 3(2)(b));

(c) damages, including the assessed value of the goods in addition to any consequential loss (s. 3(2)(c)).

A remedy may only be given under one of these heads (s. 3(3)(a)), and furthermore a remedy under s. 3(2)(a) is at the discretion of the court, whereas a remedy under s. 3(2)(b) or s. 3(2)(c) is at the election of the claimant (by virtue of s. 3(3)(b)).

  (d) On application by any person the court has a discretionary power to make an order for delivery up of the goods which either are or may become the subject matter of subsequent proceedings (e.g. see *Howard E Perry & Co Ltd v British Railways Board* [1980] 1 WLR 1375 and s. 4 of the 1977 Act). Such an application may be made under the court's power to grant interim remedies under Civil Procedure Rules (CPR), r.25.1(1).

We will examine each of these remedies in turn.

9.4.6.3   Specific delivery

Section 3(2)(a) of the 1977 Act

This order is made at the discretion of the court and thus will not usually be made in respect of ordinary articles which have no special value either intrinsically or for the claimant, because in such cases damages would provide adequate compensation.

If the court makes an order for specific delivery, a duty is imposed on the defendant to ensure that the goods are ready for collection by the claimant. The order may contain conditions regarding delivery of the goods. The order may be enforced by writ of specific delivery to recover the goods or their assessed value.

If it can be shown to the court that an order for specific delivery has not been complied with, then the court may proceed to revoke that order or any relevant part of the order and instead order payment of damages, which will be assessed on the value of the goods.

9.4.6.4   Judgment for delivery or damages

Section 3(2)(b) of the 1977 Act

Here the claimant has an election between delivery or damages together in either case with payment of any consequential damages.

Damages will be assessed by reference to the value of the goods.

The provisions allowing the court to impose conditions on specific delivery under s. 3(2)(a) apply equally under s. 3(2)(b). Such order may be enforced as under s. 3(2)(a).

9.4.6.5   Damages

A claimant may recover all such damages as are the direct and natural result of the conversion.

The 1977 Act is silent as to the time when damages should be assessed, apart from a reference in s. 6(1) regarding improvements to the goods. We must therefore rely on previously established rules.

A claimant who seeks damages for conversion based upon the value of the goods will be limited to the value of the goods at the time of conversion. If the value of the converted goods decreases after conversion, the claimant is still entitled to their original value, and consequently receives a windfall (*Solloway v McLaughlin* [1938] AC 247).

A subsequent rise in the value of goods since the time of conversion is recoverable as consequential damages provided the increase in value was foreseeable at the time of conversion (*The Playa Larga* [1983] 2 Lloyd's Rep 171 (CA)).

9.4.6.6   Basis of assessment

If there is a market price for the goods, the value of the goods is to be taken as the market price at the time of conversion. However, if there is no market price, the basis for assessing damages will be the cost of replacement as determined by the evidence.

If the value of the goods is fluctuating, the measure of damages may depend upon the claimant's awareness of the conversion.

9.4.6.7   Taxation

When considering damages for conversion, the principles in *British Transport Commission v Gourley* [1956] AC 185 are thought to be applicable. Therefore, any tax liability which would have accrued to the claimant had the claimant's goods not been converted should be taken into account in the quantification of damages.

9.4.6.8   Aggravated and exemplary damages

Aggravated damages may be awarded if the court considers they are justified by the circumstances of the conversion (*Owen and Smith v Reo Motors (Britain) Ltd* [1934] 151 LT 274).

The availability of exemplary damages was severely curtailed by the judgment of Lord Devlin in *Rookes v Barnard* [1964] AC 1129. Essentially, such damages will only be awarded in cases where the court considers that the tortfeasor should be taught a lesson and are generally reserved for exceptional cases of misconduct.

9.4.6.9   Special damage

Where a defendant is aware that the chattel converted by them is required by the claimant for a particular purpose (e.g. to be hired out for profit), the defendant may be liable to pay special damage for failure of that purpose by reason of their conversion. See, for example, *Bodley v Reynolds* [1846] 8 QB 779, in which a workman deprived of his tools recovered loss of wages.

9.4.6.10   Effect

If a defendant satisfies a judgment for damages for conversion of goods, the claimant's title is transferred to the defendant (*Ellis v John Stenning & Son* [1932] 2 Ch 81).

9.4.7   Improvement of goods

Section 6(1) of the 1977 Act restates the common law rules and provides that a person who improved goods, honestly believing that they had good title to them, is to be entitled to the value of the goods attributable to the improvement. This is known as the principle of allowance and is based upon the fact that the true owner should not be compensated for more than the value of the goods which they originally lost. Generally, any expenditure of work or materials which enhances saleability will constitute an improvement.

Section 6(2) extends the availability of the allowance from the original wrongdoer who effects the improvement to a bona fide purchaser who has obtained their supposed title from the improver, who is in this case the defendant.

Section 6(4) applies the principle of allowance to any person who acquires a limited interest in goods by way of bailment or otherwise.

9.4.8   Limitation

The Limitation Act 1980 provides that once the period of limitation, namely six years from the date of first conversion, has expired, the right to bring proceedings expires. This is an absolute bar, which is different from the basic limitation rule, which does not expressly bar the *right* to sue, but merely affords a complete defence to anyone taking the limitation point.

9.4.9   Defences

Liability in conversion is strict (*Marfani & Co Ltd v Midland Bank Ltd* [1968] 1 WLR 956 at p. 971). However, if a defendant can invoke any of the exceptions to the *nemo dat quod non habet* ('no one can give what they do not have') rule, they may escape liability for conversion.

9.4.10 Trespass

9.4.10.1 Definition

Trespass may be defined as an intentional or negligent direct interference with goods in the possession of the claimant. It is concerned with *direct and immediate* interference with the claimant's possession of a chattel.

The tort of trespass includes not only the taking away, or removal out of the claimant's possession, of their goods, but also any unpermitted contact with or impact upon another's chattel. Mere touching is sufficient, as long as it causes damage.

9.4.10.2 Elements

Whilst a claim in conversion can be founded by a claimant who has the right to possession, though not actual possession, by contrast, a claim in trespass can only be brought by the claimant if they are actually in possession at the time of the interference. There are exceptions to this rule as regards executors and administrators and trustees, but these are beyond the scope of this chapter.

9.4.10.3 Nature of the interference

The interference must be of a direct nature, and in addition there must be a blameworthy state of mind in the trespasser. Accidental interference of a non-negligent nature will not constitute a trespass.

9.4.10.4 Remedies

Damages and/or an injunction are available if the defendant is no longer in possession or control of the goods. If the defendant is in possession or control of the goods, the same remedies are available as for conversion.

Where the goods are damaged by trespass, but the claimant is not actually deprived of them, the claimant will only be entitled to damages which represent the loss actually suffered as a direct result of the trespass.

9.4.11 Negligence resulting in damage to goods

This covers negligent damage to goods, and the usual remedies for negligence apply, namely damages and/or an injunction, irrespective of whether the defendant has the goods in their possession or control. Orders for specific delivery or delivery and damages are not available.

9.4.12 Other torts

Section 1(d) of the 1977 Act applies the Act to any other tort so far as it results in damage to goods or to an interest in goods. This would cover, for example, non-natural user under the rule in *Rylands v Fletcher,* slander of title to goods, and passing off. The scope of s. 1(d) is not precisely defined, although it is considered to embrace negligent damage, loss, or destruction of goods not covered by s. 1(c).

9.4.13 Contributory negligence

Section 11(1) precludes contributory negligence as a defence in proceedings for wrongful interference which are founded on conversion or intentional trespass. However, there is internal inconsistency in the 1977 Act because such a defence is permitted for negligence and other torts, in other words, for proceedings brought under s. 1(c) or (d) of the Act.

9.4.14 Reversionary injury

A person who is entitled to goods, but has neither immediate possession nor the right to possession, is unable to sue a wrongdoer for conversion or for trespass. However, a claim will lie if the wrong committed deprives the person, either temporarily or permanently, of the benefit of their reversionary interest. The act must affect the person's reversionary interest in the goods.

The remedy for reversionary injury is confined to damages and the claimant cannot obtain an interim order for delivery up of the goods. Apart from these distinctions, the procedural provisions relating to conversion contained in the 1977 Act apply.

9.5 Exercises

9.5.1 Exercise 1

PROBLEM

Ben is a supplier of fresh fruit and owner of two fruit stores, from which Pamela often buys fruit. Ben hires a motor car to Pamela for six weeks whilst he goes on holiday. He normally uses the car for fresh fruit deliveries to his two shops on a daily basis. Pamela collects the motor car and signs a contract whereby she will hire the car from Ben for six weeks at £120 per week. After four weeks, Pamela can no longer afford the rent and decides to sell the car at an auction. James buys the car at the auction.

(a) Discuss liability and remedies.
(b) What difference would it make if Pamela had not signed a contract to hire the motor car, but instead just borrowed it from Ben's premises with his permission?

SOLUTION

By hiring the motor car to Pamela, a situation of bailment is created whereby Ben is the bailor and Pamela is the bailee. Because a contract of hire is signed between Pamela and Ben, the conditions of bailment are contained in a contract. If Pamela had not signed a contract, a situation of bailment between Pamela and Ben would still exist because Ben has entrusted goods (his car) to Pamela upon condition that she return them in the original state after six weeks. However, bailment would only exist when Pamela took delivery of the car from Ben.

By selling the motor car at an auction, Pamela has committed the tort of conversion because she has only hired the car from Ben. The ownership of the car vests in Ben.

By selling the car, Pamela is asserting a right which she does not have, namely that of ownership of the car, and she is also asserting a right which is inconsistent with the right of the true owner, namely Ben's right to possession of the car.

The remedies for conversion are contained in s. 3 of the 1977 Act. An order for specific delivery under s. 3(2)(a) of the 1977 Act is only granted at the discretion of the court, and will generally only be granted where the court considers that damages are inadequate as a remedy. However, Ben may seek an order under s. 3(2)(b) of the 1977 Act for delivery of the goods, and also giving the defendant the option of returning the goods any time before execution of the judgment. Because Pamela has sold the car at an auction to James, recovery of the car may be difficult, if not impossible, from James, who bought the car in the belief that the car once sold was his. The most appropriate remedy for Ben would be damages, which would be assessed by reference to the value of the goods lost. Furthermore, because Ben uses the car for his occupation as a fruit supplier, he will be able to claim special damages from Pamela for loss of business. However, for such damages to be recoverable, Pamela must have been aware that the car was used by Ben for this purpose. Because she shops regularly at Ben's shop, this requirement would be met.

Furthermore, Ben would have a claim for damages for breach of contract, namely the two weeks' rent that Pamela has failed to pay.

9.5.2 Exercise 2

PROBLEM

Frank and his wife Mary jointly own a computer, which they lend to Tracey for six weeks. Tracey does not return the computer to Frank and Mary because she threw it against a wall in a fit of rage when she lost some work stored on the hard drive. The entire computer is smashed and has been assessed by a computer specialist as being beyond economical repair.

(a) What remedies are available to Frank and Mary, and which is the most appropriate in this case?

(b) What steps should they take to obtain such remedy?

(c) If Frank alone recovers the value of the computer, what steps can Mary take to recover her share of the value of the computer?

Quantum of damages for personal injury

10.1 The barrister's involvement

When representing a client in a claim for damages for personal injury, a barrister will be closely involved, not only with the issues of liability, but also with the process of quantifying damages. If the issue of quantum goes to trial, you will present evidence on and argue the question of 'how much' before the court. If a settlement is reached, you are likely to be involved in, or even to conduct, the negotiation. Even at the earliest stages of your involvement in the case you are likely to be asked to advise on quantum; that is, to state how much in your opinion a judge would be likely to award. A preliminary view on quantum needs to be taken before the claimant can decide whether to bring their claim in the High Court or county court. By virtue of the Civil Procedure Rules (CPR), PD 7A, para. 3.6, if a claim for personal injury is started in the High Court, the claim form must state that the claimant expects to recover £50,000 or more.

It follows that you must understand the principles on which damages are quantified, the process by which a court would arrive at a final figure, and the practical steps to be taken in advising on quantum.

10.2 The law

10.2.1 Basis of the law

The law in this area is largely judge-made, with occasional legislative enhancement. It grew up in a piecemeal fashion over 100 years or so and originally had no overall coherence, logic, or rationale. It was not very scientific, and its overall effect tended to be to undercompensate those who have suffered serious injuries. In *Lim Poh Choo v Camden and Islington Area Health Authority* [1980] AC 174, Lord Scarman said:

Lord Denning MR in the Court of Appeal declared that a radical reappraisal of the law is needed. I agree . . . I would suggest to your Lordships that such a reappraisal calls for social, financial, economic and administrative decisions which only the legislature can take. The complexities of the present case . . . emphasise the need for reform of the law.

Few lawyers would have disagreed with this. However, over the past 25 years or so, from about 1995, some very significant steps towards a more scientific calculation of damages have been made, which should have led to claimants being more properly compensated. For a fuller explanation, and the whole story, see **10.9.2**, **10.10.3**, and **10.18**.

10.2.2 The rationale of the law

There is no force of law behind most of the rules for the quantification of damages. In theory, at least, a court may assess damages in any way it sees fit in order to do justice to the parties. However, there are two very important constraints:

(a) The method of assessment is limited by the powers of the court. In particular, except where there is a claim for provisional damages (for which, see **10.5**), the court can only ever make one order, at the date of trial, which cannot later be varied in the light of subsequent developments. So the court cannot adopt a wait-and-see approach to future uncertainties. It must assess damages in a way that will so far as possible do justice today for the claimant tomorrow. This will almost always be by the payment of a single lump sum. The only exceptions are that the court can now make an order for periodical payments under s. 2 of the Damages Act 1996 (see **10.18**), and that it can approve a structured settlement agreed by the parties themselves (see **10.19**).

(b) There is a vital principle behind the assessment of damages, which is that parties must be able to predict as closely as possible the damages that a court would award. If they cannot do so, there is little chance of their agreeing on a sum in settlement of a claim, and every case would have to go to trial. Such a result would be most undesirable. So, if parties are to be able to predict the likely damages, courts must be consistent in their approach. That is why the rules for assessment that follow are universally applied by the courts, however unsatisfactory they may seem to individual judges or in particular cases.

The methods of quantifying damages that follow in this chapter have therefore been developed over the years by judges, practitioners, and Parliament. To a very large extent, the rules are rules of practice, rather than rules of law; nevertheless, judges are bound to follow guidelines laid down by the Judicial College, the Court of Appeal, the House of Lords, and the Supreme Court. Hence the need for legislation if any major changes are to be made.

10.2.3   Sources

The practitioner's 'bible' is *Kemp & Kemp: The Quantum of Damages*, available online at Lawtel. Also useful is *Butterworths Personal Injury Litigation Service*. Lawtel is a particularly valuable online resource for all matters connected with personal injury quantum.

10.3   Basic principles

10.3.1   Application of the compensatory principle

The aim of an award of damages is to compensate the claimant for the loss caused to the claimant by their injuries and to place them, so far as it is possible to do so, in the position they would have been in had those injuries not been suffered. The claimant must be compensated, therefore, not only for the injuries themselves, but also for the effect they have had emotionally, intellectually, and financially. This cannot be done, of course, simply by the payment of money; but money is all the law has to give, and so some arbitrary yet fair relationship has to be found between the injury and the compensation.

Not all loss can be measured in money, but it still has to be assessed in financial terms.

10.3.2   Measurement of loss

Such loss as *can* be measured in money is so measured. Loss that can only partially be measured in money is assessed arithmetically to a certain extent. Wholly non-financial loss is assessed according to conventional guidelines.

10.3.3   Time of assessment

Although the cause of action accrues at the date of the injury, and all damage that flows from the injury is deemed to have been suffered at that time, nevertheless to all intents and purposes damages are assessed as at the date of the trial.

In the case of financial loss already incurred, the court will take the total amount so far; and in the case of future financial loss, the court will give any item recoverable the value it bears at the date of trial. The court will also take account of all facts about the extent of the claimant's injury or its effect on them that are known at the date of trial, and of any supervening events, such as the claimant's death or redundancy, or the onset of some disease, even if these facts or supervening events were unpredictable at the time of the injury (see *Jobling v Associated Dairies Ltd* [1982] AC 794).

10.4 Two broad heads of damages

Damages are either special or general. In any ordinary case, there will be a claim for both special and general damages.

10.4.1 Special damages

10.4.1.1 Nature and proof of special damage

Special damages represent the claimant's actual pecuniary loss between the date of injury and the date of trial; in other words, those losses that are strictly measurable in money and susceptible to precise calculation.

Every item of special damage must be specifically pleaded and specifically proved. This does not mean that every item can be given a value which is certain; rather, that every item can be given a value which is ascertainable, either by proof, by agreement between the parties, or by decision of the court. A schedule of loss and expenses, setting out the special damages claimed, must be served with particulars of claim for damages for personal injury (CPR, PD 16, para. 4.2).

10.4.1.2 Examples of items of special damage

There is in principle no limit to the range of items that can be recovered as special damages, provided they are within the rules of causation, remoteness, and the duty to mitigate, but the following list shows those items most commonly recovered.

(a) Incidental damage to property, for example damage to a motor vehicle, damage to clothing, or a broken wristwatch.

(b) Medical expenses. All reasonable medical expenses may be recovered. A claimant is not obliged to mitigate their loss by having treatment under the National Health Service (Law Reform (Personal Injuries) Act 1948, s. 2(4)).

(c) Associated expenditure, for example cost of travel to and from hospital, prescription charges.

(d) Cost of nursing care, whether in a residential institution or at home. The type of care (in a residential home or in a private arrangement), the cost of which should be awarded, depends on what is reasonable in all the circumstances, not necessarily what is in the claimant's best interests (*Sowden v Lodge* [2005] 1 All ER 581).

(e) Cost of other paid help, for example housekeeper, nanny, babysitter, gardener.

(f) Reasonable necessary expenditure, for example special equipment (crutches, wheel-chair); purchase of special car or conversion of car to hand controls; purchase of new house, special accommodation; cost of converting present or new home for claimant's special needs (e.g. building extension, enlarging bathroom, putting in a lift, ramps instead of steps, lowering work surfaces in kitchen).

(g) Increases in ordinary expenditure, for example additional transport costs, heating costs, holiday costs, cost of employing someone to do work the claimant previously did on a DIY basis.

(h) Loss of earnings from date of injury to date of trial—this is usually the major item of special damages.

(i) Loss of other fringe benefits from the claimant's employment, for example free goods, services, use of company car for private purposes, private health scheme.

(j) Loss of social security benefits. A claimant who was unemployed at the date of the accident and in receipt of social security benefits can recover the benefits they would have received but for the accident (*Neal v Bingle* [1998] 2 All ER 58).

(k) Other miscellaneous losses, for example cancellation of a holiday.

(l) Costs incurred by members of the claimant's family visiting them in hospital, looking after them, etc., including their lost earnings. These are recoverable as part of the claimant's own loss (*Kirkham v Boughey* [1958] 2 QB 338).

(m) The value of unpaid care provided by a friend or relative. Surprising as it may seem at first sight, a reasonable sum can be recovered by the claimant for the notional cost of employing someone to care for them, even where that care is being provided gratuitously, irrespective of any legal liability to pay (*Cunningham v Harrison* [1973] QB 942; *Donnelly v Joyce* [1974] QB 454). This is so whether or not the relative has given up paid employment to look after the claimant; and even where the relative has given up paid employment and the claim is valued on that basis, the loss is still viewed as the claimant's, not the relative's, loss. Similarly, the value of care provided by a charitable institution may be claimed as damages on behalf of the institution (*Drake v Foster Wheeler Ltd* [2011] 1 All ER 63). However, the loss is not recoverable where it is the defendant personally who is providing the voluntary care (*Hunt v Severs* [1994] AC 350). In order for damages to be recovered under this head, the amount of care required must go beyond the normal call of everyday life, but it is not necessary to show that but for the gratuitous care, professional care would have been required (*Giambrone v JMC Holidays Ltd* [2004] 2 All ER 891).

(n) The principle identified in (m) does not, however, apply to a relative who does gratuitous work for the claimant in their business. No damages are recoverable for the value of such work (*Hardwick v Hudson* [1999] 3 All ER 426).

(o) A claimant may also recover damages for the value of care which they used to provide gratuitously to a member of their family, but which as a result of their injury they are no longer able to provide (*Lowe v Guise* [2002] 3 All ER 454).

(p) Lost dependency. In *Haxton v Philips Electronics UK Ltd* [2014] 2 All ER 225, the claimant and her husband had both contracted mesothelioma as a result of the defendant's negligence. The claimant made a claim under the Fatal Accidents Act (see **Chapter 11**) for her loss of dependency following her husband's death, but because her life expectancy was severely reduced, she could only be awarded a small sum. However, in her personal injury claim she was able to recover the amount of the dependency she had failed to recover under the Fatal Accidents Act.

(q) Court of Protection fees; costs of administering a trust fund. Where the claimant is unable to look after their own affairs, a receiver will need to be appointed and remunerated; where the claimant is a child, a trust fund may be required. Such administrative costs are recoverable.

10.4.1.3 The schedule of loss and expense

CPR, PD 16, para. 4.2 requires the claimant to 'attach to his particulars of claim a schedule of details of any past and future expenses and losses which he claims'. Note that what is required is a full setting out of the sums claimed, not only by way of past, but also of future loss and expense. Do not be confused into thinking that future losses and expenses are special damages.

10.4.2 General damages

10.4.2.1 Nature and proof of general damages

General damages represent the loss to the claimant that cannot be precisely quantified; that is, past and future non-financial loss and future financial loss.

General damages do not have to be specifically pleaded, though any material facts giving rise to a claim for general damages should be pleaded (e.g. the injuries, loss of employment, handicap on the labour market). Nor do general damages need to be specifically proved: they can be implied to a certain extent. However, evidence is required, and in practice as much evidence as is available should be presented. A medical report must be served with the claimant's particulars of claim (CPR, PD 16, para. 4.3).

10.4.2.2 Heads of general damages

Heads of general damages are as follows:

- pain and suffering;
- loss of amenity;
- hybrid heads;
- future loss of earnings;
- loss of earning capacity;
- loss of pension rights;
- future expenses (including value of future unpaid help).

A further head of general damages, loss of expectation of life, was abolished by the Administration of Justice Act 1982 (AJA 1982), s. 1. However, mental anguish caused by a claimant's awareness that they will suffer an early death can give rise to an award: *Kadir v Mistry* [2014] EWCA Civ 1177.

Heads of damages may occasionally overlap, and where this happens care must be taken to avoid double recovery. There are various rules that have been developed by the courts to deal with overlap situations, which are explained later, where they arise.

10.5 Provisional damages

10.5.1 When may a claimant claim provisional damages?

A claimant may in certain circumstances claim provisional damages, rather than damages. Section 32A of the Senior Courts Act 1981 (SCA 1981) provides:

> *(1) This section applies to an action for damages for personal injuries in which there is proved or admitted to be a chance that at some definite or indefinite time in the future the injured person will, as a result of the act or omission which gave rise to the cause of action, develop some serious disease or suffer some serious deterioration in his physical or mental condition.*
>
> *(2) Subject to subsection (4) below, as regards any action for damages to which this section applies in which a judgment is given in the High Court, provision may be made by rules of court for enabling the court, in such circumstances as may be prescribed, to award the injured person—*
>> *(a) damages assessed on the assumption that the injured person will not develop the disease or suffer the deterioration in his condition; and*
>> *(b) further damages at a future date if he develops the disease or suffers the deterioration.*
>
> *(3) Any rules made by virtue of this section may include such incidental, supplementary and consequential provisions as the rule-making authority may consider necessary or expedient.*

The same provisions appear as in the County Courts Act 1984 (CCA 1984), s. 51, for actions in the county court.

The relevant rules mentioned in s. 32A(3) are to be found in CPR, Pt 41.

The circumstances in which a court will make an award of provisional damages were considered in *Willson v Ministry of Defence* [1991] 1 All ER 638. The judge held that:

(a) the chance of serious disease or deterioration must be measurable rather than fanciful;

(b) the 'serious deterioration' must be something distinct and beyond the ordinary deterioration that is a normal part of the claimant's condition;

(c) the risk of further injury in the future will not give rise to a provisional award where that risk of injury and its likely consequences are purely speculative.

10.5.2 Effect of a claim for provisional damages

A claim for provisional damages will result in an initial award which will be lower than an award of damages on a once-and-for-all basis, but with the possibility of a further award in the future which, when taken together with the initial award, will produce a total sum greater than an award of damages on a once-and-for-all basis would have been. The reasons for this is explained when we see how damages are quantified.

A claim for provisional damages affects only the general damages, not the special damages. A claimant may claim provisional damages or damages in the alternative. If a claimant claims damages, it is not open to a defendant to argue that the claimant should be awarded provisional damages.

10.5.3   Provisional damages are not interim payments

Be sure not to confuse provisional damages with interim payments in respect of damages under CPR, Pt 25. See Sime, *A Practical Approach to Civil Procedure*, Chapter 25.

10.6   Quantification of damages—introduction

The quantification of damages is a five-stage process:

Stage 1:   Quantify special damages.

Stage 2:   Quantify general damages.

Stage 3:   Make any necessary deductions.

Stage 4:   Contributory negligence.

Stage 5:   Add interest.

10.7   Stage 1: quantify special damages

10.7.1   A matter of arithmetic

Since special damages represent the claimant's quantifiable financial loss, this is basically just a matter of arithmetic. The claimant has to prove both the item of loss and its value. The court will therefore award such losses as are proved. If the claimant fails to prove that an item of expenditure is reasonable, the court will either not award it, or will award such sum as would have been reasonable.

10.7.2   Advising on quantum

If you are advising on quantum, look at the special damages that have been incurred, decide whether in your opinion they are reasonable, exclude what you think the claimant cannot prove or what is unreasonable, and take the result. Where the claimant is claiming the value of voluntary services, a reasonable figure for this must be claimed and proved.

Do not look into the future with special damages. Although the cut-off point for a court is the date of trial, when negotiating a settlement or advising on quantum, take the cut-off date as today, calculate special damages so far, and treat the continuing expenditure in the future as general damages. Do not invent a notional date of trial.

10.7.3   Assessing special damages

The assessment of most items of special damage is straightforward once the figures are known: medical expenses; damage to property; costs of nursing care; paid help; items of expenditure; items of increased expenditure; value of fringe benefits; miscellaneous losses; costs incurred by, and lost earnings of, claimant's relatives; Court of Protection fees—all these can simply be added up taking the exact figures that have been ascertained.

Some items of special damages are a little more complicated to assess, however, and the method for such items is as follows.

10.7.4   Assessing lost earnings

10.7.4.1   Basis of assessment

Except where the claimant is very seriously injured and the cost of caring for them is expensive, the major item of special damages is likely to be lost earnings. These are assessed not just on the basis of what the claimant was earning at the date of the accident, but on the basis of what they would have earned between accident and trial. So if, for example, the claimant is able to show that, but for their injuries, they would have had a chance of an increase in earnings, or promotion, or moving on to better paid employment, or advancing their career, or building up their business, etc., then damages will be awarded taking account of these increased earnings. The claim is for the loss of a chance. This means that the claimant does not have to show that they probably would have had an increase in earnings, only that they have lost the chance of such an increase; but damages will be assessed in accordance with the chance, so if the chance was 75 per cent, the claimant will recover 75 per cent of what the increase would have been.

Similarly, any likely decreases in income must be taken into account (e.g. because of retirement, the risk of redundancy, ailing business).

10.7.4.2   Methods of calculation

Where the claimant was a regular wage earner, the lost earnings can be calculated by reference to someone else doing the same job. If they received regular amounts of commission, bonuses, overtime, then again, their loss can be assessed in this way. Where, however, their earnings fluctuated, an average will be taken over an appropriate period. The norm is to average the last six salary payments, though a longer period may need to be taken (if, for example, overtime was available in summer but not in winter).

10.7.4.3   Taxation to be taken into account

The claimant's lost earnings are always calculated net, not gross. That is to say, you base the calculations on what the claimant earned or would have earned after deductions of tax and national insurance. This is the rule in *Gourley's* case (*British Transport Commission v Gourley* [1956] AC 185).

Since the claimant will not be liable to tax on the award of damages (Income Tax (Earnings and Pensions) Act 2003, s. 406), tax must be taken off the amount received in compensation for lost earnings, otherwise the claimant will be better off than they would have been but for their injury. Both basic rate and higher rate tax are taken into account. Where the claimant's claim is for a partial, rather than total, loss of earnings, the earnings lost are deemed to be the top slice of their income.

10.7.4.4   The *Gourley* principle and pension contributions

The *Gourley* principle also applies to an employee's compulsory contributions to a pension scheme, and earnings are taken net of such contributions, if no pension rights have been lost (*Dews v National Coal Board* [1987] 2 All ER 545). If the non-payment of pension contributions has led to a diminished pension, then usually the claimant will claim damages for lost pension rights (see **10.12**) and so must deduct their pension contributions to avoid double recovery.

10.7.4.5   Expenses incurred in connection with employment

On the same principle, it is necessary to set against the claimant's lost earnings any expenses they would have incurred in order to be able to earn that income which have been saved, for example the cost of travel to and from work or special clothing. Obviously, no such deduction needs to be made if the claimant still incurs these expenses in order to earn a lesser income.

10.7.5   The cost of a new home

There is no difficulty where the claimant is simply paying more in rent for their new accommodation: the measure is simply the increase in rent.

But where the claimant purchases new accommodation, the process is not as simple as might have been thought. The claimant cannot be awarded the capital cost of the new house less the sale value of their old house, because there will be a windfall effect for their family, dependants, and heirs. So the loss needs to be calculated in some other way.

Until recently the calculation was made in accordance with *Roberts v Johnstone* [1989] QB 878. There it was held that what the claimant has actually lost is the use of their capital tied up in the new house, and so they should be awarded the interest they could have gained by investing that sum. So the loss would be calculated by taking the difference in capital value (cost of new house less sale price of old) and awarding the claimant a percentage of that sum per year, the percentage being whatever was the appropriate rate of interest. That rate was initially 3% in accordance with *Wells v Wells* [1998] 3 All ER 481; but since 1996, the current discount rate set by the Lord Chancellor under the Damages Act 1996 (see **10.10.3.5–10.10.3.9**).

However, the Court of Appeal in *Swift v Carpenter* [2021] 3 All ER 827 decided that a new approach was necessary, particularly because the current discount under the Damages Act is negative: minus 0.25 per cent. This could only create an even bigger windfall for the claimant's estate. So the Court of Appeal decided that the proper approach now is to establish as a capital sum what award is required to fund the purchase of the new house (obviously still taking into account the proceeds of sale of the old house) and then to establish a sum to be deducted, representing the value of a reversionary interest in the windfall. This means, in effect, selecting an appropriate discount rate on the capital sum. This is not to be a fixed rate, or necessarily that set by the Lord Chancellor under the Damages Act, but a rate that reflects all the circumstances of the case, including the claimant's life expectancy and the state of the property market. In that case a discount rate of 5 per cent was applied.

Costs involved in the purchase, for example estate agent's fees, conveyancing costs, and removal costs, and any increased outgoings on the new house, are also recoverable. No deduction needs to be made for the 'Rolls Royce' effect—the fact that the claimant may incidentally be enjoying better amenities (larger garden, closer to shops), or improved quality of life ('better' area, quieter neighbourhood) than they otherwise would, providing the new house was a reasonable purchase.

10.7.6   The cost of converting a home

The claimant may not only have had to purchase new accommodation, but may also have had to convert it, or their existing home, for their special needs. Such a cost is therefore recoverable additionally to the cost of any new home. However, an adjustment must be made to take account of any change in the value of the house brought about by the conversion work (*Roberts v Johnstone*).

Not all the money spent on conversion will have had an effect on house value. Ignore any expenditure which has not, and consider only the expenditure which has had an effect. Suppose the claimant has spent £30,000 on conversion, £20,000 of which has had no effect on the value of the house, and £10,000 of which has had the effect of increasing its value. The claimant will recover £20,000 in any event. If the value of the house has increased by £10,000 or more, the claimant cannot recover the £10,000 conversion cost. If the value has increased by less than £10,000, deduct the increase in value from the £10,000 and award the difference.

If the conversion work has decreased the value of the house, then the loss in value can be recovered, as well as the conversion cost.

10.7.7   Loss of use of company car

The value of this item will depend on the extent to which the claimant was permitted to and did use the car for private purposes, and what sort of car it was. Figures provided by motoring organisations can be found in *Butterworths Personal Injury Litigation Service*, division XIV [238]–[240]. Expect a sum in the area of £3,000–£8,000 per year, even substantially more if the claimant did a high mileage in a large car. Take care to establish whether the claimant or the company paid for petrol for private use. Be careful to avoid any overlap with a claim for increased travel costs.

10.7.8   Value of unpaid care

The method of assessing this item is discretionary, and will depend to some extent on who the relative providing the care is and what they have given up in order to be able to do so. One common approach is to award the cost of employing a professional or professionals to provide the services being valued. If the claimant's spouse nurses them round the clock, then the value will be the cost of 24-hour nursing attendance, less an allowance for the amount of care they would have provided in any event as a spouse. Alternatively, damages may be assessed on the basis of the relative's lost earnings, if they have given up work to look after the claimant. If the relative has reasonably given up work to care for the claimant, the lost earnings are likely to be recoverable in full, even if the care is strictly less valuable. There may even be an added value if the relative is providing services over and above those that giving up work has enabled them to provide.

The courts frown upon artificial 'contracts' between the claimant and the carer, and will not take the amount in the contract as reliable evidence of the value of the services.

Although this item of damages is not precisely quantifiable in financial terms and is a matter of assessment, nevertheless it is strictly part of the special damages.

10.7.9   Agreement on quantum

The quantum of special damages will usually be agreed between the parties, subject to liability. Certainly, the court will expect special damages to be agreed and, if they are not, will want to know why not. Even if there is a dispute as to an item of special damages, the quantum can still be agreed on an either/or basis. See *Practice Direction (Damages: Personal Injury Actions)* [1984] 1 WLR 1127.

10.8   Stage 2: quantify general damages

10.8.1   Introduction

Each head of damages is quantified in an entirely different way, so we must look at them separately. However, the first two heads can be taken together.

10.9   Heads 1 and 2: pain and suffering, and loss of amenity

10.9.1   A single award

These are usually quantified together; that is to say, a single award will be made for pain and suffering and loss of amenity as a composite, without any indication from the court as to how much is awarded under each head.

This award will simply be a round sum, apparently plucked out of the air. Pain and suffering and loss of amenity are by their nature wholly non-financial losses, and the compensation cannot possibly be calculated; it can only be evaluated on some basis. The basis chosen for evaluation is basically convention, coupled with comparison with previous awards, experience, and sheer intuition. The process is not as arbitrary as it may sound, however. Before we look at it, we should distinguish pain and suffering and loss of amenity, which are closely connected, and sometimes overlap, yet which are not quite the same thing.

10.9.1.1   Damages for pain and suffering

Damages for pain and suffering compensate the claimant for the physical pain and the emotional and intellectual suffering caused by the injury. Shock is included, as are anxiety, embarrassment, and emotional injury. It is strictly speaking not the injury itself for which the claimant is being compensated, so a claimant who suffers multiple injuries, and is thereby rendered immediately and permanently unconscious, recovers nothing under this head, because they feel no pain and are not experiencing any mental suffering as a result of their injuries. Nevertheless, it is the injury itself which will form the starting point for evaluating pain and suffering, so the exact nature and extent of the injury is important. The more serious the injury, the longer it lasts, the greater the award. A claimant who makes a complete recovery gets less than one who is permanently handicapped or disfigured.

Emotional distress, for example fear, horror, anguish, and/or grief, which is not connected to physical or psychiatric injury, does not by itself give rise to a claim under this head.

It is necessary to look at the particular claimant and their individual circumstances. A claimant who is distressed by a facial scar suffers more than one who is not. The claimant's age and life expectancy are relevant. The shorter their expected life and the shorter the period of pain and suffering, the less the claimant will recover in damages, even where it is the injuries themselves that have reduced their life expectancy. However, the claimant's suffering may be increased by knowledge that their life expectancy has been reduced, and this must be taken into account (AJA 1982, s. 1(1)(b)). An award can be made under this head even when there is no other award for pain and suffering or loss of amenity, even in the absence of psychiatric injury: *Kadir v Mistry* [2014] EWCA Civ 1177.

10.9.1.2   Damages for loss of amenity

Damages for loss of amenity compensate the claimant for lost or reduced enjoyment of life. Loss of amenity can be general—for example, where the injuries have affected the claimant's general sense of well-being or cheerful disposition; or specific—for example, where the claimant is no longer able to enjoy a game of football or play the piano. Other examples of loss of amenity include loss of brain function, loss of any of the five senses, loss of sex life, loss of mobility, loss of ability to do one's job, loss of job satisfaction, loss of ability to form friendships or relationships, loss of marriage prospects, breakdown of marriage, and loss of enjoyment of a holiday. In this case, it is the loss of amenity itself for which the claimant is being compensated, not the suffering caused by awareness of it, so a claimant who is in a coma or so severely brain-damaged as to have no realisation of their plight can recover damages under this head (*Wise v Kaye* [1962] 1 QB 638; *Lim Poh Choo v Camden and Islington Area Health Authority* [1980] AC 174).

Loss of amenity, even more than pain and suffering, is highly subjective and specific to the claimant. As with pain and suffering, the claimant's age and life expectancy will make a difference, and the shorter the life expectancy, the *shorter* the loss of amenity. But it does not follow that the shorter the life expectancy, the *less* the loss of amenity. An injury may diminish the quality of life of an older claimant far more than it does that of a younger claimant. You must look to see precisely how each claimant has been affected by their injuries. For example, loss of hearing may be more serious for a musician than a painter; a permanent limp may be more serious for an athlete than a bank manager; a broken nose may be more serious for a model than a builder.

10.9.1.3   The difficulty of separating the two heads of damage

In the end, pain and suffering and loss of amenity have to be taken together because it is usually impossible to say where one ends and the other begins. If, for example, a claimant has an injured leg and can walk only half a mile before it starts to hurt, there is pain, there is suffering, and there is loss of amenity, but one cannot say they are three separate items of loss. The pain causes loss of mobility; inability to enjoy a walk produces suffering. It is necessary for the court to award a single lump sum.

10.9.2   Arriving at a figure for pain and suffering and loss of amenity

10.9.2.1   The first stage

The starting point for the court in selecting that figure is the evidence presented to it—medical evidence and the evidence of the claimant. A barrister's starting point in advising on quantum will be the medical reports and information contained within the claimant's statement. The first stage is to ascertain as accurately as possible the nature and extent of the injuries, the degree of pain and suffering, and the loss of amenity. Where the evidence is contradictory, the court will have to decide what evidence to accept; in advising, all you can do is bear that conflict in mind.

10.9.2.2   The second stage

The next stage is to look up the awards that have been made in past cases of a similar nature. These are found in *Kemp & Kemp*, vols 3 and 4, and in *Butterworths Personal Injury Litigation Service*, categorised according to the broad nature of the injury; also on Lawtel and Butterworths LexisNexis, where you need to search for keywords. This used to be the only way to begin, but since 1992 there has been an established tariff or a guideline range for each type of injury. These tariffs are published by the Judicial College (formerly the Judicial Studies Board) in *Guidelines for the Assessment of General Damages in Personal Injury Cases*, 15th edn (available on the Judicial College website, on Lawtel, and in *Kemp & Kemp*). You should certainly make use of these, but they are not sufficient by themselves. First, try to ascertain the correct range for the type of injury you are dealing with, then try to ascertain its whereabouts in the range in which your case falls, by comparing the facts of your case with those reported and making such value judgements as seem right, taking particular account of your claimant's individual circumstances, suffering, and losses of amenity. It is not a precise art, but it is possible to get quite close. This is what a judge will do, and it is what you do in negotiating a settlement or advising on quantum.

10.9.2.3   *Heil v Rankin*

The process of comparing awards in previous cases must be performed in the light of the decision of the Court of Appeal in *Heil v Rankin* [2000] 3 All ER 138. In that case (and seven others considered at the same time), the court took account of a Law Commission Report to the effect that awards for pain, suffering, and loss of amenity were too low, and decided that an increase was required in all awards that would previously have been over £10,000. Awards under £10,000 did not need increasing. The increase should be on a sliding scale, with the highest (those over £150,000) increasing by one-third. By way of indication, the court increased an award of £40,000 by 10 per cent, an award of £45,000 by 11 per cent, an award of £80,000 by 19 per cent, an award of £110,000 by 25 per cent, and an award of £135,000 by 30 per cent. This has become known as the *Heil v Rankin* uplift.

The 15th edition of the Judicial College Guidelines (2019) takes this adjustment into account, and so no uplift needs to be made when using the Guidelines as a starting point for assessing damages. Nor will there be any need to add an uplift when using a case decided after 23 March 2000 as a comparison. But when looking at a case before that date, in which damages were more than £10,000, it will be necessary to add a *Heil v Rankin* uplift to see what would have been awarded today. Although *Heil v Rankin* is now over 20 years old, some quantum reports in *Kemp & Kemp* are older still, and so it remains important to understand how and when to make the uplift.

This may be done approximately, using the Court of Appeal's examples as a guide; or it may be done rather more precisely, using this formula, explained in *Quantum*, 18 April 2000:

If £A is the value of an award in March 2000, immediately prior to *Heil v Rankin*, then the award after the uplift will be £A + [(£A – 10,000)/420,000 × £A]. The part in square brackets is the uplift.

But this will only be one part of a calculation which also has to take account of inflation: see **10.9.2.5**.

10.9.2.4   *Simmons v Castle*

As a result of the Jackson costs reforms, success fees under conditional or contingency fee arrangements are limited, with the result that successful claimants are likely to find that their solicitors' costs have to be paid to some extent out of the damages they receive. To counter the effect of this, the Court of Appeal in *Simmons v Castle* [2013] 1 All ER 334 announced that for awards made after 1 April 2013, general damages for pain, suffering, and loss of amenity should be increased by 10 per cent; but not where a contingency fee arrangement existed before that date. It follows that in some cases, and as time goes on, eventually all cases, another 10 per cent uplift will need to be added. To take account of this, the 15th edition of the Judicial College Guidelines sets out starting points in two columns—the first without the 10 per cent uplift, and the second with it.

10.9.2.5   Inflation

It is particularly important to look at recent awards and take account of the effect of inflation on the value of money. The tariffs for each type of injury, and the actual sums awarded, gradually increase more or less in line with inflation. The need to take accurate account of inflation was recognised by the Court of Appeal in *Housecroft v Burnett* [1986] 1 All ER 332. Before that decision, awards had been lagging behind inflation for some years.

The most accurate assessment can be made when one can find a comparable very recent award. Lawtel is particularly helpful here, but *Kemp & Kemp* and *Butterworths Personal Injury Litigation Service* are also updated regularly. In the absence of a recent comparable award, one needs to look at earlier awards and multiply them by the appropriate inflation factor. Inflation is measured in accordance with the Retail Prices Index (RPI). A table of annual multipliers can be found in *Kemp & Kemp*, vol. 2, para. 53-001 and an RPI table in para. 53-002. Alternatively, Lawtel has a very useful inflation calculator. Be very cautious, however, of adopting this approach to awards prior to *Housecroft v Burnett,* since an inaccurate result may be obtained. Generally speaking, awards more than ten years old are of little practical help.

Additional account will need to be taken of the *Heil v Rankin* uplift where the value of the award was over £10,000 in March 2000. This can lead to some fairly complex calculations, and so not surprisingly, wherever possible reliance should be placed on the Judicial College Guidelines and recent cases. But not all types of injury are covered by the Guidelines, and there is not always a comparable recent award, so such calculations will sometimes be necessary. As the years pass, and more and more recent awards are reported, it will be possible in due course to forget about the uplift. Some sample calculations follow.

10.9.2.6   Sample calculation—inflation only

Suppose you want to find out what the value of an award of £45,000 made in June 2010 is in March 2020. We assume that no *Simmons v Castle* uplift will be involved. So the adjustment needs to be made for inflation only. There are three ways of doing the calculation, two manual and one automatic.

The shorter, less accurate, manual method is to use the table in *Kemp & Kemp*, para. 53-001. At the time of writing, this was up to date only to January 2021. You will see that if you apply a multiplier of 1.35 to an award made in January 2010, you will get the value in January 2021. You can be a bit more accurate if you look also at the multiplier for January 2011, which is 1.29, and make a rough and ready guess that for June 2010 the multiplier might be about half-way between the two, so 1.32. You can also add something for inflation since January 2021. If you go online to <https://www.ons.gov.uk/economy/inflationandpriceindices/> and look at the RPI figures, you will see that annual inflation from January 2021 to January 2022 was 7.8% and from March 2021 to March 2022 it was 9%. You might split the difference and call it 8.4%. So you adjust the multiplier from 1.32 to 1.404 to give you the value of the award up to March 2022. Then £45,000 × 1.404 gives you £63,180. This calculation will usually do for advisory purposes where only an approximate sum is required.

A fuller, more accurate calculation can be made using the monthly RPI tables in *Kemp & Kemp*, para. 53-002. First look up the RPI for June 2010, which is given as 224.1. Then look up the RPI for March 2022. You may find that the table in *Kemp & Kemp* does not go that far (it is usually several months behind), so go online to <https://www.ons.gov.uk/economy/inflationandpriceindices/>, where you will find that the RPI for March 2022 was 323.5. You can then do the calculation £45,000 × 323.5 ÷ 224.1, which gives you £64,960.

The quickest and easiest method, however, is to use Kemp & Kemp's inflation calculator. You will find it under *Kemp Practice Tools* in the Personal Injury section. Simply put in the amount of the award you wish to update, and the month and year of the award, and whether you want to include the *Heil v Rankin* uplift and/or the *Simmons v Castle* uplift and with one click you get the answer. It also tells you what the relevant RPI figures used were. You will not be able to check the calculation, because it can only update to the present day, which by the time you read this will no longer be March 2022, but rest assured that, when tested, it matched the £64,960 figure given here.

10.9.2.7 Sample calculation—inflation and *Simmons v Castle* uplift

You need to add 10 per cent to the value in March 2013, and then adjust for inflation thereafter. Using the manual method described in **10.9.2.6**, you need first to calculate the value of the June 2010 award in March 2013, immediately prior to the *Simmons v Castle* uplift. First of all, look up the RPI figure for March 2013. This is 248.7. Then calculate £45,000 × 248.7 ÷ 224.1, which gives you £49,940. Add 10 per cent, which gives you £54,934. Finally, update for inflation from March 2013 to March 2022: £54,934 × 323.5 ÷ 248.7 = £71,456.

10.9.2.8 Sample calculation—inflation and *Heil v Rankin* uplift

Suppose you want to find out what the value of an award of £60,000 made in June 1997 is in December 2021. You will need to do the calculation in three stages.

First, you must update the award for inflation to March 2000. Using the RPI tables and the method explained (RPI in June 1997 was 157.5 and in March 2000 was 168.4), the sum will be £60,000 × 168.4 ÷ 157.5 = £64,152.

Next, you must give this sum the *Heil v Rankin* uplift. Using the formula set out in **10.9.2.3**, the sum is £64,152 + [(£64,152–10,000) ÷ 420,000 × £64,152]. This produces an uplift of £8,271 and so an adjusted sum of £72,423.

Finally, you must update this sum for inflation between March 2000 and March 2022. Using the RPI table again, the sum is £72,423 × 323.5 ÷ 168.4 = £139,126. This then is your answer.

But once again, the quickest and simplest method is to use Lawtel's inflation calculator, which automatically includes a *Heil v Rankin* uplift in its calculations. The answer for March 2022 was £139,127. It is very accurate!

10.9.2.9 Sample calculation—inflation and *Heil v Rankin* uplift and *Simmons v Castle* uplift

Taking again the sum of £60,000 awarded in 1997, the first two stages described in **10.9.2.8** are the same, so you get a figure of £72,423 in March 2000. You now need to update that to March 2013. The technique should now be familiar to you: the calculation is £72,423 × 248.7 ÷ 168.4 = £106,957.

Then you add the 10 per cent *Simmons v Castle* uplift to that sum, which gives you £117,653. Finally, adjust for inflation from March 2013 to February 2020: £117,653 × 323.5 ÷ 248.7 = £153,039, and that is your answer.

10.9.2.10 Whiplash injuries

There is one exception to the process described. Under Pt 1 of the Civil Liability Act 2018, for causes of action arising on or after 31 May 2021, damages for pain, suffering, and loss of amenity resulting from whiplash injuries are awarded according to a fixed tariff. The tariff is set out in para. 2 of the Whiplash Injury Regulations 2021 and ranges from £240 to £4,345, depending on the severity of the injury and its duration. There is provision in para. 3 for an uplift to be added in exceptional circumstances, but not so as to exceed the tariff amount by more than 20%. Section 4 of the Act requires the Lord Chancellor to review the tariffs every three years.

This development has come about because it is widely believed that many claimants injured in a road traffic accident have been inventing, or exaggerating the extent of, their whiplash injury, a claim which it is very hard to disprove. The cost of compensating for whiplash injuries constitutes a significant percentage of motor insurance premiums, which it is hoped will now fall.

10.9.2.11   Criminal Injuries Compensation Authority awards

Awards made by the Criminal Injuries Compensation Board were in the past assessed in the same way as awards made by courts. However, from 8 November 1995, the Criminal Injuries Compensation Act 1995 introduced a new scheme of compensation, based not on common law damages but on fixed tariffs laid down by the Home Secretary. Awards made by what is now the Criminal Injuries Compensation Authority are not likely to be reliable or helpful and should not be used.

10.9.2.12   The final figure

In the end, the figure arrived at is chosen by judgement based upon careful research and informed experience. When advising on quantum, a barrister will frequently, having formed a preliminary view, test it out on other members of chambers before setting down their final conclusion. That opinion may be expressed as a range—'in the range of £25,000–£30,000'—or as an approximate figure—'about £12,000'. It is probably better to give an approximate figure if you can, especially if an attempt at settlement is to be made. If you give a range, indicate what circumstances will put the award at the bottom and the top end of the range.

10.9.3   The problem of future uncertainty as regards pain and suffering and loss of amenity

A particular problem arises in quantifying damages for pain, suffering, and loss of amenity where the prognosis is uncertain. This will in fact almost always be the case to some extent, except where the claimant has wholly recovered from their injury. It is to the claimant's advantage usually to try and delay trial or settlement until the future is as certain as it is going to be, but this may not be possible. For example, it may not be certain whether the claimant's condition will deteriorate; whether they have recovered as far as they are going to or whether they will continue to improve; whether osteoarthritis will set in in ten years' time; whether an apparent obstacle has been overcome permanently or temporarily; whether a female claimant will be able to give birth to children or not. In such circumstances, the court has to assess the chance and value it. Broadly speaking, if there is a 10 per cent chance of an unfavourable development, the court will award 10 per cent of any increase in damages that that development would attract.

Alternatively, where the uncertainty is as to whether the claimant's condition will seriously deteriorate, or whether some serious disease will set in (but *not* in the case of any other uncertainty), the claimant has the option of claiming provisional damages under the SCA 1981, s. 32A and the CCA 1984, s. 51. This will result in a lower award now, but with the certainty of a further award in the future if the serious deterioration or disease occurs. This has to be balanced against the advantages of a once-and-for-all settlement which evaluates the chance, produces a greater sum now, and brings the litigation to an end. It is a tactical decision.

10.9.4   Hybrid heads

10.9.4.1   Overlap between loss of amenity and financial loss

There are certain miscellaneous heads of damages which are sometimes seen as losses of amenity and sometimes as financial losses. Occasionally, there is an element of both loss of amenity and financial loss, and care must be taken to avoid overlap. Some common examples of hybrid heads follow. This list is not exhaustive.

10.9.4.2   Loss of congenial employment

Awards are increasingly often being made under this head. Such damages compensate the claimant for loss of job satisfaction. If the claimant was previously employed or earning their living in a way which brought them particular pleasure, enjoyment, pride, or responsibility, and as a result of their injury is now employed in a more boring or mundane job, even if there is no loss of earnings, there is a recoverable loss under this head. It ought strictly to be part of the claimant's loss of amenity, but has come to be treated as a separate head of damages for which a lump sum of between £5,000 and £10,000 might be awarded. If there is also a claim for loss of earnings, care must be taken not to take account of loss of job satisfaction twice. A table in *Kemp & Kemp* (para. 10-075) shows some sample awards.

10.9.4.3 Loss of housekeeping ability

This head was established by *Daly v General Steam Navigation Co Ltd* [1981] 1 WLR 120. It is strictly a claim for financial loss. If a claimant has suffered an impairment of their ability to do housework, to the extent that this has diminished their happiness, it can be taken account of as part of the general loss of amenity. But otherwise, it is essentially a claim for the cost of a housekeeper and is valued on that basis, both for special damages and general damages (see **10.13.3**).

10.9.4.4 Loss of marriage prospects

Under this head, there is truly an element of both loss of amenity and financial loss. It arises where a young claimant's injury has diminished or destroyed their chances of marriage. To the extent that this affects their happiness, it is a loss of amenity. But there is also a financial loss. Only female claimants have in the past succeeded in claiming this financial loss, which is the financial support a husband would probably have provided. However, such a loss could in theory be established by a man who was engaged to a wealthy woman at the time of the accident. How a female claimant is compensated under this head is dealt with in **10.10.5.2**.

10.9.4.5 Breakdown of marriage

Sometimes a claimant's injuries can lead to marriage breakdown. This is something to be taken account of in the award for loss of amenity, but there may also be a financial loss. Provided it is not too remote, an award can be made under this head, for example, for the loss of a spouse's services. The breakdown of the marriage may also result in significant extra expenditure, particularly if there is a divorce. Unfortunately, there are conflicting authorities on whether such loss is recoverable: *Jones v Jones* [1985] QB 704; *Pritchard v JH Cobden Ltd* [1988] Fam 22.

10.10   Head 3: future loss of earnings

This head of damages arises where there is at the date of trial or settlement an annual loss of earnings which is measurable at today's values, and evidence that it will continue into the future. If at the date of trial there is no measurable annual loss, but nevertheless evidence that some loss is likely to accrue in the future, then an award under the next head, loss of earning capacity (see **10.11**) may be more appropriate.

10.10.1   The multiplier and the multiplicand

Damages are calculated on a multiplier/multiplicand basis. This means that two separate figures must be arrived at in turn and then multiplied together to produce the result. The multiplicand represents the aspect of the claimant's loss that is reasonably certain and measurable in financial terms; that is, their current annual loss. The multiplier represents that aspect of the loss that is uncertain and not precisely ascertainable; that is, how long into the future such a loss will continue.

10.10.2   Calculating the multiplicand

This is basically the claimant's net annual loss of earnings as at the date of trial, or as at the date on which you are advising on quantum. In calculating special damages, account has already been taken of any likely pay increases, promotion, career moves, business developments, etc., and these factors obviously also affect what the claimant would have been earning today. The *Gourley* principle again applies, and all calculations should be done using net sums. The calculation is simply what the claimant would have been earning net annually, minus what they are now earning net annually (if anything), minus annual expenses saved. What you are left with is the multiplicand.

This calculation of the multiplicand is straightforward where the claimant's loss of earnings is likely to continue at more or less the same level until the age at which they would have retired. But what if there is evidence that the claimant was likely to have been promoted, or that their earnings would have increased for some other reason, for example a new job or the expansion of their business; or alternatively evidence that they would have been likely to lose their job or suffer a decrease in earnings at some point in the future? The traditional approach to these problems was to make no adjustment to the multiplicand, but rather to make an adjustment to the multiplier to take account of any future uncertainties. But as we shall see in **10.10.3** when we look at multipliers, the approach these days is likely to be more scientific, and there may well be a reluctance to make speculative adjustments to the multiplier. If so, the court has two alternative approaches open to it. One is to decide on a multiplicand which represents not the annual loss of earnings today, but the average annual loss of earnings over the period to be measured, applying a single multiplier. The other approach is for the court to look at the evidence, and find as a fact, for example, that the claimant's earnings would probably have increased by £x in about five years' time, and make a split award, using two or even three multiplicands and a multiplier divided into two (or three) parts (see **10.10.4**).

10.10.3   The multiplier

10.10.3.1   What is the multiplier?

The multiplier represents the number of years for which the claimant is to be awarded their net annual loss of earnings. It is sometimes known as the 'number of years purchase'. It is important to realise that the multiplier is *not a real number of years*. In normal times (and we are not in normal times at the moment—see **10.10.3.9**) if a claimant were to be given their loss for a real number of years, the effect of accelerated receipt (i.e. the fact that the claimant receives the money earlier than they would have done had they earned it) would be to overcompensate them massively. Think, for example, of a male claimant aged 25 at the date of his accident, with a net annual loss of £10,000. He would have retired at 65 and so has lost 40 years of income. But a multiplier of 40 produces a lump sum of £400,000, from which the claimant would be able to derive an annual income far in excess of £10,000.

The multiplier is therefore an artificial figure. It takes account of accelerated receipt. It also takes account of all the variables and uncertainties with regard to the future. It is specific to the individual claimant.

10.10.3.2   The old approach to selecting the multiplier

In order to understand the method we now apply in 2020, and its rationale, we need to go into a bit of history. Until 1997, multipliers were selected in a rather artificial way. The starting points were the claimant's age, sex, state of health before the accident, and the nature of the employment lost. The more secure the job, the higher the retirement age, the higher the multiplier would be. There was then an assumption made that the claimant, when investing a lump sum award of damages, would be able to achieve a net rate of return on the investment of 4–5 per cent per year. To take account of accelerated receipt, therefore, the total lump sum needed to be reduced by about 4.5 per cent a year, and the multiplier would be arrived at on this basis. This was not generally done by accurate calculation, but rather by reference to tables in *Kemp & Kemp,* which showed the multipliers used in other cases, and conventional wisdom, which told us that the appropriate multiplier, for example, was 13 for 20 years of real time, 15 for 25 years of real time, etc. The multiplier selected was almost always a whole number of years, and the court would move the figure first arrived at up or down by a year or so to take account of contingencies like promotion, unemployment, etc.

10.10.3.3   The development of a new approach

This method had, however, become rather out of date. The 4.5 per cent discount rate assumed that the claimant would invest their damages to a substantial extent in higher risk investments, such as equities, or at least ought to. If the claimant invested in a safer way, for example in Index-Linked Government Securities (ILGS), they would probably only achieve an annual net rate of return of 2–3 per cent. Very few claimants actually invested their damages in anything more adventurous than a deposit account, and so ended up undercompensated. Further, the method ignored the existence of what are called the Ogden Tables. These are actuarial tables compiled by a working party under Sir Michael Ogden and first published in 1983. The 8th edition (2020, updated May 2021) can be found in *Kemp & Kemp* and *Butterworths Personal Injury Litigation Service*, division XIV [73]. The tables set out the multipliers that should be adopted to measure various periods of the future for claimants of every age, at different discount rates, based on statistical evidence of the population's life expectancy and mortality rate. These tables make it possible to select multipliers in a much more accurate way.

In 1994, the Law Commission made two recommendations: that the Ogden Tables should become admissible in evidence, and that multipliers should be based on an annual discount rate of 3 per cent rather than the conventional 4.5 per cent. Parliament accepted these recommendations and enacted s. 10 of the Civil Evidence Act 1995, and s. 1 of the Damages Act 1996. However, case law intervened.

10.10.3.4   Civil Evidence Act 1995, s. 10

This section provides that the Ogden Tables should be admissible in evidence. This obviates the need to call expert evidence to prove them in every case. Section 10 has never been brought into force, but in the light of the decision in *Wells v Wells* (see **10.10.3.7**), this is no longer of any importance. It may now never be brought into force.

10.10.3.5   Damages Act 1996

Section A1 of the Damages Act 1996 (added by the Civil Liability Act 2018 in place of s. 1) reads:

> *(1) In determining the return to be expected from the investment of a sum awarded as damages for future pecuniary loss in an action for personal injury the court must, subject to and in accordance with rules of court made for the purposes of this section, take into account such rate of return (if any) as may from time to time be prescribed by an order made by the Lord Chancellor.*
>
> *(2) Subsection (1) does not however prevent the court taking a different rate of return into account if any party to the proceedings shows that it is more appropriate in the case in question.*
>
> *(3) An order under subsection (1) may prescribe different rates of return for different classes of case.*
>
> *(4) An order under subsection (1) may in particular distinguish between classes of case by reference to—*
>
> > *(a)   the description of future pecuniary loss involved;*
> > *(b)   the length of the period during which future pecuniary loss is expected to occur;*
> > *(c)   the time when future pecuniary loss is expected to occur.*
>
> *(5) Schedule A1 (which makes provision about determining the rate of return to be prescribed by an order under subsection (1)) has effect.*
>
> *(6) An order under this section is to be made by statutory instrument subject to annulment in pursuance of a resolution of either House of Parliament.*

The effect of this section is to enable the Lord Chancellor to prescribe a rate of return lower than 4.5 per cent. It also enables the parties to argue for any rate of return they think is appropriate in the light of the current state of the market and the facts of the case. Once the appropriate rate of return on investment is prescribed, it becomes possible to find the correct multiplier to be taken as a starting point by reference to the Ogden Tables.

The Damages Act 1996 came into force on 24 September 1996, but it was not until June 2001 that the Lord Chancellor prescribed a rate. He was initially waiting for the decision of the House of Lords in *Wells v Wells* [1998] 3 All ER 481, but nearly two years passed before a consultation paper was issued by the Lord Chancellor's Department in March 2000, which stated that the Lord Chancellor intended at last to prescribe a rate, and at the same time to bring s. 10 of the Civil Evidence Act 1995 into force. Responses to the consultation were invited by June 2000, and on 27 June 2001 the Lord Chancellor prescribed a rate. But before we consider the effect of this order, we need to look at what happened in the meantime.

10.10.3.6   *Wells v Wells*—the background

In 1994 and 1995, several claimants were successful in persuading judges to assume a rate of return on investment of damages of 3 per cent or even less, thus obtaining a multiplier substantially greater than that which would have been applied using the conventional discount. They were able to do so with expert evidence on investment and the use of the Ogden Tables. Several of these cases went to the Court of Appeal and were reported under the name of the first, *Wells v Wells* [1997] 1 All ER 673.

The Court of Appeal came down emphatically in favour of retaining the conventional approach to multipliers, and assuming a rate of return on investment of about 4.5 per cent, thus putting the common law in clear conflict with the intention of the Law Commission and the Damages Act 1996. There was then more than a year's delay before the case went to the House of Lords.

10.10.3.7   The House of Lords' decision in *Wells v Wells*

The House of Lords decided that the conventional rate of discount of 4.5 per cent should no longer be used when selecting multipliers, and that a rate reflecting the likely rate of return when investing in ILGS should be used instead. This rate should be a standard rate, to be applied in every case until a new rate was set. This would facilitate the settlement of claims, and avoid the need to call expert evidence at trials. The rate should be 3 per cent for the time being, until either there was a very considerable change in economic circumstances and/or the Lord Chancellor set a different rate under s. 1(3) of the Damages Act 1996. The House of Lords invited him to do this as soon as possible, to avoid uncertainty. Thereafter, the rate should always be set by the Lord Chancellor under the Act, so as to avoid the need for the courts to reconsider the issue. The rate should always be set to within 0.5 of a percentage point (i.e. 2.5 per cent, 3 per cent, 3.5 per cent, etc.), so as to make it possible for the Ogden Tables always to be used in practice.

The standard rate should not, however, be regarded as absolutely fixed. It was accepted by the House of Lords in *Hodgson v Trapp* [1989] AC 807, and anticipated by s. 1(2) of the Damages Act 1996, that there may be exceptional circumstances in which an argument can be made out for assuming a different rate of return on investment, particularly where higher rate tax is likely to be payable on income. But it is likely to be rare that such an argument will succeed.

The House of Lords also held that the correct approach in future to selecting a multiplier should be to use the Ogden Tables. Once the correct rate of discount (the assumed net rate of annual return of investment) is known, the tables will provide the correct multiplier, or at least the correct starting point. At this point, therefore, a new approach to selecting the multiplier came into effect, and the use of the Ogden Tables had official sanction, even though s. 10 of the Civil Evidence Act 1995 was not yet in force.

10.10.3.8   After *Wells v Wells*

While the Lord Chancellor continued to delay setting a rate under the Damages Act 1996, pressure mounted for the courts to adopt a rate lower than 3 per cent. Sir Michael Ogden argued in an article in *The Times* that the rate should be set at 2 per cent, and in one case a judge decided to do so, but the Court of Appeal in *Warren v Northern General Hospital Trust* [2000] 1 WLR 1404 held that the courts could not alter the 3 per cent discount rate until the Lord Chancellor made an order.

10.10.3.9   The rate set by the Lord Chancellor

In June 2001, the Lord Chancellor prescribed a rate of 2.5 per cent. He accepted the need to have a single rate to cover all types of case, so he did not exercise his power under s. 1(3) of the Damages Act 1996. He also accepted the view of the House of Lords that the rate should be set as a multiple of 0.5 per cent, and that the rate of 2.5 per cent should remain unchanged for the foreseeable future. It did indeed remain unchanged for many years, but in March 2017, somewhat controversially, the Lord Chancellor prescribed a new rate of minus 0.75 per cent, taking account of the very low interest rates currently prevailing. The result was a massive increase in the appropriate multiplier, and hence a massive increase in the amount of damages awarded. It gave joy to claimant lawyers and horror to insurance companies. Now, Sch. A1 to the Damages Act 1996 (inserted by s. 10 of the Civil Liability Act 2018) prescribes a statutory process for reviewing the discount rate, which must happen every five years. This came into force in December 2018, and in July 2019 the Lord Chancellor raised the rate slightly to minus 0.25 per cent. This is therefore the rate for the foreseeable future. The Lord Chancellor specifically stated that claimants must be regarded as 'low-risk' investors.

It remains the case under the Damages Act 1996, s. 1(2) that a party may seek to persuade the court to adopt a different rate, where appropriate on the facts of the case. However, following the decision in *Warriner v Warriner* [2003] 3 All ER 447, it is hard to envisage in what circumstances a party will succeed in doing so. In that case, the Court of Appeal held that the different rate must be more appropriate in the light of the reasons given by the Lord Chancellor for setting the rate at 2.5 per cent (as it was then). So, in effect, it must be shown that there are circumstances to the case which were not considered by the Lord Chancellor. A very long life expectancy and very large damages are not such circumstances.

We therefore now have a settled approach to the selection of multipliers, which is explained in the following paragraphs. Remember that if the rate does change in the future, this will make very little difference to the process of calculation of damages. The principles by which multipliers are selected will remain unchanged; it is only the appropriate column in the Ogden Tables which will alter.

10.10.3.10 Selecting a multiplier—the new approach

The starting point in finding the multiplier for a loss of future earnings claim will be the appropriate Ogden Table (8th edition).

For loss of earnings, Tables 3–18 are the relevant ones. Choose the table appropriate to the claimant's sex and likely retirement age, then all you need to know is the claimant's age today, and the correct discount rate (minus 0.25 per cent) and the multiplier can be read off. In the event of non-standard retirement ages, you need to adjust the claimant's age. If the claimant is a 35-year-old male but would not have retired until the age of 72, you can either use Table 13 (retirement age 70) but treat the claimant as aged 33, which gives you a multiplier of 37.21; or you can use Table 15 (retirement age 75) but treat the claimant as aged 38, which gives you a multiplier of 36.45. There is a method explained in paras 33–34 of the Explanatory Notes to the Ogden Tables to produce an accurate multiplier between these two figures. You multiply 37.21 × 2 (because you have reduced the claimant's age by two years), giving 74.42, and multiply 36.45 × 3 (because you have added three years to the claimant's age), giving 109.35. Add these two sums together, a total of 183.77, and divide by 5 (the difference between the two retirement ages you have used), and you get a resulting multiplier of 36.754.

10.10.3.11 Discount for contingencies

As explained in **10.10.3.1** and **10.10.3.2** earlier, account has to be taken of uncertainties with regard to job security and any other contingencies other than mortality. The House of Lords in *Wells v Wells* recognised that this practice needed to continue in the case of multipliers for loss of future earnings. The unscientific approach of the past (add or subtract a year or two by guesswork) does not mix well with the actuarial approach and will doubtless be abandoned. There are two ways of dealing with contingencies.

The first is that advocated by the Ogden Working Party and explained in paras 54–82 of the Explanatory Notes to the Tables. It is rather more complicated than the approach that has been proposed in the past. The contingencies that need to be taken into account are the claimant's age, sex, and level of educational attainment, as well as whether the claimant was employed or unemployed and disabled or not disabled at the time of the accident. The multiplier that would be appropriate according to the main tables must then be reduced by the factor indicated in Table A, B, C, or D in para. 82. So, if you take a male aged 35, who would have retired at 65, Table 9 gives you a multiplier of 30.20. Now add the facts that he was employed and not disabled at the time of the accident, and that he had middling educational attainment (i.e. up to GCSE or A level, but not beyond) and Table A tells us that the multiplier should be discounted by a factor of 0.90. So, multiply 30.20 × 0.90 and the final multiplier is 27.18.

The other way of dealing with contingencies is much more rough and ready. It is simply to reduce the multiplier by 10 per cent. This was the conventional method before *Wells v Wells*, and it is possible that it is still followed in practice. If so, it should die out.

There will not normally be any good reason to adopt any other approach to the discount for contingencies. In particular, it is not sound to make a larger discount on the basis that the claim is really a claim for the loss of a chance—*Herring v Ministry of Defence* [2004] 1 All ER 44.

10.10.3.12   Other contingencies

There are still circumstances in which the court will or may make further adjustments to the multiplier from that suggested by the Ogden Tables. If there are any contingencies unique to the claimant that have not been taken account of already by the tables mentioned; for example, a particularly risky job, or ongoing ill health short of disability before the accident, it is still open to the court to decide that the multiplier should be further reduced, and the reduction is likely to be made in the old-fashioned, rather arbitrary, way of deducting a certain number of years.

Previously, there were other contingencies that could affect the multiplier, particularly factors like the claimant's actual earning capacity following the accident, or prospects of improving their earnings in the future. It seems unlikely that such contingencies will affect the multiplier in future. If they are to be taken account of, they will affect the multiplicand, maybe giving rise to a split award.

10.10.3.13   Factors which do not affect the choice of multiplier

(a) *Future inflation*. It has often been argued that in times of high inflation multipliers should be adjusted upwards to take account of the fact that the lump sum awarded to the claimant will diminish in value in real terms more quickly. However, high inflation is usually accompanied by higher interest rates, and so no adjustment needs to be made (*Lim Poh Choo v Camden and Islington Area Health Authority* [1980] AC 174). The theory is that inflation is already taken account of in the conventional multiplier selected. It was thought for a time that there was an exception where the award was so great that the income it produced when invested would attract tax at higher rates and not merely the basic rate, but this exception was all but ruled out by the House of Lords in *Hodgson v Trapp* [1989] AC 807.

(b) *Foreign tax*. The fact that a foreign claimant is liable to pay tax in their own country at a higher rate than they would pay in this country is not a justification for altering the discount rate or the multiplier (*Van Oudenhoven v Griffin Inns Ltd* [2000] 1 WLR 1413).

(c) *The period between injury and trial*. The length of time between injury and trial is not to be taken into account in the selection of the multiplier (*Pritchard v JH Cobden Ltd* [1988] Fam 22), though of course the court looks to the number of working years lost at the date of trial, not at the date of the injury. This does operate slightly in favour of claimants who are slow in bringing their cases to trial.

10.10.4   Split awards

Split awards for loss of future earnings are those where more than one multiplicand is worked out, and a separate multiplier applied to each. Following *Wells v Wells*, it is likely that such awards will become a lot more common in future. It is the most effective way of calculating loss where the claimant's earnings or losses are likely to change in the future. If, for example, there is evidence that the claimant would have been promoted in about ten years' time, with a corresponding increase in salary, the court is likely to take two multiplicands and split the multiplier. A method is described in paras 105–108 of the Explanatory Notes to the Ogden Tables.

For example, let us assume a female claimant, a graduate aged 43, who would have been promoted at the age of 50 and retired at the age of 60. The judge calculates two multiplicands, one for her existing loss—£35,000 per year, the other for her loss after promotion—£42,000 per year. The multiplier according to Ogden Table 8 is 17.12. However, you also need to use

Table 36, which gives multipliers for fixed periods. The multiplier for her overall loss should measure a real period of 17 years. Ogden Table 36 tells us that for a fixed period of 17 years the multiplier is 17.37. But the period before promotion is a fixed period of seven years, for which the multiplier is 7.06. The difference between 17.37 and 7.06 is 10.31, which represents the ten-year period after promotion. Now you work out 7.06 and 10.31 as percentages of 17.37. The answer is 40.64 per cent and 59.36 per cent. Next, you divide the correct multiplier, namely 17.12, into these percentages, which gives you 6.96 for the first seven years and 10.16 for the remaining ten years. Now apply the discount for contingencies other than mortality (let's say 0.89 in accordance with Table C) and you get multipliers of 6.19 and 9.04. Finally, you can do the calculation: for the loss up to the date of promotion, she gets 6.19 × £35,000 = £216,650, and for the loss thereafter she gets 9.04 × £42,000 = £379,680, giving a grand total of £596,330.

It is even possible that in appropriate cases the court will split the multiplier into three or four periods, with three or four different multiplicands and multipliers, for example where the claimant is a young man in his early twenties who had a very long and promising career ahead of him. A split award will also always be necessary in lost years cases: see **10.10.7.3**.

10.10.5   Female claimants and future loss of earnings

10.10.5.1   Possible lower awards

A female claimant may not recover damages for loss of future earnings assessed on the basis of the Ogden Tables. This is because the court must take account of the possibility that she would have given up or interrupted her employment at some time in the future in order to have children and raise a family. If she is able to satisfy the court that she would not have done so, then of course the multiplier will be unaffected. But in the absence of such evidence, the court must evaluate the chance, and it remains a statistical probability that an unmarried woman will get married, and will have children, and will give up or interrupt her employment for some years at least; so, a reduced award will result.

10.10.5.2   Loss of marriage prospects

However, an unmarried female claimant may very well also have suffered a loss of marriage prospects. This is not just a loss of amenity; it is also a financial loss—she has lost the financial support her husband would have provided had she given up work to raise a family. Although to make an award for lost marriage prospects and loss of future earnings may amount to double recovery, one can cancel the other out. In *Moriarty v McCarthy* [1978] 1 WLR 155, the court reduced the award for loss of future earnings on the ground that the claimant might have given up work to raise a family, but made an award of an amount equal to the reduction for loss of marriage prospects. More simply, the court in *Hughes v McKeown* [1985] 1 WLR 963 made no award for loss of marriage prospects, but used the same multiplier in the claim for loss of future earnings as would have been applied in the absence of any loss of marriage prospects.

10.10.6   Child claimants and future loss of earnings

When the claimant is a child who has not yet started work or chosen a career, particular difficulties arise. There can never be a measurable annual loss and so damages assessed on a multiplier/multiplicand basis are not prima facie appropriate. Indeed, where the claimant is very young, and where their earning capacity has been reduced rather than destroyed by the injury, the court is likely to make an award for loss of earning capacity rather than loss of future earnings (e.g. *Joyce v Yeomans* [1981] 1 WLR 549). But if the claimant has lost any chance of career or employment, the court may well assess damages on a multiplier/multiplicand basis (e.g. *Croke v Wiseman* [1981] 3 All ER 852).

The court will first of all need evidence of what the child's likely earnings would have been. If there is good evidence that the child's background was such that they would have been a high earner, then the court may take quite a large multiplicand (or series of multiplicands, for a split award). In the absence of such evidence, national average earnings are likely to form the basis of the multiplicand.

The multiplier will depend on the age at which the child would probably have started work. Treat the child as if that were their age in looking up the appropriate multiplier in the Ogden Tables. Reduce it for contingencies in accordance with Tables A–D, and then turn to Ogden Table 35 to determine the extra effect of accelerated receipt before the age of 18. So if, for example, the claimant is a five-year-old boy who would probably have started work at the age of 18 after taking A levels and retired at the age of 65, the multiplier will be 48.77 according to Ogden Table 9. This will be reduced by a factor of 0.90 in accordance with Table A, making 43.89. But the money will be received 13 years in advance, so Table 27 shows that the multiplier must be adjusted further by a factor of 1.0331 (43.89 × 1.0331 gives a final multiplier of 45.34).

10.10.7   Lost years

10.10.7.1   Basis of assessment

What if, as a result of their injury, the claimant's life expectancy has been reduced? Is the multiplier in the claim for loss of earnings to be based on their actual, reduced, life expectancy, or on what their life expectancy would have been but for the injury? The answer, laid down in *Pickett v British Rail Engineering Ltd* [1980] AC 136, is that the claimant can claim loss of future earnings, not only for the period they will survive, but also for the years they have lost, unless that loss is too remote to be measurable. It was thought to be too remote to be measurable if, for example, the claimant was a very young child (*Croke v Wiseman* [1981] 3 All ER 852) or if the years that had been lost could have had only a negligible effect on the choice of multiplier (e.g. a 20-year-old whose remaining life expectancy has been reduced from 60 to 50 years). However, following the adoption of the Ogden Tables as the normal starting point, it is now arguable that such a loss is always measurable, even if small.

10.10.7.2   Deduction for living expenses

But in a lost years case, a deduction will have to be made from the multiplicand to take account of the claimant's living expenses over those lost years; living expenses which they will no longer incur and so which cannot be recovered. 'Living expenses' includes all that the claimant would have spent exclusively on themselves—both needs (food, clothing, travel, etc.) and pleasures (beer, cigarettes, entertainment, etc.)—but not what the claimant would have saved or spent on the support of their dependants, or others, such as friends. Expenditure which would have been both for their own and their dependants' benefit (e.g. rent, mortgage interest, council tax, heating, electricity, gas, TV rental, the cost of running a car) has to be apportioned and a share taken from the multiplicand as the claimant's living expenses (*Harris v Empress Motors Ltd* [1983] 3 All ER 561).

10.10.7.3   Two awards

It follows that in a lost years case there will usually be two awards for loss of future earnings, each with a different multiplicand and multiplier: one in respect of the period that the claimant is likely to survive, using a multiplicand from which living expenses have not been deducted; and one in respect of the lost years, using a reduced multiplicand. For the method of calculation, see **10.10.4**.

10.10.8   Provisional damages for future loss of earnings

The court may in appropriate cases make a provisional award for future loss of earnings under SCA 1981, s. 32A or CCA 1984, s. 51. Normally, uncertainties with regard to the future are taken account of by evaluating the chance. But where the uncertainty is as to whether the claimant's condition will seriously deteriorate, causing the claimant to lose their job, the court can assess damages initially on the basis that the loss of earnings will continue at its present level, and award a further sum in the future if the loss increases due to a deterioration in condition.

10.11 Head 4: loss of earning capacity

10.11.1 The nature of the award

This head of damages arises where there is clear evidence that the claimant will not earn as much in the future as they would have done but for the injury, but there is nevertheless no measurable annual loss to found an award for loss of future earnings on a multiplier/multiplicand basis. Instead, an award for loss of earning capacity may be made. This is commonly known as a *Smith v Manchester* award, from *Smith v Manchester Corporation* [1974] 17 KIR 1. It compensates the claimant, not so much for lost earnings, but rather for lost earning capacity or the 'handicap on the labour market', and is assessed as a single lump sum.

10.11.2 When is an award of this kind appropriate?

It is possible to identify various situations in which an award of this kind is appropriate:

(a) where the claimant is back in pre-accident employment, or in work of equal value, so that there is no immediate loss, but nevertheless, as a result of the injury, they will at some time in the future be forced into an early retirement or a less well-paid job. If there is a real, or substantial, risk of this, a lump sum award can be made (*Moeliker v A Reyrolle & Co Ltd* [1976] ICR 252);

(b) where the claimant is back in pre-accident employment and is not likely to lose it, but nevertheless the injury has damaged prospects of promotion, ability to advance their career, or chances of moving on to higher-paid employment;

(c) where the claimant is handicapped on the labour market by the injury. For example, the claimant was not in settled employment or was unemployed at the date of the accident, or is not yet back at work but will be soon, and is now going to find work harder to come by, or will find that the range of jobs open to them is narrower than it was. In all these instances a *Smith v Manchester* award is appropriate;

(d) where the claimant is a child who has not yet entered the labour market (see **10.10.6**).

A recent example was the case of *Irani v Duchon* [2019] All ER (D) 45 (Nov), where as a result of his accident the claimant, an Indian national, was made redundant and there was a gap before he was able to resume employment. This had a negative effect on his ability to obtain indefinite leave to remain in the UK, and there was no good evidence on his potential earnings in India. As a result, the Court of Appeal upheld the judge's decision to award a lump sum for loss of earning capacity rather than damages on a multiplier/multiplicand basis.

10.11.3 Quantification of an award for loss of earning capacity

The award is quantified as a round lump sum, which is chosen on a fairly arbitrary basis, with some reference to awards in previous cases. Awards under this head are generally not particularly high. A typical working basis for assessment is to take one to two years' net pay, but a higher sum may be appropriate: see, for example, *Foster v Tyne and Wear County Council* [1986] 1 All ER 567, where a lump sum of five times annual net pay was approved.

10.11.4 Awards combining heads 3 and 4

Judges do not always draw a clear distinction between damages for loss of earnings and loss of earning capacity, and occasional hybrid awards can be found where damages for future loss of earnings have been assessed as a lump sum, or where damages for lost earning capacity have been quantified by means of a speculative multiplicand and multiplier. However, both these tendencies involve the kind of speculation that the modern approach since *Wells v Wells* has discouraged, and judges are well advised to use a mathematically chosen multiplier and multiplicand wherever possible.

The two heads are normally alternative to each other, but there are cases where an award under each head is appropriate, for example where the claimant has not yet gone back to work but is expected to do so in, say, a year's time; they will then resume their pre-accident employment but will still be handicapped on the labour market or have lower prospects of promotion. In such a case, the court would probably award one year's loss of earnings and a small lump sum. The courts are increasingly willing to recognise that there is a distinction between the two heads and to make an award both for future loss of earnings and for handicap on the labour market.

10.11.5 Provisional damages and loss of earning capacity

If the claimant has claimed provisional damages, this may well preclude an award being made under this head. If, for example, there is uncertainty as to whether the claimant's condition will deteriorate, but certainty that if it does, the claimant will be forced into early retirement, the court will assess damages initially on the basis that there is no loss of earning capacity, and any later award, if there is deterioration, is likely to be on a multiplier/multiplicand basis.

10.12 Head 5: loss of pension rights

10.12.1 Basis of the award

It is often the case that if a claimant has lost their employment as a result of their injury, or their employment has been interrupted, they have also lost their employer's contributions towards a retirement pension, which will accordingly be reduced. Damages can be awarded to compensate for this loss.

10.12.2 Old method of calculating damages under this head

Damages used to be calculated as follows (see *Auty v National Coal Board* [1985] 1 All ER 930):

(a) Assuming no change in the value of money, what annual pension would the claimant have received on retirement had they not been injured and had there been no interruption to the pension contributions?

(b) What annual pension will the claimant in fact receive, again assuming no change in the value of money?

(c) The difference between (a) and (b) is the annual loss. Multiply it by an appropriate multiplier representing the number of years for which they are likely to receive the pension (or, in a lost years case, would have received it).

(d) Discount the lump sum arrived at by 4 or 5 per cent per annum (the discount rate in those days—see **10.10.3.2**) for accelerated receipt. This calculation is on a year-on-year basis.

10.12.3 New method of calculation

Following *Wells v Wells* it must now be appropriate to use an actuarial method of calculation, using the Ogden Tables. *Wells v Wells* did not actually deal with the assessment of damages for a lost pension, but exactly the same principles apply.

The multiplicand can be calculated in this way—it is the difference between the annual pension the claimant would have received on retirement but for the injury and the annual pension they will now receive. The multiplier can be found from Ogden Tables 19–34. Choose the table according to the sex and retirement age of the claimant, and then read off the multiplier according to the claimant's age today and the appropriate rate of discount (minus 0.25 per cent). The tables take account not only of the element of accelerated receipt once the claimant reaches retirement age, but also the further element of accelerated receipt, given that the claimant will receive a lump sum in respect of pension loss before reaching retirement age.

The multiplier will again need to be adjusted for contingencies other than mortality. The procedure is exactly the same as in multipliers for loss of future earnings—see **10.10.3.11**.

10.12.4   A simpler method of assessment

An alternative and simpler method of valuing a loss of pension rights, which can be agreed by parties negotiating a settlement, but which does not have the court's approval, is to obtain quotations from life assurance companies. If the claimant has had their pension right on retirement reduced from, say, £15,000 to £10,000 per year, find out the market price today of a £5,000 per annum pension from age 65 for life, and take this as an appropriate sum.

10.13   Head 6: future expenses

10.13.1   Similarity to special damages

These are likely to be the same items or the same sort of items as were included in the claim for special damages; but where the expenditure has not yet been incurred, or will continue into the future for a number of years or indefinitely, the loss is future loss and forms part of the award for general damages. Any type of loss or expense that was reasonably recoverable as special damages is also recoverable if it lies in the future or will continue into the future.

10.13.2   'One-off' items

Items of expenditure that are 'one-off', such as the cost of home conversion or the purchase of special equipment, are quantified on a lump-sum basis. If the court takes the present-day value, the advantage of accelerated receipt is cancelled out by inflation.

10.13.3   Recurring items

Recurring items, such as the cost of nursing care, the cost of a housekeeper, and the value of voluntary services, are quantified on a multiplier/multiplicand basis. The multiplicand is the annual cost or value of the service as at the date of trial. The multiplier, following *Wells v Wells*, will be selected from the Ogden Tables. If the item of expenditure will last only for a certain number of years, Table 36 will be appropriate; if the item of expenditure will last indefinitely, then the multiplier represents the claimant's life expectancy and Ogden Tables 1 and 2 will be used. The only contingency that is relevant is mortality, and so no further adjustment should be made to the multiplier found by reference to the tables. There may in occasional cases (but not as a general rule) be evidence that the claimant has a particularly low or high expectation of life, in which case the court may be persuaded to make an adjustment to the multiplier. This is likely to be done by assuming a different age for the claimant when reading the multiplier off the table. In the event that the claimant's injuries have substantially reduced life expectancy to a given number of years, then Table 36 will be the appropriate table.

The discount rate is that specified by the Lord Chancellor—currently minus 0.25 per cent, as in claims for loss of future earnings. Attempts have been made to argue that the discount rate should be lower in claims for the cost of future care, relying on s. 1(2) (now s. A1(2)) of the Damages Act 1996, but the courts are extremely reluctant to depart from the standard rate. In *Cooke v United Bristol Healthcare NHS Trust* [2004] 1 All ER 797, several claimants tried to get around the convention by arguing that the multiplicand should increase in stages over future years (because the costs of care are increasing faster than the general rate of inflation). However, the Court of Appeal refused to adopt this approach. It is hard to see when, if ever, s. A1(2) can actually be applied.

There may frequently be several items of recurring expense, and each will need to be calculated with its own multiplicand and multiplier. Note that not all future expenditure will last indefinitely. For example, if the claimant is claiming for the cost of a gardener, when the claimant used to do their own gardening, it is arguable that they should not recover this loss for life, because even if the claimant had not been injured, they would probably have given up doing the gardening at some stage before death.

A claim for the cost of nursing care may well have to be calculated on a split basis, because as the claimant gets older, the cost will increase. In such cases, the court will allow one multiplicand for, say, ten years, and a higher multiplicand thereafter. The multiplier will be split in the way explained in **10.10.4**.

The cost of purchasing a new house is a recurring item: the multiplicand is 2.5 per cent of the increased capital value (see **10.7.5**) and the multiplier represents the claimant's life expectancy.

Where the item of recurring expenditure is not an annual expense, the easiest way to calculate the loss is to spread the multiplicand over a number of years. For example, if the claimant will need a new wheelchair every five years for the rest of their life, at a cost of £1,000 at present-day values, take a multiplicand of £200 and a multiplier from Ogden Table 1 or 2.

10.13.4   The domestic element in the cost of care

Where there is a claim for the cost of future care of the claimant, as well as a claim for the claimant's lost earnings, care must be taken to avoid duplication or overlap of damages in the area of living expenses. It is quite likely that part of the cost of looking after the claimant in an institution will match what the claimant would have spent in looking after themselves (e.g. food and clothing). If no deduction were made, the claimant would therefore be compensated for some of the loss twice over. Rather than deducting living expenses from the award for loss of earnings, instead the 'domestic element' is deducted from the claim for the cost of care (*Lim Poh Choo v Camden and Islington Area Health Authority* [1980] AC 174). This involves an adjustment to the multiplicand, not the multiplier.

The domestic element is narrower than living expenses as defined by *Pickett v British Rail Engineering Ltd* [1980] AC 136: it is merely that portion of the living expenses that is replaced by the cost of care, and does not include any portion of the joint expenditure or what the claimant would have spent on pleasures. (It is irrelevant that the claimant can no longer enjoy those pleasures.)

10.13.5   Cost of investment advice

If a claimant is to receive a large award of damages for future loss, they will very likely need to pay for professional advice on how to invest it, and will also incur charges from fund managers investing the money. The question arises whether such sums can be recovered as future expenses. It was held in *Page v Plymouth Hospitals NHS Trust* [2004] 3 All ER 367 that these expenses are not recoverable as damages. In setting the discount rate to be used when selecting the multiplier, the Lord Chancellor has assumed that damages will be invested in index-linked gilt-edged stock, for which these expenses will not be incurred. The discount rate would have been greater if the kind of investment requiring advice and management had been contemplated, so it would be too generous to a claimant to take account of these expenses in awarding damages. In *Eagle v Chambers* [2005] 1 All ER 136, the Court of Appeal held that the same rule must apply to panel brokers' fees charged by the Court of Protection.

10.14   Stage 3: make any necessary deductions

10.14.1   Introduction

Following injury, the claimant may have received benefits or made savings, as well as suffered losses. On the compensatory principle, therefore, any gains made as a result of the injury should be deducted from any claim for losses suffered. However, the courts require a clear causative link between injury and benefit, and not all benefits received have to be deducted. There are various rules for different types of benefit. Some have been considered already: see **10.7.4.3, 10.7.4.4, 10.7.6, 10.10.7.2,** and **10.13.4**.

10.14.2 Social security benefits

Social security benefits may well have been received by the claimant, but will be recovered by the State on payment of damages: see **10.17**. Therefore, they should be disregarded in the assessment of damages (i.e. no deduction should be made). This is expressly provided for in s. 17 of the Social Security (Recovery of Benefits) Act 1997.

10.14.3 Contractual sick pay

Any sick pay received by the claimant from their employer under a contract of employment is equivalent to earnings and so must be deducted from any claim for lost earnings. For statutory sick pay, see **10.17**.

10.14.4 Insurance

Where the claimant was insured against accidental injury and receives the benefits of that insurance policy, no deduction is to be made (*Bradburn v Great Western Railway* (1874) LR 10 Ex 1). The rule is the same even where the insurance premium was paid on the claimant's behalf by another (such as an employer). But where the claimant's employer runs a sick pay scheme through an insurance policy, by which the claimant is contractually entitled to sick pay under the contract of employment, such sick pay is treated as part of their earnings and is to be deducted (*Hussain v New Taplow Paper Mills Ltd* [1988] 1 All ER 541). However, where the insurance premiums have been paid by the tortfeasor, the insurance benefit is to be deducted (*Gaca v Pirelli General plc* [2004] 3 All ER 348).

10.14.5 Pensions

Where the claimant receives a pension as a result of their injuries, no deduction is to be made, whether the pension was payable as of right or was discretionary, whether it was contributory or non-contributory (*Parry v Cleaver* [1970] AC 1, reaffirmed by the House of Lords in *Smoker v London Fire and Civil Defence Authority* [1991] 2 AC 502). State retirement pensions are also not deductible (*Hewson v Downs* [1970] 1 QB 73; *Hopkins v Norcros plc* [1992] ICR 338).

However, in *Longden v British Coal Corp* [1998] 1 All ER 289, the House of Lords allowed a small exception to this rule. Where the claimant had received an incapacity pension consisting of a lump sum as well as an annual payment, the proportion of that lump sum that related to the period after the claimant would have retired was to be deducted from any claim for lost retirement pension.

10.14.6 Redundancy payments

Where the claimant has been made redundant and received a redundancy payment, this will not normally be deducted, since the payment has nothing to do with the injury or incapacity to work (*Mills v Hassall* [1983] ICR 330). However, where the claimant has been made redundant or has been offered and accepted voluntary redundancy, but would not have been made redundant or would not have accepted redundancy but for the injury, then the redundancy payment is deductible (*Colledge v Bass Mitchells and Butlers Ltd* [1988] 1 All ER 536).

10.14.7 Benevolent donations

It sometimes happens, particularly following well-publicised disasters, that the claimant has benefited from a fund created by voluntary donations. Any such benefits are not deductible (*Redpath v Belfast and County Down Railway* [1947] NI 167).

Similarly, no account is to be taken of gifts from family or friends, or an ex gratia payment by the claimant's employer (*Cunningham v Harrison* [1973] QB 942). A voluntary payment by an employer may be deductible, however, where the employer is the liable defendant (*Hussain v New Taplow Paper Mills Ltd* [1988] 1 All ER 541), and particularly where the payment is expressed to be treated as an advance against any damages that may be awarded (*Williams v*

BOC Gases Ltd [2000] ICR 1181). Indeed, as a general rule, any redundancy payments made by the tortfeasor will be treated as deductible (*Gaca v Pirelli General plc* [2004] 3 All ER 348). No deduction is made in respect of voluntary services provided by family and friends (see **10.4.1.2(m)** and **10.7.8**).

10.14.8   Maintenance at public expense

If the claimant is being or has been maintained wholly or partly at public expense in a hospital, nursing home, or other institution, any saving made must be deducted from any damages for lost earnings or earning capacity (AJA 1982, s. 5). This deduction is roughly equivalent to the deduction of the domestic element (see **10.13.4**).

10.14.9   Foreign repayable benefits

If the claimant has received a foreign State benefit which they are by law obliged to repay if they recover damages, then no deduction will be made from the damages to take account of this benefit, even if it would otherwise be deductible (*Berriello v Felixstowe Dock & Railway Co* [1989] 1 WLR 695). To do so would penalise either the claimant or the provider of the benefit.

10.14.10   Statutory compensation

Where a claimant has received compensation payable under the Pneumoconiosis, etc. (Workers' Compensation) Act 1979, and then recovers damages in respect of the same disease for which they received that compensation, those damages must be reduced by the full amount of the compensation received. By analogy, the same principle is likely to apply in respect of any other statutory compensation that may be payable for industrial injury or disease.

10.15   Stage 4: contributory negligence

10.15.1   Introduction

Damages may well have to be reduced to take account of the claimant's contributory negligence. The circumstances in which such a reduction is to be made are set out in **4.5.2**.

10.15.2   Quantification

If there has been a finding of contributory negligence, the total sum of damages quantified so far must be reduced accordingly. If the finding is 25 per cent contributory negligence, reduce the total award by 25 per cent. If advising on quantum, form an opinion as to whether there is likely to be a finding of contributory negligence and, if so, reduce your estimate of damages accordingly.

10.15.3   Reduction for contributory negligence is made last

Note that any reduction for contributory negligence is made after taking account of any other deductions.

This sequence of deductions operates in the claimant's favour. To take an example: damages are assessed at £2,500; contributory negligence is 50 per cent; and the amount to be deducted is £500.

If contributory negligence was taken account of first, the claimant would receive: £(2,500 × 50%) − £500 = £750.

In fact, the other deductions are made first, and the claimant receives £(2,500−500) × 50% = £1,000.

10.16 Stage 5: add interest

10.16.1 Introduction

Interest will be awarded by the court under SCA 1981, s. 35A or CCA 1984, s. 69. By s. 35A(2) and s. 69(2), the award is prima facie mandatory, unless there are special reasons to the contrary. The sections give no guidelines as to interest rates or periods, which are in the court's discretion, but there are rules of practice.

10.16.2 Interest on special damages

Interest is awarded on special damages at half the 'appropriate rate' from the date of accident to the date of trial (*Jefford v Gee* [1970] 2 QB 130). The date of trial is the date of judgment on damages, not liability (*Thomas v Bunn* [1991] 1 AC 362).

The appropriate rate is the rate of interest allowed on the High Court Special Investment Account over the relevant period. This rate of interest is fixed from time to time by the Lord Chancellor. At the time of writing, it is 0.1 per cent, so half the appropriate rate is 0.05 per cent.

10.16.3 Interest on general damages

Interest is awarded on damages for pain and suffering and loss of amenity from the date of service of proceedings to the date of trial (*Pickett v British Rail Engineering Ltd* [1980] AC 136). The rate was set at 2 per cent a year by *Wright v British Railways Board* [1983] 2 All ER 698. It was thought that, following *Wells v Wells*, the rate should be 3 per cent, but this was ruled out in *Lawrence v Chief Constable of Staffordshire* The Times, 25 July 2000. The rate therefore remains at 2 per cent.

No interest is awarded on any damages for future loss.

10.17 Recovery of benefits

10.17.1 Introduction

Since 1989, it has been government policy that when a claimant receives a compensation payment in respect of injuries, any social security benefits which they have received in the meantime should be repaid to the State. The scheme was first introduced by the Social Security Act 1989, amended a few times, and consolidated into the Social Security Administration Act 1992. There were certain injustices in the scheme, notably that benefits could be recovered from a claimant's damages for pain, suffering, and loss of amenity as well as loss of earnings, so that in some cases a claimant could be left with very little in the way of damages at all. A revised scheme was therefore introduced by the Social Security (Recovery of Benefits) Act 1997. A fundamental change is that benefits are no longer recovered from the claimant, but from the compensator.

10.17.2 How the scheme works

10.17.2.1 The basic outline

By ss. 1 and 6 of the Social Security (Recovery of Benefits) Act 1997, a person who makes a compensation payment (whether on their own behalf or not) to any other person in consequence of any accident, injury, or disease must pay an amount equal to the total amount of the recoverable benefits to the Secretary of State.

By s. 8, they may then deduct the amount paid to the Secretary of State from the compensation to be paid to the claimant under the appropriate head of damages, but not so as to reduce the amount payable to the claimant under that head below nil. So, if the claimant has received more in benefits in respect of a particular type of loss than they are to receive by way of compensation, the claimant does not lose compensation under other heads to make up the difference.

On the other hand, the compensator must repay benefits in full to the Secretary of State, so if the benefits are greater than the compensation under the relevant head, the compensator will pay more in total than would have been the case if there had been no recovery of benefits. However, by s. 22, if the compensator was insured in respect of liability to the claimant, then they are also insured in respect of liability to the Secretary of State.

10.17.2.2   Recoverable benefits

The recoverable benefits are the listed benefits which have been or are likely to be paid to the claimant during the relevant period (Recovery of Benefits Act 1997, s. 1(1)). The listed benefits are set out in Sch. 2 to the 1997 Act. The effect of s. 8 is that each benefit is recoverable from compensation in respect of a particular type of loss only. The table in Sch. 2 is recreated in **Table 10.1**.

By s. 24 of the 1997 Act, the Secretary of State can amend Sch. 2 by statutory regulation.

10.17.2.3   The relevant period

The relevant period is defined by s. 3 of the 1997 Act. In the case of accident or injury, it is five years from the date of the accident or injury. In the case of disease, it is five years from the date on which the claimant first claimed benefit in respect of that disease. In either case, the relevant period comes to an end before the end of the five years when the defendant makes a compensation payment.

Table 10.1 **List of recoverable benefits from Sch. 2 to the Social Security (Recovery of Benefits) Act 1997**

Head of compensation	Benefit
1. Compensation for earnings lost during the relevant period	Universal credit
	Disablement pension
	Employment and support allowance
	Incapacity benefit
	Invalidity pension and allowance
	Jobseeker's allowance
	Reduced earnings allowance
	Severe disablement allowance
	Sickness benefit
	Statutory sick pay
	Unemployability supplement
	Unemployment benefit
2. Compensation for cost of care incurred during the relevant period	Attendance allowance
	Daily living component of personal independence payment
	Disablement pension increase
3. Compensation for loss of mobility during the relevant period	Mobility allowance
	Mobility component of personal independence payment

10.17.2.4   Certificates of recoverable benefits

How does the person making the compensation payment know how much to pay to the Secretary of State and how much to deduct from the compensation payment? They are given the necessary information by a certificate issued by the Compensation Recovery Unit. By s. 4 of the 1997 Act, before the compensator makes any compensation payment, they must apply for a certificate of recoverable benefits, which informs the compensator how much they must pay to the Secretary of State if the compensation payment is made within a specified time. If the compensator does not make the payment within that time, they must apply for a new certificate.

10.17.3   Court orders

The scheme applies in exactly the same way whether the compensation is paid by a court order, by agreement, or voluntarily. But where the court makes an order for the payment of damages (other than a consent order), then by s. 15 of the 1997 Act it must specify the amount awarded under each of the heads of compensation set out in Sch. 2.

10.17.4   Other provisions

The description in **10.17.3** is only an abbreviated outline of the effect of the 1997 Act. There are other provisions dealing with reviews and appeals against the amounts of recoverable benefits, recovery of overpayments, payments by more than one person in respect of the same injury, and other matters. In particular, there is a power to make regulations exempting small payments (up to a specified sum) from the scheme, though no such exemption has been made.

10.17.5   Contributory negligence and recovery of benefits

Recovery bites into damages actually paid after the assessment process is complete, so any reduction for contributory negligence will already have been made before the compensation payment is reduced to take account of the amount paid to the Secretary of State.

10.17.6   Interest on damages to be recovered

A claimant is entitled to receive interest on all the special damages assessed, not just those damages which will in fact be paid after the defendant has made a deduction in consequence of the recovery of benefits (*Wisely v John Fulton (Plumbers) Ltd* [2000] 2 All ER 545). However, the defendant can set off the benefits repaid to the Department for Work and Pensions against both the damages and the interest on those damages (*Griffiths v British Coal Corp* [2001] 1 WLR 1493).

10.18   Periodical payments

Section 2 of the Damages Act 1996, as substituted by s. 100 of the Courts Act 2003, and in force from 1 April 2005, gave statutory authorisation to the payment of damages by periodical payments. Here are the main subsections:

> *(1) A court awarding damages for future pecuniary loss in respect of personal injury—*
> > *(a) may order that the damages are wholly or partly to take the form of periodical payments, and*
> > *(b) shall consider whether to make that order.*
> *(2) A court awarding other damages in respect of personal injury may, if the parties consent, order that the damages are wholly or partly to take the form of periodical payments.*
> *(3) A court may not make an order for periodical payments unless satisfied that the continuity of payment under the order is reasonably secure.*
> *(8) An order for periodical payments shall be treated as providing for the amount of payments to vary by reference to the retail prices index (within the meaning of section 833(2) of the Income and Corporation Taxes Act 1988) at such times, and in such a manner, as may be determined by or in accordance with Civil Procedure Rules.*

(9) But an order for periodical payments may include provision—

    (a) disapplying subsection (8), or

    (b) modifying the effect of subsection (8).

This is not so much a change to the method of assessing damages, but rather an alternative method of paying them. As an addition to its other powers, the court can now order damages to be paid wholly or partly by way of periodical payments. It had the power to do so previously with the consent of the parties, but it may now do so even without their consent in relation to future pecuniary loss. It also has a duty in every case to consider whether to make such an order.

So, for example, rather than making a lump sum award for future medical expenses, calculated on the basis of a multiplicand of £24,000 a year and an appropriate multiplier taken from the Ogden Tables, the court may instead order the defendant to pay the claimant periodical payments of £2,000 per month for life. The figure of £2,000 will be automatically updated in line with inflation under s. 2(8) or (9).

There are a lot more detailed provisions in ss. 2A and 2B of the Damages Act 1996, especially with regard to ensuring that continuity of payment is reasonably secure.

Although it was expected that periodical payments orders under s. 2 would quickly become the norm, rather than lump sum awards, this has not happened. There are considerable difficulties in making such orders, because of the complexity of the calculations, the amount of evidence required, and the level of detail required in the court's order. At first, it was thought that periodical payments would only be likely to be more appropriate in high-value cases, and that lump sum awards would continue to be the norm in ordinary low-to-average-value claims. However, that was partly because claimants were reluctant to seek periodical payments, especially for the cost of care. Since it seemed likely that such payments would be index-linked to the Retail Prices Index (RPI) under s. 2(8), while all the indications are that medical and caring costs rise at well above the rate of inflation, such an order did not seem to be in the claimant's best interests.

However, in *Flora v Wakom (Heathrow) Ltd* [2006] 4 All ER 982, the Court of Appeal held that index-linking to RPI under s. 2(8) was merely a default position to be followed when the order for periodical payments did not name any other index. There was nothing in the Act to suggest that RPI would be the normal index, or that exceptional circumstances had to exist before any other index was used. The courts were therefore free under s. 2(9), if it was just to do so, to adopt any index that was consistent with the principle that the claimant should be fully compensated for their loss, only resorting to the RPI under s. 2(8), when there was no better or fairer alternative.

The matter was considered again by the Court of Appeal in *Thompstone v Tameside and Glossop Acute Services NHS Trust* [2008] 2 All ER 553. The court reinforced the principle that the judge has an absolute discretion to depart from the RPI as a default index and adopt any other index that on the evidence is appropriate, giving overriding consideration to the claimant's needs (as opposed to preferences), giving very little weight to the defendant's preference, and seeking to achieve as far as possible 100 per cent compensation. It seems likely that, as a result of this decision, periodical payments orders will become a lot more frequent, certainly in high-value cases.

10.19 Structured settlements

10.19.1 What is a structured settlement?

Parties negotiating a settlement are not bound to follow the conventional methods if they agree not to do so. They may agree not to use actuarial calculations; they may agree to take full notice of inflation. In particular, unlike a judge, they are not obliged to agree to a once-and-for-all lump sum. They may instead negotiate a structured settlement. A structured settlement is an agreement between the parties that damages will not be paid as a conventional lump sum, but rather in the form of future annual payments and future lump sums. It is not so much an alternative way of quantifying damages, as an alternative way of paying them.

A structured settlement is not something that can be imposed by a court, but must be agreed between the parties. It can then be approved by the court and incorporated into a *Tomlin* order if necessary. The first case in which a judge approved a structured settlement was reported in July 1989 (*Kelly v Dawes*, reported as a news item in *The Times*, 27 September 1990) and since then there has been an increasing number of such settlements.

The result of an effective structured settlement is likely to be that the claimant's needs are better provided for, that the claimant actually receives more money over their lifetime than with a conventional award, and that the defendant's insurer actually pays less.

10.19.2   When is a structured settlement appropriate?

The cases in which structured settlements have been agreed are all ones in which the claimant has suffered serious or very serious injuries, which have resulted in substantial ongoing future loss for the rest of the claimant's life. A structured settlement is of little use where there has been a complete recovery, or when the claimant's injuries are relatively minor, or where the bulk of damages are to compensate the claimant for past losses.

But where the future losses are high, because the claimant will need continued care or incur significant expense throughout their life, there is a real advantage to be gained in a structured settlement, provided the extra cash generated is not outweighed by the costs of setting up and administering the settlement. At present, this is likely to be where the sum to be paid by way of future instalments is more than about £100,000, though this threshold has already come down from £200,000 and is likely to fall further as the various professionals involved in the implementation of structured settlements gain more experience.

10.19.3   How does a structured settlement work?

10.19.3.1   Investment of a conventional lump sum

When seriously injured claimants receive a conventional lump sum award, it is intended to compensate not only for the expense already incurred, but also to pay for all future needs. Claimants will therefore doubtless invest a proportion of it and use both capital and income to provide for themselves for the rest of their lives.

The most effective way of ensuring that the money does not run out before death, the time of which may be very uncertain, is to purchase an index-linked annuity from a life office. The claimant will then receive an annual sum representing both capital and interest, which will rise in line with inflation. But the claimant will receive the annual sum net of income tax.

10.19.3.2   The structured settlement

The essence of a structured settlement is that the defendant's insurers will pay some of the damages as an immediate lump sum to provide for the claimant's past and present needs, and will use the rest of the sum available to purchase an index-linked annuity for the claimant. The life office will pay the insurers the annual sum net of tax, but the insurers can recover that tax from HM Revenue and Customs (HMRC), under an agreement made between the Revenue and the Association of British Insurers in 1987, and will then pay the claimant the gross value of the annuity. The claimant thus receives more.

Because the claimant receives more a year than they would if they were to receive a conventional lump sum, it is possible for the defendant's insurers to negotiate a lower sum to be invested in the purchase of the annuity. Both sides therefore gain from the arrangement. If the parties focus on the claimant's annual needs, and then find out how much it would cost to purchase an index-linked annuity at that annual value for the claimant's life, they may well then be able to agree on that sum as the lump sum to be invested (after making allowance for costs). That sum is likely to be lower than the sum that would otherwise have been awarded.

10.19.4   How is a structured settlement worked out?

The first step will be to work out or agree the value of the claimant's claim for damages on a conventional basis. Only if that sum is known can either side appreciate the benefits of a structured settlement, or whether those benefits will outweigh the costs.

There will then need to be a cooperative effort between a considerable number of people: the claimant's and the defendant's legal advisers, the defendant's insurers, a life assurance broker, an accountant with experience of structured settlements, a life office, and HMRC. If the claimant is a patient, the Court of Protection will also be involved, and if a claim has been commenced, the approval of the court is likely to be required.

Only if the scheme is in the correct form will HMRC agree to treat the future instalments as payments of capital, and so refund the tax deducted by the life office.

The costs and professional fees are what make the setting up and administration of a structured settlement more expensive than a simple payment of damages. However, provided the sum to be invested is large enough, these are likely to be offset by the tax savings and lower capital sums involved.

10.19.5   The importance of maintaining flexibility

Although the central ingredient of a structured settlement is the purchase of an annuity on the claimant's behalf by the defendant's insurers, there are many other ingredients that may be appropriate in individual cases. The claimant's situation and likely future needs will be different in every case, and it is important that the settlement should be *structured* to cater for any possible or anticipated changes in the claimant's situation.

For example, a structure which involves gradually increasing annual sums may be required if the claimant's condition is likely to deteriorate. Another way of dealing with this might be to purchase two annuities, one deferred. It may be wise to build in occasional future lump sums to enable the claimant to cope with specific anticipated events in the future.

The value of a structured settlement will be lost if it becomes an inflexible form of settlement revolving solely around the annuity.

10.19.6   Recovery of benefits

Structured settlements do not prevent recovery of benefits. Section 18 of the Social Security (Recovery of Benefits) Act 1997 enables regulations to be made setting out how benefits to be recovered will bite into sums paid by way of structured settlements and periodical payments ordered by the court under s. 2 of the Damages Act 1996. The Social Security (Recovery of Benefits) Regulations 1997 (SI 1997/2205) make the necessary provisions.

Quantum of damages for a fatal accident

11.1 Rights of claim

11.1.1 Introduction

There are two rights of action that arise as a result of a fatal accident, both statutory. These are an action on behalf of the deceased's estate under the Law Reform (Miscellaneous Provisions) Act 1934 (LR(MP)A 1934) and a claim on behalf of the deceased's dependants under the Fatal Accidents Act 1976 (FAA 1976). These Acts were both amended by the Administration of Justice Act 1982 (AJA 1982) (ss. 3 and 4), as a result of which (except in the case of deaths occurring before 1983) the two *rights* of action are entirely separate from each other and there is no overlap between them, though both will be founded on the same *cause* of action.

11.1.2 The right of action under LR(MP)A 1934

11.1.2.1 Section 1 of the Act

Section 1 of LR(MP)A 1934 provides:

(1) Subject to the provisions of this section, on the death of any person after the commencement of this Act all causes of action subsisting against or vested in him shall survive against, or, as the case may be, for the benefit of, his estate. Provided that this subsection shall not apply to causes of action for defamation.

*(1A) The right of a **person** to claim under section 1A of the Fatal Accidents Act 1976 (bereavement) shall not survive for the benefit of his estate on his death.*

(2) Where a cause of action survives as aforesaid for the benefit of the estate of a deceased person, the damages recoverable for the benefit of the estate of that person—

    (a) shall not include—

        (i) any exemplary damages;

        (ii) any damages for loss of income in respect of any period after that person's death;

    (b) ...

    (c) Where the death of that person has been caused by the act or omission which gives rise to the cause of action, shall be calculated without reference to any loss or gain to his estate consequent on his death, except that a sum in respect of funeral expenses may be included.

11.1.2.2 The effect of the provision

The effect of this provision is that any cause of action which the deceased had at their death can still be pursued by their estate, so that if the deceased could have sued the defendant in negligence for damages for personal injury, their estate may step into their shoes and do so instead. The deceased's estate may claim damages in respect of any losses that had already accrued at the moment of death. So the estate will recover any damages that the deceased could have recovered if they had instituted a claim for personal injury, pursued it, and obtained judgment, all in the instant before death; with the important exception of the damages the deceased could have recovered for loss of earnings in their lost years, which are not recoverable (s. 1(2)(a)(ii)), and the further exception of any claim for bereavement the deceased may have had (s. 1(1A)).

11.1.2.3 Dependants' losses not recoverable

The estate *cannot* recover damages in respect of any loss *resulting* from death, or which arises because of the death (s. 1(2)(c)). Such loss is not the deceased's own loss, but is their dependants' loss, and can be recovered by them under FAA 1976. The single exception to this is funeral expenses, where the funeral was paid for out of the deceased's estate.

11.1.2.4 Damages form part of deceased's estate

The claimant(s) will be the deceased's personal representative(s)—the executor(s) or administrator of the estate. Damages recovered under LR(MP)A 1934 form part of the estate and will be distributed in accordance with the terms of the deceased's will or the rules of intestacy.

11.1.3 The right of action under FAA 1976

11.1.3.1 Sections 1–5 of the Act

Sections 1–5 of the FAA (as amended) provide:

> **1 Right of action for wrongful act causing death**
>
> (1) If death is caused by any wrongful act, neglect or default which is such as would (if death had not ensued) have entitled the person injured to maintain an action and recover damages in respect thereof, the person who would have been liable if death had not ensued shall be liable to an action for damages, notwithstanding the death of the person injured.
>
> (2) Subject to section 1A(2) below, every such action shall be for the benefit of the dependants of the person ('the deceased') whose death has been so caused.
>
> (3) In this Act 'dependant' means—
>> (a) the wife or husband or former wife or husband of the deceased;
>> (aa) the civil partner or former civil partner of the deceased;
>> (b) any person who—
>>> (i) was living with the deceased in the same household immediately before the date of the death; and
>>> (ii) had been living with the deceased in the same household for at least two years before that date; and
>>> (iii) was living during the whole of that period as the husband or wife or civil partner of the deceased;
>> (c) any parent or other ascendant of the deceased;
>> (d) any person who was treated by the deceased as his parent;
>> (e) any child or other descendant of the deceased;
>> (f) any person (not being a child of the deceased) who, in the case of any marriage to which the deceased was at any time a party, was treated by the deceased as a child of the family in relation to that marriage;
>> (fa) any person (not being a child of the deceased) who, in the case of any civil partnership in which the deceased was at any time a civil partner, was treated by the deceased as a child of the family in relation to that civil partnership;
>> (g) any person who is, or is the issue of, a brother, sister, uncle or aunt of the deceased.
>
> (4) The reference to the former wife or husband of the deceased in subsection (3)(a) above includes a reference to a person whose marriage to the deceased has been annulled or declared void as well as a person whose marriage to the deceased has been dissolved.
>
> (4A) The reference to the former civil partner of the deceased in subsection (3)(aa) above includes a reference to a person whose civil partnership with the deceased has been annulled as well as a person whose civil partnership with the deceased has been dissolved.
>
> (5) In deducing any relationship for the purposes of subsection (3) above—
>> (a) any relationship by marriage or civil partnership shall be treated as a relationship by consanguinity, any relationship of the half blood as a relationship of the whole blood, and the stepchild of any person as his child, and
>> (b) an illegitimate person shall be treated as the legitimate child of his mother and reputed father.
>
> (6) Any reference in this Act to injury includes any disease and any impairment of a person's physical or mental condition.

1A Bereavement

(1) An action under this Act may consist of or include a claim for damages for bereavement.

(2) A claim for damages for bereavement shall only be for the benefit—

    (a) of the wife or husband or civil partner of the deceased;

    (aa) of the cohabiting partner of the deceased; and

    (b) where the deceased was a minor who was never married or a civil partner—

        (i) of his parents, if he was legitimate; and

        (ii) of his mother, if he was illegitimate.

(2A) In subsection (2) 'cohabiting partner' means any person who—

    (a) was living with the deceased in the same household immediately before the date of the death; and

    (b) had been living with the deceased in the same household for at least two years before that date; and

    (c) was living during the whole of that period as the wife or husband or civil partner of the deceased.

(3) Subject to subsection (5) below, the sum to be awarded as damages under this section shall be £15,120.

(4) Where there is a claim for damages under this section for the benefit of both the parents of the deceased, the sum awarded shall be divided equally between them (subject to any deduction falling to be made in respect of costs not recovered from the defendant).

(5) The Lord Chancellor may by order made by statutory instrument, subject to annulment in pursuance of a resolution of either House of Parliament, amend this section by varying the sum for the time being specified in subsection (3) above.

2 Persons entitled to bring the action

(1) The action shall be brought by and in the name of the executor or administrator of the deceased.

(2) If—

    (a) there is no executor or administrator of the deceased, or

    (b) no action is brought within six months after the death by and in the name of an executor or administrator of the deceased, the action may be brought by and in the name of all or any of the persons for whose benefit an executor or administrator could have brought it.

(3) Not more than one action shall lie for and in respect of the same subject matter of complaint.

(4) The plaintiff in the action shall be required to deliver to the defendant or his solicitor full particulars of the persons for whom and on whose behalf the action is brought and of the nature of the claim in respect of which damages are sought to be recovered.

3 Assessment of damages

(1) In the action such damages, other than damages for bereavement, may be awarded as are proportioned to the injury resulting from the death to the dependants respectively.

(2) After deducting the costs not recovered from the defendant any amount recovered otherwise than as damages for bereavement shall be divided among the dependants in such shares as may be directed.

(3) In an action under this Act where there fall to be assessed damages payable to a widow in respect of the death of her husband there shall not be taken into account the remarriage of the widow or her prospects of remarriage.

(4) In an action under this Act where there fall to be assessed damages payable to a person who is a dependant by virtue of section 1(3)(b) above in respect of the death of the person with whom the dependant was living as husband or wife or civil partner there shall be taken into account (together with any other matter that appears to the court to be relevant to the action) the fact that the dependant had no enforceable right to financial support by the deceased as a result of their living together.

(5) If the dependants have incurred funeral expenses in respect of the deceased, damages may be awarded in respect of those expenses.

(6) Money paid into court in satisfaction of a cause of action under this Act may be in one sum without specifying any person's share.

4 Assessment of damages: disregard of benefits

In assessing damages in respect of a person's death in an action under this Act, benefits which have accrued or will or may accrue to any person from his estate or otherwise as a result of his death shall be disregarded.

5 Contributory negligence

Where any person dies as the result partly of his own fault and partly of the fault of any other person or persons, and accordingly if an action were brought for the benefit of the estate under the Law Reform (Miscellaneous

Provisions) Act 1934 the damages recoverable would be reduced under section 1(1) of the Law Reform (Contributory Negligence) Act 1945, any damages recoverable in an action under this Act shall be reduced to a proportionate extent.

11.1.3.2 Basis of the right of action and recovery

The right of action under FAA 1976 arises because of, and only because of, the deceased's death. It belongs to the dependants, who can recover damages in respect of the loss they have suffered as a result of the deceased's death. They can recover nothing of what the deceased themselves could have recovered: such damages belong to the estate and are recoverable under LR(MP)A 1934. They can recover nothing in respect of losses they would have suffered even if the deceased had survived: such damages could either have been recovered by the deceased, or the dependants will have a separate right of action in their own name (e.g. in respect of their own personal injuries).

11.1.3.3 Who brings the claim?

Although the right of action belongs to the dependants and damages will in the end be paid to them, the claim is prima facie brought by the executor or administrator of the estate (s. 2(1)). Not every de facto dependant has a right of action, only those brought within the Act by s. 1(3), (4), and (5).

11.1.3.4 Dependants must have a cause of action

The dependants must also have a cause of action. For the purposes of their claim, they 'borrow' whatever cause of action the deceased had, the same cause of action which survives for the benefit of the estate under LR(MP)A 1934. If the deceased had no cause of action, the dependants also have none.

11.1.4 The relationship between the two claims

There will almost invariably be a claim under both Acts, with the same claimant and using the same cause of action to establish liability. Beyond that there is no longer any connection between the claims. Each is for different damages on behalf of different persons. The only exception to this is funeral expenses, which can be recovered under either Act, depending on who paid for the funeral (LR(MP)A 1934, s. 1(2)(c); FAA 1976, s. 3(5)).

Before 1983, there was a symbiotic relationship between the two claims: the estate could recover damages in respect of the deceased's earnings over the lost years, which could only be assessed by reference to the FAA award; and damages awarded to the estate under LR(MP)A 1934 usually had to be taken into account in quantifying the FAA award. This relationship was, thankfully, effectively severed by AJA 1982, which inserted s. 1(2)(a)(ii) into LR(MP)A 1934 and rewrote FAA 1976, s. 4, but you need to be aware of this history to understand reported cases.

11.1.5 Where the deceased has commenced a claim for personal injury

It is not uncommon that an injured person commences a claim for personal injury, but dies before the claim is complete, or soon after damages are awarded. What is the position then of the estate and dependants?

11.1.5.1 Where the claim is still pending

In these circumstances, the estate has the right to continue the claim under LR(MP)A 1934, but that will not be sufficient in itself because the estate cannot recover any damages in respect of the deceased's future loss of earnings (s. 1(2)(a)(ii)). It is these damages which would have provided for the dependants after the deceased's death and so the dependants will need to recover their loss by a separate claim under FAA 1976. This is a distinct claim, and may be pursued even when the deceased's personal injury claim has been discontinued (*Reader v Molesworth Bright Clegg* [2007] 3 All ER 107).

11.1.5.2   Where the deceased had recovered damages in full

The dependants' claim under FAA 1976 is likely to be limited to bereavement and funeral expenses. The damages awarded to the deceased were intended to restore them to the position they would have been in had they not been injured (including, if necessary, damages for lost earnings in the lost years), and so the dependants cannot show that they have suffered any additional loss of dependency as a result of the death.

11.1.5.3   Where the deceased had recovered provisional damages

The position is now governed by s. 3 of the Damages Act 1996, which provides:

> (1) *This section applies where a person—*
>> (a) *is awarded provisional damages; and*
>> (b) *subsequently dies as a result of the act or omission which gave rise to the cause of action for which the damages were awarded.*
>
> (2) *The award of the provisional damages shall not operate as a bar to a claim in respect of that person's death under the Fatal Accidents Act 1976.*
>
> (3) *Such part (if any) of—*
>> (a) *the provisional damages; and*
>> (b) *any further damages awarded to the person in question before his death,*
>
> *as was intended to compensate him for pecuniary loss in a period which in the event falls after his death shall be taken into account in assessing the amount of any loss of support suffered by the person or persons for whose benefit the claim under the Fatal Accidents Act 1976 is brought.*
>
> (4) *No award of further damages made in respect of that person after his death shall include any amount for loss of income in respect of any period after his death.*
>
> (5) *In this section 'provisional damages' means damages awarded by virtue of subsection (2)(a) of section 32A of the Senior Courts Act 1981 or section 51 of the County Courts Act 1984 and 'further damages' means damages awarded by virtue of subsection (2)(b) of either of those sections.*
>
> (6) *Subsection (2) above applies whether the award of provisional damages was before or after the coming into force of that subsection; and subsections (3) and (4) apply to any award of damages under the 1976 Act or, as the case may be, further damages after the coming into force of those subsections.*
>
> (7) *. . .*

Section 3 sorts out a problem that existed when a claimant commenced a claim for personal injury, and was awarded provisional damages, but then died. In such a case, the dependants were precluded from suing for their lost dependency under FAA 1976 and it was unclear whether the estate, under LR(MP)A 1934, could continue the personal injury claim and seek a further award under s. 32A of the Senior Courts Act 1981 (SCA 1981), including damages for lost earnings in the 'lost years'.

Section 3 adopts the sensible solution. In such cases, a barrier is brought down on the personal injury claim—the estate can only seek a further award under s. 32A in respect of the deceased's losses up to the date of death. Instead, the dependants can bring a claim under FAA 1976 for their lost dependency, but account must be taken of any damages the deceased received as compensation for losses in the period after death and which the dependants may have inherited.

11.2   Quantification of damages under LR(MP)A 1934

11.2.1   General principles

Since the claim is basically a claim by the deceased for damages for personal injury, damages will be quantified upon the same principles and in the same stages as a personal injury claim. The total sum, however, is likely to be relatively small, since there is no claim for any future loss. It is only likely to be substantial if there was a significant delay between accident and death.

11.2.2   Special damages

Special damages are likely to be small, unless they include, for example, damage to a motor vehicle, lost earnings between accident and death, or funeral expenses. On the other hand, there will usually be some special damages sufficient to justify a claim under LR(MP)A 1934, even if nothing else is recoverable under this Act.

11.2.3   General damages

The only head of general damages recoverable is pain and suffering and loss of amenity, and then only if there was a significant period of time between the accident and death. If death was instantaneous, or nearly instantaneous, nothing is recoverable, since any pain and suffering is in reality part of the death (*Hicks v Chief Constable of South Yorkshire* [1992] 1 All ER 690). If the deceased was unconscious between the accident and death, damages for loss of amenity only are recoverable. The longer the deceased survived after the accident, the greater the award will be, but it is still going to be small compared to what would be given to an injured claimant who has a lifetime's pain, suffering, and loss of amenity ahead of them.

11.2.4   Deductions

The award will be subject to any deductions that would have been made in a personal injury claim (see **10.14**).

11.2.5   Contributory negligence

The award will be subject to any reduction for the deceased's contributory negligence (see **10.15**).

11.2.6   Interest

Interest will be added as in personal injury claims (see **10.16**).

11.2.7   Recovery of benefits

The compensator will be liable to repay benefits under the Social Security (Recovery of Benefits) Act 1997, but will be able to reduce the damages paid to the deceased's estate in the usual way (see **10.17**).

11.3   Quantification of damages under FAA 1976

11.3.1   The sole head of damages

With the single and simple exception of damages for bereavement (s. 1A), the loss recoverable under FAA 1976 is wholly financial loss, and what is being assessed is the value of the 'dependency', which is the only head of damages. The dependency consists of:

- the amount the deceased would have applied to the benefit of their dependants;
- any additional expense the dependants have been put to as a result of the death; and
- any additional losses the dependants have suffered as a result of the death over the period for which they would have remained dependent.

If the dependants have suffered loss of income, it does not matter what the source of that income was. So, for example, if the deceased's only source of income was State benefits, and as a result of their death those benefits are no longer payable, the dependants can recover their loss to the extent that the lost benefits were applied to their support (*Cox v Hockenhull* [1999] 3 All ER 577).

11.3.2   The seven-stage process

The quantification of damages is a seven-stage process:

Stage 1:   Calculate the pre-trial loss.
Stage 2:   Assess the future loss.

Stage 3:   Add lump sums.

Stage 4:   Add bereavement.

Stage 5:   Contributory negligence.

Stage 6:   Add interest.

Stage 7:   Apportion between dependants.

11.4   Stage 1: calculate the pre-trial loss

11.4.1   What is the pre-trial loss?

The pre-trial loss is the total value of the dependency so far; that is, from the date of death to the date of trial (or the date of settlement, or the date on which you are advising as to quantum). It is roughly equivalent to the special damages in a personal injury claim.

Like special damages it is, in theory at least, precisely ascertainable: in reality a great deal of estimation may be required, but it should still be quantified as accurately as possible.

11.4.2   The approaches that may be adopted

The basic principle of assessment is exactly the same in every case: the court is trying to put a value on each of the three aspects of the dependency (see **11.3.1**). However, the items that will be included within the dependency vary according to the relationship between the dependants and the deceased, and so the court's approach to the assessment tends to vary as well. There are three main approaches that may be adopted:

(a) the item-by-item approach—where each item of loss and expenditure is added up one by one;

(b) the earnings-minus-living-expenses approach—where the court looks at what the deceased earned, takes away personal living expenses, and assumes whatever is left to be the dependency;

(c) the conventional percentage approach—where the court assesses the likely dependency as x per cent of the deceased's earnings.

These three approaches are not mutually exclusive: the court may use a little of each. Where the claim is for the death of a breadwinner, however, the modern practice is to use the conventional percentage approach almost exclusively.

Whether an item is to be included or not is simply a matter of evidence. What approach the court adopts to assessment will also depend on the evidence, or the lack of it, and convenience. It is easiest to look at the assessment process according to certain, well-established types of claim, but there is no rule that any item of dependency can only be recovered in certain types of claim; it is recoverable wherever it exists. Do not therefore be misled into generalisation: every case depends on its own facts.

The value of the dependency is fixed at the moment of death. There is a good illustration of this principle in the case of *Paramount Shopfitting Co Ltd v Rix* [2021] EWCA Civ 1172. In that case the deceased ran a business with his own work and skill, out of which he supported his wife. After his death she took over the running of the business with the help of her son, and it was now more profitable than it had been during her husband's lifetime. The defendant argued that therefore she had suffered no loss of dependency, as she was now better off than she would have been if her husband had not died. However, the court held that she was entitled to a dependency valued at the date of death, and the increased income from the business thereafter should not be taken into account.

11.4.3   Claims for the death of a breadwinner

11.4.3.1   The item-by-item approach

This approach is only likely to be possible, but will be the most reliable, where there exist detailed household accounts. It is, however, difficult to persuade a judge to use this approach, rather than the quick and simple conventional percentage approach.

Where the deceased was the breadwinner, and the dependants are their spouse and children, or just their spouse, the items likely to form a part of the dependency are:

- housekeeping money;
- rent, mortgage instalments;
- council tax;
- repairs, maintenance, decoration, cleaning;
- fuel bills;
- telephone and internet costs;
- clothing;
- school fees;
- costs of running a car, travel, and transport;
- holidays and outings;
- gifts, entertainments, sports and leisure, pets;
- pocket money;
- insurance;
- digital subscriptions;
- one-off purchases, for example furniture, computers, luxury goods.

11.4.3.2   Deductions

From each of these, any element of the deceased's own living expenses must be deducted (housekeeping money, for example, is likely to include an element of their food and keep). Expenditure that is joint—that is, where there is no saving as a result of death (e.g. rent, fuel bills)—does not have to be reduced. (Note the difference between this rule and the rule for living expenses in a lost years claim: see **10.10.7.2**.)

11.4.3.3   Other losses

To this add any other losses. For example, a widow(er) may, as a result of their spouse's death, have had to give up work for a while and so have lost earnings; the family may have lost other free perks from the deceased's employers. Also add any loss of benefits in kind or additional expenditure the dependants have been put to. Common examples are:

(a) the value of DIY work around the home, where the deceased used to carry out repairs and improvements, which can have considerable annual value (take care to include only the value of the work, not the cost of materials);

(b) the value of fruit and vegetables grown by the deceased in the garden or allotment;

(c) the loss of use of a company car for private purposes;

(d) the loss of other employee's perks: for example health insurance, free goods or services, school fees.

11.4.3.4   Total the loss

If the evidence of the family's expenditure is on a weekly basis, calculate the amount per week and multiply by the number of weeks between death and trial. Similarly, if the accounts are monthly. Some benefits in kind are more easily valued on an annual basis, in which case bring them in at that stage.

11.4.3.5   The 'earnings-minus-living-expenses' approach

Where the evidence is not complete enough for the item-by-item approach, the court may use the quicker and easier earnings-minus-living-expenses approach. Take the deceased's net earnings (weekly or monthly) and deduct their personal living expenses. Living expenses under FAA 1976 include all that the deceased spent exclusively on themselves, both needs and pleasures, but *not* a portion of any expenditure for the joint benefit of the deceased and their dependants. What is left will be the prima facie value of the dependency, to which can be added any additional losses or benefits in kind. This approach is now almost entirely obsolete.

11.4.3.6 The conventional percentage approach

These days, the court is likely to save time and trouble by going directly to a conventional percentage figure. This is 75 per cent where the dependants are spouse and child(ren) or 67 per cent where the spouse is the sole dependant; that is, the court assesses the dependency as 75 per cent or 67 per cent of the deceased's net earnings (see *Harris v Empress Motors Ltd* [1984] 1 WLR 212).

11.4.3.7 Arriving at a percentage

Whatever approach has been used, it is usually helpful to express the dependency as a percentage of the deceased's net earnings. This makes it easier to take account of any likely increases in pay over the pre-trial period.

11.4.3.8 Changes in the value of the dependency between death and trial

These must be taken into account—both actual changes and changes that would have occurred but for the deceased's death. The most obvious example of an actual change is a child who becomes financially independent at some point during the pre-trial period. The child's dependency obviously comes to an end, or at least is very substantially reduced from that time.

But there is usually likely to be some evidence of changes that would have occurred as well. The deceased's earnings might well have increased during the pre-trial period through pay rises, promotion, career moves, building up a business, etc. If this is the case, the question arises, would the dependency have increased as well? If there would have been no increase, simply value the dependency as at the date of death and multiply by the appropriate number of weeks or months. If the increase in the dependency would have been in proportion to the increased earnings, the percentage approach is helpful. The dependency continues to be the same fixed percentage of the increased net pay. But if there would have been an increase proportionally greater or smaller than the increase in earnings, then an adjustment will have to be made to the percentage. Similar considerations apply if the deceased's earnings would have fallen during the pre-trial period, for example as a result of retirement. In the absence of evidence to the contrary, assume that the dependency would have increased or decreased in line with the change in income, applying the fixed percentage.

11.4.3.9 Deceased's savings

If the deceased saved regularly, the money may or may not be part of the dependency, according to how they would eventually have spent it. If some of it would eventually have been applied to the dependants' benefit, then a suitable portion of the savings can be added to the weekly or monthly dependency. If savings were irregular, it may be more appropriate to add a lump sum at Stage 3.

11.4.3.10 Widow's remarriage or prospects of remarriage

These are not to be taken into account in assessing her dependency (FAA 1976, s. 3(3)). However, if the claim is for the death of a breadwinner wife, the husband's remarriage or prospects must be taken into account.

11.4.3.11 Widow's earnings or earning capacity

Where a widow has lost earnings as a result of the death, this loss forms part of the dependency. Where a widow was a working woman both before and after the death, clearly her earnings are irrelevant to her claim under FAA 1976. A non-working widow's earning capacity can usually be ignored (*Howitt v Heads* [1973] QB 64). If she goes out to work after her husband's death, her earnings should probably be ignored, even if she would not have worked but for her husband's death: the earnings are simply a realisation of her earning capacity, not a gain resulting from the death.

11.4.3.12   Family living beyond its means

It may be that the amount the deceased was spending on their dependants was more than they were earning. If this was being paid for out of capital, then the dependency can be valued at its actual rate, but account must be taken of how long the capital would have lasted. If it was being subsidised by a loan or overdraft, the value of the dependency will be reduced to take account of the amount the deceased would have had to repay.

11.4.4   Claim for the death of a wife/mother

11.4.4.1   Preliminary note

This section is written on the basis that the breadwinner spouse was a husband and father, and the dependent spouse was a wife and mother, as this is what is almost invariably the case in the relevant case law. However, the same principles apply if the roles are reversed.

11.4.4.2   The items forming the dependency

Where the wife was working, the value of her contribution to the family expenses can be quantified in much the same way as for a husband (see **11.4.3**). But whether the wife was working or not, the main item in the dependency is likely to be the value of her services as a wife and mother. There may also be a claim for lost benefits in kind—where the wife did DIY work, or made clothes for her husband and children, for example.

11.4.4.3   Assessing the value of a wife's services

The value of a wife's services is not easily quantified, and is very much in the court's discretion. At the very least, it is likely to be assessed as the cost of employing a home help and/or a housekeeper. Nevertheless, there is a good argument for looking at a wife's services more broadly and valuing each service she performed for the family, not just those that a housekeeper can perform (*Regan v Williamson* [1976] 1 WLR 305). Where the wife was in full-time employment, the amount of time she had available to care for the family is less than it would have been if she were a full-time housewife, and so the value of her services is proportionally less (see, e.g., *Cresswell v Eaton* [1991] 1 All ER 484). Where the wife was a poor mother, the value of her services will be lower (see *Stanley v Saddique* [1992] QB 1).

If the husband has reasonably given up his work in order to stay at home and look after the home and children, then the dependency may be assessed on the basis of the husband's lost earnings (*Mehmet v Perry* [1977] 2 All ER 529). Similarly, if a relative has given up full-time work in order to be able to do so, the dependency may be based on that relative's loss of earnings. But if the relative's full-time care replaces only part-time care by the mother, a discount will need to be made (*Cresswell v Eaton*).

Where a father is the defendant being sued in respect of his wife's death, and he has given up work to look after their children, the value of the services he is providing should be set off against the value of the mother's services lost, so as to reduce the children's claim (*Hayden v Hayden* [1992] 4 All ER 681).

11.4.5   Claims for the death of a parent

Where the dependants claiming are simply the children, either because both parents were killed simultaneously, or the family was a one-parent family, or because the surviving parent has no claim since they are the defendant being sued, some special considerations apply.

To the extent that the children's claim is for the death of their father who provided financial support, it can be quantified as in **11.4.3**. To the extent that the children's claim is for the death of their mother, it cannot be quantified simply on the basis of the cost of employing a housekeeper, for they have lost more than this. It may be appropriate to assess the cost of providing a full-time nanny for the children, if they are young, and this loss is recoverable even if no nanny in fact needs to be employed because the children are being looked after by a relative (*Hay v Hughes* [1975] QB 790). Alternatively, particularly when the children are older, it may be more appropriate to assess their loss on the basis of the cost of providing a foster home; at the very least some account must be taken of the fact that they will not need a nanny throughout the period of their dependency (*Spittle v Bunney* [1988] 3 All ER 1031).

If the children have been legally adopted since the death of their parents, their dependency from the date of adoption will be limited to any difference between the value of the dependency provided by their father (assuming he was the breadwinner) and that provided by their adoptive father. The care provided by the adoptive mother replaces that provided by the natural mother and so a claim for the value of their mother's services comes to an end on adoption (see *Watson v Willmott* [1991] 1 QB 140).

11.4.6   Claims for the death of a child

Where the claim is made by parents in respect of the death of their child, the dependency is likely to be assessed item by item and to be fairly small. If the child was adult, and was in fact supporting their parents at the date of death, account must be taken of the likelihood that this support would have diminished or ceased if they left home or got married. In the case of a minor child, the parents have lost little more than the chance that they might have received some support in the future, plus the occasional gifts.

11.4.7   Claims by other dependants

A claim by a cohabitee or civil partner can be assessed in the same way as a claim by a husband or wife; claims by grandchildren or grandparents, if appropriate, in the same way as claims by children and parents. In the case of other relatives, the claim is likely to be very small and can be quantified item by item.

11.4.8   Funeral expenses

Having calculated all the rest of the pre-trial loss, add funeral expenses if they were incurred by the dependants.

11.5   Stage 2: assess the future loss

The future loss to the dependants consists of (a) the loss of dependency over the remainder of the deceased's working life; and (b) the loss of dependency flowing from the deceased's pension, where the dependants would have received any benefit from it. A widow cannot, however, recover in respect of her husband's retirement pension if she has instead received a widow's pension under the same scheme from her husband's employers (*Auty v National Coal Board* [1985] 1 All ER 930).

11.5.1   The multiplicand

The multiplicand is the annual value of the dependency as at the date of trial. It takes account of all the items dealt with under Stage 1, and includes the three aspects of the dependency (see **11.3.1**). It also takes account of any likely changes in the value of the dependency that would have occurred between the date of death and the date of trial. Everything that has been said in **11.4** with regard to the dependency applies equally to the future loss. The multiplicand is the answer to the question, 'What is the annual loss as at today's date?'

Although a widow's earning capacity can usually be ignored, it may need to be taken into account where, for example, a widow has lost her job because of her husband's death, but can reasonably be expected to resume work soon (*Cookson v Knowles* [1977] QB 913). A widow's future earnings or earning capacity may also be taken into account in assessing the value of the children's dependency where they are claiming for the death of their father (*Dodds v Dodds* [1978] QB 543).

As with personal injury claims, there is likely to be a growing tendency to make split awards in the future. Where there is evidence that the deceased's earnings would have increased at some point after death, the court will achieve the most accurate assessment of the dependency by taking separate multiplicands for separate periods, and apportioning the multiplier. There may be a single multiplicand for the whole of the period of dependency (the deceased's and the dependants' joint lives), or the period may be divided into the years before retirement, and the pension years, with the first multiplicand being based on the deceased's net earnings and the second based on the annual value to the dependants of the deceased's pension.

11.5.2   The multiplier

11.5.2.1   Introduction

As in personal injury cases, the multiplier is not a real number of years, but is discounted to take account of accelerated receipt and contingencies. It represents the number of years for which the dependency would have lasted. This is prima facie the deceased's and dependants' joint lives. In the case of a deceased husband and widow, the dependency would have lasted until the first of them died.

Following the decision in *Wells v Wells* [1998] 3 All ER 481, it would seem incongruous not to take an actuarial approach to the quantification of damages. The conventional approach was even more intuitive and unscientific in fatal accident claims than it was in personal injury claims. But *Wells v Wells* was concerned only with personal injury claims, and until very recently no more modern approach had been approved by the Court of Appeal or House of Lords/Supreme Court. However, a major change was made by the Supreme Court in *Knauer v Ministry of Justice* [2016] 4 All ER 897 (see later in **11.5.2.8**). Section D to the Explanatory Notes to the Ogden Tables explains how the tables can be used to quantify damages in fatal accident cases with reasonable accuracy. This approach results in a much more complicated calculation than that in personal injury cases, too complex to reproduce here, but it is likely that moves towards this method will now be made. Section D does contain several worked examples, to which you can refer if necessary.

11.5.2.2   The conventional approach

Before *Wells v Wells*, the multiplier was selected in a manner very similar to that used in personal injury cases (see **10.10.3.2**). The period being measured was the period from the deceased's date of death (not the date of trial as in personal injury claims) and the end of the period of dependency. This had to be estimated taking into account the deceased's age, the age(s) of the dependant(s), the deceased's likely retirement age, the deceased's and dependants' life expectancy, and a large number of other variables such as job security, promotion prospects, and health. A fairly substantial discount was made for contingencies and uncertainties, and a discount for accelerated receipt based on a notional rate of return on investment of 4–5 per cent. Tables in *Kemp & Kemp* enabled comparisons with previous cases to be made, and the final result was usually a rough and ready approximation.

11.5.2.3   The conventional approach today

Even without an approved new method of calculation, it seems that the conventional approach is too out of date to use. At the very least, a discount rate of minus 0.25 per cent should surely be used, which renders tables of multipliers in pre-*Wells* cases useless, and necessitates reference to the Ogden Tables. This would suggest that the following method might be appropriate.

First, decide whether to assess the dependencies for the pre-retirement years and the pension years together or separately. If they are to be taken together, then use Ogden Tables 1 and 2, looking under the minus 0.25 per cent column. In the case of a husband and wife, look up the multiplier for a male of the age the deceased was at the date of his death, and the multiplier for a female of the age the widow was at that date: whichever is the smaller figure will be the correct multiplier to take as a starting point.

Alternatively, the working years and retirement years may be calculated separately. Use Tables 3–14 to find the multiplier for the dependency up to the deceased's retirement, and

Tables 15–26 for the pension loss after that date. A widow is entitled to recover a sum in respect of her husband's retirement pension where she would have derived a benefit from it.

11.5.2.4   Discount for contingencies

The multiplier found by the method described in **11.5.2.3** must then be discounted to take account of contingencies other than mortality, as in personal injury cases. There is no easy guide as to how this should be done. It is necessary to take account of contingencies relating not only to the deceased, but also to all of the dependants. The result in the past was a rather bigger discount than might have been made in a personal injury case. This ought logically to continue to be the case. In the absence of anything better, since this is still a less-than-accurate method of selecting the multiplier, it is likely that the courts will continue to make the conventional discount of 10 per cent, at least, making further adjustments as necessary.

11.5.2.5   Other contingencies

There are a large number of other contingencies which may have a specific effect, and cause the multiplier to be adjusted upwards or downwards:

(a) Evidence of the deceased's actual life expectancy. If this can be shown to be plainly lower or greater than average for a person of the deceased's age, an adjustment may need to be made.

(b) The possibility of divorce. The fact that at the deceased's death the marriage was showing signs of collapse does not mean that the dependency is automatically reduced: a dependant's right to financial support continues even after divorce, and so the dependency might well have been unaffected. However, the possibility also exists that after divorce the deceased would have remarried, which might have resulted in a diminished level of support for the first spouse, so the risk of divorce may be a relevant factor (*Martin v Owen* The Times, 21 May 1992).

(c) Children's ages and marriage prospects. The court should be aware of how long any children would have remained dependent on the deceased. The actual dependency of young children is obviously longer than that of adult or nearly adult children, and may be a factor affecting the multiplier. Similarly, the age at which the children will cease full-time education and become financially independent is material. These matters will certainly make a difference when the children alone are the dependants. However, they will not normally do so when there is also a dependent spouse. When children cease to be dependent, the usual expectation is that the dependency of the spouse simply increases proportionately, so no adjustment needs to be made.

(d) The fact that a cohabitee had no enforceable right to financial support by the deceased (FAA 1976, s. 3(4)). This must result in some reduction in the multiplier, since the cohabitee's dependency was less secure than that of a spouse.

11.5.2.6   Factors which do not affect the multiplier

The following factors do not affect the choice of multiplier to be used in assessing future loss:

(a) A widow's remarriage or prospects of remarriage. This is expressly excluded from consideration by FAA 1976, s. 3(3).

(b) The likelihood of future inflation (*Cookson v Knowles* [1979] AC 556). This is the same principle as for personal injury (see **10.10.3.13(a)**). The decision in *Hodgson v Trapp* (see **10.10.3.7**) must by implication apply also to claims under FAA 1976.

11.5.2.7   A single multiplier

Although there may be several dependants, nevertheless in the vast majority of cases the dependency has conventionally been assessed as a single sum, there being just one multiplier to take account of all the dependants' claims. This is because, if the deceased had a certain amount of money available to support any dependants, that sum would have been spread among them in some way or other, but would not have been affected overall by their individual needs. However, in an increasing number of cases, where the circumstances of the case seem to demand it, the court these days assesses the multiplier and multiplicand for each dependant separately, and indeed this is the approach recommended by the Ogden Tables.

11.5.2.8   The multiplier runs from the date of trial

Until very recently, the law required the multiplier in fatal accident cases, unlike personal injury cases, to run from the date of death, not the date of trial (*Graham v Dodds* [1983] 2 All ER 953). This meant that the period from death to trial had to be deducted from the multiplier chosen. So if, for example, the multiplier selected was 16, and the period from death to trial was three years nine months, the multiplier applied to the future loss would be 12.25. This could result in some injustice where there was a long period between death and trial, which might almost swallow up the entire multiplier.

So, the Supreme Court in *Knauer v Ministry of Justice* [2016] UKSC 9, [2016] 4 All ER 897 determined that previous authority should be departed from, and the multiplier should in future run from the date of trial, as in personal injury cases. It is too early to say what effect this will have in practice, but the clear intent is to better compensate the dependants of the deceased, so that the end result is likely to be an increase in the overall sums awarded. It is also probable that courts will start to follow the approach advocated in section D of the Explanatory Notes to the Ogden Tables.

11.5.3   Split awards

As suggested in **11.5.1**, it may become increasingly common for the court to make split awards when calculating the future dependency. It may value different periods of the dependency with a different multiplicand, it may take the working years separately from the pension years, it may take the dependency of each dependant separately. The manner of calculation will be as explained in **10.10.4**.

11.5.4   Taking Stages 1 and 2 together

When advising on the quantum of damage, if there is no evidence as to how the dependency would have increased after death, then there is little point in assessing the pre-trial loss and the future loss separately. Simply value the dependency as at the date of trial and apply a suitable multiplier from that date.

11.6   Stage 3: add lump sums

There can be added to the total sum arrived at thus far any lump sums which it can be shown that the dependants would have benefited from in the future—for example, the deceased's savings or capital.

11.7   Stage 4: add bereavement

The spouse or civil partner of the deceased or the parents of an unmarried child (but no other dependants) can recover damages for bereavement, quantified as a fixed lump sum (FAA 1976, s. 1A). The sum can be specified from time to time by the Lord Chancellor and is currently £15,120 (but £12,980 for causes of action accruing from 1 April 2013 to 30 April 2020). The parents of an unmarried child cannot recover damages for bereavement where that child was under 18 at the date of injury but over 18 on the date of death (*Doleman v Deakin* The Times, 30 January 1990).

Although FAA, s. 1 treats a person who has cohabited with the deceased as a spouse for two years or more as a dependant, that does not extend to s. 1A, enabling them to recover damages for bereavement. However, the Court of Appeal in *Smith v Lancashire Teaching Hospitals* [2017] EWCA Civ 1916 found this to be in breach of Articles 8 and 14 of the European Convention on Human Rights and made a declaration of incompatibility under the Human Rights Act 1998.

11.8 Stage 5: contributory negligence

The total sum quantified so far must be reduced if there has been a finding of contributory negligence by the deceased. Take off the appropriate percentage.

Contributory negligence by a dependant must also be taken into account, but only as regards that dependant's share of the dependency (an example of a situation where the dependency for each dependant will have to be assessed separately).

11.9 Stage 6: add interest

Interest will be awarded by the court under SCA 1981, s. 35A. By s. 35A(2), the award is prima facie mandatory, unless there are special reasons for the contrary. The guidelines for the award of interest were laid down by *Cookson v Knowles* [1979] AC 556.

- Interest is awarded on the pre-trial loss from the date of death to the date of trial at half the 'appropriate rate'. For the meaning of 'appropriate rate', see **10.16.2**.

- Interest is awarded on damages for bereavement at the full appropriate rate from the date of death to the date of trial (*Prior v Hastie* [1987] CLY 1219).

- No interest is awarded on damages for future loss.

There is no discretion to vary these rules under normal circumstances (*Fletcher v A Train & Sons Ltd* [2008] 4 All ER 699).

When advising on the quantum of damages, it is not usual to make any attempt to calculate interest.

11.10 Stage 7: apportion between dependants

Although there is usually only one multiplier and damages are awarded as a single lump sum, the court must indicate how that sum is to be divided up between the dependants (FAA 1976, s. 3(2)). The apportionment must bear some relationship to the comparative value of each dependant's dependency, but does not have to be exact.

The only difficulties arise when apportioning between a widow and child(ren). The widow always gets the larger share, which will include the joint dependency of the family as a whole. The children, on the other hand, get all that is truly their share of the dependency, not just 'pocket money' (*Benson v Biggs Wall & Co Ltd* [1982] 3 All ER 300). The greater the number of children, the younger the children are, the larger their share. There is a table showing reported apportionment in *Kemp & Kemp* at para. 36-195.

Damages for bereavement are not, of course, apportioned.

11.11 Deductions

You might have expected Stage 5 to be 'make any necessary deductions', but it is not, because there are no deductions. This is the effect of FAA 1976, s. 4, which provides that any benefits which have accrued, or will accrue, to the dependants as a result of the deceased's death are to be disregarded. No deduction needs to be made, therefore, in respect of sums inherited from the estate, damages recovered under LR(MP)A 1934, widow's pension, widow's benefit, insurance money, charitable donations, or anything else, even where the result is that the dependants are better off than they would have been but for the death (see, e.g., *Pidduck v Eastern Scottish Omnibuses Ltd* [1990] 2 All ER 69 and *McIntyre v Harland & Wolff plc* [2007] 2 All ER 24). Nor can any deduction be made for the value of benefits in money's worth: for example, where a father's second wife is providing a higher standard of motherly services than the children's deceased mother ever did (*Stanley v Saddique* [1992] QB 1). However, s. 4 does not prevent the value of a father's services being set off against the value of the deceased mother's services (*Hayden v Hayden* [1992] 4 All ER 681).

Where children were cared for by their mother, who died in the fatal accident, and their care has been taken over by their father, who but for the accident would probably have made no contribution to their welfare, the father's care is a benefit to be disregarded under s. 4. However, the damages received by the children for the loss of their mother's services are held on trust for the father, who is to be reimbursed for the services he has provided and will provide in the future (*ATH v MS* [2003] QB 975).

11.12   No recovery of benefits

A person making a compensation payment under the FAA 1976 is not liable to repay benefits under the Social Security (Recovery of Benefits) Act 1997 (Social Security (Recovery of Benefits) Regulations 1997 (SI 1997/2205), reg. 2(2)(a)).

Real property law remedies

12.1 Possession orders

12.1.1 The primary remedy

The primary remedy available to the owner of land is repossession by means of an action for recovery of land. The procedure which an owner must follow to obtain possession will vary depending on whether the occupier is occupying the land or premises as a tenant, a licensee, or as a trespasser. A fairly complicated statutory procedure must be followed if the occupier has occupation rights which are protected by the Housing Act 1985, the Housing Act 1988, the Housing Act 1996, the Rent Act 1977, or the Landlord and Tenant Act 1954. The procedure for most actions for possession of premises is governed by Pt 55 or Pt 56 of the Civil Procedure Rules 1998 (CPR).

12.1.2 Possession claims against trespassers

CPR, Pt 55 provides the landowner with a rapid remedy against anyone who occupies the land without their consent. The landowner need only issue a claim form claiming possession. Particulars of claim need to be filed and served with the claim form stating the claimant's interest in the land and the circumstances in which it was occupied without licence or consent (see CPR, PD 55A, para. 2.6). If the claimant does not know the name of the person in occupation, the claim can be brought against 'persons unknown', in addition to any named defendants (CPR, r.55.3(4)). The majority of cases should be commenced in the county court, but a small number of exceptional cases may justifiably be issued in the High Court (see *Practice Note Chancery Division and Queen's Bench Division of the High Court in London, Possession Claims Against Trespassers*, 30 November 1996). Where the proceedings have been commenced against persons unknown, service is effected by attaching the claim form, particulars of claim, and any evidence to the main door or other relevant part of the property, and if practicable, by also inserting copies of those documents through the letter box. Five clear days, or two clear days in the case of non-residential premises, after service of the claim form, the court may make an order for possession. Where the occupier entered as a trespasser, the court has no power to suspend the order. However, even in this situation, the court may have to consider whether it is proportionate to make a possession order bearing in mind any rights a defendant may have under the European Convention on Human Rights (ECHR), Articles 10 and 11 (see *Mayor of London v Hall* [2010] EWCA Civ 817; *City of London Corp v Samede* [2012] EWCA Civ 160). The order will be effective even though the landowner cannot discover the names of the occupiers. This procedure is used most commonly against squatters, although it is also available against ex-licensees. The court has power under the Housing Act 1980, s. 89 to suspend an order against certain ex-licensees (e.g. an occupier under a restricted contract or secure tenancy) for 14 days, or up to six weeks in cases of exceptional hardship.

12.1.3   Interim possession orders

Section III of CPR, Pt 55 contains rules that enable a landowner to obtain a possession order against occupiers who entered the land as trespassers. An application for an interim possession order (IPO) can only be made if the conditions in CPR, r.55.21 are satisfied and the only claim that is made is for possession of premises (it is not available if possession is claimed together with another remedy, such as damages). The application must be made within 28 days of the date on which the claimant knew or reasonably ought to have known that the defendant was in possession (CPR, r.55.21). The claimant applies for an IPO by a claim form (N5), and application notice in N130, supported by a witness statement in Form N133. The claimant must serve the claim form and all relevant documents listed in CPR, r.55.23 within 24 hours of the issue of the application. The court may make an order not less than three days after the date of issue of the application. The order commands the occupier to vacate the premises within 24 hours of service and informs the occupier of the date for a hearing in the presence of both parties not less than seven days later. In deciding whether to make an IPO, the court will have regard to whether the claimant is prepared to give the undertakings set out in CPR, r.55.25(1). If an IPO is made, it must be served by the claimant within 48 hours after it is sealed, together with the claim form and the written evidence in support (CPR, r.55.26). Under the Criminal Justice and Public Order Act 1994, s. 76 it is a criminal offence for such an occupier to remain in the premises after this 24-hour period has elapsed and the occupier may be arrested by a uniformed constable without warrant. The 1994 Act also imposes criminal liability on a landowner who obtains an interim possession order by knowingly or recklessly making false or misleading statements (s. 75). The IPO will expire on the date of the hearing of the claim, but at the hearing the court can make a final order for possession, dismiss the possession claim, and give directions for the claim for possession to continue or enforce any of the claimant's undertakings (CPR, r.55.27). The defendant is given power to set aside an IPO under CPR, r.55.28.

12.1.4   Damages for trespass

A landowner may claim damages against a trespasser for trespass. Such a claim will include compensation for the use and occupation of the land, which is normally awarded on the basis of the current letting value of the property. Where the occupier is a former tenant and holds over as a tenant at will/on sufferance, this part of the claim is generally known as a claim for 'mesne profits', becoming damages for trespass when the owner terminates the tenancy at will/on sufferance, for example by demanding possession.

12.1.5   Landlord and tenant—determination of the lease

Where premises are let to a tenant, a landlord may be able to regain possession of the premises by determining the lease. There are a number of ways in which a lease can be determined including:

(a) *Surrender.* The tenant may surrender the lease before the end of the contractual term. A surrender at law must be made by deed (Law of Property Act 1925 (LPA 1925), s. 52), but in equity a surrender will be effective if it is made in writing and satisfies LPA 1925, s. 53(1)(a). An agreement to surrender in the future must comply with s. 2 of the Law of Property (Miscellaneous Provisions) Act 1989. An implied surrender by operation of law may be effected without writing: *Proudreed Ltd v Microgen Holdings plc* [1996] 1 EGLR 89. An implied surrender is based on the principle of estoppel (*Allen v Rochdale BC* [2000] Ch 221; *Artworld Financial Corp v Safaryan* [2009] L & TR 20; *Padwick Properties Ltd v Punj Lloyd Ltd* [2016] EWHC 502 (Ch)). The conduct of both the landlord and the tenant must unequivocally amount to an acceptance that the tenancy has ended. In all cases, the surrender by the tenant will only end the tenancy if the landlord assents. The tenant remains liable for any breach of covenant that occurred before the surrender took place.

(b) *Determination by exercising an option or a break clause in the lease.* Determination of the tenancy is likely to be effective only if there is strict compliance with the terms of the clause, although minor errors will not necessarily invalidate a notice if a reasonable recipient would not be misled by them: *Mannai Investment Co v Eagle Star Assurance Co* [1997] AC 749 (HL). In determining whether a notice complies with the terms of a break clause in the lease, the first stage is to consider what, as a matter of true construction, the notice says, and the second stage is to determine whether the notice complies with the terms of the lease (see *Siemens Hearing Instruments Ltd v Friends Life Ltd* [2014] EWCA Civ 382).

(c) *Notices to quit.* Periodic tenancies need to be determined by a notice to quit, which expires at the end of a current period, and the relevant period will depend on whether it is a yearly, monthly, weekly, or quarterly periodic tenancy. Care needs to be taken to ensure that the notice to quit expires on the correct date and that it gives the correct length of notice. Note too that in most cases (for excluded tenancies and licences, see the Protection from Eviction Act 1977, s. 3A) where premises are let as a dwelling, a notice to quit will not be valid unless it is given not less than four weeks before the date on which it is to take effect (Protection from Eviction Act 1977, s. 5), and such notices need to be in writing and contain prescribed information (see Notice to Quit (Prescribed Information) Regulations 1988 (SI 1988/2201)).

(d) *Forfeiture.* This is only available where the lease expressly provides for forfeiture by re-entry for breach of covenant or where there is a breach of a condition. Procedures vary according to the type of covenant breached. In general terms, forfeiture can be effected by physical re-entry or by service of proceedings although, in practical terms, most forfeitures take place by the issue and service of court proceedings because s. 2 of the Protection from Eviction Act 1977 provides that while any person is lawfully residing in the premises or any part of them, it shall not be lawful to enforce a right to forfeiture otherwise than by proceedings in court. If there is someone present in the premises, but not 'residing' there, effecting forfeiture by physical re-entry may amount to an offence under s. 6 of the Criminal Law Act 1977. There are also statutory restrictions on forfeiture where the tenant is insolvent, where a right of forfeiture is being exercised for non-payment of rent or service charges, where the tenant is claiming the right to enfranchise under the Leasehold Reform Act 1967 or the Leasehold Reform, Housing and Urban Development Act 1993 (as amended by the Leasehold Reform Amendment Act 2014, with effect from 13 May 2014), and where a restraint order has been made under the Proceeds of Crime Act 2002 and this applies to the tenancy of the premises.

   (i) *Non-payment of rent.* The landlord must make a formal demand for rent unless either the lease permitting forfeiture contains a provision dispensing with this requirement—every well-drafted lease will contain such a provision—or, in some circumstances, when there is more than six months' rent in arrears (see s. 210 of the Common Law Procedure Act 1852). Where a landlord wants to forfeit for non-payment of residential ground rents in respect of long leases (i.e. terms exceeding 21 years), they must first serve notice in accordance with s. 166(1) or, if applicable, s. 167 of the Commonhold and Leasehold Reform Act 2002 and the regulations made pursuant to that Act.

   (ii) *Breach of other covenants.* In most cases, other than non-payment of rent, LPA 1925, s. 146 requires a notice to be served which: (a) specifies the breach complained of; (b) if the breach is remediable, requires the tenant to remedy it; (c) where the landlord wants financial compensation, calls on the tenant to pay it.

Where the breach is remediable, a reasonable time must elapse between service of the s. 146 notice given to remedy the breach and the right of re-entry or forfeiture. What is a reasonable time will depend on the facts of each case.

   In respect of long leases, there are also restrictions imposed on the service of a s. 146 notice by ss. 166–172 of the Commonhold and Leasehold Reform Act 2002. Restrictions on the ability to forfeit a residential tenancy for non-payment of service charges are imposed by the Housing Act 1996, s. 81 as amended by the Commonhold and Leasehold Reform Act 2002, s. 170. Section 81 of the Housing

Act 1996 prevents landlords from exercising a right of re-entry or forfeiture of premises let as a dwelling for a failure to pay service charges unless the amount claimed is either admitted or agreed by the tenant or it has been determined by the court or an arbitral tribunal (in which case, forfeiture proceedings cannot be commenced until 14 days after the determination).

In the case of long leases of a dwelling, a landlord cannot exercise a right of re-entry or forfeiture for a tenant's failure to pay rent or service charges or administration charges unless the amount unpaid exceeds £500, or the amount has been outstanding for more than three years (s. 167 of the Commonhold and Leasehold Reform Act 2002).

Where a landlord wishes to forfeit for breach of a repairing covenant, the landlord must first serve a s. 146 notice and give the tenant a reasonable time to remedy the disrepair. A right of re-entry or forfeiture cannot be enforced until a time reasonably sufficient to enable the repairs to be done has elapsed from the date of service of the notice on the tenant (see s. 18 of the Landlord and Tenant Act 1927). Additional requirements for forfeiture for disrepair are imposed where the Leasehold Property Repairs Act 1938 applies.

An assured tenancy cannot be terminated by forfeiture (see Housing Act 1988, s. 5, as amended on 1 November 2016) and special provisions apply to the forfeiture of secure tenancies (see Housing Act 1985, s. 82).

Forfeiture will not be available if the breach has been waived, for example by the landlord accepting rent with knowledge of the breach unless the breach is a continuing one, for example of a repairing covenant, in which case forfeiture for past breaches may be waived but the landlord can still forfeit in respect of any future breaches.

Even if the landlord takes steps to forfeit the lease, a tenant may still apply to the court for relief from forfeiture. This will be granted more readily in the case of forfeiture for non-payment of rent than where the forfeiture is for breach of some other covenant. The jurisdiction to grant relief derives from the Common Law Procedure Act 1852, s. 210, the Senior Courts Act 1981, s. 38 or the County Courts Act 1984, ss. 138–140 (non-payment of rent), or under LPA 1925, s. 146(2) (all other breaches).

12.1.6 Possession claims against residential occupiers

Generally, when a landlord is dealing with a tenant or a licensee of a dwelling house, regard should be had to the provisions of the Protection from Eviction Act 1977 (as amended by the Housing Act 1988) which:

(a) impose criminal penalties for the unlawful eviction and harassment of residential occupiers (Protection from Eviction Act 1977, s. 1(3));

(b) create a statutory tort for harassment and unlawful eviction (Housing Act 1988, ss. 27 and 28) (damages for this statutory liability are assessed in accordance with ss. 27 and 28 of the 1988 Act);

(c) require a notice to quit served in respect of a tenancy to be of at least four weeks' duration and to contain prescribed information;

(d) require the service of a four-week notice containing prescribed information to terminate most periodic licences;

(e) require a landlord to effect forfeiture through court proceedings rather than by a physical re-entry onto the land;

(f) in the case of residential tenants and licensees not entitled to the statutory protection given by the Rent Act 1977 (protected tenants), the Housing Act 1985 (secure tenants), or the Housing Act 1988 (assured tenants), restrict the owner to recovering possession through court proceedings;

(g) provide a civil claim for damages against a landlord who unlawfully evicts a residential occupier in breach of these requirements.

Further, in the case of tenants entitled to statutory protection under the Rent Act 1977 (protected tenants), the Housing Act 1985 (secure tenants), or the Housing Act 1988 (assured tenants), the landlord is restricted in the exercise of their common law rights to possession, for example on service of a notice to quit (thus ending the tenancy), and will normally have to also obtain a court order for possession by proving the existence of statutory grounds for possession, and where a possession order has been obtained, the tenancy will end when the order is executed (see Housing Act 1988, s. 5 and Housing Act 1985, s. 82). Note, however, that most assured tenancies granted after 28 February 1997 will take effect as assured shorthold tenancies, and as such will be subject to an easily satisfied mandatory ground for possession (Housing Act 1988, s. 19A, inserted by the Housing Act 1996, s. 96). In *McDonald v McDonald* [2016] UKSC 28, the Supreme Court held that the Housing Act 1988, the Protection from Eviction Act 1977, and the Housing Act 1980 contained provisions showing how the courts should balance the Article 8 rights of residential tenants and the rights of private-sector landlords to the peaceful enjoyment of their property when the tenancy ended. Therefore, when hearing a possession claim by a private-sector landlord against a residential occupier, the court should not consider the proportionality of the eviction under Human Rights Act 1998, s. 6(1) and the ECHR, Article 8(2).

12.1.7 Possession claims against business occupiers

Security of tenure for business tenants is achieved by the Landlord and Tenant Act 1954. The effect of this Act is that once the contractual term has been determined, the tenancy continues automatically unless and until it is terminated by a method laid down by the Act (s. 24). The tenancy can be terminated by the landlord serving a notice in the prescribed form under s. 25 or by the tenant serving a notice requesting a new tenancy under s. 26 (note that a tenant has also the right to terminate the continuation tenancy by serving a notice under s. 27). After a s. 26 or a s. 25 notice has been served, either the landlord or the tenant is entitled to apply to the court for an order terminating the tenancy and/or the grant of a new tenancy as applicable under s. 24(1). The tenant is entitled to a new tenancy unless the landlord can make out one of the grounds of opposition set down in s. 30 of the Act. Even if the landlord successfully opposes the grant of a new tenancy by making out one of the grounds of opposition, the tenant may be entitled to compensation for disturbance, depending on which ground is established.

12.2 Additional remedies

As between landlord and tenant, various additional remedies are available.

12.2.1 Damages for breach of covenant

Actions for breach of covenant typically involve: breaches of covenants to insure; covenants for quiet enjoyment; covenants against assignment or subletting (which may be subject to statutory modification by the Landlord and Tenant Act 1927, s. 19(1), (1A)–(1E) and the Landlord and Tenant Act 1988); covenants against alteration or change of use; or, most commonly of all, covenants to repair the premises.

The measure of damages for breach of covenant will be assessed on the usual basis. However, as the claim is usually framed in contract, damages for distress or exemplary damages are not usually available (*Perara v Vandiyar* [1953] 1 WLR 672). Nevertheless, in some cases, such as a breach of the covenant of quiet enjoyment, it is possible to plead the claim in tort as well, in which case exemplary and aggravated damages can also be awarded.

In relation to repairing covenants, a tenant may achieve some degree of protection under LPA 1925, s. 147 by which they can apply to the court for relief from liability in respect of certain internal decorative repairs. Tenants can also gain some protection if the Leasehold Property (Repairs) Act 1938 applies to the lease, in that in the circumstances prescribed by that Act, the landlord cannot enforce its right to damages for breach of covenant except with the leave of the court, which will only be granted if the landlord proves one or more of the circumstances set out in s. 1(5).

Where a tenant sues a landlord for breach of a repairing covenant, the amount of damages they may recover is prima facie the difference in value of the premises to the tenant measured by the condition the premises are now in compared to the condition they would have been in had the landlord complied with their obligations (*Hewitt v Rowlands* [1924] LJKB 1080; and see also *Calabar Properties Ltd v Stitcher* [1984] 1 WLR 287; *Grand v Gill* [2011] 1 WLR 2253; and *Moorjani v Durban Estates Ltd* [2015] EWCA Civ 1252). Damages can include the cost of repair and redecoration, and alternative accommodation costs, as well as general damages for inconvenience and discomfort.

Where the landlord is seeking damages for disrepair, a 'statutory ceiling' is imposed on the amount they can recover by s. 18(1) of the Landlord and Tenant Act 1927, which provides that damages should not exceed the amount (if any) by which the value of the reversion is diminished owing to such breach, and no damages at all can be recovered if, at or shortly after termination of the tenancy, the premises are to be pulled down or altered in such a way as to render the repairs valueless. This statutory ceiling often operates to prevent the landlord recovering damages for the cost of remedying the disrepair if this is more than the diminution in value of the reversion. However, it only applies to a claim for damages, not to a debt claim.

12.2.2 Action to enforce payment and distress

Up until 6 April 2014, a landlord could enforce payment of rent either by an action for the money or by distress (seizing the tenants' goods). However, the common law right to distrain for arrears of rent was abolished, with effect from that date, by s. 71 of the Tribunals, Courts and Enforcement Act 2007. This Act introduces a new procedure for taking control of goods for rent arrears recovery in leases of commercial premises (see Pt 3 and Schs 12 and 13). By s. 81, a landlord of commercial premises can also exercise a statutory right to recover rent from a sub-tenant.

12.3 Mortgagee's remedies

There are a number of options open to a mortgagee when mortgagors fail to keep up with instalment payments under a mortgage.

12.3.1 Action for money due

The mortgagee can sue for the money due once the date for repayment has arrived. This is unlikely to be the best remedy for the mortgagee, unless perhaps the mortgagor has substantial other assets and the value of the property mortgaged has fallen below the amount owed. More often, the mortgagee will use other powers to enforce a sale and then, if there is a shortfall, sue the mortgagor for the difference.

An action by a mortgagee for arrears of interest is statute-barred after six years from the date on which the interest became due (Limitation Act 1980, s. 20(5)). Actions to recover the principal are statute-barred after 12 years from the date on which the right to receive the principal debt accrued (Limitation Act 1980, s. 20(1)). However, the mortgagee will still be entitled to enforce the security by an order for sale or by an order for possession, and it can recover the debt out of the proceeds of sale, even if an action to recover the principal and/or interest is statute-barred: *West Bromwich Building Society v Wilkinson* [2005] 1 WLR 2303; *National Westminster Bank plc v Ashe* [2008] 1 WLR 710. Note too that time may run again for recovery of the debt if the mortgagor acknowledges it (Limitation Act 1980, ss. 29, 30; *Bradford & Bingley v Cutler* [2008] EWCA Civ 74). Even if a claim for mortgage interest is statute-barred, a mortgagor who wishes to redeem the mortgage will only be allowed to do so if the whole debt and any outstanding interest is paid: *Holmes v Cowcher* [1970] 1 WLR 834.

12.3.2 Foreclosure

A mortgagee can apply for an order for foreclosure when the mortgagor is in breach of obligations under the mortgage which provide that the principal sum secured under the mortgage becomes due. If a foreclosure order is granted and made absolute, the legal title to the mortgaged property is automatically transferred to the mortgagee and the mortgagor loses all rights in the property. So, in a subsequent sale of the property any proceeds above the amount owed under the mortgage can be retained by the mortgagee. Section 88(2) and (6) of LPA 1925 deals with the effect of foreclosure on freehold mortgages, and mortgages of leasehold property are governed by LPA 1925, s. 89(2).

Because of the potential unfairness to the mortgagor, foreclosure is a procedurally cumbersome remedy and there is uncertainty for the mortgagee. An order can be set aside even after it has been made absolute (*Campbell v Holyland* (1877) 7 ChD 166). Also, the mortgagor can apply for, and the court readily grants, an order substituting an order for sale for the foreclosure (LPA 1925, s. 91(2)). This means that the mortgagor receives any proceeds of sale left after discharging the debt, costs, and expenses of sale in the same way as if the mortgagee had exercised its powers of possession and sale in the first place. For these reasons, foreclosure is rarely used by institutional lenders.

12.3.3 Possession

Many institutional lenders' standard mortgage conditions give the mortgagee a right to possession of the property without there being any breaches of the mortgagor's obligations. It is very rare that a mortgagee will enforce the right to possession without there being arrears of repayment instalments and without having obtained an order for possession. The right to possession is usually exercised only as a preliminary step to exercising the power of sale. However, in a potentially far-reaching decision, *Ropaigealach v Barclays Bank plc* [1999] 3 WLR 17, the Court of Appeal reasserted the view that as mortgagees were entitled to possession, they could use their common law right to re-enter the property peacefully and take possession, and that s. 36 of the Administration of Justice Act 1970 had not extinguished this right. However, even if a mortgagee can take possession without a court order, it would be unwise to do so if the premises are occupied in case the mortgagee is charged with committing an offence under s. 6 of the Criminal Law Act 1977.

If there are arrears outstanding, the mortgagee will usually be granted an order for possession unless (rarely) the mortgagor successfully applies to have the mortgage set aside for, for example, undue influence or (much more commonly) if the mortgagor can claim the benefit of one of the statutory regimes which provide some protection (see Administration of Justice Act 1970, s. 36 for residential occupiers of 'dwelling houses' or the Consumer Credit Act 1974, as amended by the Consumer Credit Act 2006, for commercial or residential 'regulated agreements').

Under s. 36 of the 1970 Act, possession will be suspended if the mortgagor can satisfy the court that the arrears on the instalments due (not the principal sum secured) are likely to be paid, or breach of any other obligation is remedied, within a 'reasonable time'. If so, then under s. 36(2) and (3), the court may adjourn the proceedings, or stay or suspend execution of a judgment or order for possession, or postpone the date for delivery of possession, for such period or periods as the court thinks reasonable, and subject to such conditions in relation to payment of the mortgage instalments or the remedying of any default as the court thinks fit. For examples of the operation of these provisions, see *Jameer v Paratus AMC* [2012] EWCA Civ 1924, *Zinda v Bank of Scotland plc* [2012] 1 WLR 728, and *Deutsche Bank Suisse SA v Khan* [2013] EWCA Civ 1149.

Section 8 of the Administration of Justice Act 1973 enlarged the protection given to a mortgagor by s. 36 of the 1970 Act. It provides that where the mortgagor is allowed to repay the principal debt by instalments, but there is a provision for accelerated payment (e.g. in the event of demand or default in the payment of one or more instalments), then the amount 'due' for the purposes of s. 36 is limited to the amount of the instalments in arrears, rather than the full amount due under the mortgage.

What amounts to a reasonable time will depend on the facts of each case; it can include the time it would take for the mortgagor to sell the property to discharge the arrears (*Target Home Loans Ltd v Clothier & Clothier* [1993] 25 HLR 48). However, the court order must define the period of postponement or suspension of possession because there is no power under s. 36 to postpone possession for an indefinite period. In deciding what is a reasonable period, the court can take the remaining term of the mortgage as its starting point (*Cheltenham and Gloucester Building Society v Norgan* [1996] 1 WLR 343). The court has power to exercise its discretion under s. 36 more than once to grant a variation or an extension of a time period set initially (*LBI HF v Stanford* [2015] EWHC 3130 (Ch)).

By the Mortgage Repossessions (Protection of Tenants etc.) Act 2010, lenders are required to give notice to occupiers and unauthorised tenants of residential premises which are subject to a mortgage if they intend to execute a possession order obtained against the borrower. The court, on the application of the tenant, can postpone the date for delivery of possession or suspend or stay execution of the order for a period not exceeding two months. By s. 2, lenders are required to give 14 days' notice to anyone in the property of their intention to execute a possession order that they have obtained.

12.3.4 Sale

The power of sale is the mortgagee's primary remedy, as it enables the mortgagee to sell the property and discharge the sums due out of the proceeds of sale. A power to sell is implied into every mortgage made by deed (LPA 1925, s. 101). The power of sale can be, and usually is, exercised without the need for a court order and this has been held to be not incompatible with the mortgagor's rights under the ECHR (see *Horsham Properties Group Ltd v Clark* [2009] 1 WLR 1255).

The exercise of that power is conditional upon any one of the following requirements being satisfied (see LPA 1925, s. 103):

(a) a notice requiring payment of the mortgage money has been served on the mortgagor and there has been a default for three or more months in the payment of part of it or all of it; or

(b) the interest payments must be two or more months in arrears; or

(c) there must be a breach of some provision of the mortgage deed other than the covenant for payment of the mortgage money or interest.

One advantage of a sale over foreclosure is that the power to sell is generally exercisable without a court order.

Once possession is obtained, it is not usually necessary to obtain a court order to sell the mortgaged property.

The mortgagee in possession owes the mortgagor a duty of care in relation to the property while in possession and in relation to carrying out the sale, although the extent of the duties is not entirely clear. There is a duty to take reasonable care to obtain a 'proper price', which effectively means 'the best price reasonably obtainable' (*Cuckmere Brick Co Ltd v Mutual Finance Ltd* [1971] Ch 949; *Garland v Ralph Pay & Ransom* [1984] 271 EG 106; *Parker-Tweedale v Dunbar Bank plc* [1991] Ch 12; *Downsview Nominees Ltd v First City Corp Ltd* [1993] AC 295; *Morgan v Lloyds Bank plc* [1998] 3 Lloyd's Rep 73; and *Glatt v Sinclair* [2011] EWCA Civ 1317).

In fixing the price, there will always be an acceptable margin of error and, in the absence of a specific purchaser willing to buy the property at a higher price, a mortgagee will not be in breach of its duty provided the price agreed falls within the acceptable bracket: see *Michael v Miller* [2004] 2 EGLR 141; *Freeguard v Royal Bank of Scotland (No 3)* [2005] EWHC 978 (Ch); and *Dean v Barclays Bank plc* [2007] EWHC 1390 (Ch). The same duties are imposed on a mortgagee selling chattels (*Alpstream AG v Pk Airfinance Sarl* [2015] EWCA Civ 1318; *Close Brothers Ltd v Ais (Marine) 2 Ltd* [2017] EWHC 2782 (Admiralty Court)).

In relation to timing, the power of sale can be exercised at any time, but the mortgagee must not sell without taking appropriate steps to secure the best available price at the time in question, and must ensure a proper exposure of the property to the market: *Predeth v Castle Phillips Finance Co Ltd* [1986] 279 EG 1355. Provided the mortgagee acts in good faith and fairly towards the mortgagor, there is no duty to wait until market conditions improve (see *Bank of Cyprus (London) Ltd v Gill* [1980] 2 Lloyd's Rep 51 and *Palk v Mortgage Services Funding plc* [1993] 2 WLR 415). See also *Bell v Long* [2008] 2 BCLC 706 and *AIB Group (UK) plc v Personal Representatives of James Aiken (Deceased)* [2012] NIQB 51.

Conduct of the sale can be given to the mortgagor (*Cheltenham and Gloucester plc v Booker* [1997] 29 HLR 634).

A mortgagee is entitled to recover all costs, charges, and other expenses which are properly incurred in the course of the sale or the attempted sale of the property (LPA 1925, s. 105). This is in addition to the principal debt and any interest due on that debt.

If a mortgagee is in breach of its duty to sell at a proper price, then it will be liable to the mortgagor for damages representing the difference between the actual sale price and the price the mortgagee could have obtained, or alternatively the debt owing to the mortgagee will be reduced by this amount.

An order for sale can also be made by the court under LPA 1925, s. 91, and this is primarily used by equitable mortgagees or chargees, or by the mortgagor (see *Toor v State Bank of India* [2010] EWHC 1097 (Ch)). The court also has power to vest the legal estate in the new purchaser (or the mortgagee) by virtue of s. 90 of the LPA 1925.

12.3.5   Appointment of a receiver

There is a power to appoint a receiver in the case of all mortgages made by deed (LPA 1925, s. 101). In the absence of a deed, a mortgagee may still apply, in appropriate cases, for a receiver to be appointed. An LPA receiver is deemed to be the agent of the mortgagor.

12.4   Order for sale under the Trusts of Land and Appointment of Trustees Act 1996

Trustees for the sale of land enjoy all the powers of an absolute owner of the land (Trusts of Land and Appointment of Trustees Act 1996, s. 6), although they must exercise those powers in the best interests of the beneficiaries under the trust. By s. 11 of the 1996 Act, beneficiaries entitled to an interest in possession in the land have the right to be consulted, so far as is practicable, in relation to the exercise of any function relating to land subject to the trust. Beneficiaries may also have a right to occupy the land in the circumstances set out in ss. 12 and 13 of the 1996 Act.

An application to the court for an order in relation to the trust can be made by any trustee of land or the proceeds of sale of the land, or by any person who has an interest in the property which is the subject of the trust (1996 Act, s. 14). Although this obviously includes beneficiaries, it is not limited to such persons. By s. 14(2), the court has power to make any order it thinks fit in relation to the exercise of the functions of the trustees, including an order relieving them of any obligation to obtain the consent of, or to consult, any person, or an order declaring the nature and extent of a person's interest in the property subject to the trust.

The factors that the 1996 Act require the court to take into account in deciding whether to order a sale are based on the case law which developed interpreting the old s. 30 of LPA 1925. Those principles are, to a large extent, codified in s. 15 of the 1996 Act, which provides that the matters to which the court should have regard include:

(a) the intentions of the persons who created the trust;

(b) the purposes for which the property subject to the trust is held;

(c) the welfare of any minor who occupies or might reasonably be expected to occupy any land subject to the trust as their home; and

(d) the interests of any secured creditor of any beneficiary.

The wishes and circumstances of any beneficiaries can also be taken into account in the circumstances set out in s. 15(2) and (3) of the 1996 Act.

Case law decided under s. 30 of the Law of Property Act 1925 should be treated with caution and may be of very limited value (*Mortgage Corp v Shaire* [2001] Ch 743). Where the application for sale is brought by the trustee in bankruptcy, s. 355A of the Insolvency Act 1986 sets out the factors that the court will take into account. There have been a great many cases which demonstrate how the courts apply these factors when considering the competing needs of the secured creditors against those of the bankrupt and their family. In some cases, an order for sale may be postponed where it would cause exceptional hardship to the bankrupt's family (see, e.g., *Martin-Sklan v White* [2007] BPIR 76 and *Re Haghighat* [2010] EWCA Civ 1521). An order for sale is likely to be made at the request of a creditor or trustee in bankruptcy of one beneficiary if there is sufficient equity in the property to enable the other beneficiary of the trust to buy another home (*Edwards v Bank of Scotland plc* [2010] EWHC 652 (Ch)). The court has power under s. 14 to order one beneficiary under a trust of land to sell or transfer their interest to another beneficiary (*Bagum v Hafiz* [2015] EWCA Civ 801). The court's wide powers under s. 14 also include the power to grant an extension of a lease to 999 years at a peppercorn rent if that accorded with the intention of the parties under the trust (*Kyaw v Claassen* [2015] EWHC 3337 (Ch); *Parkes v Wilkes* [2017] EWHC 1556 (Ch)).

12.5 Easement

Where there is an infringement of an easement, a claim for an injunction and/or damages may be brought. The claimant may also ask for a declaration as to the extent or scope of an easement (*Lomax v Wood* [2001] 1 All ER 80). In extreme cases, the remedy of abatement may be used (see *Lagan Navigation Co v Lambeg Bleaching, Dyeing & Finishing Co* [1927] AC 226). This is a self-help remedy usually consisting of removing the obstacle complained of.

12.6 Registered land

The usual remedy for people who claim they have suffered loss as a result of an omission of their interests in the records at the Land Registry is to apply for financial compensation from the Land Registry itself (Land Registration Act 1925). However, on 13 October 2003, the 1925 Act was repealed and replaced by the Land Registration Act 2002 (LRA 2002). The new Act provides for the appointment of an independent adjudicator.

If the loss is as a result of failure to register, rather than a mistake at the registry, there may be a professional negligence claim against those who handled any dealings with the interest.

An application can be made to rectify the register to ensure that for the future it includes the interest claimed (LRA 2002, Sch. 4). The court can make an order for alteration of the register to correct a mistake, bring the register up to date, or to give effect to any estate, right, or interest excepted from the effect of registration. The Registrar also has power to alter the register without a court order in the circumstances set out in Sch. 4, para. 5. It is unlikely that rectification would be ordered where the result would adversely affect the title of the registered proprietor unless the proprietor has caused or contributed to the error by fraud or negligence or there are other special circumstances which make it unjust not to rectify (LRA 2002, Sch. 4, paras 3 and 6).

Note that the LRA 2002 changed the position on adverse possession. After 13 October 2003, the Limitation Act 1980 applies to unregistered land only. The LRA 2002 applies to registered land—a squatter who has been in adverse possession for ten years may apply for registration in place of the registered proprietor (LRA 2002, Sch. 6).

12.7 Exercise

PROBLEM

Mr and Mrs Bowler had a joint mortgage with the Great and Good Building Society. They were two months in arrears in their instalment payments after they both had lost their jobs. At a hearing at the Kingswood County Court, they argued that they would be able to pay off the arrears within four years. The district judge rejected their defence and granted possession. The Bowlers moved in with relatives. The building society did not get an order for sale, but put the property up for sale straightaway. It has been on the market for about six months. The building society has just informed the Bowlers it has had an offer of £45,000 for the property, which it is likely to accept. The Bowlers paid £47,000 for the property in 2011. The mortgage was for £44,000. The Bowlers have just sought legal advice. They say they have been told by a friend who is an estate agent that the firm the building society is using has done very little to market the property and that if the property had been well marketed and looked after over the last six months it would have fetched over £48,000.

SOLUTION

- The Bowlers are out of time to lodge an appeal against the granting of the order for possession (14 days from the order being made) and it does not appear in any case that they would be able to show that no reasonable judge would have granted the order.
- The building society did not need to get an order to allow it to sell, as it could rely on its statutory power, or a power granted in the mortgage.
- The building society as mortgagee in possession does owe the Bowlers a duty of care. It is clear that it will be in breach if it does not take reasonable steps to protect the property from, for example, vandalism, but it does not have to repair, redecorate, etc. to make the property more attractive to potential buyers. The Bowlers may be able to argue that the building society should have rented the property out for the six months and so the property would have been better kept and rental income would have been received (*Brandon v Brandon* [1862] 10 WR 287). However, the building society might well be able to defend such a claim by saying that it was not 'wilful default' not to rent out the property because it might have made it more difficult to sell.
- There is a common law duty, and, in the case of a building society, a statutory duty to take 'reasonable care' to obtain the best price for the property (Building Societies Act 1986, Sch. 4, para. 1(1)(a); *Cuckmere Brick Co Ltd v Mutual Finance Ltd* [1971] Ch 949). On the facts known at present, it is unlikely that the Bowlers could obtain an injunction to prevent sale, as there is no clear breach of these duties. They could sue the building society for damages, but they would have difficulty both in establishing a breach and showing the measure of loss. The sale was put in the hands of an estate agent. Provided some efforts were made to market the property which were within the broad range of acceptable marketing strategies, it would be hard to show a breach of the duty of care by either the building society or the estate agent. The cases tend to support the view that the lender is not obliged to wait for the market to improve or take special steps to sell the property (*Predeth v Castle Philips Finance Co Ltd* [1986] 2 EGLR 144).
- If (which appears unlikely on present information) a claim succeeded, the damages the Bowlers would receive would be based on what they should have received from the sale if there had been no breach. As this is speculative, the court is traditionally conservative in estimating what price would have been achieved. They would have received the price less the costs of sale (which might have been higher) and the sums owed to the lender as well as the lender's costs. It is likely that if the proposed sale goes ahead, the Bowlers will still owe the building society some money. This shortfall would be taken into account in calculating damages.
- If the sale goes ahead and there is a shortfall, the building society can sue the Bowlers for that amount notwithstanding the sale. If they have no means, the building society may not think it worth pursuing the claim, at least in the short term.

13 Remedies in the law of trusts

13.1 Introduction

Students should note that the following outline is purely for general guidance, not least in that many academic courses emphasise basic principles rather than trust remedies. Such a brief account involves generalisations, and any remedy that appears appropriate must be fully researched for application to a particular case. This chapter is intended to provide a guide to approach and thought processes, rather than a comprehensive answer.

13.2 Identifying precisely what issues require to be resolved

In trying to decide which remedy is appropriate in a particular case, certain issues require to be resolved.

13.2.1 What is the problem?

- There is some doubt about whether a trust has arisen or the terms of a trust (see **13.3**).
- There is a trust, and the terms are clear, but there is doubt as to whether a particular action can be carried out (see **13.4**).
- There is a trust with clear terms, but something has been done which does not appear to be within the terms of the trust (see **13.5**).

13.2.2 Be clear as to the viewpoint from which you approach the problem

- From the position of the settlor.
- From the position of a trustee.
- From the position of a beneficiary.

Do note that for any of these you might be making or defending a claim.

13.2.3 Which court has jurisdiction?

- Trust matters are assigned to the Chancery Division, with proceedings commenced in the Business and Property Courts (Trusts and Probate List).
- County courts have jurisdiction in certain trust matters.

13.3 Doubts about the validity of the trust

Any difficulty as to whether a trust has arisen and, if so, what its terms are, is primarily a matter of substantive law. Consider the relevant substantive law to see if, on the facts of the case, a valid trust has or has not arisen and, if so, what its terms are.

If advising the settlor, your aim will be to avoid the need for recourse to any remedies by clarifying or altering any doubtful provisions. If the trust has been set up and is operating, the settlor may be able to make alterations if the trust instrument provides for this; otherwise, it is no longer the settlor's concern.

The trustees are at risk from future claims by beneficiaries, or potential beneficiaries, if they apply the trust funds in ways which, when challenged later, prove to be incorrect because a provision was invalid. In advising the trustees, you need to balance the benefit of protection for the trustees from such possible claims against the need not to waste trust funds on unnecessary applications to court.

If, after careful consideration of the substantive law, you consider that there is no real doubt, then an application should not be made to court and the trustees will be able to resist a charge that they acted in 'wilful default' by showing that they relied on legal advice. If there is any serious doubt about the meaning but, under whatever interpretation is proved correct, the beneficiaries and all potential beneficiaries are *sui juris*, then they can give their consent to the trustees' interpretation. Otherwise, it is necessary for the trustees to apply to the court to construe the trust document or testamentary disposition by means of a claim under the Civil Procedure Rules (CPR), Pt 8. All those whose interests may be affected by the outcome should be made defendants. The remedy sought is directions as to the answers to particular questions relating to the meaning of provisions in the document. Other consequential remedies can be sought, such as drawing up accounts and directions for application of property *cy-près* where there is a failed charitable disposition (see also Chapter 28 of the *Drafting* manual).

It is rare, although not impossible, for beneficiaries or individuals claiming to be beneficiaries to bring a construction claim. Usually, they are defendants and can argue their point of view in that capacity. If the trustees do not apply for a construction claim, a disappointed potential beneficiary would have to consider bringing a claim for breach of trust (see **13.5**).

13.4   Doubts about powers

Although a trust may be clearly valid, there may be doubts about whether a particular transaction can or cannot properly be carried out within its terms. Answers here are again largely a matter of specific legal principle, and the following notes merely make some general suggestions. The starting point must always be to identify precisely what the terms of the trust are and to seek to interpret them.

The settlor can alter the settlement to give the trustees new powers only if the trust deed permits. If it does not, the problem is for the trustees alone.

The trustees have to consider whether they consider it is necessary or advisable to have a particular power. The beneficiaries can give their views, but the trustees must make the decisions, and they are under no obligation to consult or follow the wishes of the beneficiaries (unless the trust deed says they must consult).

If it is considered by the trustees that the power is necessary, and the beneficiaries are *sui juris*, their consent can be obtained to waive their rights to sue in the future in relation to what would amount to a breach of trust. In the case of a charitable trust, the Charity Commission can authorise certain transactions which are not expressly permitted in the trust deed.

In all other circumstances it will be necessary for the trustees to apply to court.

The general power to help in such a case is provided by the Trustee Act 1925 (TA 1925), s. 57, which provides that where some transaction is required in the management or administration of any property vested in trustees which is in the opinion of the court expedient, but which cannot be carried out because no power to carry it out has been given to the trustees, then the court may confer the necessary power on the trustees, subject to such conditions as the court thinks fit. This power is wide and flexible (see, e.g., *Mason v Fairbrother* [1983] 2 All ER 1078).

An alternative, which may be of assistance in appropriate circumstances where the terms of the existing trust are causing difficulty, is an application under the Variation of Trusts Act 1958.

13.5   Possible breach of trust

If the existence and terms of a trust are clear, but some action has been performed or not performed and a beneficiary objects to its performance or non-performance, there may have been a breach of trust. What actions and omissions amount to a breach are beyond the scope of this chapter, which only outlines how to approach a case, but where there is a breach, a range of remedies may be available (see **13.6**).

13.5.1   Identifying a potential breach

Beneficiaries (whether with a fixed or future interest or just a right to be considered under a discretionary trust) can bring a claim for breach of trust if it appears that the trustees have failed in their duties in any way. This could be by positive actions or by failing to control other trustees or agents.

The main difficulty in advising beneficiaries is that they often have very little information on the administration of the trust and so it is difficult to decide what sort of breaches may have occurred. The beneficiaries have a right to see the trust documents and accounts, and, if they do not have these, the first step is to demand them (*Re Londonderry's Settlement* [1965] Ch 918).

13.5.2   Analysing the potential breach

First, it is necessary to identify specifically:

- what exactly is alleged to be a breach;
- whether there is more than one potential breach;
- when each possible breach was committed.

Then, the person(s) who may have committed the breach must be identified. For example:

- one or more of the trustees;
- anyone else, for example an agent acting for the trustees;
- any beneficiary who might be liable for instigating a breach.

Next, it must be decided which of the potential defendants should actually be sued:

- Who is likely to have sufficient assets to indemnify the beneficiary?
- Is the case against a possible defendant legally or factually weak?
- Are there any reasons for not suing a potential beneficiary, such as family reasons?

Lastly, what has been lost from the trust as a result of the alleged breach must be identified as precisely as possible:

- in terms of capital;
- in terms of income;
- in terms of specific assets.

It is only in the light of a proper and accurate analysis of these areas that the lawyer can review the range of possible and/or appropriate remedies.

13.5.3   Liability

While a trustee is prima facie liable only for their own acts, they will also be liable for the acts of a co-trustee where that trustee:

- has stood by while a breach of trust was committed;
- leaves trust administration in the hands of a co-trustee without inquiry;

- leaves the trust funds in the sole control of a co-trustee;
- fails to take appropriate steps on becoming aware of a breach of trust.

Where on the facts more than one trustee is responsible for a breach, liability will be joint and several (see *Bahin v Hughes* [1886] 31 ChD 390). Execution can be levied by a successful claimant beneficiary against any trustee held liable. As between trustees, however, liability is shared equally, so if one trustee pays more than their appropriate share for a breach, they can claim a contribution from any other trustees found liable.

The court has a power to exempt a person from liability to make a contribution, and therefore potentially to make another trustee solely liable. This can be done where:

(a) one trustee alone received or misappropriated trust funds or otherwise benefited from the breach;

(b) one trustee was a solicitor who advised on the breach;

(c) one trustee is also a beneficiary, making that trustee liable to the extent of their beneficial interest (*Chillingworth v Chambers* [1896] 1 Ch 685).

A solicitor trustee's partners cannot be held vicariously liable for a fraudulent breach of trust (*Walker v Stones* [2000] 4 All ER 412). For a consideration of when it is appropriate to relieve a trustee of a small estate of liability to account, see *Re Evans (deceased)* [1999] 2 All ER 777.

For guidance on drafting particulars of claim in a breach of trust action, see the **Drafting** manual, Chapter 28.

13.6 The range of remedies

13.6.1 Financial compensation

The measure of compensation varies with the type of breach committed, but basically it is always based on a liability to make good the loss caused to the trust. This is calculated by applying the same principle that applies to common law damages: to restore the beneficiary to the position they would have been in if there had been no breach of trust; they cannot recover losses which would have been suffered in any event if there had been no breach of trust: *Target Holdings Ltd v Redferns* [1995] 3 All ER 785, reaffirmed in *AIB Group (UK) plc v Mark Redler & Co Solicitors* [2015] 1 All ER 326.

Note that, normally, capital loss will be compensated from the date of loss with interest. So long as the interest on capital represents the loss of capital growth, a claim for lost income will also lie; but take care to avoid double recovery where interest represents lost income.

It should be appreciated that in most cases money claimed will be repaid to the trust for proper administration, rather than paid directly to a claimant beneficiary.

The following categories give some guide to the measure applied in particular circumstances.

13.6.1.1 Payment of trust funds to wrong person

Liability is to make good to the trust the amount wrongly paid out with interest.

13.6.1.2 Improper sale of authorised investments

Liability, at the option of the beneficiary, is:

(a) to make good the value at which the authorised investment was sold, less any proceeds of sale of any improper investment purchased with the proceeds; or

(b) to repurchase the authorised investment with credit for the proceeds of sale of any improper investment purchased; or

(c) to place the beneficiaries in the position they would have been in if the authorised investment had not been sold (*Re Massingberd* (1890) 63 LT 296).

In any event, the trustee can claim no credit if the authorised investment has also fallen in value.

13.6.1.3 Unauthorised investment

If the unauthorised investment results in a loss, the liability is to sell it and make good any loss with interest. If the unauthorised investment results in a loss of interest, the liability is to make up the difference between the interest that was received and the interest that might have been received from an authorised investment.

If the unauthorised investment results in a profit, the liability is that the profit can be claimed for the trust. Alternatively, if all beneficiaries are of age and *sui juris*, they can adopt the unauthorised investment (*Re Lake* [1903] 1 KB 439).

If unauthorised activity results in no loss to the trust, and the resulting assets are held for the beneficiaries, there is no loss to be compensated, for example a building is built on trust land without authority (*Vyse v Foster* [1872] LR 8 Ch App 309).

13.6.1.4 Improper retention of unauthorised investment

The liability is the difference between the price for which the investment is finally sold, and what it would have fetched if sold at the correct time.

13.6.1.5 Non-investment

Money can be held in a bank account while an investment is being sought (TA 1925, s. 11), but should not be left uninvested for an unreasonable time.

The liability for non-investment is to make good any interest lost due to failure to invest. If there is a failure to invest in a specified investment, the liability is to purchase as much of that investment as could have been purchased at the time the duty to purchase arose (*Nestlé v National Westminster Bank plc* [1993] 1 WLR 1260).

13.6.1.6 Use of trust funds for private purposes

If the trustee makes private use of the trust funds, the liability is:

(a) to make good any capital loss, with interest (at a higher rate and compound if the money has been used in the trustee's business (*Attorney-General v Alford* [1855] 4 De G M & G 843)); alternatively

(b) to pay over to the trust any actual profit received (or if funds have been mixed, an appropriate part of any profit).

In an interesting example, the House of Lords held that beneficiaries had a right to choose between a lien and a proportionate share of an asset, irrespective of whether there had been a mixing of funds (*Foskett v McKeown* [2000] 3 All ER 97).

13.6.1.7 Fraud

If a trustee acts fraudulently, their liability is not only to make up any capital loss, but also to pay compound interest.

13.6.1.8 Interest on financial compensation

Interest will normally be awarded on capital ordered to be repaid to the trust. Interest is normally at a basic flat rate (based on the special investment account rate), but a higher rate may be granted in cases of fraud, where a higher rate of interest ought to have been received by the trust, or where the trustee has personally benefited from a higher rate of return. Simple interest will normally be awarded, compound interest in limited cases.

13.6.1.9 Taxation of financial compensation

No deduction will be made to take account of tax that might have had to be paid on the assets but for the breach (*Bartlett v Barclays Bank Trust Co Ltd (No 2)* [1980] 2 All ER 92; *Re Bell's Indenture* [1980] 1 WLR 1217).

13.6.2   Taking an account

The claim for an account has a long history, first in common law and then as a remedy available in a Chancery Court to support a legal or equitable right. An account can usefully be claimed by a beneficiary against a trustee or an executor, as well as in partnership, agency, and real property cases. For rules regarding the taking of an account, see CPR, Pt 40, and for a summary order for an account, CPR, Pt 25. Note that it is normally appropriate in a breach of trust action to seek the taking of an account and the payment of sums found due, rather than seeking damages.

13.6.2.1   Nature of an account

An account consists of a schedule of all sums due from one side to the other, setting off sums due the other way, to reach a figure due to compensate the applicant. It can take into consideration any relevant payments, for example rent received.

An application for an account should be accompanied by an application for an order that any sum found due be paid over to the trust.

An account can be ordered only where a breach has been proved, not merely to see if there has been a breach (*Re Wrightson* [1908] 1 Ch 789).

13.6.2.2   Obligation to replace assets

An account is appropriate to a trust claim rather than a claim for damages as the obligation is to replace assets. Rules of assessment of damages such as remoteness have no place in assessing trust loss.

An account can be ordered with regard to the whole of the trust property or to the part with regard to which a breach has been proved (*Re Tebbs* [1976] 1 WLR 924).

13.6.2.3   Accounts and wilful default

Where there is an omission to act rather than an active breach, an account is taken on the basis of wilful default; that is, on the basis of what would have been received but for the wilful default (this does not necessarily imply a conscious failure to act so long as the failure involves a breach of trust). At least one act of wilful default must be referred to in the statement of case and proved to get an account on this basis.

13.6.2.4   Defence to the claim

It is a defence to a claim for an account that the parties have already stated in writing sums due between them, arriving at a balance figure. This will not succeed, however, if there has been any mistake or fraud to vitiate the account.

13.6.3   Following and tracing and constructive trusts

Following and tracing are rights *in rem* against a particular item of property or an item that has been substituted for it, rather than against a trustee. Such remedies will be particularly useful where a beneficiary has a good reason for wishing to recover a particular item of property, either because of what the item is or because the trustee is unlikely to have sufficient assets to satisfy a claim personally (see *Re Diplock* [1948] Ch 465 and *Foskett v McKeown* [2000] 3 All ER 97).

Although tracing was available at common law, it is now subject to equitable principles, and will therefore not be granted if it would be inequitable to do so.

Where a trustee has obtained other property which was not the subject of the trust but as a result of their position as a trustee, it is likely to be imposed with a constructive trust, and the trustee is obliged to bring it into the trust.

These remedies are considered further in **Chapter 14**.

13.7 Exercise

PROBLEM

Juliet, who is 16 years old, is a beneficiary under a trust set up by her grandfather, Colin Lewis. She has not seen the terms of the trust, but knows that her three cousins are also beneficiaries. She has received varying amounts of money and, since she was 11, her school fees have been paid from the trust.

At the beginning of term Juliet's father, Steve, was informed by her school that the fees had not been paid by the trustees, despite a number of reminders. Steve was unable to contact the trustees, who are his uncle Joe and an accountant friend of his father, Fred Treece. Steve eventually spoke to Joe's wife. She was very evasive, but said that Joe was having a bit of trouble with Fred and that he had discovered a few problems with Fred's handling of the finances. She said Joe had gone to Fred's house in Cumbria to try to sort things out. Steve paid the school fees himself to avoid Juliet having any disruption to her schooling.

Steve is now very concerned about the trust. He has seen some accounts, although they are not very recent. He showed them to an accountant friend, who said that the bulk of the trust fund seemed to be in investments which are very safe but produce very low income and that there were a number of odd-looking withdrawals from the fund.

SOLUTION

There appears to be enough evidence to commence a breach of trust claim. The claim can be brought by Juliet (acting through her father as next friend). The other beneficiaries do not have to be involved, as the remedy sought is not damages for loss, but reconstitution of the trust fund. She does not have to show she has personally lost financially, only that the trustees have breached their duties. The trustees would have to make up the loss to the fund and account for any profits they had made in breach of their duties.

Steve does not have a direct claim against the trustees for the school fees, as he is not a beneficiary and (presumably) there is no contract between him and the trustees.

Up-to-date accounts and a copy of the trust deed should be formally requested from the trustees as Juliet has a right to copies (*Re Londonderry's Settlement* [1965] Ch 918).

Juliet can choose whether to proceed against Fred and Joe or just one of them at this stage and wait to commence proceedings against the other. If it is discovered that the trustees, in breach of their duties, have transferred trust assets to other people, then tracing remedies against that property can be considered.

Juliet will have personal claims against the trustees, as well as being able to trace any trust property in their hands and any profits they have made.

Joe will be liable for any fraudulent losses caused by Fred if Joe has not supervised and checked up on him properly.

Depending on the precise wording of the trust document, there is no obvious breach of trust in leaving the fund in safe investments. There is no duty to speculate! However, there may well be a breach if they have not diversified the funds, kept a balance between investment production and capital growth, and kept the investments under review. If it was found that the trustees breached these duties, there would have to be an inquiry into what the funds would have been worth if properly invested. The courts are likely to go for a very conservative estimate (*Nestlé v National Westminster Bank plc* [1993] 1 WLR 1260).

The situation needs to be kept under careful watch. If more evidence comes to light, injunctive relief to protect the funds may be expedient. Juliet could also consider applying to have the trustees replaced or an additional trustee appointed. This can be done in the breach of trust application or, if urgent, by an interim application.

Other equitable remedies

This can only be a brief outline of some of the other important equitable remedies. For further discussion, see *Goff and Jones: Law of Unjust Enrichment* (9th edn, Sweet & Maxwell, 2016) and *Snell's Equity* (34th edn, Sweet & Maxwell, 2020).

14.1 Personal and proprietary claims

Remedies such as suing for damages for tort or breach of contract are personal remedies, which means that if the person sued is insolvent, the client is unlikely to recover any money (subject to any security taken as part of a contractual arrangement).

A few remedies, most notably trust remedies and tracing, give rights *in rem*, which means that the remedy is strictly against the property rather than the wrongdoer, so it is unaffected by the insolvency of the wrongdoer. Provided the claim is made out, and the property can be identified, it belongs to the person seeking the remedy, and no other creditor can make claims to it.

14.2 Tracing

Tracing is available where property is taken and dealt with contrary to a person's fiduciary duties. It is mainly used in the context of breaches of trust, but it is not confined to these. A tracing order can be made to recover the property itself or the proceeds of sale if they can be sufficiently identified.

14.2.1 Mixed funds

Where proceeds have been paid into a mixed fund, the basic rule is that the first payment in is related to the earliest payment out (*Devaynes v Noble, Clayton's Case* [1816] 1 Mer 572). However, where the money is paid into a bank account, the trustee will be deemed to spend their own money before spending a beneficiary's money (*Re Hallett's Estate* (1880) 13 ChD 696).

A beneficiary may be able to claim a charge on property bought from a mixed fund (*Re Hallett's Estate*). It may also be possible for a beneficiary to claim a proportion of any profit made from a mixed fund (*Re Tilley's Will Trusts* [1967] Ch 1179).

14.2.2 Limits to the right to trace

There are limits to the right to trace. A trustee or someone in a fiduciary capacity must admit the claim of a beneficiary, giving priority to it, as must a volunteer. An innocent person will share property equally with a beneficiary who claims a right to trace. Once property has passed to a purchaser for value without notice, a right to trace will be extinguished.

14.3 Constructive trusts

On the facts of a particular case, a constructive trust may arise in equity to provide an additional or alternative remedy. There has been much academic debate as to whether a constructive trust can strictly speaking be regarded as a 'remedy', rather than simply as an operation of substantive law. It is clearly so regarded in the United States, but while there is some authority for regarding it as a remedy in the United Kingdom (see especially Lord Denning MR in *Hussey v Palmer* [1972] 1 WLR 1286), there is no agreement on the matter. The technical distinction has little relevance so long as the facts justify the finding of a constructive trust.

In general terms, a constructive trust can arise wherever there is a fiduciary relationship; it does not require the existence of a formal trust (*English v Dedham Vale Properties Ltd* [1978] 1 WLR 93). The broad basis for finding a constructive trust is to prevent unjust enrichment (*Carl Zeiss Stiftung v Herbert Smith & Co (No 2)* [1969] 2 Ch 276; *James v Williams* [2000] Ch 1 (CA)).

A constructive trust has been held to arise in the following circumstances:

(a) where a person in a fiduciary position gains any unauthorised personal benefit or profit from that position (see *Keech v Sandford* [1726] Sel Cast King 61);

(b) where particular property is subject to a fiduciary duty (see *Tito v Waddell (No 2)* [1977] Ch 106);

(c) where property has been acquired as a result of information obtained by someone acting as a fiduciary (see *Boardman v Phipps* [1967] 2 AC 46, but see *Sabnam Investments v Dunlop Heywood* [1999] 3 All ER 652);

(d) where a stranger to a trust has actual or constructive knowledge of a trust and knowingly receives trust property. There is a very large number of reported cases dealing with the degree of knowledge required and whether there was sufficient proof of knowledge on the facts. If dealing with this issue, it is especially important to check recent case law. An interesting example is *Bank of Credit and Commerce International (Overseas) Ltd (in liquidation) v Akindele* [2000] 4 All ER 221;

(e) where a person who dishonestly procures or assists in a breach of trust is liable to make good any resulting loss (see *Belmont Finance Corp Ltd v Williams Furniture Ltd* [1979] Ch 250 and *Royal Brunei Airlines Sdn Bhd v Tan* [1995] 3 WLR 64);

(f) where an agent acting for a trust can become a constructive trustee if they:

    (i) become chargeable with some part of the trust property; or

    (ii) knowingly assist in a dishonest or fraudulent design on the part of the trustee; or

    (iii) act without proper instructions.

(See *Blyth v Fladgate* [1892] 1 Ch 337.)

However, an agent such as a solicitor will not become a constructive trustee simply by acting as an agent (see *Barnes v Addy* (1874) LR 9 Ch App 224; *Mara v Browne* [1896] 1 Ch 199; and *Williams-Ashman v Price and Williams* [1942] Ch 219).

14.4 Subrogation

Subrogation involves a person being able to take over the rights or assets of another party to avoid a third party benefiting unjustly from a benefit conferred on them by the first person. The right of subrogation is well established in insurance law. So, for example, where an insurer has paid an employee insurance money in respect of injuries suffered at work, the insurer can take over any rights the insured employee may have had against their employer (or third parties). See further *Goff and Jones: The Law of Unjust Enrichment*, pp. 553 *et seq.*

14.5 Quasi-contract

The main quasi-contract remedies are *quantum meruit* and *quantum valebat*. For these remedies, there may have been a contract and a dispute over whether there was a breach. Even if the issues are decided in favour of one party, the court may order that party to pay the other a 'reasonable' amount for any benefit conferred or asset transferred if it would be unjust to allow the person to retain that benefit without compensation.

14.6 Benefits conferred in an emergency

Similar principles of avoidance of unjust enrichment underlie the cases where a person has been allowed to claim remuneration for goods provided in an emergency to a person under a legal incapacity or for services rendered in an attempt to save life or prevent injury (*Williams v Wentworth* [1842] 5 Beav 325; *Great Northern Railway Co v Swaffield* [1874] LR 9 Ex 132).

14.7 Rights to contribution and recoupment

There are various situations where a person has a common law or statutory right to recover some or all of the money they have paid out in satisfying a claim by a third party from someone else whom that third party could have claimed against or who was somehow involved in the situation which gave rise to the third party's claim. The most important statutory remedy is under the Civil Liability (Contribution) Act 1978. Common law examples arise with joint tenants, partners, and joint contractors.

14.8 Benefits conferred through mistake, duress, or undue influence

This is a complex and rapidly changing area. Basically, if the claim succeeds, a person may be able to rescind a contract, mortgage, trust, or other obligation and recover money or property notwithstanding that there appeared to be, in form at least, a valid contract or gift or other transfer. In dealing with any of these areas, it is necessary to establish whether the claim falls within one of the recognised categories which give rise to relief, whether it can be argued it would only involve a small extension of one of those categories, or whether you will need to try to rely on a general principle of prevention of unjust enrichment, unconscionable bargains, etc. If the latter is the case, it is obviously going to be more difficult to convince a court that the remedy is obtainable.

Two cases extended and clarified the scope of remedies in cases of payments made under mistakes of law: *Kleinwort Benson Ltd v Lincoln City Council* [1998] 3 WLR 1095 (HL) and *Nurdin and Peacock plc v DB Ramsden & Co Ltd* [1999] 1 All ER 941. Restitutionary remedies in the case of benefits conferred under contracts which later were held to be void were considered extensively in the 'interest rate swap transaction' cases which followed the decision that local authorities had no power to enter into such transactions. Key decisions in this area include *Hazell v Hammersmith & Fulham London BC* [1991] 1 All ER 545, *Kleinwort Benson Ltd v Sandwell BC* [1994] 4 All ER 890, *Westdeutsche Landesbank Girozentrale v Islington London BC* [1996] AC 669, and *Guinness Mahon & Co Ltd v Kensington & Chelsea Royal London BC* [1998] 2 All ER 272.

14.9 Benefits conferred as a result of fraud or criminal conduct

Irrespective of whether the law recognises general principles of prevention of unjust enrichment, a person has always been able to seek a remedy to prevent someone from benefiting from their fraudulent conduct or other criminal conduct. The remedy could be rescission or return of property.

14.10 Fraudulent preferences and avoidance of voluntary transfers

Where a person becomes insolvent, the creditors may be able to call in property voluntarily transferred by that person to others or used to 'fraudulently' pay off one creditor at the expense of others. Any property called in would form part of the debtor's estate and would be distributed to creditors in accordance with the normal rules of priority of creditors and equal treatment for creditors of equal ranking. See further the Insolvency Act 1986, ss. 238–241.

Judicial review

Judicial review is a very important area of law, which affects a wide range of cases. However, there are clear limits to its scope.

15.1 Scope of judicial review

There are several restrictions on the availability of judicial review. In summary, those restrictions are:

- Judicial review is available only in 'public law' cases.
- Usually, judicial review may be used only as the remedy of last resort.
- The applicant must have 'sufficient interest'.
- The applicant must act 'promptly'.

Each of these restrictions will be examined in more detail in the sections which follow.

15.2 Public law cases only

Judicial review procedure is governed by the Civil Procedure Rules (CPR), Pt 54. CPR, r.54.1(2)(a) defines a claim for judicial review as meaning a claim to review the lawfulness of (a) an enactment; or (b) 'a decision, action or failure to act in relation to the exercise of a public function'. It is therefore only 'public law' claims which can be made by way of judicial review. It follows that judicial review is limited to claims against:

- public bodies exercising public functions; and
- so-called 'inferior' courts.

15.2.1 Public bodies

Judicial review may be sought in respect of decisions of a diverse range of public bodies and authorities. The term 'public body' includes bodies set up by statute, along with government departments and non-statutory bodies which exercise public functions. See *R v Panel on Takeovers and Mergers, ex p Datafin plc* [1987] QB 815 (where a non-statutory body regulating certain business dealings in the City of London was held to be susceptible to judicial review) and *R v Advertising Standards Authority Ltd, ex p Insurance Services plc* [1990] 2 Admin LR 77 (where the Advertising Standards Authority, another non-statutory body, was held to be susceptible to judicial review).

In *R (on the application of Kaur) v Institute of Legal Executives Appeal Tribunal* [2011] 1 All ER 1435, the Court of Appeal entertained an application for judicial review relating to the Institute of Legal Executives. This professional body is amenable to judicial review mainly because it discharges a statutory duty as an approved regulator under the Legal Services Act

2007. The same applies to the Solicitors Regulation Authority (see, for example, *Ali v Solicitors Regulation Authority* [2021] EWHC 2709 (Admin)), and to the Bar Standards Board (see, for example, *Diggins v Bar Standard Board* [2020] EWHC 467 (Admin)).

Where, however, a body derives its functions and authority from contract, judicial review is not available. See *Law v National Greyhound Racing Club* [1983] 1 WLR 1302 (where the Greyhound Racing Club was held not to be susceptible to judicial review) and *R v Disciplinary Committee of the Jockey Club, ex p Aga Khan* [1993] 1 WLR 909 (where the same decision was reached in the case of the Jockey Club). This is because, in such cases, the applicant can pursue a remedy for breach of contract.

This principle is illustrated by *R v Muntham House School, ex p R* [2000] ELR 287. A pupil at the school was excluded and judicial review of that decision was sought. Most of the fees were in practice paid by a local educational authority, but the school was not a publicly funded school in the sense of receiving grants or other direct funding from the public sector. The local authority entered into a purely contractual relationship with the school to place a child there. Therefore, it was held that the decision by the school to exclude a pupil did not have a sufficient public law character to make it amenable to judicial review.

In *R (on the application of Mullins) v Appeal Board of the Jockey Club* [2005] EWHC 2197 (Admin), the court equated the requirement that the body must be carrying out a public function with the test applied by the House of Lords in *Aston Cantlow and Wilmcote with Billesley Parochial Church Council v Wallbank* [2004] 1 AC 546 to determine whether a body is a public authority for the purposes of the Human Rights Act 1998, namely that the essential test is whether the functions of the body are 'governmental' in nature.

Where the public body is a charity, it may be preferable to pursue a remedy under charity legislation. For example, in *Scott v National Trust* [1998] 2 All ER 705, it was held that the National Trust, being a charity of exceptional importance to the nation and being subject to special statutory provisions, constitutes a public body. However, because it is a charity, a challenge should be brought under the special procedure set out in what is now s. 115 of the Charities Act 2011; the availability of this alternative remedy meant that judicial review would not normally be granted.

The principles were summarised by Dyson LJ in *R (on the application of Beer (t/a Hammer Trout Farm)) v Hampshire Farmers Markets Ltd* [2004] 1 WLR 233 (at [16]):

[U]nless the source of power clearly provides the answer, the question whether the decision of a body is amenable to judicial review requires a careful consideration of the nature of the power and function that has been exercised to see whether the decision has a sufficient public element, flavour or character to bring it within the purview of public law. It may be said with some justification that this criterion for amenability is very broad, not to say question-begging. But it provides the framework for the investigation that has to be conducted. There is a growing body of case law in which the question of amenability to judicial review has been considered . . .

The difficulty of defining what is, and what is not, a public function is illustrated by *L v Birmingham City Council* [2007] UKHL 27, [2008] 1 AC 95, where the House of Lords held (by a 3:2 majority) that a distinction had to be drawn between the function of a local authority in making arrangements for those in need of care and accommodation who are unable to make such arrangements for themselves and that of a private company in providing such care and accommodation under contract with the authority, on a commercial basis rather than by subsidy from public funds, in order for the authority to fulfil its duty. The actual provision of such care and accommodation by the private company, as opposed to its regulation and supervision pursuant to statutory rules, is not an inherently public function. It followed that a resident of a private care home placed there by a local authority, though retaining public law rights against the authority which had arranged the accommodation, did not have such rights against the care home.

15.2.2 Inferior courts

Judicial review is also a means by which the decisions of certain courts may be challenged. Decisions of magistrates' courts may be challenged in this way. However, decisions of the

Crown Court may only be challenged by judicial review if the decision does not relate to a trial on indictment, since the Senior Courts Act 1981 (SCA 1981), s. 29(3), excludes from the scope of judicial review 'matters relating to trial on indictment'. In *DPP v Manchester Crown Court and Huckfield* [1993] 1 WLR 1524, Lord Browne-Wilkinson suggested (at p. 1530) that one 'pointer' to the true construction of s. 29 would be:

> . . . to ask the question, 'Is the decision sought to be reviewed one arising in the issue between the Crown and the defendant formulated by the indictment (including the costs of such issue)?' If the answer is 'Yes,' then to permit the decision to be challenged by judicial review may lead to delay in the trial: the matter is therefore probably excluded from review by the section. If the answer is 'No,' the decision of the Crown Court is truly collateral to the indictment of the defendant and judicial review of that decision will not delay his trial: therefore it may well not be excluded by the section.

In *Director of Public Prosecutions v Manchester Crown Court and Ashton* [1994] 1 AC 9, the House of Lords held that s. 29(3) applies to matters which affect the conduct of a Crown Court trial (covering orders made before the trial) and matters which are an integral part of the trial process (which covers orders made during, or even at the very end of, the trial, together with some pre-trial orders).

Despite the breadth of this definition, the question of what matters relate to trial on indictment has generated a considerable body of case law. In *A (F) v Crown Court at Kingston* [2017] EWHC 2706 (Admin), for example, it was held that the court did not have jurisdiction to consider an application for judicial review of a decision of the Crown Court to withhold bail between the verdict of the jury and sentencing, since this was a decision clearly related to a trial on indictment.

However, in *R v Crown Court at Maidstone, ex p London Borough of Harrow* [2000] QB 719, it was held that, where a Crown Court judge has no jurisdiction to make the order they purported to make, it could not be categorised as a matter relating to a trial on indictment so as to fall within the exclusion in s. 29(3), and so that purported order was thus amenable to judicial review. Similarly, in *R (M) v Kingston Crown Court* [2014] EWHC 2702 (Admin), [2016] 1 WLR 1685, the court said (at [32]) that, where an order is made relating to a trial on indictment, it may nonetheless be quashed 'in circumstances where the defect is so severe that it deprived the court below of jurisdiction to make it . . . The question is whether there is a jurisdictional error of such gravity as to take the case out of the jurisdiction of the Crown Court.' The same approach was taken in *R (DPP) v Sheffield Crown Court* [2014] EWHC 2014 (Admin), [2014] 1 WLR 4639, where Lord Thomas CJ (considering whether the court had jurisdiction to hear an application for judicial review of a costs order made by the Crown Court under s. 19 of the Prosecution of Offences Act 1985) said that, 'if there was no jurisdiction for the judge to make the order under s. 19 of the 1985 Act, no question could arise as to the lack of this court's jurisdiction . . . to set aside the order of the judge'. This approach was followed in *R (DPP) v Aylesbury Crown Court* [2017] EWHC 2987 (Admin), where Sharp LJ concluded (at [7]) that the Divisional Court has jurisdiction, despite the bar in s. 29(3), if there is 'a jurisdictional error of sufficient gravity to take the case out of the jurisdiction of the Crown Court'.

So far as magistrates' courts are concerned, the High Court has jurisdiction to entertain appeals on points of law or jurisdiction both by way of judicial review and through appeals by way of case stated under s. 111 of the Magistrates' Courts Act 1980. In *R v Oldbury Justices, ex p Smith* (1995) 159 JP 316, it was said that where appeal by way of case stated is available, it is generally preferable to challenge a decision of a magistrates' court by that means rather than judicial review (because judicial review is to be regarded as a remedy of last resort and because, on an appeal by way of case stated, the Divisional Court is presented with all the findings of fact made by the magistrates). However, in *R v North Essex Justices, ex p Lloyd* [2001] 2 Cr App Rep (S) 15, the Divisional Court said that the most appropriate procedure for challenging a decision of a magistrates' court where the issue is the extent of its jurisdiction is judicial review (since this saves the cumbersome procedure of appealing by way of case stated, and has the advantage that the matter comes before a High Court judge who decides whether or not to give permission to apply for judicial review: see the judgment of Lord Woolf CJ, at [11]). In *R (on the application of P) v Liverpool City Magistrates* [2006] ELR 386, Collins J said that judicial review is appropriate where it is alleged that there was unfairness in the way that the justices conducted the case, but case stated is appropriate where it is alleged that justices have misdirected themselves or got the law wrong in their approach to a decision.

B v Carlisle Crown Court [2009] EWHC 3540 (Admin) concerned an application for judicial review of the Crown Court following the hearing of an appeal from a magistrates' court. Langstaff J, at [16], said that it was plain from the observations of Lord Bingham CJ in *Chester v Gloucester Crown Court* [1998] EWHC Admin 692 that 'appeal by case stated would normally be the preferable way of proceeding, particularly where matters of evidence are concerned' and that 'the procedural advantages of the case-stated procedure are such as to make it undoubtedly more appropriate in most cases where an applicant has been dissatisfied by the result of an appeal from the magistrates' court to the Crown Court'. His Lordship went on to say (at [17] and [18]):

I conclude . . . that this court does have power to consider an application brought by way of judicial review in circumstances such as those I have described, but I have concluded that it is necessary for this court to exercise any power which it possesses sparingly. It should not become the position that applications for judicial review are regarded as an alternative to a proper route of appeal which would ordinarily be by case stated, in particular if a question as to a matter of law or matter of evidence, or sufficiency of evidence, arose. It would be a sad day if appellants generally felt that they could appeal indirectly, by judicial review, a decision of the Crown Court, which, after all, is provided as the route of appeal from the Magistrates' Court and has no onward appeal to the Court of Appeal. It must therefore be in exceptional circumstances, in general terms, that judicial review is appropriate at all; and indeed it will usually be the case that applications which ought to be brought (if at all) by case stated, and are brought by way of judicial review, may find that permission is refused at the permission stage.

. . . The jurisdiction, though exercised sparingly, must be approached on a case-by-case basis. In those cases where there is said to be a material irregularity in the procedure adopted in the court hearing the appeal, judicial review may well be an appropriate route. It is my view that that route is appropriate in this case.

A defendant who wishes to appeal against conviction and/or sentence has a right of appeal to the Crown Court under the Magistrates' Courts Act 1980, s. 108. In *R v Hereford Magistrates' Court, ex p Rowlands* [1998] QB 110, Lord Bingham CJ (at p. 118) said that appeal to the Crown Court is the 'ordinary avenue of appeal for a defendant who complains that the magistrates' court reached a wrong decision of fact, or a wrong decision of mixed law and fact'. On the other hand, appeal by way of case stated is the:

ordinary avenue of appeal for a convicted defendant who contends that the justices erred in law: the usual question posed for the opinion of the High Court is whether on the facts which they found the justices were entitled to convict the defendant; but sometimes the question is whether there was any evidence upon which the justices could properly convict the defendant, which has traditionally been regarded as an issue of law . . . [I]f a magistrates' court convicts a defendant after radically departing from well-known principles of justice and procedure, the defendant may challenge his conviction as wrong in law by way of case stated.

His Lordship went on to say, at p. 120, that judicial review is the 'usual if not invariable means of pursuing challenges based on unfairness, bias or procedural irregularity in magistrates' courts'.

Judicial review is particularly appropriate where the *procedure* adopted by the lower court is being questioned. For example, judicial review has been held to be appropriate in the following instances:

(a) the unreasonable refusal of an adjournment to enable a defendant to prepare his case (*R v Thames Magistrates' Court, ex p Polemis* [1974] 1 WLR 1371);

(b) refusing an adjournment where a defence witness could not attend on the day of the trial without first considering the effect on the defence of having to go ahead without that witness (*R v Bracknell Justices, ex p Hughes* (1990) 154 JP 98);

(c) failure by the prosecution to notify the defence of the existence of witnesses who could support the defence case (*R v Leyland Justices, ex p Hawthorn* [1979] QB 283);

(d) failure by the prosecution to inform the defence that the key prosecution witness had a previous conviction for wasting police time, arising out of the making of a false allegation (*R v Knightsbridge Crown Court, ex p Goonatilleke* [1986] QB 1, where the accused was charged with shoplifting);

(e) ordering a defendant to pay costs without considering his means to pay them (*R v Newham Justices, ex p Samuels* [1991] COD 412).

Decisions of coroners' courts are also susceptible to challenge by way of judicial review (see, e.g., *R (Speck) v HM Coroner for the District of York* [2016] EWHC 6 (Admin), [2016] 4 WLR 15; *R (on the Application of T) v HM Senior Coroner for the County of West Yorkshire (Western Area)* [2017] EWCA Civ 318).

Because the scope of judicial review is limited to the review of 'inferior' courts, it does not extend to decisions of the High Court itself, the Court of Appeal, or the Supreme Court.

15.2.3 Upper Tribunal

The High Court also exercises a supervisory jurisdiction over the Upper Tribunal, which was established by the Tribunals, Courts and Enforcement Act 2007. In *R (on the application of Cart) v Upper Tribunal* [2011] UKSC 28, [2012] 1 AC 663, the Supreme Court had to decide whether and (if so) on what basis, the right to judicial review of a decision of the Upper Tribunal should be restricted. Each appeal under consideration arose out of the refusal of the Upper Tribunal to give permission to appeal from a decision of the First-tier Tribunal. The court ruled that the availability of judicial review should be limited to the grounds on which permission to make a second-tier appeal to the Court of Appeal would be granted (under s. 13(6) of the Tribunals, Courts and Enforcement Act 2007), namely where an 'important point of principle or practice' was raised, or where there was 'some other compelling reason' for the case to be heard. Baroness Hale (at [37]) said that 'there is nothing in the 2007 Act which purports to oust or exclude judicial review of the unappealable decisions of the Upper Tribunal. Clear words would be needed to do this, and they are not there'. Her Ladyship added (at [56]) that adopting the second-tier appeal criteria would enable 'a further check, outside the tribunal system, but not one which could be expected to succeed in the great majority of cases'. She went on to say (at [57]) that this approach:

would be a rational and proportionate restriction upon the availability of judicial review of the refusal by the Upper Tribunal of permission to appeal to itself. It would recognise that the new and in many ways enhanced tribunal structure deserves a more restrained approach to judicial review than has previously been the case, while ensuring that important errors can still be corrected.

The effect of *Cart* was considered in *PR (Sri Lanka) v Secretary of State for the Home Department* [2012] 1 WLR 73. In that case, Carnwath LJ observed (at [33]) that the 'second appeals test' was 'designed to ensure best use of the limited judicial resources' of the court and that the 'emphasis was to be on important points of law or principle. The alternative "compelling reasons" test . . . was to be an "exceptional" remedy, a "safety valve".' His Lordship went on (at [35]) to emphasise the narrowness of the exception: the prospects of success should normally be 'very high'; the exception might apply where the first decision was 'perverse or otherwise plainly wrong' (e.g. inconsistent with authority of a higher court) or where a procedural failure in the Upper Tribunal might make it 'plainly unjust' to refuse a party a further appeal (where the practical effect would be to deny that party a right of appeal altogether).

CPR, r.54.7A applies where an application is made, following refusal by the Upper Tribunal of permission to appeal against a decision of the First-tier Tribunal, for judicial review of the decision of the Upper Tribunal refusing permission to appeal, or in relation to the decision of the First-tier Tribunal which was the subject of the application for permission to appeal. Rule 54.7A(7) states that the court will give permission to proceed only if it considers:

> (a) that there is an arguable case, which has a reasonable prospect of success, that both the decision of the Upper Tribunal refusing permission to appeal and the decision of the First Tier Tribunal against which permission to appeal was sought are wrong in law; and
>
> (b) that either –
>> (i) the claim raises an important point of principle or practice; or
>> (ii) there is some other compelling reason to hear it.

15.2.4   Judicial review versus private law remedies

Even if the body whose decision is under challenge is a public body (see **15.2.1**), and so a body against which judicial review may be sought, judicial review is available only to challenge decisions made by such bodies when they are acting in a public law (rather than private law) capacity. If there is a 'private law' remedy (e.g. for breach of contract), the applicant should bring a claim based on that private law claim, rather than seeking judicial review. See *Roy v Kensington and Chelsea and Westminster Family Practitioner Committee* [1992] 1 AC 624, where Lord Bridge of Harwich said (at pp. 628–629) that it 'is appropriate that an issue which depends exclusively on the existence of a purely public law right should be determined in judicial review proceedings and not otherwise'. However, 'where a litigant asserts his entitlement to a subsisting right in private law, whether by way of claim or defence, the circumstance that the existence and extent of the private right asserted may incidentally involve the examination of a public law issue cannot prevent the litigant from seeking to establish his right' by means of an ordinary civil claim. So, for example, a person who claims to have been unfairly dismissed from the employment of a public body cannot challenge that decision by way of judicial review.

In *The Trustees of Dennis Rye Pension Fund v Sheffield City Council* [1998] 1 WLR 840, the Court of Appeal gave guidance for those cases on the borderline between private law and public law. Lord Woolf MR made the following observations (at p. 848):

(a) If it is not clear whether judicial review or a private law claim is the most appropriate way to proceed, it is safer to make an application for judicial review.

(b) If a case is brought by way of an ordinary claim (seeking a private law remedy) and the defendant applies to strike the claim out on the ground that it should have been brought by way of judicial review, the court should ask itself whether it is clear that permission would have been granted had the claimant sought to bring judicial review proceedings.

(c) If the claimant brings an ordinary (private law) claim and it is equally, or more, appropriate than an application for judicial review, and the defendant tries to strike the claim out on the basis that it should have been a judicial review claim, the claim should not be struck out.

(d) In cases where the claimant brings an ordinary claim, but it is unclear whether proceedings should have been brought by way of judicial review instead, it should be borne in mind that the court can order the case to be heard as a judicial review claim instead of striking the claim out.

(e) The choice made by the claimant as regards the type of claim will not normally be regarded as an abuse of process where that choice has no significant disadvantages for the parties, the public, or the court.

In *R (on the application of Shoesmith) v Ofsted* [2011] ICR 1195, it was held that the dismissal of a Director of Children's Services (DCS) had been unlawful because of the lack of procedural fairness leading to it. Maurice Kay LJ said (at [91]) that a DCS has ultimate executive responsibility and accountability for children's services and that it is a position 'created, required and defined by and under statute'. It followed that, 'if a local authority were to dismiss a DCS in total disregard for the rules of natural justice, . . . whatever alternative remedy might be available in the employment tribunal, the dismissal would be amenable to judicial review'. The court referred to *Kay v Lambeth London Borough Council* [2006] 2 AC 465, where Lord Bingham (at [30]) had noted the principle that 'if other means of redress are conveniently and effectively available to a party they ought ordinarily to be used before resort to judicial review'. In the present case, however, a successful claim for judicial review would be 'far more valuable to [the claimant] in both financial and reputational terms than any decision of the employment tribunal could ever be, given the low cap on compensation'. Moreover, given the complexity of the case, if the claimant were to carry on with proceedings in the employment tribunal, 'the most successful outcome might mean that her capped compensation would be greatly diminished, if not entirely swallowed up, by irrecoverable legal costs' (at [99]).

15.3 Availability of alternative remedies

As we have seen, judicial review is generally regarded as a remedy of last resort. It follows that other forms of redress must generally have been sought first. In *R v Inland Revenue Commissioners, ex p Preston* [1985] AC 835 at p. 852, Lord Scarman said that 'a remedy by way of judicial review is not to be made available where an alternative remedy exists'. Similarly, in *R v Chief Constable of Merseyside Police, ex p Calveley* [1986] QB 424, Lord Donaldson of Lymington MR said (at p. 433) that the court, in the exercise of its discretion, will very rarely make judicial review available where there is an alternative remedy by way of appeal, and Glidewell LJ said (at p. 440) that 'where application is made for judicial review but an alternative remedy is available, an applicant should normally be left to pursue that remedy. Judicial review in such a case should only be granted in exceptional circumstances.' Thus, if there is a mechanism for appealing against the decision complained of, that mechanism ought to be used; if the result is unfavourable, it may well be possible to challenge the appellate decision by means of judicial review. In *Harley Development Inc v Commissioners of Inland Revenue* [1996] 1 WLR 727, the Privy Council said that where a comprehensive statutory appeals procedure exists but was not used by the applicant, an application for judicial review would only be entertained in exceptional circumstances.

However, this is not a hard-and-fast rule; there are many cases where judicial review has been granted despite the existence of an alternative remedy. In *R v Huntingdon District Council, ex p Cowan* [1984] 1 WLR 501, Glidewell J said (at p. 507):

Where there is an alternative remedy available but judicial review is sought, then in my judgement the court should always ask itself whether the remedy that is sought in the court, or the alternative remedy which is available to the applicant by way of appeal, is the most effective and convenient, in other words, which of them will prove to be the most effective and convenient in all the circumstances, not merely for the applicant, but in the public interest. In exercising discretion as to whether or not to grant relief, that is a major factor to be taken into account.

In the criminal context, in *R v Hereford Magistrates' Court, ex p Rowlands* [1998] QB 110, Lord Bingham CJ, at p. 125, said that the court did not 'consider that the existence of a right of appeal to the Crown Court, particularly if unexercised, should ordinarily weigh against the grant of leave to move for judicial review, or the grant of substantive relief, in a proper case' (the words 'proper case' should be emphasised).

In *R v Secretary of State for the Home Department, ex p Capti-Mehmet* [1997] COD 61, Laws J reiterated the principle that an applicant for judicial review will usually be required to exhaust all alternative remedies before the court will grant leave to apply for judicial review and that this rule applies unless there are exceptional circumstances justifying departure from it. His Lordship went on to say that a failure to exhaust alternative remedies brought about by the error or incompetence of the applicant's legal representatives will not, of itself, constitute an exceptional circumstance; however, such failures do not weigh as heavily against the applicant as a deliberate decision not to exhaust alternative remedies. Exceptional circumstances may arise from a combination of factors which individually would be insufficient. Relevant factors include whether the applicant gave an early intimation of an intention to challenge the decision. Strong legal merits, such that the court is satisfied that the applicant was denied 'substantial justice' before the inferior court, body, or tribunal, will weigh powerfully in favour of finding that exceptional circumstances exist.

A similar approach was taken in *R v Falmouth & Truro Health Authority, ex p South West Water Ltd* [2001] QB 445. This case was mainly concerned with the abatement of a statutory nuisance. However, Simon Brown LJ (at p. 473) made some general comments on cases where there is an alternative to judicial review, such as a statutory appeal: 'If the applicant has a statutory right of appeal, permission [for judicial review] should only exceptionally be given.' The judge considering the application for permission should, however, have regard to all relevant circumstances, including the 'comparative speed, expense and finality of the alternative process, the need and scope for fact-finding, the desirability of an authoritative ruling on any point of law arising, and (perhaps) the apparent strength of the applicant's substantive challenge'.

15.4 Sufficient interest

In order to seek judicial review, the applicant must have 'sufficient interest' in the matter to which the application relates, sometimes known as 'standing' (or *locus standi*). The applicant must therefore be able to show a legitimate expectation of being heard. This generally requires that the applicant must be directly affected by the decision which is being challenged. In *Council of Civil Service Unions v Minister for the Civil Service* [1985] AC 374, Lord Diplock (at pp. 408–409) said that to have a legitimate expectation in respect of a decision, the applicant must be affected by the decision, in that the decision has the effect of:

   (a) altering rights or obligations of that person which are enforceable by or against him in private law, or

   (b) depriving him of some benefit or advantage which either:

      (i) he has in the past been permitted by the decision-maker to enjoy and which he can legitimately expect to be permitted to continue to do until there has been communicated to him some rational ground for withdrawing it on which he has been given an opportunity to comment, or

      (ii) he has received assurance from the decision-maker that it will not be withdrawn without giving him first an opportunity for advancing reasons for contending that they should not be withdrawn.

Such expectation may be based, for example, on an express promise by the decision-maker (as in *R v Liverpool Corporation, ex p Liverpool Taxi Fleet Operators' Association* [1972] 2 QB 299), or on the practice adopted in the past by the decision-maker (e.g. *R v Secretary of State for the Home Department, ex p Ruddock* [1987] 1 WLR 1482).

15.5 The need to act promptly

Section 31(6) of the SCA 1981 provides:

> . . . *where the High Court considers that there has been undue delay in making an application for judicial review, the court may refuse to grant:*
>
> > *(a) leave for the making of the application; or*
> > *(b) any relief sought on the application,*
>
> *if it considers that the granting of the relief sought would be likely to cause substantial hardship to, or substantially prejudice the rights of, any person or would be detrimental to good administration.*

CPR, r. 54.5(1) says that the claim form seeking judicial review must be filed 'promptly' and 'in any event not later than three months after the grounds to make the claim first arose'. It follows from the wording of this provision that a claim may fail for delay even if it is brought within the three-month period. In *R (on the application of Derwent Holdings Ltd) v Trafford BC* [2009] EWHC 1337 (Admin), for example, the court refused an application for permission to seek judicial review of a decision to grant planning permission because, although the application was made just within the three-month time limit, it had not been made 'promptly' and no adequate explanation had been given for the delay in commencing proceedings.

CPR, PD 54A, para. 4.1 says that where the claim is for a quashing order in respect of a judgment, order, or conviction, the date when the grounds to make the claim first arose is the date of the judgment, order, or conviction.

If the three-month period has expired, the court may grant an extension of time, but only if there is 'good reason' for doing so. In *R (on the application of Cukurova Finance International Ltd) v HM Treasury* [2008] EWHC 2567 (Admin), Moses LJ said (at [32]) that, when deciding whether to extend time for bringing a claim for judicial review, the court should start by considering to what extent there are good reasons for extending time and, if there is good reason, to what extent relief would be likely to cause hardship, would be prejudicial, or would be detrimental to good administration. It follows that, even if the court considers that there is good reason for extending the period, permission may nonetheless be refused if the court takes the view that the granting of the remedy would cause hardship or prejudice or be detrimental to good administration.

However, it should be noted that, in *Caswell v Dairy Produce Quota Tribunal for England and Wales* [1990] 2 AC 738 at p. 747, Lord Goff had expressed the view that it was appropriate that permission to apply for judicial review out of time should be granted where the judge finds that there is a good reason for extending time; the question of whether the remedy should be withheld on the ground of prejudice or hardship or detriment to good administration should be dealt with at the substantive hearing.

Where there has been delay, any explanation for that delay should be given in the application for permission to seek judicial review.

In *R v Criminal Injuries Compensation Board, ex p A* [1998] QB 659, the Court of Appeal made the point that 'the better the prospects of success, the readier will the court be to extend time even where the delay is unjustifiable, that is, the merits themselves can contribute to or even supply the "good reason"' (per Simon Brown LJ at p. 677). When this case went to the House of Lords (*R v Criminal Injuries Compensation Board, ex p A* [1999] 2 AC 330), it was held that, where permission to apply for judicial review has been given without notice, an application to set permission aside might be made, although such applications are not to be encouraged. Unless permission is set aside, the question of permission cannot be reopened at the substantive hearing on the basis that there were no grounds for extending time. What the court can do, under s. 31(6) of the SCA 1981, is to refuse to grant relief on the basis of the applicant's delay (per Lord Slynn of Hadley at p. 341).

In *R v Newbury District Council, ex p Chieveley Parish Council* [1998] 10 Admin LR 676, it was noted by the Court of Appeal that important decisions can be taken by public and private bodies, and by individuals, on the strength of some decisions, such as the granting of planning permission. It is therefore in the interests of good administration that any challenge should be made quickly. The court held that this was so even if there is no evidence of actual hardship or prejudice to the rights of third parties.

15.6 Procedure for seeking judicial review

The procedure for seeking judicial review is contained in CPR, Pt 54 and PD 54A. Under CPR, r.54.4, the court's permission to proceed is required in order to bring a claim for judicial review. Thus, an application for judicial review has two stages: an application for permission to seek judicial review and then (if permission is granted) the substantive application for judicial review.

15.6.1 Pre-action protocol for judicial review

There is a pre-action protocol for judicial review claims. Paragraph 5 of the pre-action protocol states that judicial review 'should only be used where no adequate alternative remedy, such as a right of appeal, is available'. Paragraph 9 goes on to say that the parties should consider whether some form of alternative dispute resolution procedure would be more suitable than litigation and, if so, endeavour to agree which form to adopt. Both the claimant and defendant may be required by the court to provide evidence that alternative means of resolving their dispute were considered.

Observance of the pre-action protocol is not required in very urgent cases, for example, where the claimant is about to be removed from the United Kingdom, or where there is an urgent need for an interim order to compel a public body to act where it has unlawfully refused to do so (e.g. the failure of a local housing authority to secure interim accommodation for a homeless claimant). In such cases, a claim may be made immediately (para. 6). Even in emergency cases, however, it is good practice to send to the defendant the draft claim form which the claimant intends to issue.

Paragraph 7 provides that, where the use of the protocol is appropriate, the court will normally expect all parties to have complied with it and will take into account compliance or non-compliance when giving directions for case management of proceedings or when making orders for costs.

An integral part of the pre-action protocol is the letter before claim. The purpose of this letter is to identify the issues in dispute and establish whether the issues can be narrowed or litigation can be avoided (para. 14). Annex A of the pre-action protocol contains a suggested standard format for the letter. Paragraphs 16 and 17 of the protocol go on to summarise the key contents of the letter before claim:

- the date and details of the decision, act, or omission being challenged;
- a clear summary of the facts and the legal basis for the claim;
- details of any relevant information that the claimant is seeking and an explanation of why this is considered relevant;
- details of any interested parties known to the claimant (who should also be sent a copy of the letter before claim for information).

Paragraph 18 states that a claim should not normally be made until the proposed reply date given in the letter before claim has passed, unless the circumstances of the case require more immediate action to be taken.

The next part of the pre-action protocol deals with the letter of response from the defendant. Paragraph 20 states that defendants should normally respond within 14 days. Failure to do so will be taken into account by the court and sanctions may be imposed unless there are good reasons. Paragraph 21 goes on to add that, where it is not possible to reply within the proposed time limit, the defendant should send an interim reply and propose a reasonable extension. Where an extension is sought, reasons should be given and, where required, additional information requested. This will not affect the time limit for making a claim for judicial review, nor will it bind the claimant if they consider the extension to be unreasonable. The paragraph does warn that where the court considers that a subsequent claim is made prematurely it may impose sanctions.

Annex B contains a suggested format for the response. Paragraph 23 states that if the claim is wholly denied or conceded only in part, the reply should say so in clear and unambiguous terms, and should:

- (where appropriate) contain a new decision, clearly identifying what aspects of the claim are being conceded and what are not, or give a clear timescale within which the new decision will be issued;
- (where appropriate) provide a fuller explanation for the decision;
- address any points of dispute, or explain why they cannot be addressed;
- enclose any relevant documentation requested by the claimant or explain why the documents are not being enclosed; and
- (where appropriate) confirm whether or not any application for an interim remedy will be opposed.

A copy of this response should be sent to all the interested parties identified by the claimant and contain details of any other parties whom the defendant considers also have an interest (para. 24).

15.6.2   Seeking permission to apply for judicial review

Claims for judicial review are dealt with in the Administrative Court (part of the High Court of Justice). Documents have to be filed at the Administrative Court Office at the Royal Courts of Justice in London.

Under the *Practice Direction (Administrative Court: Establishment)* [2000] 1 WLR 1654, the parties to an application for judicial review are described in the proceedings as being: 'The

Queen on the application of [name of applicant], claimant v [the name of the public body against whom the proceedings are brought], defendant'.

15.6.3 The paperwork

Following compliance with the pre-action protocol, the first step in a claim for judicial review is to file a claim form. As well as the matters that normally have to appear in a claim form (see CPR, r.8.2), r.54.6 provides that the claimant has to state:

(a) the name and address of any person the claimant considers to be an interested party (defined in r.54.1(2)(f) as any person, other than the claimant and defendant, who is 'directly affected' by the claim);

(b) that the claimant is requesting permission to proceed with a claim for judicial review;

(c) any remedy (including any interim remedy) being claimed.

The claim form has to be accompanied by the documents required by CPR, PD 54, para. 5.6, which provides that the claim form must include or be accompanied by:

- a detailed statement of the claimant's grounds for bringing the claim for judicial review;
- a statement of the facts relied on;
- any application to extend the time limit for filing the claim form;
- any application for directions.

Practice Direction 54A, para. 5.7 provides that the claim form must also be accompanied by:

- any written evidence in support of the claim (or application to extend time);
- a copy of any order that the claimant seeks to have quashed;
- where the claim for judicial review relates to a decision of a court or tribunal, an approved copy of the reasons for reaching that decision;
- copies of any documents on which the claimant proposes to rely;
- copies of any relevant statutory material;
- a list of essential documents for reading in advance by the court (with page references to the passages relied on).

The claim form must be served on the defendant, and (unless the court otherwise directs) on any person the claimant considers to be an interested party, within seven days after the date of issue (CPR, r.54.7).

Where the claim for judicial review relates to proceedings in a court or tribunal, any other parties to those proceedings must be named in the claim form as interested parties (PD 54A, para. 5.1). It follows that where a defendant in a criminal case seeks judicial review of a decision of a magistrates' court or the Crown Court, the prosecution must always be named as an interested party (para. 5.2).

Under CPR, r.54.8, a person served with the claim form who wishes to take part in the judicial review must file an acknowledgement of service not more than 21 days after the service of the claim form. The acknowledgement of service must be served on the claimant, and on any other person named in the claim form, not later than seven days after it is filed. These time limits may *not* be extended by agreement between the parties (CPR, r.54.8(3)). The acknowledgement of service must (if the person filing it intends to contest the claim) set out a summary of the grounds for contesting the claim (and must state the name and address of anyone whom the person filing it considers to be an interested party): see CPR, r.54.8(4).

CPR, r.54.9 says that a person who fails to file an acknowledgement of service may not (unless allowed by the court) take part in any hearing to decide whether permission to proceed should be given. However, if that person complies with any direction of the court regarding the filing and service of detailed grounds for contesting the claim (or supporting it on additional grounds), together with any written evidence, they may take part in the substantive hearing of the claim for judicial review.

15.6.4   Determining the application for permission

PD 54A, para. 8.4 provides that the court will generally, in the first instance, consider the question of permission without a hearing. Where there is a hearing, neither the defendant nor any other interested party needs to attend the hearing unless the court directs otherwise (para. 8.5). Where the defendant or any interested party does attend a hearing, the court will not generally make an order for costs against the claimant (para. 8.6).

If the applicant has sufficient standing to bring the claim for judicial review and there has not been undue delay, the judge will go on to consider the merits of the application. The test applied by the single judge is whether the claimant's application for judicial review discloses an arguable case.

In *R v Secretary of State for the Home Department, ex p Begum* [1990] Imm AR 1, it was held that if the judge is satisfied that there is no arguable case, the application for permission should be refused. If the judge is satisfied that there is an arguable case, permission should be given. If the judge is uncertain whether or not there is an arguable case, the application for permission should be adjourned to enable a hearing to take place so that oral arguments from both the claimant and the defendant (and other interested parties) may be heard.

Under s. 31(3C) of the SCA 1981, when considering whether to grant permission, the court may of its own motion consider whether the outcome for the applicant would have been substantially different if the conduct complained of had not occurred, and must consider that question if the defendant asks it to do so. If it appears to the court to be 'highly likely that the outcome for the applicant would not have been substantially different', the court must refuse to grant permission (s. 31(3D)), unless the court considers that it is appropriate to disregard this requirement for reasons of 'exceptional public interest' (s. 31(3E)). In such a case, there may be a hearing, under CPR 54.11A, to determine whether permission should be given.

15.6.5   Refusal of permission

CPR, r.54.12 provides that if the court, without a hearing, refuses permission to proceed, or gives permission that is subject to conditions or on certain grounds only, the court will serve its reasons for making the decision along with the order itself.

Under CPR, r.54.12(3), 'the claimant may not appeal but may request the decision to be reconsidered at a hearing' and (under r.54.12(4)) must file a request for such a hearing within seven days of the service of the court's reasons for the decision.

CPR, r.54.13 states that neither the defendant, nor anyone else served with the claim form, may apply to set aside an order giving the claimant permission to proceed.

In *R v Secretary of State for Trade & Industry, ex p Eastaway* [2000] 1 WLR 2222, the House of Lords held that, under CPR, Pt 52, permission (from the lower court or the Court of Appeal) is required to appeal to the Court of Appeal against refusal by a judge to grant permission to apply for judicial review. No further appeal lies to the Supreme Court.

Where, at the judicial review hearing, the claimant seeks to rely on grounds other than those for which the court gave permission to proceed, the court's permission is required (CPR, r.54.15). In *R (on the application of Smith) v Parole Board* [2003] 1 WLR 2548, the Court of Appeal held that a judge hearing a substantive judicial review application should require substantial justification before allowing a claimant to advance an argument in relation to which permission was refused at a contested oral permission hearing. However, if the judge comes to the conclusion that there is good reason to allow argument on that ground, bearing in mind the interests of the defendant, they can give permission for that to happen, even if no new legal or factual situation has arisen (per Lord Woolf CJ at [16]).

15.6.6   Procedure if permission is given

Under CPR, r.54.14, once the claimant has been given permission to proceed, the defendant (and anyone else served with the claim form who wishes to contest the claim or to support it on additional grounds) must, within 35 days after service of the order giving permission, serve:

- detailed grounds for contesting the claim (or supporting it on additional grounds); and
- any written evidence.

Any person may apply for permission to file evidence or to make representations at the judicial review hearing (CPR, r.54.17). Under s. 87 of the Criminal Justice and Courts Act 2015, a party to judicial review proceedings may not be ordered to pay the intervener's costs in connection with the proceedings unless the court considers that there are exceptional circumstances that make it appropriate to do so.

Where all the parties agree, the court may decide the claim for judicial review without a hearing (CPR, r.54.18). In *BP v Secretary of State for the Home Department* [2011] 1 WLR 3187, it was held that, where permission to apply for judicial review has been granted, the effect of CPR, r.54.18 is that the claimant is entitled to a hearing, and the claim can only be decided without a hearing where all the parties agree to the case being dealt with in that way.

Otherwise, the claimant must file and serve a skeleton argument not less than 21 working days before the date of the hearing of the judicial review claim (PD 54A, para. 15.1). The defendant (and any other party wishing to make representations at the hearing) must file and serve a skeleton argument not less than 14 working days before the date of the hearing (para. 15.2). The skeleton arguments must (under para. 15.3) contain:

- a list of issues;
- a list of the legal points to be taken (together with any relevant authorities, with page references to the passages relied on);
- a chronology of events (with page references to the bundle of documents);
- a list of essential documents for advance reading by the court;
- a list of persons referred to.

In *Tweed v Parades Commission for Northern Ireland* [2007] 1 AC 650, the House of Lords gave guidance on disclosure of documents in the context of judicial review. Since a challenge to an administrative decision by way of judicial review raises predominately legal issues, disclosure will not ordinarily be necessary for fairly disposing of the matters in issue. However, the courts should adopt a flexible approach and judge the need for disclosure on the facts of the individual case. Where the claim raises the issue of the proportionality of a decision restricting a protected Convention right, this will call for careful factual assessment in the context of the relevant margin of appreciation; it follows that the court, on an application for disclosure, should take account of those factors when considering whether to make the order sought. Even in cases involving issues of proportionality, however, disclosure should be carefully limited to the issues which require it in the interests of justice.

15.6.7 Expedited hearing

The sheer number of cases where judicial review is sought means that claims can take a long time to be dealt with. In urgent cases, an expedited hearing may be sought. In such a case, the claim form must contain a request for an expedited hearing and must set out the reasons why such a hearing is sought.

15.6.8 Hearing an application for judicial review

Criminal cases are heard by a Divisional Court (normally two High Court judges, although in complex cases there may be three); civil cases are heard by a single judge (unless the judge who gives permission for the application to proceed directs that the case be heard by a Divisional Court).

The hearing takes the form of legal argument based on the contents of the statements of case and the written evidence. Since the evidence is in written form, witnesses are not usually called.

In *R (on the application of G) v Ealing LBC* [2002] EWHC 250 (Admin), it was held that although there is no specific provision in CPR, Pt 54 for the court to receive oral evidence and to order the cross-examination of witnesses on their witness statements/affidavits, the court has the power (under CPR, r.32.1 or through its inherent jurisdiction) to do so. This power will, however, only be exercised in exceptional cases.

In *R (on the application of McVey) v Secretary of State for Health* [2010] EWHC 437 (Admin), Silber J said (at [35]) that, in a claim for judicial review, the proper approach to disputed evidence is as follows:

(i) The basic rule is that where there is a dispute on evidence in a judicial review application, then in the absence of cross-examination, the facts in the defendants' evidence must be assumed to be correct;

(ii) An exception to this rule arises where the documents show that the defendant's evidence cannot be correct; and that

(iii) The proper course for a claimant who wishes to challenge the correctness of an important aspect of the defendant's evidence relating to a factual matter on which the judge will have to make a critical factual finding is to apply to cross-examine the maker of the witness statement on which the defendant relies.

At the hearing, counsel for the claimant speaks first, followed by counsel for the defendant; counsel for the claimant then has the right to reply.

15.6.9 Costs

Practice Statement (QBD (Admin Ct): Judicial Review: Costs) [2004] 1 WLR 1760 stipulates that a grant of permission to pursue an application for judicial review (whether made on the papers or after oral argument) will be deemed to contain an order that costs will be 'costs in the case'. Should the judge granting permission wish to make a different order, that fact should be reflected in the order granting permission.

In *Davey v Aylesbury District Council* [2008] 1 WLR 878, the Court of Appeal gave guidance on recovery of costs incurred prior to the grant of permission to seek judicial review. Sedley LJ (at [21]) said that, on the conclusion of full judicial review proceedings in a defendant's favour, the nature and purpose of the particular claim is relevant to the exercise of the judge's discretion as to costs. In contrast to a judicial review claim brought wholly or mainly for commercial or proprietary reasons, a claim brought partly or wholly in the public interest, albeit unsuccessful, may properly result in a restricted order (or no order) for costs. If awarding costs against the claimant, the judge should consider whether they are to include preparation costs. It will be for the defendant to justify these. If the judge makes an order for costs in a defendant's favour but does not distinguish between pre-permission and post-permission costs, the order has to be regarded as including any reasonably incurred preparation costs. However, a defendant who chooses to attend and oppose an oral application for permission cannot ordinarily expect to recover the costs of doing so, even if permission is refused, although such costs may be allowed in exceptional circumstances (see *R (on the application of Mount Cook Land Ltd) v Westminster City Council* [2003] EWCA Civ 1346).

15.7 Grounds for seeking judicial review

In *Council of Civil Service Unions v Minister for the Civil Service* [1985] AC 374, Lord Diplock (at p. 410) identified three broad heads under which judicial review might be sought: illegality, irrationality, and procedural impropriety.

15.7.1 Illegality

Lord Diplock defined illegality in this context by saying that 'the decision-maker must understand correctly the law that regulates his decision-making power and must give effect to it'

(*Council of Civil Service Unions v Minister for the Civil Service* [1985] AC 374 at p. 410). In other words, the decision must be within the decision-maker's jurisdiction. An act is outside jurisdiction ('*ultra vires*') where the decision-maker purports to exercise a power which they do not possess, or else use a power for a purpose other than the purpose for which the power was granted.

Where a discretionary power is being exercised, the decision-maker must not adhere to a fixed policy without having regard to the circumstances of the particular case under consideration (*R v Secretary of State for the Home Department, ex p Findlay* [1985] AC 318). There is no objection to a decision-maker having a policy, provided consideration is given to each individual case to see if there is any reason why the policy should not apply to that case (see *R v Port of London Authority, ex p Kynoch Ltd* [1919] 1 KB 176).

15.7.2 Irrationality

Another word for irrationality is 'unreasonableness'. The classic definition of unreasonableness was set out by Lord Greene MR in *Associated Provincial Picture Houses Ltd v Wednesbury Corp* [1948] 1 KB 223 at p. 234: a decision may only be quashed as irrational if it is 'so unreasonable that no reasonable [decision-maker] could ever have come to it'.

In many cases, the basis for claiming that the decision is an unreasonable one will be that the decision is flawed by irrelevance. In *Wednesbury* (at pp. 233–234), Lord Greene MR said that the court is entitled to investigate whether a decision-making body 'has taken into account matters which it ought not to take into account, or conversely, has refused to take into account matters or neglected to take into account matters which it ought to take into account'.

For example, in *R v Lewisham London Borough Council, ex p Shell (UK) Ltd* [1988] 1 All ER 938, a local authority boycotted Shell's products because that company had connections in South Africa (which was then subject to a system of racial apartheid); this boycott was declared unlawful, because the decision was motivated by considerations which were (legally) irrelevant.

The courts are generally reluctant to usurp the function of the original decision-maker. For example, in *R (on the application of Isiko) v Secretary of State for the Home Department* [2001] 1 FLR 930 (an immigration case), the Court of Appeal said that, in reviewing a decision of the executive to see if it complies with the Human Rights Act 1998, the court will not substitute its decision for that of the executive, but will decide whether the decision-maker has exceeded the discretion given to them. The scope of the discretion has to be exceeded before a decision can be recognised as unlawful. In the area of immigration and deportation, for example, difficult choices have to be made between the rights of the individual and the needs of society and it is appropriate for the courts to recognise that there is an area of judgement within which the judiciary will defer, on democratic grounds, to the considered opinion of the elected body or person whose decision was said to be incompatible with an individual's Convention rights. Nonetheless, where a fundamental right is engaged, the court will insist that that fact is recognised by the decision-maker, who is therefore required to demonstrate that the proposed action does not interfere with the individual's right, or if it does, that there exist considerations which amount to substantial objective justification for the interference. The graver the impact of the decision in question upon the individuals affected by it, the more substantial the justification that is required. Within that framework, the court would give due deference to the primary decision-maker (per Schiemann LJ at [31]).

However, in *R v Secretary of State for the Home Department, ex p Daly* [2001] 2 AC 532, Lord Steyn (at [28]) pointed out that differences in approach between the traditional *Wednesbury* ground of review and the approach of proportionality (the approach adopted by the European Court of Human Rights) may sometimes yield different results. His Lordship expressed the view (at [27]) that the doctrine of proportionality 'may require the reviewing court to assess the balance which the decision-maker has struck, not merely whether it was within the range of rational or reasonable decisions'. The proportionality test may therefore 'go further than the traditional grounds of review in as much as it might require attention to be directed to the relative weight accorded to interests and considerations'. This does not, said Lord Steyn (at [28]), mean that there has been a shift to 'merits review': the respective roles of judges and administrators are fundamentally different and will remain so. Even in cases involving Convention rights, the intensity of review in a public law case will depend on the subject matter in hand.

In *R (on the application of Samaroo) v Secretary of State for the Home Department* [2001] UKHRR 1150, the applicants were challenging deportation decisions. The Court of Appeal held that in deciding what proportionality requires in any particular case, the issue will usually have to be considered in two distinct stages. Dyson LJ (at [19]) said that, at the first stage, the question is: 'Can the objective of the measure be achieved by means which are less interfering with an individual's rights?' The 'essential purpose of this stage of the inquiry is to see whether the legitimate aim can be achieved by means that do not interfere, or interfere so much, with a person's rights under the Convention'. That inquiry must be undertaken by the decision-maker in the first place. His Lordship (at [20]) said that, at the second stage, 'it is assumed that the means employed to achieve the legitimate aim are necessary in the sense that they are the least intrusive of Convention rights that can be devised in order to achieve the aim'. The question at this stage is: 'Does the measure have an excessive or disproportionate effect on the interests of affected persons?' Dyson LJ went on to say (at [25]) that:

Where the legitimate aim cannot be achieved by alternative means less interfering with a Convention right, the task for the decision-maker, when deciding whether to interfere with the right, is to strike a fair balance between the legitimate aim on the one hand, and the affected person's Convention rights on the other.

Moreover (at [28]), achieving a:

fair balance involves comparing the weight to be given to the wider interests of the community with the weight to be given to an individual's Convention rights. Some rights are regarded as of especial importance and should for that reason be accorded particular weight . . . the more serious the interference with a fundamental right and the graver its effects, the greater the justification that will be required for the interference.

How much weight the decision-maker gives to each factor will be the subject of (at [39]):

careful scrutiny by the court. The court will interfere with the weight accorded by the decision-maker if, despite an allowance for the appropriate margin of discretion, it concludes that the weight accorded was unfair and unreasonable. In this respect, the level of scrutiny is undoubtedly more intense than it is when a decision is subject to review on traditional Wednesbury grounds, where the court usually refuses to examine the weight accorded by the decision-maker to the various relevant factors.

Another aspect of reasonableness is that judicial review may be granted to prevent a public authority from acting in a way that defeats the claimant's legitimate expectations. For example, in *R (on the application of Nadarajah) v Secretary of State for the Home Department* [2005] EWCA Civ 1363, it was said that 'where a public authority has issued a promise or adopted a practice which represents how it proposes to act in a given area, the law will require the promise or practice to be honoured unless there is good reason not to do so' (per Laws LJ at [68]). A public body's promise or practice as to future conduct may only be departed from in circumstances where to do so is the public body's legal duty, or is otherwise a proportionate response, having regard to a legitimate aim pursued by the public body in the public interest (ibid). This principle applies both to procedural and substantive expectations.

In *R (SC v Secretary of State for Work and Pensions and others) v Equality and Human Rights Commission* [2021] UKSC 26, Lord Reed noted (at [146]) that:

the administrative law test of unreasonableness is generally applied in contexts such as economic policy and social policy with considerable care and caution; and the same is true of the Convention test of proportionality. Both tests have to be applied in a way which reconciles the rule of law with the separation of powers.

His Lordship went on to note that, in *R (DA) v Secretary of State for Work and Pensions* [2019] UKSC 21, [2019] 1 WLR 3289, Lord Wilson had said (at [65]):

in relation to the Government's need to justify what would otherwise be a discriminatory effect of a rule governing entitlement to welfare benefits, the sole question is whether it is manifestly without reasonable foundation.

Lord Reed concluded (at [158]) that:

a low intensity of review is generally appropriate, other things being equal, in cases concerned with judgements of social and economic policy in the field of welfare benefits and pensions, so that the judgement of the executive or legislature will generally be respected unless it is manifestly without reasonable foundation. Nevertheless, the intensity of the court's scrutiny can be influenced by a wide range of factors, depending on the circumstances of the particular case, as indeed it would be if the court were applying the domestic test of reasonableness rather than the Convention test of proportionality. In particular, very weighty reasons will usually have to be shown, and the intensity of review will usually be correspondingly high, if a difference in treatment on a 'suspect' ground [in particular, one that has a discriminatory effect] is to be justified.

Mistake of fact resulting in unfairness can also be a ground for judicial review if the five conditions summarised in *E v Secretary of State for Home Department* [2004] EWCA Civ 49, [2004] QB 1044 (at [66]) and more recently in *R (DPP) v Sunderland Magistrates' Court* [2018] EWHC 229 (Admin) (at [11]) are met, namely that:

(1) All the participants had a shared interest in co-operating to achieve the correct result. (2) There was a mistake as to an existing fact (which could include a mistake as to the availability of evidence on a particular matter). (3) The fact or evidence has been 'established'—in the sense that it is uncontentious and objectively verifiable. (4) The person relying on the mistake, and/or his advisers, was not responsible for the mistake. (5) The mistake played a material (but not necessarily decisive) part in the court's reasoning.

15.7.3 Procedural impropriety

Most claims of procedural impropriety involve alleged breaches of the rules of natural justice. There are two fundamental rules of natural justice:

(a) The rule against bias (sometimes described by the Latin phrase *nemo judex in re sua* or *nemo judex in causa sua*, which means that no one should be a judge in their own cause). A decision-maker should not have an interest in the outcome of the case under consideration. The test for bias was laid down by the House of Lords in *Porter v Magill* [2002] 2 AC 357 at [103], where Lord Hope of Craighead said:

. . . the question is whether the fair-minded and informed observer, having considered the facts, would conclude that there was a real possibility that the tribunal was biased.

It should be noted that this formulation takes account of two types of bias: actual and perceived. A decision may be vitiated by bias either because of evidence that the decision-maker was, in fact, biased, or because of the existence of circumstances from which a reasonable bystander could reasonably conclude that there was a real possibility that the decision-maker was biased.

(a) The right to a fair hearing (sometimes described by the Latin phrase *audi alteram partem*, which means 'hear the other side'). In *Ridge v Baldwin* [1964] AC 40, for example, a chief constable was dismissed from office without receiving any notice of his proposed dismissal and without being given any opportunity to argue against his dismissal. The House of Lords held it to be essential to a fair decision-making process that the person who is the subject of the decision should:

(i) have notice of the allegations which they have to meet; and

(ii) have an adequate opportunity to meet those allegations by making representations (whether orally or in writing) and, in appropriate cases, by calling evidence in support of those representations.

In *R (on the application of Woolcock) v The Secretary of State for Communities and Local Government* [2018] EWHC 17 (Admin), Hickinbottom LJ noted (at [50]) that, 'In considering procedural fairness, the function of the court is not merely to review the reasonableness of the decision-maker's judgement of what fairness required: the court must determine for itself whether a fair procedure was followed.'

15.7.4   The giving of reasons

In *R v Secretary of State for the Home Department, ex p Doody* [1994] 1 AC 531, the House of Lords held that even though there is no general duty to give reasons for a decision, in many cases the reasons for the decision will have to be revealed 'as an effective means of detecting the kind of error which would entitle the court to intervene' (per Lord Mustill at p. 565). Reasons given by any tribunal for reaching a decision should be intelligible and adequate, and should meet the substance of the arguments advanced by the parties. A tribunal has to show that it has successfully grasped the main contentions advanced by the parties and tell them in broad terms why they have lost or won (*Ogango v Nursing and Midwifery Council* [2008] EWHC 3115 (Admin) at [23], per Cranston J).

In *R v Ministry of Defence, ex p Murray* [1998] COD 134, it was held that where a statute confers the power to make decisions affecting individuals but does not contain an express requirement that the decision-maker must give reasons for the decision, the court will imply such a requirement if, but only if, the interests of fairness so require.

In *Adami v Ethical Standards Officer of the Standards Board for English* [2005] EWCA Civ 1754, it was held that a judge hearing a statutory appeal from a specialist tribunal which has given inadequate reasons for its decision has a discretion to remit the matter to the tribunal so that it can supply adequate reasons.

15.7.5   The effect of the Human Rights Act 1998

In *Smith and Grady v United Kingdom* [2000] 29 EHRR 493, the European Court of Human Rights noted that the effect of Article 13 of the European Convention on Human Rights is to require the provision of a domestic remedy allowing the competent national authority both to deal with the substance of the relevant Convention complaint and to grant appropriate relief. However, Article 13 does not go so far as to prescribe a particular form of remedy, Contracting States being afforded a margin of appreciation in conforming to their obligations under this provision. However, when the present case (which concerned the outlawing of homosexuality in the armed forces) came before the Court of Appeal, that court made it clear that, since the Convention did not (at that time) form part of English law, questions as to whether the application of that policy violated the applicants' rights under Article 8 and, in particular, as to whether the policy had been shown by the authorities to respond to a pressing social need or to be proportionate to any legitimate aim served, were not questions to which answers could properly be offered. The sole issue before the domestic court was whether the policy could be said to be 'irrational'. Lord Bingham MR had held that a court was not entitled to interfere with the exercise of an administrative discretion on substantive grounds, save where the court was satisfied that the decision was unreasonable in the sense that it was beyond the range of responses open to a reasonable decision-maker. In judging whether the decision-maker had exceeded this margin of appreciation, the human rights context was important, so that the more substantial the interference with human rights, the more the court would require by way of justification before it was satisfied that the decision was reasonable. It was, however, further emphasised that, notwithstanding any human rights context, the threshold of irrationality which an applicant was required to surmount was a high one. The Court of Appeal had gone on to hold that the policy in question could not be said to be beyond the range of responses open to a reasonable decision-maker and, accordingly, could not be said to be 'irrational'. However, the European Court concluded that, in such circumstances, it was clear that the threshold at which the domestic courts could find a policy irrational was placed so high that it effectively excluded any consideration by the domestic courts of the question whether the interference with the applicants' rights answered a pressing social need or was proportionate to the national security and public order aims pursued, principles which lie at the heart of the European Court's analysis of complaints under Article 8 of the Convention. The Court accordingly found that there had been a violation of Article 13 of the Convention.

The right to a fair trial under Article 6 may also be relevant in claims for judicial review. In *R (on the application of Beeson) v Dorset CC* [2003] HRLR 11, the Court of Appeal said that, if there is no reason of substance to question the objective integrity of the first-instance process (whatever may be said about its appearance), the added safeguard of judicial review 'will very likely satisfy the Article 6 standard unless there is some special feature of the case to show the contrary' (per Laws LJ at [30]). However, in *Tsfayo v United Kingdom* [2009] 48 EHRR 18, the European Court of Human Rights had to consider the adequacy of judicial review as a remedy in a case concerning the refusal of housing benefit. The court held that, where a decision is reviewed by a body that is not independent of the parties to the dispute (in this case, a review board staffed by councillors from the local authority whose decision was being challenged), the existence of judicial review is not a sufficient safeguard for the purposes of Article 6 of the Convention (the right to a fair trial), since the High Court does not have jurisdiction to rehear evidence or to substitute its own views as to the credibility of the parties. It follows that, in such a case, there exists no possibility for the central factual issue at dispute to be determined by an independent and impartial tribunal. The court therefore held that there had been a breach of Article 6.

It is submitted that the position may be summarised as follows. For the judicial review process to comply with Article 13 in a case where Convention rights are engaged, the court must take full account of those Convention rights and must be prepared to look at the merits of the decision being reviewed, not just the procedure by which that decision was reached. This requires the court to consider whether the decision is a proportionate way of achieving a legitimate aim. In those cases where Convention rights are not engaged, it is of course open to the court to adopt the traditional approach, that the sole issue is whether the decision was a rational decision reached by the correct procedure.

15.8 Remedies

The remedies which may be granted following an application for judicial review are set out in CPR, r.54.2 and include:

(a) a 'quashing order' (formerly known as *certiorari*): this has the effect of quashing the decision being challenged;

(b) a 'mandatory order' (formerly known as *mandamus)*: this has the effect of requiring the defendant to do something, most commonly to compel a decision-maker to reconsider the original decision;

(c) a 'prohibiting order' (formerly known as 'prohibition'): the effect of this remedy is similar to that of an injunction, in that it prevents a public body from acting or continuing to act in a way which is unlawful.

The Senior Courts Act 1981, s. 31(5) and (5A) provides that, if the decision in question was made by a court or tribunal and it is quashed on the ground that there has been an error of law and, without the error, there would have been only one decision which the court or tribunal could have reached, then the High Court (in addition to quashing the decision) may either remit the matter to the court or tribunal which made the decision (with a direction to reconsider the matter and reach a decision in accordance with the findings of the High Court), or else substitute its own decision for the decision in question (see also CPR, r.54.19).

Additionally, under CPR, r.54.3, the court has the power to grant what would normally be regarded as 'private law' remedies, namely:

(a) *Declaration.* The effect of a declaration is to state the law on a particular point. So, if a decision is quashed because the decision-maker misunderstood the law, the court can grant a declaration setting out the correct interpretation of the law.

(b) *Injunction.* This has the same effect as a prohibiting order but with one difference, which is that an injunction may be an interim remedy (i.e. pending the full hearing), whereas a prohibiting order may not be granted as an interim remedy.

A claim for judicial review may include a claim for damages but cannot be used to claim damages only (CPR, r.54.3(2)).

More than one remedy may be sought in the same application.

The grant of any judicial review remedy is discretionary. Reasons for refusing to grant the remedy sought include such matters as:

(a) the conduct of the applicant, so that the applicant does not deserve assistance (in *R (on the application of Santos) v Stratford Magistrates' Court* [2012] EWHC 752 (Admin), for example, the claimant sought judicial review of a refusal by a magistrates' court to state a case; the claim was rejected because the claimant had not raised the disputed issue in the magistrates' court at the original trial);

(b) adverse consequences to the public as a whole, or the impact on third parties (see, e.g., *R v Panel on Take-Overs and Mergers, ex p Guinness plc* [1990] 1 QB 146);

(c) if no harm has been done, in that the following of the proper procedure by the decision-maker would have made no difference (e.g. *R v Secretary of State for the Environment, ex p Walters* [1998] 30 HLR 328, where the Court of Appeal held that even if a decision-maker fails to comply with a statutory consultation process, the court is entitled to refuse to grant relief in judicial review proceedings). Section 31(2A) of the SCA 1981 (inserted by s. 84 of the Criminal Justice and Courts Act 2015) provides that the court must refuse to grant relief on an application for judicial review, 'if it appears to the court to be highly likely that the outcome for the applicant would not have been substantially different if the conduct complained of had not occurred', unless (by virtue of s. 31(2B)), the court 'considers that it is appropriate to do so for reasons of exceptional public interest'.

15.9 Interim remedy

There is a power to grant an interim remedy in judicial review proceedings. In *R v Ministry of Agriculture, Fisheries & Food, ex p Monsanto* [1999] QB 1161, it was held that the court should apply the principles which govern the grant of an interim injunction (see *American Cyanamid v Ethicon* [1975] AC 396) to the question of whether to grant an interim remedy in judicial review proceedings.

15.10 Future developments in judicial review

The Judicial Review and Courts Bill (introduced in July 2021) proposes two significant changes to judicial review. The first relates to remedies. The Bill proposes that a quashing order may include a provision that it is not to take effect until a date specified in the order (i.e. a discretion to suspend the quashing order), or a provision removing or limiting any retrospective effect of the quashing order (so that court declares an action or decision to be unlawful only from a particular point in time). The second proposal would reverse the effect of *Cart* (see **15.2.3**) by stating that the decision (or purported decision) of the Upper Tribunal to refuse permission to appeal is final, and not liable to be questioned or set aside in any other court (thereby removing the ability to judicially review a decision of the Upper Tribunal to refuse permission to appeal from the First-tier Tribunal).

15.11 FURTHER READING

There are a number of textbooks on judicial review, including:

Fordham, M., *Judicial Review Handbook*, 7th edn, Bloomsbury Publishing, 2020.

Southey, H., Westing, A., Bunting, J., *Judicial Review: A Practical Guide*, 3rd edn, Jordan Publishing, 2017.

Supperstone, M., Goudie, J., Walker, P., *Judicial Review*, 6th edn, LexisNexis, 2017.

Hare, I., Donolley, C., Bell, J., Carnwath, R., *De Smith's Judicial Review*, 9th edn, Sweet & Maxwell, 2022.

Remedies for unlawful discrimination

16.1 Introduction

The law of discrimination has developed considerably since the first effective legislation in the mid-1970s. Introduced to address discrimination on grounds of sex, marital status, and race, it has now been extended to other areas, notably disability, sexual orientation, religion or belief, and age. Article 14 of the European Convention on Human Rights (ECHR) makes discrimination unlawful in respect of Convention rights. Most cases have arisen in the context of employment, and some categories of discrimination only apply to the employment context. However, the principles apply to other areas, and major case law developments have arisen from these.

This chapter introduces the basic concepts required to understand the law of discrimination, but then focuses on the remedies available. If you wish to explore the basic concepts further, you will find a fuller exposition in the **Employment Law in Practice** manual. To apply the law to real situations, however, you are advised to refer to the main practitioner texts, for example (in the employment field) *Harvey on Industrial Relations and Employment Law*, which is available within Lexis Library or as a looseleaf encyclopaedia.

16.2 Legal framework

Both international and domestic provisions provide for unlawful discrimination:

- Equality Act 2010;
- Treaty on the Functioning of the European Union (TFEU) Article 157 (ex Article 141 Treaty of Rome);
- Equal Pay Directive 75/117;
- Equal Treatment Directive 76/207;
- European Union (Withdrawal) Act 2018;
- Human Rights Act 1998 (incorporating Article 14 of the European Convention on Human Rights);
- Race Directive 2000/43;
- Framework Directive on Equal Treatment in Employment 2000/78.

Although the UK has left the EU, the European Union (Withdrawal) Act 2018, s. 2 maintains in force EU-derived legislation and s. 6 provides that case law contained in UK and European Court judgments before 31 December 2020 continues to be binding. *Harvey* has an updating service which may usefully be consulted regularly.

16.2.1   What types of discrimination are made unlawful?

16.2.1.1   The nature of the discrimination

Four types of discrimination are recognised by the law: direct discrimination, indirect discrimination, harassment, and victimisation. Remedies for these four are not necessarily available in all circumstances. Further special provisions apply to disability discrimination.

16.2.1.2   The protected characteristics

These may be found in the Equality Act 2010 (EqA 2010), ss. 4–12:

- age (s. 5);
- disability (s. 6);
- gender reassignment (s. 7);
- marriage and civil partnership (s. 8);
- race (s. 9);
- religion or belief (s. 10);
- sex (s. 11);
- sexual orientation (s. 12).

16.2.1.3   Other anti-discrimination provisions

The Human Rights Act 1998 prohibits discrimination on wider grounds: 'sex, race, colour, language, religion, political or other opinion, national or social origin, association with a national minority, property, birth or other status', but only in relation to Convention rights brought into UK law.

16.3   Basic concepts explained

16.3.1   Direct discrimination

The Equality Act 2010 provides a new definition of the established concept of direct discrimination, which is now defined in s. 13(1) as follows:

> *A person (A) discriminates against another (B) if, because of a protected characteristic, A treats B less favourably than A treats or would treat others.*

'Because of' is sufficiently broad to include those discriminated against because they actually have the protected characteristic, those who are thought to have the characteristic (discrimination by perception), and those who are associated with someone who has the characteristic (discrimination by association).

This definition applies to all protected characteristics, although s. 18(7) excludes discrimination on grounds of pregnancy and maternity. Section 18 makes specific provisions in respect of these protected characteristics.

Segregation on grounds of race is unlawful, but not segregation on grounds of sex, although sex segregation in schools may be unlawful (*HM Chief Inspector of Education, Children's Services and Skills v Interim Executive Board of Al-Hijrah School (Secretary of State for Education and others intervening)* [2017] All ER (D) 79 (Oct)).

The concept of 'race' has proven complex. It is defined as including colour, nationality, or ethnic or national origins (s. 9(1)). 'Ethnic origins' was further explained by the House of Lords in *Mandla v Dowell Lee* [1983] 2 AC 548, recognising that the concept of ethnicity encompasses cultural identity as well as racial identity. This means that discrimination on the grounds of caste may, in certain circumstances, fall within the concept of race discrimination (*Chandhok v Tirkey* [2015] IRLR 195 (EAT)).

Direct discrimination, if established, may never be justified, except in the case of age discrimination (s. 13(2)) and disability discrimination (s. 15). Note the Supreme Court decision in *Seldon v Clarkson Wright and Jakes* [2010] IRLR 590 that in age discrimination cases the only acceptable justifications are likely to be those of a 'public interest' nature.

The claimant has the burden of establishing a prima facie case against the respondent: *Royal Mail Group Ltd v Efobi* [2021] UKSC 33. A finding of unlawful discrimination should follow unless the respondent can prove that there was no unlawful discrimination. Guidance is available from *Barton v Investec Henderson Crosthwaite Securities Ltd* [2003] IRLR 332.

16.3.1.1   How is pregnancy dealt with?

The Equality Act 2010, s. 18 makes special provision for pregnancy and maternity discrimination, this being the reason for the exclusion of these characteristics from the direct discrimination provisions. The wording of the provisions avoids the need to make comparisons with men, as had been the case under the original sex discrimination provisions. Thus, a claim may be made by a woman treated unfavourably (as opposed to less favourably) on grounds of pregnancy or maternity.

Pregnancy is also an inadmissible reason for dismissal, entitling the dismissed employee to make an unfair dismissal claim without serving the normal one-year qualifying period and making it unnecessary to prove that the dismissal was unreasonable in all the circumstances (Employment Rights Act 1996, s. 99).

Outside the employment field (and in employment cases not involving dismissal), a remedy is available on a similar analysis (see the decision of the House of Lords in *Webb v EMO Air Cargo (UK) Ltd* [1995] IRLR 645).

16.3.2   Indirect discrimination

Before the implementation of EqA 2010, different provisions applied to the different protected characteristics. The concept has now been simplified and the former disparate definitions codified to provide consistency.

Section 19 provides:

> *(1) A person (A) discriminates against another (B) if A applies to B a provision, criterion or practice which is discriminatory in relation to a relevant protected characteristic of B's.*
>
> *(2) For the purposes of subsection (1), a provision, criterion or practice is discriminatory in relation to a relevant protected characteristic of B's if—*
>
> > *(a) A applies, or would apply, it to persons with whom B does not share the characteristic,*
> >
> > *(b) it puts, or would put, persons with whom B shares the characteristic at a particular disadvantage when compared with persons with whom B does not share it,*
> >
> > *(c) it puts, or would put, B at that disadvantage, and*
> >
> > *(d) A cannot show it to be a proportionate means of achieving a legitimate aim.*

One significant change is the extension of indirect discrimination to disability (s. 19(3)). There are no provisions for indirect discrimination on grounds of pregnancy or maternity.

The new provisions replace the previous test of 'condition or requirement' with 'provision, criterion or practice' and apply the same test to all relevant protected characteristics (indicated in s. 19(3)). They also amend the concept of justification to one of proportionality. These changes remedy the complications caused by diverse provisions and mean that earlier case law establishing the meaning of 'condition or requirement' will no longer be relevant. However, other case law continues to be relevant, as it indicates the ways in which this legislation may be used in practice and the shift from 'justifiable' to 'proportionate' reflects the European Court of Justice case law in this area.

16.3.2.1   How is disproportionate impact proven?

Statistical evidence may well be necessary. The courts recognise that this should not be over-elaborate (*Perera v Civil Service Commission* [1983] IRLR 166), and the Court of Appeal has expressed support for a common-sense approach (*London Underground Ltd v Edwards (No 2)* [1998] IRLR 364). This is a technical area. For more discussion, see s. 8.8.1 of the ***Employment Law in Practice*** manual.

16.3.2.2   How can a claim of indirect discrimination be defended?

To apply the concept of proportionality to establish a defence, a balancing exercise is expected between the needs of the alleged discriminator and those of the alleged victim. In fact, the Framework Directive uses the term 'appropriate and necessary'. The Explanatory Memorandum to the Sex Discrimination Act 1975 (Amendment) Regulations 2008 (now spent since the repeal of the 1975 Act by the Equality Act 2010) explained that this term was not used because of its very strict interpretation in English jurisprudence and that 'proportionality' incorporates the concept of necessity.

Guidance on applying the test may be found in *R (on the application of Elias) v Secretary of State for Defence* [2006] IRLR 934. A useful example of a proportionality defence being accepted is *Azmi v Kirklees Metropolitan BC* [2007] IRLR 484 and an example of its failure may be seen in *Allen v GMB* [2008] IRLR 690.

16.3.3   Harassment

The Equality Act 2010, s. 26 now provides for this to be a separate head of discrimination and is worded to avoid the difficulties under the earlier legislation:

> (1) *person (A) harasses another (B) if—*
>   (a) *A engages in unwanted conduct related to a relevant protected characteristic, and*
>   (b) *the conduct has the purpose or effect of—*
>   (i) *violating B's dignity, or*
>   (ii) *creating an intimidating, hostile, degrading, humiliating or offensive environment for B.*
> (2) *A also harasses B if—*
>   (a) *A engages in unwanted conduct of a sexual nature, and*
>   (b) *the conduct has the purpose or effect referred to in subsection (1)(b).*
> (3) *A also harasses B if—*
>   (a) *A or another person engages in unwanted conduct of a sexual nature or that is related to gender reassignment or sex,*
>   (b) *the conduct has the purpose or effect referred to in subsection (1)(b), and*
>   (c) *because of B's rejection of or submission to the conduct, A treats B less favourably than A would treat B if B had not rejected or submitted to the conduct.*

The effect of these provisions is to make three types of behaviour unlawful:

- Harassment related to a protected characteristic. This includes the harassment of people because of a protected characteristic they have, one the harasser believes them to have, or because they are associated with someone having a protected characteristic (such as the carer of a disabled person). A person harassed because they object to an employer's racist actions is protected.

- Sexual harassment. This is unwanted conduct of a sexual nature. This is defined as addressing the nature of the conduct rather than the gender of the victim. It can include verbal, non-verbal, or physical conduct including unwelcome sexual advances, touching, forms of sexual assault, sexual jokes, displaying pornographic photographs or drawings, or sending emails with material of a sexual nature.

- Less favourable treatment based on a person's rejection of or submission to unwanted sexual conduct. This provision is designed to cover the situation where a victim of unwanted sexual conduct who rejects it suffers treatment which is damaging but which does not constitute harassment. This might include a denial of overtime opportunities or a promotion. While this sort of treatment may be most commonly imposed on those who reject unwanted sexual conduct, the legislation also protects those who succumb to it.

The Protection from Harassment Act 1997 (PHA 1997) provides civil remedies and criminal penalties for conduct (including speech) which causes or may cause distress. This must involve at least two occasions and covers action at work. There is no need to establish that it is related to a protected characteristic. The civil remedy is an action in tort.

16.3.4 Victimisation

This is provided for by EqA 2010, s. 27. People who suffer less favourable treatment because they carry out a protected act are victimised and are entitled to a remedy. Protected acts include bringing claims, giving evidence, making allegations, or doing other things by reference to the discrimination legislation (or intending to do so). Victimisation after employment has ended is actionable (*Jessemey v Rowstock Ltd* [2014] IRLR 368 (CA)).

16.3.5 May affirmative action programmes be lawful?

Although the results of past discrimination continue to disadvantage many individuals, the law makes all discrimination (including 'positive discrimination') in the specified fields unlawful. A well-publicised example is *Bayfield v J Walter Thompson Group Ltd* [2021] 2200540/2019. Limited exceptions, however, exist where properly approved affirmative action programmes may be lawful (see EqA 2010, s. 158).

16.4 Disability discrimination

16.4.1 Who is able to make a claim?

The EqA 2010, s. 6 defines disability and s. 6(4) applies the general provisions of the Act to disability. A remedy is available for people who have a disability, defined as a physical or mental impairment causing a substantial long-term adverse effect on the ability to carry out normal day-to-day activities (EqA 2010, Sch. 1, Pt 1). Progressive conditions such as multiple sclerosis are included.

In deciding whether this test is met, tribunals should consider what claimants cannot do rather than what they can do (*Goodwin v The Patent Office* [1999] IRLR 4). There is no formal list of activities but typically they are likely to include:

- mobility;
- manual dexterity;
- physical coordination;
- continence;
- the ability to lift and carry;
- speech, hearing, and eyesight;
- memory or ability to concentrate, learn, or understand; and
- perception of the risk of danger.

For guidance see the Equality Act 2010 Guidance on Disability Definitions: <https://assets.publishing.service.gov.uk/government/uploads/system/uploads/attachment_data/file/570382/Equality_Act_2010-disability_definition.pdf>.

16.4.2 Discrimination arising from disability

The Equality Act 2010, s. 15 provides:

> (1) A person (A) discriminates against a disabled person (B) if—
>> (a) A treats B unfavourably because of something arising in consequence of B's disability, and
>> (b) A cannot show that the treatment is a proportionate means of achieving a legitimate aim.
>
> (2) Subsection (1) does not apply if A shows that A did not know, and could not reasonably have been expected to know, that B had the disability.

The wording of this provision avoids the need for a comparison to be drawn, easing the task for the claimant, but introduces a justification defence for employers.

This wording is designed to overturn the widely criticised House of Lords' decision in the local authority housing case of *London Borough of Lewisham v Malcolm* [2008] IRLR 700. The problem had been that where a disabled person behaved in a particular way because of their disability, and was less favourably treated as a result, they could not use as a comparator a non-disabled person who, not being disabled, had not behaved in that particular way.

A common situation to which this applies is where a disabled employee has higher than usual rates of absence. An employer who dismisses because of the level of absences (treating the disabled employee as they would have treated any other employee) will not necessarily have unlawfully discriminated, but (s. 15(1)(b)) will bear the burden of justifying the decision in order to escape liability.

Explanation and examples of these provisions may be found in Chapter 5 of the Equality and Human Rights Commission (EHRC) Equality Act Code of Practice (<https://www.equalityhumanrights.com/sites/default/files/employercode.pdf>).

16.4.3   Duty to make reasonable adjustments

The Equality Act 2010, s. 21(2) provides that it is unlawful discrimination to fail to comply with a duty to make reasonable adjustments for a disabled person. That duty comprises of three requirements, provided for in s. 20:

> *(3) The first requirement is a requirement, where a provision, criterion or practice of A's puts a disabled person at a substantial disadvantage in relation to a relevant matter in comparison with persons who are not disabled, to take such steps as it is reasonable to have to take to avoid the disadvantage.*
>
> *(4) The second requirement is a requirement, where a physical feature puts a disabled person at a substantial disadvantage in relation to a relevant matter in comparison with persons who are not disabled, to take such steps as it is reasonable to have to take to avoid the disadvantage.*
>
> *(5) The third requirement is a requirement, where a disabled person would, but for the provision of an auxiliary aid, be put at a substantial disadvantage in relation to a relevant matter in comparison with persons who are not disabled, to take such steps as it is reasonable to have to take to provide the auxiliary aid.*

These refer, respectively, to changing a practice, changing the built environment, and providing equipment or services. The duty protects employees, job applicants, and those who may be job applicants (EqA 2010, Sch. 8, Pt 2). Detailed provisions may be found in s. 20 and Sch. 8 and in Chapter 6 of the EHRC Equality Act Code of Practice (<https://www.equalityhumanrights.com/sites/default/files/employercode.pdf>).

16.4.4   Harassment

Those suffering harassment on grounds of disability are protected by s. 26 (see **16.3.3**).

16.4.5   Discrimination by way of victimisation

Those victimised for taking action under the EqA 2010 may bring a claim under s. 27 (see **16.3.4**).

16.5   Discrimination in employment

This is the field most commonly affected by the discrimination legislation. All the provisions identified in **16.2** affect the employment relationship.

Note that where the claimant complains of sex discrimination in pay or other terms of the contract of employment, the claim should be under EqA 2010, Pt 1, Ch. 3, and special procedural rules apply to such claims (see **16.8**).

There is a defence peculiar to the employment field. Discrimination which would otherwise be unlawful may be lawful if it relates to an occupational requirement (EqA 2010, Sch. 9). Paragraph 1(1) provides:

> *(1) A person (A) does not contravene [a direct discrimination provision] by applying in relation to work a requirement to have a particular protected characteristic, if A shows that, having regard to the nature or context of the work—*

(a) *it is an occupational requirement,*

(b) *the application of the requirement is a proportionate means of achieving a legitimate aim, and*

(c) *the person to whom A applies the requirement does not meet it (or A has reasonable grounds for not being satisfied that the person meets it).*

An example is employing only women to supervise a female changing room, but the reason must be an objective one and not a subjective one based on assumptions about customers' preferences. See *Bougnaoui and ADDH v Micropole SA* [2017] IRLR 447, where the European Court of Justice rejected a requirement that a Muslim woman not wear a hijab.

This is a departure from the previous legislation (which had listed accepted occupational requirements) as it establishes a principle to be applied rather than a list to fall within.

16.5.1 Individual remedies for discrimination in employment cases

16.5.1.1 Jurisdiction and time limit

Employment tribunals have jurisdiction to hear these claims (EqA 2010, s. 120).

The time limit is three months from the last discriminatory act complained of, although the tribunal may extend the period if it is 'just and equitable' to do so (a relatively broad provision). A prospective claimant must seek 'early conciliation' through the Advisory, Conciliation and Advisory Service (ACAS) in order to seek a conciliated settlement of the claim. The limitation period will be suspended during the early conciliation process (one month, extendable if there is a reasonable prospect of achieving settlement within the extended period).

16.5.1.2 What orders can the tribunal make?

A tribunal can make the following orders:

(a) a declaration of the rights of each party (EqA 2010, s. 124(2)(a));

(b) an award of compensation, including compensation for injury to feelings (EqA 2010, s. 124(2)(b));

(c) a recommendation of action to be taken within a specified time, in default of which additional compensation can be ordered (EqA 2010, s. 124(2)(c)).

16.5.2 Tribunal procedure

Tribunal procedures are regulated by the Employment Tribunal (Constitution and Rules of Procedure) Regulations 2013 (SI 2013/1237). For a more detailed exposition, see the *Employment Law in Practice* manual. There are a number of features peculiar to these proceedings.

16.5.2.1 ACAS discrimination questions approach

The Equality Act 2010, s. 138, which provided for a claimant to require responses from the respondent to a statutory questionnaire, was repealed with effect from 6 April 2014. It has been replaced by guidance from ACAS <http://www.acas.org.uk/media/pdf/m/p/asking-and-responding-to-questions-of-discrimination-in-the-workplace.pdf>. A key attribute of the s. 138 procedure was the ability of tribunals to infer discrimination from evasive or ambiguous answers. The new guidance permits tribunals to consider such factors in taking their decisions, so it appears that the impact of these changes are minor.

16.5.2.2 The role of ACAS

ACAS has a duty to promote settlement in employment tribunal cases. Before a claim may be issued, the claimant must undertake early conciliation, whereby ACAS is engaged to seek to achieve a settlement. If that fails, the claim may proceed, but either party may seek further help from ACAS if seeking to achieve settlement.

16.5.2.3 Preliminary hearings

These are designed to address case management matters or to weed out hopeless cases. Either party may request such a hearing or the tribunal itself may decide to hold one. Evidence is not usually heard. Where the tribunal concludes that either the claim or defence has no reasonable prospect of success, it may require the party to pay a deposit of up to £1,000 before continuing to bring or defend the claim.

16.5.2.4   Appeals

An appeal against an employment tribunal decision lies to the Employment Appeal Tribunal (EAT) and must be made within 42 days of the extended written reasons being sent to the parties.

16.6   Discrimination in other fields

16.6.1   Education

Discrimination in education is addressed by EqA 2010, Pt 6. Much of the provision in relation to disability has been provided for by the Special Educational Needs and Disability Act 2001.
   Discrimination is actionable in the following situations:

- in terms of admission;
- by not accepting an application;
- in access to benefits, etc.;
- by excluding, or causing other detriment.

There are statutory exemptions which apply to single-sex establishments and further education courses in physical training.

16.6.1.1   Remedies for discrimination in education

This protection does not apply to the protected characteristics of age, marriage, or civil partnership. In other cases, an application may be made to a county court (EqA 2010, s. 114(1)).
   The Special Educational Needs and Disability Act 2001 established the Special Educational Needs and Disability Tribunal. This tribunal now sits within the Health, Education and Social Care Chamber of the First-tier Tribunal (SI 2010/2655, art. 4).

16.6.2   Services, public functions, and premises

Discrimination in the field of services and public functions is covered by EqA 2010, Pt 3. Discrimination in the disposal, management, or leasing of premises is covered by EqA 2010, Pt 4. Discrimination in this field will be actionable on denial of the services or premises concerned or on denial of equal quality or terms.
   Examples might include:

- access to and use of any place which members of the public or a section of the public are permitted to enter;
- accommodation in a hotel, boarding house, or other similar establishment;
- facilities by way of banking or insurance or for grants, loans, credit, or finance;
- facilities for education;
- facilities for entertainment, recreation, or refreshment;
- facilities for transport or travel;
- the services of any profession or trade or any local or other public authority.

These provisions do not apply to the protected characteristics of age, marriage, or civil partnership.
   A claim will lie in respect of premises if discrimination is shown in the following instances:

- in offering or refusing housing, etc.;
- in the operation of any waiting list;

- in access to any benefits;
- by denying access to any benefits, etc.;
- by eviction or causing other detriment.

16.6.3 Individual remedies for discrimination in the provision of goods, facilities, etc.

The remedy lies in an application to the county court.

For procedure, see Civil Procedure Rules (CPR), Section 3I (WB Vol 2). Notice must be given to the EHRC, which may support the claim by giving advice or assistance and can recoup its costs from any damages ordered to be paid to the claimant by the court.

16.6.3.1 Time limit

A claim must be brought within six months of the act complained of.

16.6.3.2 What are the powers of the court?

The court may make orders which it could make on a successful claim in the law of tort, that is:

- a declaration of rights;
- an order for damages (at large), including an order for damages for injury to feelings;
- an injunction to prohibit or mandate certain acts.

16.6.4 Preparing a case

Whether acting for a claimant or a respondent in individual discrimination claims it is important to approach the case preparation in a systematic way which reflects the conceptual basis of the legislation and the procedural provisions that exist. These are presented in **Table 16.1**.

16.7 Compensation in cases of individual discrimination

16.7.1 Compensation in direct and indirect discrimination cases

Compensation is available in all cases where loss can be shown (EqA 2010, ss. 119, 124(2)(b) and (6)).

The main element of most compensation claims will be the conventional measure: the actual loss caused by the discrimination. However, where injury to feelings can be shown, compensation will be made for that and in appropriate circumstances (e.g. where an employer has behaved particularly badly), aggravated damages may also be awarded. Exemplary damages may be available on the standard grounds in *Rookes v Barnard* [1964] AC 1129 since the House of Lords held that the remedy was not restricted to causes of action in existence in 1964 (*Kuddus v Chief Constable of Leicester Constabulary* [2002] 2 AC 122).

16.7.2 What may be awarded for injury to feelings?

A significant element of many awards is given to cover injury to feelings. Guidance is available from the Court of Appeal in *Vento v Chief Constable of West Yorkshire Police* [2003] IRLR 102, where three bands were identified:

(a) the top band should normally be between £15,000 and £25,000, for example where there has been a sustained campaign of harassment; awards above £25,000 should only be made in exceptional cases;

(b) the middle band of £5,000–£15,000 should be used in serious cases falling short of the top band;

(c) the lower band of £500–£5,000 is appropriate for less serious cases, for example one-off events. In general, awards of less than £500 are to be avoided altogether, because they risk being so low as to be derisory.

Table 16.1 **Discrimination checklist—how to prepare a case**

Checklist claimant	Checklist respondent
1. *Is there an actionable claim?* 　(a) Does the discriminatory act relate to a field covered by the legislation? 　(b) Is it an act that gives an individual a right of claim? 　(c) When did the act occur? 　(d) When do time limits run out? 2. *Is this a case of direct or indirect discrimination?* 　See respondent's checklist for matters to be considered in each type of claim. 3. *How is the discrimination to be proved?* 　(a) What evidence is provided in the papers? 　(b) What does the lay client say happened? 　(c) Is a conference necessary to establish the lay client's side of the case? 　(d) What further evidence is required (including statistical evidence in indirect discrimination cases)? 　(e) Where can the evidence be obtained? 　　(i) If an informal questionnaire has been sent according to the ACAS Guidance: 　　Have replies been received? Are they clear and unequivocal? If they are not, what inferences should the court/tribunal draw? 　　(ii) If an informal questionnaire has not been sent, consider sending one. 　　(iii) Is a code applicable and has it been broken? 　(f) What has happened to the claimant since the discriminatory act? 　　(i) What financial loss has the claimant suffered? 　　(ii) To what extent have the claimant's feelings been injured? 　　(iii) What evidence is required to establish financial loss and/or injury to feelings? 　(g) Has the requirement for early conciliation been complied with?	1. *What allegations of discrimination have been made?* 2. *Is the application within time limits?* 3. *In direct discrimination cases, does the respondent admit allegations?* 　(a) If not, with what facts does the respondent disagree? 　　(i) What evidence supports the respondent's view of the facts? 　　(ii) How is that evidence to be proven? 　　(iii) What interpretation of the law might avoid a finding of discrimination? 　(b) If the respondent admits discrimination, identify: 　　(i) what the respondent is willing to do for the claimant; 　　(ii) what would be the result of action? 　　(iii) negotiate a settlement—consider a compromise agreement. 4. *If the allegation is of indirect discrimination:* 　(a) Was a provision, criterion, or practice applied? 　(b) Does it have a disproportionately adverse impact on the claimant's protected characteristic? 　(c) What statistical evidence might undermine the allegation of disproportionate impact? 　(d) Was the claimant put at a disadvantage as a result? What evidence is there of disadvantage? 　(e) Was the provision, criterion, or practice proportionate? If so, why, and how is this to be established? 5. *Is the whole application one in which the principle* de minimis non curat lex *could apply?* 6. *What submissions could be made to reduce damages?* 7. *What might be done to avoid discrimination or agree recommended action for the future?*

In *Vento*, the court awarded £18,000 for injury to feelings and a further £5,000 in aggravated damages.

These figures are revised annually every April by Presidential guidance. The bands for claims presented on or after 6 April 2021 are: lower level: £900–£9,000; middle level: £9,000–£27,000; upper level: £27,000–£45,000, or higher in the most serious cases. Moreover, the Court of Appeal has decided (*De Souza v Vinci Construction (UK) Ltd* [2017] EWCA Civ 879) that the 10 per cent *Simmons v Castle* uplift (see **10.9.2** *Kyaw v Claassen* [2015] EWHC 33374) applies to tribunal awards for psychiatric injury or injury to feelings.

16.8　Equal pay

Where discrimination on grounds of sex is alleged to arise within the contract of employment, claims should be made under EqA 2010, Pt 5, Ch. 3 or, where no remedy is available under those provisions, under Article 157 (ex 141) TFEU. The Act provides that there is an 'equality clause' in all contracts of employment, breach of which entitles the claimant to a remedy. Both men and women may make use of these provisions, although claims by women are far more common.

16.8.1 The remedy

The remedy is a claim to an employment tribunal which, if the claim is established, may import the more favourable term into the claimant's contract. The tribunal may make a declaration of rights and may award compensation as appropriate, including compensation for arrears of unequal pay.

16.8.1.1 How is a claim established?

The claimant must cite a comparator of the other gender within the same employment, whose job involves:

- like work;
- work rated as equivalent (e.g. by a job evaluation study); or
- work of equal value.

If this is established, the claimant will be entitled to the same contractual terms as the chosen comparator.

16.8.1.2 Is there a defence available to the employer?

An employer may successfully defend an equal pay claim by establishing that the contractual difference is genuinely due to a material factor other than sex (EqA 2010, s. 69). Examples would include employees working on incremental salary scales where a newly appointed woman sought equal pay with a man who did the same job, but earned more, having moved up the salary scale over a period of years. Where there is evidence that experience genuinely enhances performance, the employer may have a defence. In *Wilson v Health and Safety Executive* [2009] IRLR 282, a ten-point incremental scale was prayed in defence of such a claim. The claimant alleged that inspectors became fully proficient after five years. The EAT remitted the claim to the tribunal to assess whether there was a serious doubt as to the justifiability of the ten-year incremental scale.

The test for whether such a material factor defence is valid is closely related to that for justification of indirect discrimination (*Bilka-Kaufhaus GmbH v Weber von Hartz* (Case 170/84) [1987] ICR 110) (see **16.3.2.2**).

16.8.2 Procedure

Where a claim is based on the comparator doing like work or work rated as equivalent, the tribunal procedure is similar to other tribunal proceedings (see the Employment Tribunal (Constitution and Rules of Procedure) Regulations 2013 (SI 2013/1237), Sch. 1). Equal value claims, however, are treated differently (see 2013 Regulations, Sch. 3). The tribunal may make an initial evaluation on the evidence and, where it is sufficiently clear, rule that the jobs are, or are not, of equal value. Where it is not sufficiently clear, the tribunal will commission a report from an independent expert. That report will then be subject to argument from the parties and the tribunal will take the final decision of fact (see EqA 2010, s. 131).

16.9 Enforcing the law

As well as enforcement in the courts and tribunals by individuals suffering from discrimination, the legislation has established the Equality and Human Rights Commission, which may not only support selected individual cases, but may also conduct formal investigations. These are intended to deal with more widespread discrimination, for example practices throughout a particular industry, employer, or authority which are considered to have a discriminatory effect.

The Equality Act 2006 (EqA 2006), s. 1 established the new EHRC, which came into existence on 18 April 2006. On 1 October 2007, it took over the work of the existing Commissions. Details of the work of the EHRC are available from its website: <http://www.equalityhumanrights.com>.

Codes of Practice have been prepared which are admissible in evidence before courts and tribunals as to the standards to be expected in a variety of fields and circumstances. They are now provided for by EqA 2006, s. 14.

16.9.1   Formal investigations

The EHRC may institute an investigation on its own initiative provided that it believes that there has been an unlawful discriminatory act (EqA 2006, s. 20). The Secretary of State may require it to conduct an investigation. Where a number of individuals have suffered from discriminatory practices, such an informal investigation may provide them with an effective remedy. These enforcement powers and procedural stages are presented in **Figure 16.1**.

16.9.1.1   What are the procedures for a formal investigation?

The EHRC must draw up terms of reference stating that the persons named are believed to have done or be doing specified unlawful acts. If required to investigate by the Secretary of State, all parties named must be given notice of the investigation.

The EHRC may, by notice, require a person who:

- is believed to be committing unlawful discriminatory acts; or
- applies a requirement or condition which results in an unlawful act of indirect discrimination or victimisation, whether or not there is a specific victim; or
- advertises in a discriminatory way; or
- gives instructions to others to discriminate; or
- induces others to discriminate; or
- is subject to such a notice being ordered by the Secretary of State

to provide specific written information or to attend for oral examination and produce such documents as may be required which are in that person's possession or control, subject to the rules of evidence governing the production of documents in the High Court. If a failure to comply with such a notice occurs or is reasonably believed to be likely, an order can be obtained from the county court.

16.9.1.2   What are the possible results of a formal investigation?

Following a formal investigation, the EHRC may:

(a)   recommend future action;

(b)   recommend a change in the law;

(c)   deliver the report to the Secretary of State (when that investigation was requested by the Secretary of State), who must publish it;

(d)   publish the report or make it available for inspection (subject to a fee if required);

(e)   serve a notice stating that the EHRC is minded to serve a non-discrimination notice (NDN) on the person formally investigated. This minded notice must specify the grounds on which the NDN is contemplated, and give an opportunity for representations to be made either orally or in writing within 28 days. The EHRC must take account of any such representations before issuing an NDN.

16.9.1.3   What is a non-discrimination notice?

This is a notice that requires the person served to commit no further such acts of discrimination. Where the notice requires a change of practice, then the EHRC must be informed that

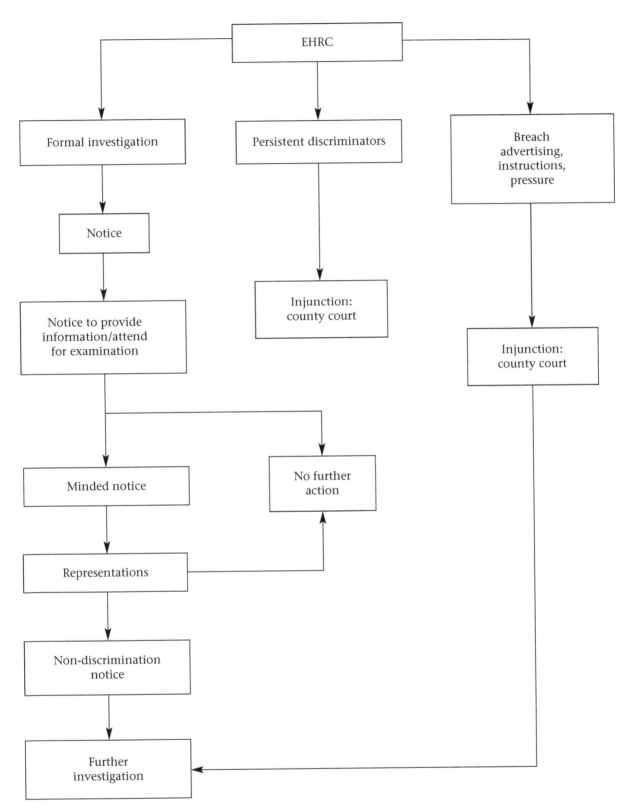

Figure 16.1 Powers of the EHRC to enforce the law (details of these powers may be found in 16.9.1–16.9.2).

the change in practice has been made. It may also require the person served to provide the EHRC with further information and specify the time and manner in which that information is to be provided, which must be no later than five years from the date of the notice.

An appeal against an NDN must be made within six weeks of the NDN being served. Appeals in relation to employment matters will be heard in the employment tribunal, and those in relation to other fields of discrimination will be heard in the county court for the district in which the acts to which the requirements relate were done. In race discrimination cases, this must be a designated county court.

The NDN should be accompanied by a statement of the findings of fact. The notice of appeal should specify each finding of fact that is challenged, each allegation of fact which it is intended to prove, and any other grounds on which it is alleged that the requirements contained in the NDN are unreasonable.

Appeals are governed by CPR, Pt 52.

16.9.1.4   What are the powers of the court or tribunal on appeal?

If the requirement contained in the NDN is considered unreasonable because it is based on an incorrect finding of fact or for any other reason, the court or tribunal must quash the requirement. The court or tribunal may direct that a requirement be substituted for the quashed requirement. It is possible to challenge all or any of the findings of fact on which the requirements contained in the notice were based.

16.9.2   Claim against the persistent discriminator

The EHRC may apply to a county court for an injunction restraining a person who, within five years of a finding of discrimination made in an employment tribunal or county court or within five years of the issue of an NDN, discriminates or who continues to apply a condition or requirement which is discriminatory but which has no specific victim, from continuing to act unlawfully.

16.10   Exercises

16.10.1   Exercise 1

PROBLEM

The ABC Building Society is unwilling to advance money for the improvement of terraced houses without front gardens in an area where many members of black, Asian, and minority ethnic (BAME) groups live. Your instructing solicitors have presented you with a copy of a report which states that 86 per cent of BAME families living in that area live in terraced houses without front gardens and that 46 per cent of white families living there live in terraced houses without front gardens.

Please advise in the following situations on appropriate procedure and remedies, treating each as independent of the other:

(a) A, who owns a terraced house without a front garden in this area and is a member of an ethnic minority group, believes she has been indirectly discriminated against. The ABC Building Society has refused to advance money on a mortgage for improvements to her home as a result of this policy.

(b) The local Law Centre has received a number of complaints from residents in the same situation as A, but who are unwilling to take action themselves as they fear that they will be seen as troublemakers and be denied any chance of a mortgage if they were to do so.

SOLUTION

(a) This concerns facilities by way of banking or loans for finance which is a field in respect of which race is a protected characteristic (see EqA 2010, ss. 4, 9, 29). As 14 per cent of BAME families can comply with the requirement (86 per cent cannot) and 54 per cent of white families can comply (46 per cent cannot), the proportions suggest that this meets the requirement that a considerably smaller proportion of A's racial group can comply with the provision, criterion, or practice compared with the proportion of people not in A's racial group who can comply.

A's remedy is to file a claim under the EqA 2010 in the county court where the ABC Building Society carries on business or in the district where the act took place (perhaps the relevant branch of the society). ABC Building Society will have a defence if it can justify the condition irrespective of race—a financial motive for the condition will not be sufficient reason to constitute justification.

There is no need for A to prove that ABC Building Society had an intention to discriminate. Generally, A will be able to recover injury to feelings plus other losses subject to proof of causation. It is unlikely that A would obtain an injunction against ABC Building Society and the likely remedy would be a declaratory order and a recommendation as to action to avoid further discrimination.

(b) The Law Centre should make a complaint to the EHRC. The Equality Act 2006, s. 20 gives the EHRC power to investigate allegations of discriminatory behaviour. The EHRC may issue a recommendation to the ABC Building Society and investigate whether this has been complied with. If not, it may issue an NDN, which ABC Building Society may appeal in the county court. Failure to comply with an NDN entitles the EHRC to file an action in the county court. A possible action exists in the European Court of Human Rights, although both routes require a long period of time, and A and others needing immediate protection may not see the benefit.

16.10.2 Exercise 2

PROBLEM

Mrs Smith has been sexually harassed at work by her section supervisor, Mr James. Her complaints consisted of: Mr James asking her out, touching her, and pressing against her whenever he had cause to come into her office, and telling others in the company that she was free with sexual favours and that when he had finished with her he would pass her on.

When Mrs Smith first complained to Mr James's line manager, she was told that she should be flattered. It was only a week later, after she had spoken to the Human Resources Manager, that her complaint was taken seriously.

Mr James has now been dismissed and Mrs Smith has decided to continue to work for her employers. You are asked to advise her as to her remedies (if any), the best forum in which to pursue them, and the amount of damages she is likely to recover.

17

European Convention on Human Rights and Fundamental Freedoms

17.1 Introduction

17.1.1 The Human Rights Act in post-Brexit UK

In 2020, the United Kingdom formally departed from the European Union (often termed 'Brexit'). This changed the UK's relationship with the European Court of Justice (ECJ) but, for now, the European Court of Human Rights (ECtHR) retains its oversight of the UK's application of the European Convention on Human Rights (ECHR) via the UK's Human Rights Act 1998 (HRA 1998). This horizon is, however, set to change as the UK government has announced (December 2021) a wholesale review of the HRA 1998.

This chapter states the law as at 22 January 2022.

17.1.2 The European Convention on Human Rights and Human Rights Act 1998

The Convention for the Protection of Human Rights and Fundamental Freedoms, commonly referred to as the 'European Convention on Human Rights' principally concerns civil and political rights. The ECHR is an international treaty of the Council of Europe, which was adopted in 1950, ratified by the United Kingdom in 1951, and entered into force in 1953. It provides a mechanism for individuals to enforce their Convention rights against State parties. It is administered by the Council of Europe and the ECtHR.

The ECHR was incorporated into UK law via the HRA 1998, which came into force in October 2000. The HRA 1998 made available, for the first time, a remedy for breach of the ECHR in the UK courts. This means that, in appropriate cases, all UK courts are tasked with deciding whether public bodies have acted compatibly with the ECHR. The HRA 1998 further imposes on all UK courts a duty to interpret legislation compatibly with the ECHR, so far as it is possible to do so, and where it is not possible, they can issue a 'declaration of incompatibility'—which sends a clear steer to legislators to adjust the law to make it Convention-compliant. No UK court, including the Supreme Court, has the power to 'strike down' legislation if it is incompatible with the ECHR. The HRA 1998 also requires UK courts, including the Supreme Court, to 'take account' of decisions of the ECtHR based in Strasbourg. The UK courts can decline to do so, particularly if the Strasbourg Court has not sufficiently appreciated or accommodated particular aspects of the UK's domestic constitutional position.

The ECHR and the ECtHR exist separately from the European Union. This means the UK's exit from the European Union did not, of itself, change the UK's relationship with the Convention or the Strasbourg Court. However, in December 2021, the UK government launched a consultation to 'update[e] the Human Rights Act [and] replace it with a Bill of Rights, in order to restore a proper balance between the rights of individuals, personal responsibility and the wider public interest'. This indicates the relationship will be, at the very least, significantly reviewed. The consultation can be followed at: <https://consult.justice.gov.uk/human-rights/human-rights-act-reform/>.

17.1.3 The Council of Europe

The Council of Europe (CoE) is a pan-European organisation of 47 Member States, including all 27 Member States of the European Union, and the UK. The CoE was established in 1949, following the atrocities of the Second World War, with the following aims:

(a) to protect human rights, pluralist democracy, and the rule of law;

(b) to promote awareness and encourage the development of Europe's cultural identity and diversity;

(c) to seek solutions to problems facing European society (discrimination against minorities, xenophobia, intolerance, environmental protection, organised crime, etc.);

(d) to help consolidate democratic stability in Europe by backing political, legislative, and constitutional reform.

The Council of Europe has passed more than 200 international treaties or conventions, including the ECHR and the European Convention for the Prevention of Torture and Inhuman or Degrading Treatment or Punishment (1987). Once signed and ratified, conventions are legally binding on Member States.

The UK remains a member of the CoE since its departure from the EU.

17.1.4 The European Court of Human Rights

The ECtHR is an international court based in Strasbourg in France. The ECtHR has jurisdiction to decide complaints ('applications') submitted by individuals and States concerning violations of the Convention allegedly committed by a State party to the Convention and that directly and significantly affected the applicant. It has 47 judges—one from each Member State of the Council of Europe which has ratified the ECHR; some of these States have also ratified one or more of the Additional Protocols to the Convention, which protect additional rights. The ECHR and the ECtHR exist separately from the European Union. The Supreme Courts of the UK's relationship with the Strasbourg Court is not, therefore, changed by the UK's exit from the European Union.

Since 2018, the Court also has advisory jurisdiction. Under Protocol 16 to the European Convention, which entered into force on 1 August 2018, the highest domestic courts in the States that are a party to the Protocol may request European Court advisory opinions on questions of interpretation of the European Convention and its protocols. The questions must arise out of cases pending before the domestic court.

An application to the Court will only be declared admissible if it meets the following criteria:

(a) exhaustion of domestic remedies;

(b) within the application deadline from the final domestic judicial decision;

(c) a complaint against a State party to the ECHR;

(d) the applicant suffered a significant disadvantage.

From 1 February 2022, the application deadline outlined in (b) reduces from six to four months, although the four-month time limit will only apply where the final domestic decision was given on or after 1 February 2022.

If an application fails to meet any of these requirements, it will be declared inadmissible and cannot proceed any further. There is no appeal from a decision of inadmissibility.

In terms of allocation of court business, a single judge may determine the admissibility of an application, whereas a committee of three judges is required to decide both admissibility and merits, and only if there is well-developed case law on the issue at hand. More complex matters go before a Chamber of seven judges, and the Grand Chamber composed of 17 judges is reserved for a select number of cases that usually involve an important or novel question. Chamber judgments become final after three months and Grand Chamber judgments are final. The Court's final judgments are binding on the Member State concerned (i.e. on the government, not the courts).

17.1.5   Classification of Convention rights

Convention rights are classified as being either absolute, qualified, or limited.

Absolute rights are those which cannot be restricted in any circumstances, not even in times of war or other public emergency. These are Articles 2 (right to life), 3 (the prohibition of torture and inhuman or degrading treatment), 4(1) (the prohibition of slavery), and 7 (the prohibition of retrospective criminal penalties).

Qualified rights are those which are subject to restriction clauses which enable the general public interest to be taken into account. They are Articles 8 (right to respect for private and family life), 9 (freedom to manifest religion or belief), 10 (freedom of expression), 11 (freedom of assembly), 14 (discrimination), and Protocol 1, Article 1 (the right to property).

Limited rights are those in relation to which the government can enter a derogation. These are Articles 4(2) and (3) (the prohibition of forced or compulsory labour), 5 (liberty), 6 (fair trial), 9(1) (freedom of thought), 12 (right to marry), Protocol 1, Article 2 (the right to education), Protocol 1, Article 3 (the right to free elections), and Protocol 6, Article 1 (abolition of the death penalty).

The operation of the restrictions was considered by the Privy Council in *Brown v Stott (Procurator Fiscal, Dunfermline)* [2001] 2 WLR 817, where the Privy Council held that there was no breach of the privilege against self-incrimination under Article 6 for a prosecutor to rely on an obligation of a registered keeper of a motor vehicle to supply information as to the identity of the driver under s. 172 of the Road Traffic Act 1988. The section did not represent a disproportionate response to the high incidence of death and injury on the roads by reason of the misuse of cars and the Convention had to be read as balancing Community rights with individual rights.

17.1.6   Convention concepts

Popular Convention concepts include the 'margin of appreciation', the Convention being considered to be a 'living instrument', and the 'hierarchy of authority'.

17.1.6.1   Margin of appreciation

The limits of the ECtHR's supervisory role are defined by the doctrine of the 'margin of appreciation', which recognises that national authorities are in the main best placed to decide how human rights should be applied. It is not the Strasbourg Court's task to take the place of national courts, but rather to review the decisions they deliver in the exercise of their domestic authority. Lord Hope stated in *R v DPP, ex p Kebilene* [2000] 2 AC 326 at pp. 380–1:

> By conceding a margin of appreciation to each national system, the court has recognised that the Convention, as a living system, does not need to be applied uniformly by all states but may vary in its application according to local needs and conditions. This technique is not available to the national courts when they are considering Convention issues arising within their own countries. But in the hands of the national courts also the Convention should be seen as an expression of fundamental principles rather than as a set of mere rules. The question which the courts will have to decide in the application of these principles will involve questions of balance between competing interests and issues of proportionality . . .

17.1.6.2   Living instrument

Attitudes and cultures change over time. The Convention is regarded as a 'living instrument' which evolves and develops and 'must be interpreted in the light of present-day conditions' (*Tyrer v United Kingdom* (1978) 2 EHRR 1). The Strasbourg case law provides a floor, not a ceiling, and old Convention case law must be approached with caution.

17.1.6.3   Hierarchy of authority

The decisions of the Commission (previously) and the ECtHR are not binding on domestic courts. The governments do, however, regard themselves to be bound and will generally take steps to give effect to the Court's decisions, for example by amending legislation.

17.2   The Human Rights Act 1998

As described at **17.1.2**, the HRA 1998 enables certain rights contained in the ECHR to be directly enforceable in domestic courts, which revolutionised the courts' interpretation and application of legislation. Section 1 and Sch. 1 define the 'Convention rights' which have been incorporated, subject to any designated derogations or reservations. Article 13 (the right to an effective remedy) was not specifically included as a 'Convention right' within this definition.

17.2.1   Convention rights

17.2.1.1   The vertical effect

The rights operate vertically; that is, they affect relations between private individuals and public authorities. Individuals have an additional cause of action against public authorities.

Section 6 of the Act created a new public law wrong in relation to the acts or proposed acts of public authorities such as local councils, police forces, prisons, health services, and courts and tribunals. Under s. 7, a victim who alleges a breach of Convention rights against a public authority can make a claim under s. 7(1)(a) based on the breach alone, or under s. 7(1)(b) based on other pre-existing rights of action in domestic law. This has become widely known as the 'vertical effect' of the Act.

17.2.1.2   The horizontal effect

The horizontal effect of the Act suggests that the Convention will affect relations between individuals; that is, because the courts are defined by s. 6 of the Act as public authorities. Relations between individuals will be affected indirectly, as the courts need to act compatibly with the Convention when adjudicating in an action between individuals.

17.2.1.3   Limitation period

Section 7(5) provides that the general limitation period for action under s. 7(1)(a) is one year from the date on which the act took place or 'such longer period as the court or tribunal considers equitable having regard to all the circumstances'. There is no limitation for those seeking to rely on breaches in other proceedings under s. 7(1)(b).

17.2.2   The main provisions

17.2.2.1   Section 1: the Convention rights

Under s. 1 HRA 1998, 'the Convention rights' mean the rights and fundamental freedoms set out in Articles 2–12 and 14 of the Convention, Articles 1–3 of the First Protocol, and Articles 1 and 2 of the Sixth Protocol, as read with Articles 16–18 of the Convention. These rights are declared to have effect for the purposes of the Act.

17.2.2.2   Section 2: interpretation of Convention rights

Section 2 provides that any court or tribunal determining a question which has arisen in connection with a Convention right must take into account the jurisprudence of the Strasbourg bodies (the ECtHR, the Commission of Human Rights, and the Committee of Ministers), whether before or after the coming into force of the Act, so far as, in the opinion of the court or tribunal, it is relevant to the proceedings.

17.2.2.3   Section 3: interpretation of legislation

This section provides that primary and subordinate legislation is to be read and given effect in a way which is compatible with Convention rights, so far as it is possible to do so, and applies to all legislation, whenever enacted. Courts have engaged in generous statutory interpretation in three ways: by 'reading in', namely inserting words into a statute; by 'reading out', by omitting words from a statute; and by 'reading down', where a particular meaning is chosen to enable compliance. Courts have generally been reluctant in particular to 'read out' provisions. If it is not possible to read legislation so as to give effect to the Convention, the validity, continuing operation, or enforcement of the legislation will not be affected, but a declaration of compatibility may be appropriate. Past examples of cases where statutory provisions have been interpreted to meet Convention rights include:

(a) In *R v Lambert* [2001] 3 WLR 206, the House of Lords held that s. 28(2) of the Misuse of Drugs Act 1971 could be interpreted in accordance with the obligation under s. 3 as only imposing an evidential burden of proof on the defendant which would enable it to be compatible with Article 6(2).

(b) In *Sheldrake v DPP* [2005] 1 AC 264, the House of Lords held that s. 5(2) of the Road Traffic Act 1988 imposed a legal burden on a defendant charged with being in charge of a motor vehicle, with an alcohol concentration above the prescribed limit, contrary to s. 5(1)(b) of the Act. It was also held that the statutory defence in s. 11(2) of the Terrorism Act 2000 to a charge of membership of a proscribed organisation was to be interpreted as imposing an evidential burden only.

17.2.2.4   Section 4: declaration of incompatibility

Section 4 provides that '*if the court is satisfied that the provision is incompatible with a Convention right, it may make a declaration of that incompatibility*'. This declaration of incompatibility is available to the higher courts (the High Court and above). A declaration of incompatibility does not affect the continuing operation or enforcement of the legislation in question, nor does it bind the parties to the proceedings in which it is made. Under the HRA 1998, there is no legal obligation on the government to take remedial action following a declaration of incompatibility or on Parliament to accept any remedial measures the government may propose.

Since the HRA 1998 came into force on 2 October 2000 until the end of July 2021, 44 declarations of incompatibility have been made. Of these: ten were overturned on appeal (and there is no scope for further appeal); five related to provisions already amended by primary legislation; eight have already been addressed by Remedial Order, and 15 by primary or secondary legislation (other than by Remedial Order) with a further four awaiting being addressed by Remedial Order or by primary legislation. For more detail, see the Ministry of Justice's annual report, *Responding to human rights judgments:* <https://www.gov.uk/government/publications/responding-to-human-rights-judgments-2020-to-2021>.

Some examples of declarations of incompatibility from the case law are:

(a) In *R (on the application of Anderson) v Secretary of State for the Home Department* [2003] 1 AC 837, a panel of seven judges in the House of Lords held unanimously that the court would make a declaration of incompatibility of s. 29 of the Crime (Sentences) Act 1997 with Article 6(1) as the section left to the Home Secretary alone the decision on how long a prisoner sentenced to mandatory life for murder should remain in prison for punitive purposes. The tariff or minimum term should be fixed by an independent and impartial tribunal, and the Home Secretary was not such a tribunal.

(b) In *Bellinger v Bellinger* [2003] 2 AC 467, the House of Lords held that s. 11(c) of the Matrimonial Causes Act 1973 was incompatible with Articles 8 and 12, as a post-operative transsexual was unable to have her marriage legally recognised. This was remedied by primary legislation. The Gender Recognition Act 2004 since provides that transsexual persons will be legally recognised upon issue of a full gender recognition certificate enabling them to marry persons of the opposite gender to their acquired gender.

(c) In *R (on the application of Uttley) v Secretary of State for the Home Department, Administrative Court* [2003] EWHC 950 (Admin) a declaration of incompatibility with Article 7 was made in respect of s. 33 of the Criminal Justice Act 1991 as the terms of the licence of a sentenced appellant imposed a heavier penalty than the one provided by the law at the time of the commission of the offences for which he was sentenced.

17.2.2.5   Section 5: right of Crown to intervene

This section provides that where a court is considering making a declaration of incompatibility, the Crown is entitled to notice. This enables the appropriate Minister to be involved in the proceedings at an early stage to prepare for any remedial action under s. 10.

17.2.2.6   Section 6: acts of public authorities

Section 6 introduced a new public law wrong by providing that it is unlawful for a public authority to act in a way which is incompatible with a Convention right. A 'public authority' includes a court or tribunal, but does not include either House of Parliament.

In *Aston Cantlow Parochial Church Council v Wallbank* [2003] 3 WLR 283, the House of Lords held that a parochial church council, enforcing a lay rector's liability for repairs to the chancel of a church, was not a public authority, and in any event enforcing such a liability did not infringe the Convention rights of the rector.

17.2.2.7   Section 7: proceedings

Section 7 enables a victim of an unlawful act by a public authority to bring proceedings in the appropriate court or tribunal against the authority or rely on the Convention right or rights concerned in any legal proceedings. A victim is a person who has been directly affected by the act or has been at risk of being so affected.

17.2.2.8   Section 8: judicial remedies

This section provides that the court may grant such relief or remedy, or make such order as it considers 'just and appropriate' including damages, provided that the court has power to make such orders. Section 8(3) provides that damages may only be awarded if necessary to afford 'just satisfaction', and s. 8(4) provides that in determining whether to award damages, or the amount to award, the court must take account of the principles applied by the ECtHR in relation to the award of compensation under Article 41 of the Convention. In *R (on the application of Bernard) v Enfield BC* [2003] HRLR 4, Sullivan J awarded £10,000 damages under s. 8(1) of the Act against the London Borough of Enfield for a breach of Article 8 due to the local authority's failure to provide suitable accommodation for a severely disabled wheelchair-dependent woman over a period of 20 months. In *R (on the application of Greenfield) v Secretary of State for the Home Department* [2005] 1 WLR 673, it was held by the House of Lords that when assessing awards of damages under s. 8 of the Act, the principles applied in the ECtHR to awards of compensation should be applied in the domestic courts.

17.2.2.9   Section 9: judicial acts

This section provides that proceedings in respect of judicial acts may be brought on appeal or by judicial review.

17.2.2.10   Section 10: power to take remedial action

The provisions of s. 10 confirm the power of a Minister of the Crown to take remedial action to amend legislation in order to remove an incompatibility where legislation has been declared incompatible under s. 4.

17.2.2.11   Section 11: safeguard for existing human rights

In accordance with s. 11, reliance on the Convention rights referred to in the Act does not restrict any other rights or freedoms.

17.2.2.12   Section 12: freedom of expression

Section 12 provides that courts must have particular regard to the importance of freedom of expression, and is of benefit to the media.

17.2.2.13   Section 13: freedom of thought, conscience, and religion

This section provides that courts must have regard to the importance of freedom of thought, conscience, and religion, and is of benefit to certain religious organisations.

17.3   Rights and freedoms under the Convention

17.3.1   Purpose of the Convention

Article 1 of the Convention states the obligation of Contracting States to secure to everyone within those States' jurisdiction the rights and freedoms defined in the Convention.

17.3.2   Restrictions on the rights and freedoms

Many of the rights and freedoms set out in the Convention contain restrictions. They are classified as absolute, qualified, or limited rights.

17.3.2.1   Limitations on rights

Articles 1, 3, 4(1), and 7 are classified as absolute rights as they may never be the subject of derogation, even in times of national emergency, although see the commentary in this section on the limits to Article 1.

All rights which are not absolute are, in principle, derogable. This is a formal procedure requiring the lodging of an instrument of derogation with the Secretary General of the Council of Europe.

The rights contained in Articles 8–11 are qualified. The conditions under which the State may lawfully interfere with or restrict the exercise of each right is set out in the second paragraph to each Article. Article 14 and Protocol 1, Article 1 are also said to be qualified rights.

Articles 4(2) and 4(3), 5, 6, 9(1) (freedom of thought), 12, Protocol 1, Article 2, Protocol 1, Article 3, and Protocol 6, Article 1 are regarded as limited rights.

Generally, any such limitation must satisfy the following criteria:

(a) It must be according to the rule of law (see *Sunday Times v United Kingdom* (1979–80) 2 EHRR 245).

(b) It must be in pursuit of a 'legitimate aim', for example national security, public safety, the economic well-being of the country, the prevention of disorder or crime, the protection of health or morals, or the protection of the rights and freedoms of others.

(c) It must be proportionate. 'Necessary in a democratic society' has been defined as 'proportionate to the legitimate aim pursued' (*Handyside v United Kingdom* (1976) 1 EHRR 737). In *Silver v United Kingdom* (1983) 5 EHRR 344, it was stated that 'the interference must, inter alia, correspond to a pressing social need and be proportionate to the legitimate aim pursued'. In *Soering v United Kingdom* (1989) 11 EHRR 439, at para. 89, it was stated that 'inherent in the whole of the Convention is a search for a fair balance between the demands of the general interests of the community and the requirement of the protection of the individual's fundamental rights'.

17.3.3   Human rights in the Convention

Schedule 1 to the HRA 1998 sets out the Convention rights which are directly enforceable in domestic courts. They are as follows:

Part 1	*Article 2*	Right to life.
	Article 3	Prohibition of torture and inhuman or degrading treatment or punishment.
	Article 4	Prohibition of slavery and forced labour.
	Article 5	Right to liberty and security.

Article 6	Right to a fair trial:

(a) In civil and criminal matters, the right to a fair and public hearing within a reasonable time by an independent and impartial tribunal established by law. In some circumstances the press and public may be excluded.

(b) Presumption of innocence on a criminal charge.

(c) Minimum rights on a criminal charge:

(i) to be informed promptly in an understandable language and in detail of the nature and cause of the accusation;

(ii) to have adequate time and facilities for the preparation of one's defence;

(iii) to defend oneself in person or through legal assistance of one's own choosing, or to be given free assistance where no means to pay and interests of justice so require;

(iv) to examine or have examined witnesses and obtain the attendance of witnesses on one's behalf under the same conditions as witnesses against oneself;

(v) to have the free assistance of an interpreter if one cannot understand/speak the language in court.

Article 7	Freedom from retrospective criminal law, and the principle of legal certainty and restrictive interpretation in criminal matters.
Article 8	Right to respect for private and family life, home, and correspondence.
Article 9	Freedom of thought, conscience, and religion.
Article 10	Freedom of expression.
Article 11	Freedom of peaceful assembly and association.
Article 12	Right to marry and found a family.
Article 14	Prohibition of discrimination in the enjoyment of Convention rights.
Article 16	Restrictions on political activity of aliens.
Article 17	Prohibition of abuse of rights.
Article 18	Limitation on use of restrictions on rights.
Part 2	*The First Protocol*
Article 1	Protection of property.
Article 2	Right to education.
Article 3	Right to free elections.
Part 3	*The Sixth Protocol*
Article 1	Abolition of the death penalty.
Article 2	Death penalty in time of war.

17.3.3.1 Article 2: right to life

Article 2 states:

> 1. Everyone's right to life shall be protected by law. No one shall be deprived of his life intentionally save in the execution of a sentence of a court following his conviction of a crime for which this penalty is provided by law.
>
> 2. Deprivation of life shall not be regarded as inflicted in contravention of this article when it results from the use of force which is no more than absolutely necessary:
> (a) in defence of any person from unlawful violence;
> (b) in order to effect a lawful arrest or to prevent the escape of a person lawfully detained;
> (c) in action lawfully taken for the purpose of quelling a riot or insurrection.

This is a fundamental right which places a corresponding positive duty on public authorities to protect life and a negative obligation to refrain from the unlawful taking of life.

Article 2 is often referred to as an 'absolute right', meaning that this right that can never be interfered with by the State. In practical terms, the right to life is not absolute, although the limitation of the ECHR provisions were disapplied when the UK ratified Protocol 6, and death sentences were abolished from remaining statutes. The UK cannot reintroduce the death penalty in future, except for acts committed in time of war or imminent threat of war. There are situations, however, when a person's right to life is not breached, such as when a public authority (such as the police) uses necessary force to stop them carrying out unlawful violence, or stops a riot or uprising, as long as the force was essential and proportionate.

In the case of *R (Purdy) v DPP* [2009] EWCA Civ 92 Mrs Purdy, the sufferer of incurable, progressive multiple sclerosis, sought clarification as to whether her husband would be prosecuted for the offence of assisting a suicide should he help her die. The Supreme Court ruled that the code of criminal prosecutors was not sufficiently clear on the circumstances in which a prosecution under the Assisted Suicide Act 1961, s. 2(1) would be brought. In 2010, the Director of Public Prosecutions (DPP) published a policy (updated in October 2014) identifying the facts and circumstances which he will take into account when deciding whether or not to prosecute. An Assisted Dying Bill was introduced into Parliament in late 2021, with the aim of enabling terminally ill adults to be permitted specified assistance to end their own life; a previous attempt in 2012 to introduce a similar Bill was unsuccessful.

Article 2 case law inevitably engages a broad spectrum of circumstances. In *Edwards v United Kingdom* (2002) 35 EHRR 487, the applicants' son was stamped on and kicked to death by his cellmate in Chelmsford prison. The deceased was suffering from mental illness and the assailant was suffering from paranoid schizophrenia, yet they were placed in a cell together. It was held that there were violations of Articles 2 and 13.

In terms of jurisdictional limits, in *R (on the application of Smith) v Oxfordshire Assistant Deputy Coroner* (2011) 1 AC 1, the Supreme Court held by a 6:3 majority that the HRA 1998 has no application to members of the armed forces serving overseas when they are outside their military bases. However, deaths of military personnel on active service overseas which do occur within the jurisdiction of the United Kingdom and which appear to result from State failure should be subject to comprehensive investigation. In contrast, in *Al-Skeini v United Kingdom* (2011) 53 EHRR 18, the Grand Chamber of the ECtHR ruled that from 1 May 2003 to 28 June 2004 the United Kingdom had jurisdiction under Article 1 (obligation to respect human rights) of the ECHR in respect of Iraqi civilians killed during security operations carried out by UK soldiers in Basra. The Court went on to find in *Al-Skeini* that there had been a failure to conduct an independent and effective investigation into the deaths of the relatives of five of the six applicants, in violation of Article 2 (right to life) of the Convention. The Court awarded €17,000 to five of the six applicants, in addition to €50,000 in costs jointly.

17.3.3.2   Article 3: prohibition of torture and freedom from inhuman or degrading treatment
Article 3 states:

No one shall be subjected to torture or to inhuman or degrading treatment or punishment.

There is an absolute prohibition on torture and inhuman or degrading treatment or punishment. The case law is, again, extensive. In February 2018, the UK Supreme Court in *Commissioner of Police of the Metropolis (Appellant) v DSD and another (Respondents)* [2018] UKSC 11 ruled that the Article 3 rights in favour of two victims of sexual assault had been breached by systemic failures by the Metropolitan Police to detect their attacker, the serial rapist John Worboys. Between 2003 and 2008, Worboys committed sexual offences against many women who were passengers in his black taxicab.

Both women brought proceedings against the police, alleging failure to conduct effective investigations into Worboys' crimes. They claimed that these failures constituted a violation of their rights under Article 3 of the ECHR, to the effect that the State has a duty to conduct an effective investigation into crimes involving serious violence to the individual.

In *Hilal v United Kingdom* (2001) 33 EHRR 31, the Court held that there was a violation where a decision was made to deport an overstayer to Tanzania, as his life would have been endangered by his return. In *Keenan v United Kingdom* (2001) 33 EHRR 38, the ECtHR held that there was a violation due to the treatment of a mentally disordered prisoner who committed suicide in the segregation unit of the prison the day after an adjudication in which he was ordered to serve an additional period of 28 days in custody. In *McGlinchey v United Kingdom* (2003) 37 EHRR 821, the Court held that there had been a violation of Article 3 on account of the failure of prison authorities to provide requisite medical care to a heroin addict who died in custody. In *Secretary of State for the Home Department v Wainwright* [2003] 3 WLR 1137, the House of Lords held that a strip search of visitors to an inmate in a prison did not give rise to a new common law tort of invasion of privacy.

In *R (on the application of Limbuela) v Secretary of State for the Home Department* [2006] 1 AC 396, the House of Lords held that refusal of asylum support had resulted in severe conditions suffered by asylum seekers, and amounted to a breach of Article 3. In *A v Secretary of State for the Home Department* [2006] 2 AC 221, the House of Lords held that the Special Immigration Appeals Commission should refuse to admit evidence if it concluded on a balance of probabilities that such evidence had been obtained by torture. If in doubt, however, the evidence should be admitted, subject to considerations of weight to be given to such evidence. The United Kingdom's obligations under Article 3 were considered by the ECtHR in the case of *Sufi and Elmi v United Kingdom* (Case 8319/07) [2011] ECHR 1045 (28 June 2011). Two Somali nationals faced deportation from the United Kingdom on conviction for a number of serious criminal offences. They claimed that their removal to Somalia would place their lives at risk and/or expose them to a real risk of ill treatment. They also relied on Article 8 (right to respect for family and private life). The Court ruled that the state of chaos prevailing in Somalia was so dire that repatriation there would amount to a breach of the prohibition on torture and inhuman treatment under Article 3. However, in *GS (India) and others v SSHD* [2015] EWCA Civ 40, the Court of Appeal confirmed that foreign nationals may be removed from the United Kingdom even if this meant their lives would be drastically shortened due to a lack of health care in their home States, as this does not breach Article 3 or 8 of the ECHR, except in the most exceptional cases.

17.3.3.3 Article 4: prohibition of slavery and forced labour

Article 4 states:

1. *No one shall be held in slavery or servitude.*
2. *No one shall be required to perform forced or compulsory labour.*
3. *For the purpose of this article the term 'forced or compulsory labour' shall not include:*
    (a) *any work required to be done in the ordinary course of detention imposed according to the provisions of Article 5 of this Convention or during conditional release from such detention;*
    (b) *any service of a military character or, in case of conscientious objectors in countries where they are recognised, service exacted instead of compulsory military service;*
    (c) *any service exacted in case of an emergency or calamity threatening the life or well-being of the community;*
    (d) *any work or service which forms part of normal civic obligations.*

Article 4(1) contains an absolute prohibition on slavery or servitude. The ECtHR has ruled that, although it is not explicitly mentioned in the ECHR, trafficking in human beings falls within the scope of Article 4: *Rantsev v Cyprus and Russia* [2010] ECHR 25965/04 (7 January 2010).

17.3.3.4 Article 5: right to liberty and security

Article 5 states:

1. *Everyone has the right to liberty and security of person. No one shall be deprived of his liberty save in the following cases and in accordance with a procedure prescribed by law:*
    (a) *the lawful detention of a person after conviction by a competent court;*
    (b) *the lawful arrest or detention of a person for non-compliance with the lawful order of a court or in order to secure the fulfilment of any obligation prescribed by law;*
    (c) *the lawful arrest or detention of a person effected for the purpose of bringing him before the competent legal authority on reasonable suspicion of having committed an offence or when it*

is reasonably considered necessary to prevent his committing an offence or fleeing after having done so;

(d) *the detention of a minor by lawful order for the purpose of educational supervision or his lawful detention for the purpose of bringing him before the competent legal authority;*

(e) *the lawful detention of persons for the prevention of the spreading of infectious diseases, of persons of unsound mind, alcoholics or drug addicts or vagrants;*

(f) *the lawful arrest or detention of a person to prevent his effecting an unauthorised entry into the country or of a person against whom action is being taken with a view to deportation or extradition.*

2. Everyone who is arrested shall be informed promptly, in a language which he understands, of the reasons for his arrest and of any charge against him.

3. Everyone arrested or detained in accordance with the provisions of paragraph 1 (c) of this article shall be brought promptly before a judge or other officer authorised by law to exercise judicial power and shall be entitled to trial within a reasonable time or to release pending trial. Release may be conditioned by guarantees to appear for trial.

4. Everyone who is deprived of his liberty by arrest or detention shall be entitled to take proceedings by which the lawfulness of his detention shall be decided speedily by a court and his release ordered if the detention is not lawful.

5. Everyone who has been the victim of arrest or detention in contravention of the provisions of this article shall have an enforceable right to compensation.

The right under Article 5 is limited by the circumstances set out in the Article.

Once a sentence of long-term detention is imposed, Article 5(4) requires periodic review by a judicial body of the sentence to ensure that it remains justified. The reviewing body must be independent of the executive, for example the First-tier Tribunal (Mental Health); the Discretionary Lifer Panel of the Parole Board. In *T v United Kingdom; V v United Kingdom* (2000) 30 EHRR 121, there was held to have been a violation of Article 5(4) where there had been no review of the offenders' tariff once the Home Secretary's decision to set it had been quashed by the House of Lords in judicial review proceedings. Similarly, in *Curley v United Kingdom* (2000) 31 EHRR 401, a violation of Article 5(4) was found in the case of an offender detained during Her Majesty's pleasure whose release was always subject to the approval of the Secretary of State. In addition, Article 5(5) was breached because the offender had no enforceable claim for compensation under domestic law.

The use by the UK government of closed courts to review the detention of terrorism suspects, without the suspect or their lawyer being present, was held not to breach Article 5 as the independent 'special advocate' performed a counterbalancing role, putting arguments on behalf of the detainee: *A v United Kingdom* [2009] No 3455/05. In the same case the Grand Chamber found, in respect of some of the applicants, that the closed procedure could not be fair when decisive evidence was contained in the closed material that they had no chance to challenge.

17.3.3.5   Article 6: right to a fair trial

Article 6 states:

1. In the determination of his civil rights and obligations or of any criminal charge against him, everyone is entitled to a fair and public hearing within a reasonable time by an independent and impartial tribunal established by law. Judgment shall be pronounced publicly but the press and public may be excluded from all or part of the trial in the interest of morals, public order or national security in a democratic society, where the interests of juveniles or the protection of the private life of the parties so require, or to the extent strictly necessary in the opinion of the court in special circumstances where publicity would prejudice the interests of justice.

2. Everyone charged with a criminal offence shall be presumed innocent until proved guilty according to law.

3. Everyone charged with a criminal offence has the following minimum rights:

(a) *to be informed promptly, in a language which he understands and in detail, of the nature and cause of the accusation against him;*

(b) *to have adequate time and facilities for the preparation of his defence;*

(c) *to defend himself in person or through legal assistance of his own choosing or, if he has not sufficient means to pay for legal assistance, to be given it free when the interests of justice so require;*

> (d) *to examine or have examined witnesses against him and to obtain the attendance and examination of witnesses on his behalf under the same conditions as witnesses against him;*
>
> (e) *to have the free assistance of an interpreter if he cannot understand or speak the language used in court.*

This Article has given rise to extensive litigation.

The right to consult with a solicitor in a police station is fundamental to the preparation of a defence and is protected under Article 6(3). It has been held that, where adverse inferences can arise from an accused's silence when being questioned in the police station, access to a solicitor is of 'paramount importance' (*Murray v United Kingdom* (1996) 22 EHRR 29). See also *Magee v United Kingdom* (2001) 31 EHRR 822 and *Averill v United Kingdom* (2001) 31 EHRR 839, where the ECtHR held that violations of Article 6(1) and Article 6(3)(c) had occurred due to the lack of access to a lawyer for 48 hours and 24 hours respectively, during interrogation. In *Brennan v United Kingdom* (2002) 34 EHRR 507, the Court held that there was a violation of Article 6(1) and Article 6(3)(c) where a police officer remained within sight and earshot of a legal consultation.

The right to silence is an important right. In *Condron v United Kingdom* (2001) 31 EHRR 1, there was held to have been a violation due to failure of the trial judge to adequately direct the jury on an inference to be drawn from the suspects' silence whilst in custody. The ECtHR made the following points:

(a) The right to silence is at the heart of the notion of fair procedure under Article 6 and particular caution is required before a domestic court can invoke an accused's silence against them.

(b) The power to draw adverse inferences from the silence of the accused cannot of itself be considered incompatible with Article 6, but is a matter to be determined in light of all the circumstances of the case.

(c) It is incompatible with the right to silence to base a conviction solely or mainly on the accused's silence or refusal to answer questions, or give evidence.

(d) However, where a situation clearly called for an explanation from an accused, then their silence can be taken into account in assessing the persuasiveness of the evidence against them.

(e) In the instant case, it was more than merely desirable that the jury should have been directed that if they were satisfied that the applicants' silence at the police interview could not sensibly be attributed to their having no answer, or none that would stand up to cross-examination, then they should not draw the adverse inference.

In *Beckles v United Kingdom* (2003) 36 EHRR 162, the ECtHR held that there was a violation due to the failure of the trial judge to adequately direct the jury on the inference from silence. (See **Evidence** manual for more detail.)

It is essential that adequate disclosure is given to the defence in criminal trials. In *Edwards v United Kingdom* (1992) 15 EHRR 417, the Court held that 'it is a requirement of fairness under Article 6, indeed one which is recognised under English law, that the prosecution must disclose to the defence all material evidence for or against the accused'. The decision of the ECtHR in the case of *Rowe and Davis v United Kingdom* (2000) 30 EHRR 1, although avoiding a comprehensive critique of the domestic system for dealing with the disclosure of 'sensitive' material, established the following principles:

(a) The right to a fair trial means that the prosecution authorities should disclose to the defence all material evidence in their possession for and against the accused.

(b) That duty of disclosure is not absolute, and 'in any criminal proceedings there may be competing interests, such as national security or the need to protect witnesses at risk of reprisals or keep secret police methods of investigation which must be weighed against the rights of the accused'.

(c) Only such measures restricting the rights of the defence to disclosure as are strictly necessary are permissible under Article 6(1).

(d) Any difficulties caused to the defence by a limitation on its rights must be sufficiently counterbalanced by the procedure followed by the court.

The Court held that there was a violation of Article 6(1) due to failure of the prosecution to leave decisions on disclosure to the judge. Following that decision, the Court of Appeal held that the convictions should be quashed (*R v Davis, Johnson and Rowe* [2001] 1 Cr App R 8). In *Atlan v United Kingdom* (2002) 34 EHRR 833, the ECtHR held that there was a violation of Article 6(1) for failure to lay relevant evidence before the trial judge to rule on disclosure.

Trials of very young defendants should not be subjected to the full publicity of criminal trials as in the case of adults. Measures ought to be taken to ensure that they receive a fair trial. In *T v United Kingdom; V v United Kingdom* (2000) 30 EHRR 121, it was held that the child killers of James Bulger had been denied a fair hearing in breach of their rights under Article 6. One of the reasons for this was that the trial took place in the glare of unprecedented media attention which, combined with other factors such as the layout of the courtroom, in the opinion of the Court, increased the defendants' sense of discomfort. Following the decision of the ECtHR in that case, the Court of Appeal laid down a *Practice Direction* to address the limitations of practice and procedure in relation to trials of young defendants in the Crown Court (see the **Criminal Litigation and Sentencing** manual).

In *Davies v United Kingdom* (2002) 35 EHRR 720, a delay of over five years in proceedings by the Secretary of State for Trade and Industry was held to be in violation of Article 6(1). In *Mellors v United Kingdom* (2004) 38 EHRR 189, the Court held that there had been a violation of Article 6(1) due to the unreasonable length of criminal proceedings. In *Cuscani v United Kingdom* (2003) 36 EHRR 11, the ECtHR held that there was a violation of Article 6(1) and Article 6(3)(e) due to the absence of an interpreter at the trial of the defendant, an Italian, manager of 'The Godfather Restaurant' in Newcastle, on VAT charges, for which he was sentenced to four years' imprisonment, as he had a very poor command of English. In *R v Looseley, Attorney-General's Reference (No 3 of 2000)* [2001] 1 WLR 2060, L had supplied heroin to an undercover police officer who had telephoned him to place an order for the drugs. The House of Lords held that the police had done no more than provide L with an unexceptional opportunity to commit the offence, and his appeal was dismissed. The acquitted defendant in the Attorney-General's Reference was charged with supplying heroin to undercover police officers who were offering contraband cigarettes for sale. It was held that the trial judge had been entitled to stay the proceedings as the officers had instigated the offence by offering inducements to a person who had not previously dealt in heroin. In *Teixeira de Castro v Portugal* (1998) 28 EHRR 101, it was held that the right to a fair trial will be violated where police officers or participant informers have stepped beyond an 'essentially passive' investigation of a suspect's criminal activities, and have 'exercised an influence such as to incite the commission of an offence'. Such influence would amount to entrapment.

In *R v Lyons* [2003] 1 AC 976, the House of Lords considered appeals against convictions where the ECtHR had previously held that there were violations of Article 6(1) in the *Guinness* serious fraud trial following the use at trial of evidence obtained under compulsion in an earlier Department of Trade and Industry investigation. The House of Lords held that the convictions were not unsafe, as the law was applied as at the date of trial. The HRA 1998 did not have retrospective effect, even though the ECtHR had found that the trials were unfair (*Saunders v United Kingdom* (1996) 23 EHRR 313 and *IJL, GMR and AKP v United Kingdom* (2001) 33 EHRR 225).

In 2012, the ECtHR ruled that the UK government could not deport Abu Qatada to Jordan because of the risk of a trial using evidence obtained by torture: *Othman (Abu Qatada) v United Kingdom* (Application No 8139/09) [2012] ECHR 56 (17 January 2012). Despite the Court finding that there would be no risk of ill treatment to Abu Qatada himself, the Strasbourg Court agreed with the English Court of Appeal that the use of evidence obtained by torture during a criminal trial would amount to a flagrant denial of justice under Article 6. The stalemate was only broken when Abu Qatada pledged that he would leave the United Kingdom if the United Kingdom and Jordanian governments agreed and ratified a treaty clarifying that evidence gained through torture would not be used against him in his forthcoming trial. In July 2013, following the ratification of such a treaty, Abu Qatada was deported from the United Kingdom.

In *Matthews v Ministry of Defence* [2003] 1 AC 1163, it was held that the provision in s. 10(1)(b) of the Crown Proceedings Act 1947 which prevented an ex-serviceman from bringing a personal injury claim against the Ministry of Defence was a substantive bar and was not incompatible with Article 6(1), which applied to procedural limitations, and was not engaged.

In *Edwards and Lewis v United Kingdom* [2003] Crim LR 891, the ECtHR held that there was a violation of Article 6(1) as the applicants had been convicted and sentenced to prison terms on the basis of evidence of undercover police officers who were stated to have entrapped the applicants into committing offences of possession, intent to supply heroin, and possession of counterfeit notes.

In *R v H; R v C* [2003] 1 WLR 3006, the Court of Appeal held that where there was a public interest immunity application, it was only in exceptional cases that the judge should invite the Attorney-General to appoint special independent counsel.

17.3.3.6 Article 7: no punishment without law

Article 7 states:

> 1. No one shall be held guilty of any criminal offence on account of any act or omission which did not constitute a criminal offence under national or international law at the time when it was committed. Nor shall a heavier penalty be imposed than the one that was applicable at the time the criminal offence was committed.
>
> 2. This article shall not prejudice the trial and punishment of any person for any act or omission which, at the time when it was committed, was criminal according to the general principles of law recognised by civilised nations.

This Article prohibits the retrospective application of the criminal law.

17.3.3.7 Article 8: right to respect for a private and family life, home, and correspondence

Article 8 states:

> 1. Everyone has the right to respect for his private and family life, his home and his correspondence.
>
> 2. There shall be no interference by a public authority with the exercise of this right except such as is in accordance with the law and is necessary in a democratic society in the interests of national security, public safety or the economic well-being of the country, for the prevention of disorder or crime, for the protection of health or morals, or for the protection of the rights and freedoms of others.

Article 8 has proved one of the most mutable, fluid, and oft-cited of all the Convention rights. Neither the Commission nor the Court has attempted to define Article 8's remit, permitting it to adapt and extend to protect a range of interests that do not fit into other Convention heads.

Article 8 creates both a negative obligation upon the State not to interfere with privacy rights, and a positive duty to take measures to prevent private parties from interfering with these rights: *(1) X (2) Y v the Netherlands* (1985) 8 EHRR 235.

There are four express protected interests under Article 8: (1) private life; (2) home; (3) family; and (4) correspondence. Most actions have been decided under the right to respect for private life, although they may involve incidental claims to respect for home, family, or correspondence.

High-profile examples of arguments engaging privacy are those cases involving celebrities, based on the principle of the law of confidentiality. In *Douglas v Hello!* [2001] 2 WLR 992, an injunction restraining *Hello!* against publishing pictures of the wedding of the celebrities Michael Douglas and Catherine Zeta-Jones was discharged by the Court of Appeal, which held that:

(a) there was clearly a serious triable issue as to whether the photographs had been taken at a private function;

(b) English law recognised the right to privacy in Article 8, but there were different degrees of privacy which materially affected the interaction between the right to privacy and the right to freedom of expression conferred by Article 10;

(c) the wedding was far from being a private one, for the major part of the couple's privacy rights had been sold as part of a commercial transaction; and

(d) the balance of convenience militated against the grant of an injunction.

In *Beckham and Beckham v MGN Ltd* Lawtel 30 July 2001, an injunction was continued against the publishers to prevent publication of pictures in the *Sunday People* of David and Victoria Beckham's new house as they argued that their security could have been breached. In *A v B plc and another, Garry Flitcroft v Mirror Group Newspapers Ltd* [2002] 3 WLR 542, an injunction had been granted restraining newspaper publishers from disclosing or publishing information concerning sexual relationships between the claimant, a professional footballer who was a married man with children, the second defendant, and another woman. The injunction was set aside as the law of confidentiality would not grant the same protection in relation to transient relationships as it would to those concerning relationships in marriage.

In *AB (Jamaica) v Secretary of State for the Home Department* [2008] 1 WLR 1893, the Court of Appeal held that the breach of immigration control by an overstayer who had married a British citizen was not so significant that it warranted disruption of the family's life by her and her daughters' removal to Jamaica. It was also unreasonable to expect her British husband to leave the United Kingdom to settle in Jamaica.

In *Re P (A Child) (Adoption: Unmarried Couples)* [2009] 1 AC 173, the House of Lords held that it was unlawful for the Family Division of the High Court of Northern Ireland to reject a couple as prospective adoptive parents on the ground that they were not married. In 2008, the ECtHR had decided that the blanket indefinite retention of suspects' DNA and fingerprint samples was an unjustified interference with Article 8 (*S and Marper v United Kingdom* (2009) 48 EHRR 50). The Protection of Freedoms Act 2012 now provides a specific regime for the use and retention of these samples, depending on the type of offence, and whether the suspect is simply arrested or eventually convicted.

17.3.3.8 Article 9: freedom of thought, conscience, and religion

Article 9 states:

> *1. Everyone has the right to freedom of thought, conscience and religion; this right includes freedom to change his religion or belief and freedom, either alone or in community with others and in public or private, to manifest his religion or belief, in worship, teaching, practice and observance.*
>
> *2. Freedom to manifest one's religion or beliefs shall be subject only to such limitations as are prescribed by law and are necessary in a democratic society in the interests of public safety, for the protection of public order, health or morals, or for the protection of the rights and freedoms of others.*

Article 9 covers the sphere of private, personal beliefs and religious creeds, and the Strasbourg Court has accepted beliefs ranging from veganism (*United Kingdom* Application No 00018187/91 (1993) Unreported) to Scientology (*Sweden* Application No 0007805/77 (1979) 16 DR 68).

This Article was argued unsuccessfully in the Court of Appeal on behalf of a Rastafarian who claimed a defence of religious use to a charge of possession of cannabis with intent to supply (*R v Taylor* [2002] 1 Cr App R 37).

17.3.3.9 Article 10: freedom of expression

Article 10 states:

> *1. Everyone has the right to freedom of expression. This right shall include freedom to hold opinions and to receive and impart information and ideas without interference by public authority and regardless of frontiers. This article shall not prevent States from requiring the licensing of broadcasting, television or cinema enterprises.*
>
> *2. The exercise of these freedoms, since it carries with it duties and responsibilities, may be subject to such formalities, conditions, restrictions or penalties as are prescribed by law and are necessary in a democratic society, in the interests of national security, territorial integrity or public safety, for the prevention of disorder or crime, for the protection of health or morals, for the protection of the reputation or rights of others, for preventing the disclosure of information received in confidence, or for maintaining the authority and impartiality of the judiciary.*

This Article has been relied on, together with s. 12 HRA 1998, by the media, to counter arguments founded on Article 8.

In *R (on the application of ProLife Alliance) v BBC* [2003] 2 WLR 1403, it was held that the BBC and other broadcasters were entitled to refuse to broadcast a party election broadcast which contained graphic images of abortion on the ground that it was offensive to public feeling. Article 10(1) was qualified by Article 10(2).

The balance between Article 8, the right to private life, and Article 10, the freedom of expression, came under the spotlight in the United Kingdom in the 2011 media debate surrounding privacy injunctions. These super-injunctions, which forbid the media from revealing their existence, revisited a familiar debate: what is the proper role of the courts in balancing the media's right to reveal the (usually extra-marital) activities of public figures against the right for that person to enjoy a private life.

17.3.3.10   Article 11: freedom of assembly and association

Article 11 states:

> 1. *Everyone has the right to freedom of peaceful assembly and to freedom of association with others, including the right to form and to join trade unions for the protection of his interests.*
> 2. *No restrictions shall be placed on the exercise of these rights other than such as are prescribed by law and are necessary in a democratic society in the interests of national security or public safety, for the prevention of disorder or crime, for the protection of health or morals or for the protection of the rights and freedoms of others. This article shall not prevent the imposition of lawful restrictions on the exercise of these rights by members of the armed forces, of the police or of the administration of the State.*

This Article relates to a right considered to be one of the foundations of a democratic society and is not restrictively interpreted. In *Wilson v United Kingdom* (2002) 35 EHRR 523, the Court held that there was a violation of Article 11 where domestic law allowed for employers to cease to recognise trade unions in the workplace and to abandon previous collective bargaining agreements.

In *R (on the application of Laporte) v Chief Constable of Gloucestershire* [2007] 2 AC 105, the House of Lords held that the police had acted unlawfully in preventing coach passengers from reaching the site of an anti-war demonstration because it was unreasonable to have concluded that a breach of the peace was imminent at the point where the coaches had been stopped and escorted away. The interference with the demonstrators' rights was disproportionate and in violation of Articles 10 and 11.

17.3.3.11   Article 12: right to marry and found a family

Article 12 states:

> *Men and women of marriageable age have the right to marry and to found a family, according to the national laws governing the exercise of this right.*

Although Article 12 offers two separable rights, to marry and to found a family, it is through the lens of Article 8 that the majority of claims have been decided relating to family, and personal relationships. This means that Article 12 case law is limited.

In *R v Registrar General for Births, Deaths and Marriages, ex p CPS* [2003] QB 1222, the Court of Appeal held that there was no power to prevent a prisoner on remand from marrying a woman who was a prospective witness at his forthcoming trial and who would cease to be compellable by reason of s. 80 of the Police and Criminal Evidence Act 1984.

Although the wording of Article 12, which was drafted in the 1950s and envisaged only a heterosexual marriage model, the UK's civil partnership laws have since 2004 allowed same-sex couples to live in legally recognised partnerships. The Marriage (Same Sex Couples) Act 2013 took this a step further and finally legalised same-sex marriages in England and Wales with effect from March 2014.

17.3.3.12   Article 13: right to an effective remedy

Article 13 states:

> *Everyone whose rights and freedoms as set forth in this Convention are violated shall have an effective remedy before a national authority notwithstanding that the violation has been committed by persons acting in an official capacity.*

This right was omitted from the Convention rights referred to in HRA 1998.

17.3.3.13   Article 14: prohibition of discrimination

Article 14 states:

> *The enjoyment of the rights and freedoms set forth in this Convention shall be secured without discrimination on any ground such as sex, race, colour, language, religion, political or other opinion, national or social origin, association with a national minority, property, birth or other status.*

This is not an independent prohibition, but lends support to other Convention rights, for example in *Abdulaziz, Cabales and Balkandali v United Kingdom* (1985) 7 EHRR 471, immigration rules were held to be discriminatory against women seeking permission for their husbands to enter the United Kingdom (i.e. discriminatory of their enjoyment of their right to a family life under Article 8). In *Willis v United Kingdom* (2002) 35 EHRR 547, the Court held that there was a violation of Article 14 and Protocol 1, Article 1 where the applicant had been refused social security benefits to which he would have been entitled had he been a woman in a similar position, namely the widowed mother's allowance and a widow's payment. Further, in *Ghaidan v Godin-Mendoza* [2004] 2 AC 447, the House of Lords held that sexual orientation was an impermissible ground for discrimination and that a gay partner was entitled to be a survivor to a protected tenancy.

The Equality Act 2010 sought to codify into a single Act the numerous anti-discrimination laws that had been implemented piecemeal throughout the preceding four decades, including the Equal Pay Act 1970, the Sex Discrimination Act 1975, the Race Relations Act 1976, the Disability Discrimination Act 1995, and certain statutory instruments protecting discrimination in employment on grounds of religion or belief, sexual orientation, and age.

17.3.3.14   Article 15: derogation from the Convention

Article 15 states:

> 1. *In time of war or other public emergency threatening the life of the nation any High Contracting Party may take measures derogating from its obligations under this Convention to the extent strictly required by the exigencies of the situation, provided that such measures are not inconsistent with its other obligations under international law.*
>
> 2. *No derogation from Article 2, except in respect of deaths resulting from lawful acts of war, or from Articles 3, 4 (paragraph 1) and 7 shall be made under this provision.*
>
> 3. *Any High Contracting Party availing itself of this right of derogation shall keep the Secretary General of the Council of Europe fully informed of the measures which it has taken and the reasons therefor. It shall also inform the Secretary General of the Council of Europe when such measures have ceased to operate and the provisions of the Convention are again being fully executed.*

The derogation from Article 5(3) (no detention without prompt trial) was held by the Court in *Brannigan v United Kingdom* (1993) 17 EHRR 539 to have satisfied Article 15 as there was an emergency in Northern Ireland threatening the life of the nation, and detention for seven days without access to a court was necessary. A wide margin of appreciation was allowed to the United Kingdom.

The UK government derogated from some of its obligations under the Convention when it enacted the Anti-terrorism, Crime and Security Act 2001 following the 11 September terrorist incidents and the military action in Afghanistan. In *A v Secretary of State for the Home Department* [2005] 2 AC 68, the House of Lords held, however, that detention of several non-national suspected terrorists was incompatible with the Convention and was disproportionate. The case was subsequently considered by the ECtHR, where it was held in *A v United Kingdom* The Times, 20 February 2009, that there were violations of Article 5(1) and Article 5(5) in the cases of nine applicants, and of Article 5(4) in the cases of four applicants.

17.3.3.15 Articles 16, 17, and 18: additional restrictions and rights

Articles 16–18 state:

Article 16: Restrictions on political activity of aliens

Nothing in Articles 10, 11 and 14 shall be regarded as preventing the High Contracting Parties from imposing restrictions on the political activity of aliens.

Article 17: Prohibition of abuse of rights

Nothing in this Convention may be interpreted as implying for any State, group or person any right to engage in any activity or perform any act aimed at the destruction of any of the rights and freedoms set forth herein or at their limitation to a greater extent than is provided for in the Convention.

Article 18: Limitation on use of restrictions on rights

The restrictions permitted under this Convention to the said rights and freedoms shall not be applied for any purpose other than those for which they have been prescribed.

17.3.3.16 Articles 1–3 of the First Protocol

Articles 1–3 of Protocol 1 state:

Article 1: Protection of property

Every natural or legal person is entitled to the peaceful enjoyment of his possessions. No one shall be deprived of his possessions except in the public interest and subject to the conditions provided for by law and by the general principles of international law.

The preceding provisions shall not, however, in any way impair the right of a State to enforce such laws as it deems necessary to control the use of property in accordance with the general interest or to secure the payment of taxes or other contributions or penalties.

Article 2: Right to education

No person shall be denied the right to education. In the exercise of any functions which it assumes in relation to education and to teaching, the State shall respect the right of parents to ensure such education and teaching in conformity with their own religious and philosophical convictions.

Article 3: Right to free elections

The High Contracting Parties undertake to hold free elections at reasonable intervals by secret ballot, under conditions which will ensure the free expression of the opinion of the people in the choice of the legislature.

17.3.3.17 Articles 1 and 2 of the Sixth Protocol

Articles 1 and 2 of Protocol 6 state:

Article 1: Abolition of the death penalty

The death penalty shall be abolished. No one shall be condemned to such penalty or executed.

Article 2: Death penalty in time of war

A State may make provision in its law for the death penalty in respect of acts committed in time of war or of imminent threat of war; such penalty shall be applied only in the instances laid down in the law and in accordance with its provisions. The State shall communicate to the Secretary General of the Council of Europe the relevant provisions of that law.

17.4 Reports and further reading

17.4.1 Court reports

Butterworths Human Rights Direct <http://www.lexisnexis.co.uk>.
Criminal Law Review (Human Rights Case Reports).

European Court of Human Rights (Judgments) <http://www.echr.coe.int>.

European Human Rights Reports (EHRR).

Lawtel <http://www.lawtel.com>.

The Times Law Reports.

17.4.2   Textbooks and periodicals

Leach, P., *Taking a Case to the European Court of Human Rights,* 4th edn, Oxford University Press, 2018.

Stanton, J., *Blackstone's Statutes on Public Law & Human Rights 2021/22*, Oxford University Press, 2021.

Reid, K., *A Practitioner's Guide to the European Convention on Human Rights,* 6th edn, Sweet & Maxwell, 2019.

Wadham, J., Mountfield, H., Prochaska, E., Dessai, R., *Blackstone's Guide to the Human Rights Act 1998*, 7th revised edn, Oxford University Press, 2015.

European Human Rights Law Review.

Legal Action.

New Law Journal.

Solicitors Journal.

Class problems in contract and tort

In each of the following problems, you are given a brief set of facts. In each case, you should advise the client on appropriate remedies, taking as practical an approach as possible.

18.1 Martin Pender

Your instructing solicitors act for Martin Pender, whose business is that of car leasing. By a leasing agreement dated 3 January 2020 Mr Pender ('the owner') leased, and Jest Videos Company plc ('the hirer') took, for a term of three years from 1 February 2020, five cars at a rental of £22,500 per annum, payable yearly in advance on 1 February 2020 and the two subsequent anniversaries of that date. Clause 7 of the agreement provided that in the event of default being made in any yearly payment for 14 days or more after the due date, the owner might take possession of the goods.

During December 2019 the owner, in the expectation that the hirer would sign a leasing agreement, bought five new Ford Focus motor cars for £15,000 each, which he had painted in accordance with the company's wishes, in company colours. The cost of the modifications was £7,500.

On 1 February 2019, the hirer took possession of the cars and paid the first year's rent. The hirer failed to pay the rent due on 1 February 2021, and on 16 February the owner repossessed the cars.

Between 16 February and 1 April 2021 the owner carried out, at a cost of £3,750, repairs necessary to put the cars in a state fit for re-leasing, and on the latter date released the cars to Dodgems Incorporated for two years at a rent of £11,250 per annum. Counsel may assume that no terms which would have been more favourable to the owner could have been found, and that it is unlikely that the cars can be leased again at the end of the two-year period, when they will probably be worth about £7,500 each.

As a result of the hirer's default in paying the amount due on 1 February 2021, the owner did not have in hand sufficient funds to fulfil an agreement which he had made to purchase a Renault van from the manufacturers with delivery and payment set for 1 March 2021. The owner managed to complete this purchase by borrowing £12,500 for six months at 20 per cent per annum from Grasping Finance Ltd. Interest on this loan amounted to £1,250 and Grasping Finance Ltd charged an 'arrangement' fee of £375.

Liability is unlikely to be an issue.

Counsel will please advise as to quantum.

18.2 Mr and Mrs Roberts

Mr and Mrs Roberts are the owners of farmland in Northumberland. In 2010, they granted a licence for three years to the Northern Gravel Company ('the Company') to extract gravel from one of their fields. The Company extracted a large amount of gravel, leaving a pit measuring 100 m by 150 m, with a depth of 15 m.

On 4 August 2015, Mr and Mrs Roberts entered into a second licence with the Company, granting it the right to tip certain types of rubbish in the pit. Clause 3 of the licence provided:

> (a) *The Company shall tip rubbish up to a level one metre below the natural surface of the pit.*
> (b) *Upon completion of the tipping the Company shall place one metre of topsoil evenly over the whole of the pit and such topsoil shall be free from all impediments and materials which may turn a plough.*

The Company completed tipping at the pit in September 2018. It then set about complying with clause 3(b) of the licence. The Company claimed to have discharged its obligation by August 2019. However, in October 2019, when the field was being ploughed, the mechanical plough was fouled by an underground obstruction and badly damaged. Mr and Mrs Roberts immediately gave instructions for boring tests to be carried out, which revealed that there is only 70 cm of topsoil and that there is a great deal of rubbish in it, including large concrete blocks.

Unfortunately, Mr and Mrs Roberts have only just come to instructing solicitors concerning the matter, having relied on their land agent previously to obtain rectification of the position.

If possible, Mr and Mrs Roberts would wish to force the Company to place another 30 cm of topsoil on the site after the rubbish has been removed from the existing soil. Counsel is asked to advise:

(a) whether it will be possible to obtain an order for specific performance against the Company;

(b) what will be the measure of damages if specific performance is not ordered and at what date damages will be assessed. The value of the field is now £40,000, but it would have been £60,000 if it were ploughable. The value of the whole farm is £500,000; with the field restored the farm would be worth £510,000. The cost of doing the necessary work to restore the field was £20,000 in 2019, but is now £30,000;

(c) what further damages may be recoverable in any event. As a result of the damage to the plough (which cost £1,000 to repair), Mr and Mrs Roberts were unable to plough another of their fields in time to sow a winter crop and so lost profit of £6,000. Further, they have not been able to use the field in which the Company tipped rubbish for the planting of crops for the last three years, but only less profitably for the grazing of cattle, a loss of £4,000 per annum.

18.3   Newtown Theatre Company

Instructing solicitors act for Newtown Theatre Company Ltd (NTC), a new company set up to run a theatre in Newtown and to tour the surrounding districts. Counsel is instructed in relation to the employment of two actors, Mr Murray Clive, the well-known film and TV star, and Mr Siegfried Blackstone.

Mr Clive was engaged by NTC on the terms of a letter on NTC notepaper dated 15 September 2022, which reads as follows:

Dear Mr Clive

This is to confirm the terms of the agreement made yesterday at your meeting with our Mr Selsdon.

1. You will be employed to act for our company from 18 September 2022 to 17 September 2023 at a salary of £3,000 per week.
2. You will act in such roles, and carry out such other duties incidental to the business of the company, as the company's management may direct.
3. You will be entitled to four weeks' paid holiday to be taken in accordance with the direction of the company's management.
4. You will not during the period of the agreement act in any other stage production in the United Kingdom.

Yours sincerely
Newtown Theatre Co. Ltd

On 3 October, NTC decided that its Christmas production would be *Aladdin* and cast Mr Clive in the role of Widow Twankey. Yesterday, Mr Clive did not turn up to rehearsal, but sent a note saying that he was leaving the company and would be starting new employment with the Grabham Theatre Company in ten days' time.

Mr Blackstone was employed specifically for the production of *Aladdin*, in which he plays the Genie. His contract runs from 18 September 2022 to 31 January 2023. He is paid £1,000 per week. He has no written agreement, but was engaged orally by Mr Selsdon on behalf of NTC.

NTC has no specific information, but Mr Selsdon has heard a rumour that Mr Blackstone may have accepted an offer from a film company and will leave its employment shortly before the opening on 1 November. In such an event, the company would be forced to abandon the production as it would be impossible to find a replacement, and there would be about £200,000 wasted expenditure on the publicity and settings, as well as the loss of box office profits.

The Company wishes to take proceedings against Mr Clive and wishes to be advised as to its position in relation to both Mr Clive and Mr Blackstone. In particular, it wishes to know whether there is any possibility of preventing Mr Clive or Mr Blackstone from leaving NTC or, if not, on what basis damages would be awarded.

Counsel is requested to advise NTC what, if anything, can be done to protect its legitimate business interest.

18.4 Gordon Priestly

Mr Priestly previously lived in London with his wife Mary and two children aged eight and six. In 2021, the family decided to move into the country, where they would be able to afford a larger house. They wanted a larger house for two reasons: to provide a home for Mr Priestly's mother, who is getting on in years and not well able to look after herself; and to have a music studio in which to place a grand piano and in which Mary Priestly could supplement the family income by giving music lessons.

They were unable to find just the house they were looking for, but in September 2021 purchased a Victorian house called Mon Repos, Hobbs Green, Sussex, which stood in large grounds and could easily have an extension added.

Mr Priestly engaged Mr James Foyle, an architect, to design a two-storey extension which provided a large living area on the ground floor and a studio and bedroom on the floor above. Mr Foyle delivered the plans and specification in December 2021 and Mr Priestly engaged a local builder, Premier Builders Ltd, to construct the extension, commencing January 2022. He did not employ Mr Foyle or anyone else to supervise the building works, preferring to rely on his own experience as an interior designer.

After the usual delays, Premier Builders Ltd completed the extension in June 2022 at a final agreed cost of £80,000. Mr Priestly then employed a local firm of decorators, R.B. Ricketts & Son, to decorate the extension to his design. The decorations included some ornamental plastering on the ceiling of the ground floor of the extension. Before R.B. Ricketts started work, Mrs Priestly's piano was moved into the upstairs studio (suitably protected with dust sheets and plastic wrapping), in order to save storage costs.

On the day they started work, Mr Ricketts senior pointed out to Mr Priestly that the floor of the upper storey seemed very springy and expressed some concern about this, but neither he nor Mr Priestly discussed the matter further. The ornamental plastering was completed and on 29 June 2022 Mr Ricketts junior, a large man who must weigh about 14 stone, was standing on a ladder while painting in the studio, when suddenly the ladder fell through the floor. He was scarcely able to run out of the way before the piano also fell through the hole, taking most of the floor (and ceiling of the room downstairs) with it.

Mr Priestly called in another architect, Mr Basil Soole, to investigate the damage and supervise the repairs. Mr Soole found no fault with Mr Foyle's design, but reported that Premier

Builders Ltd had constructed the floor in breach of the specification, good practice, and the building regulations, in four main respects:

(a) The joists to the timber first-floor construction should have been at not more than 600 mm centres in order to comply with Building Regulation B19(3)(i). The joists fitted by Premier Builders were at varying centres, never less than 800 mm and at five places as much as 950 mm centres. There was therefore insufficient support for the floor.

(b) The floorboards should have been of a thickness of not less than 22 mm in order to comply with Building Regulation B21(2)(ii). They were in fact 15 mm throughout the extension.

(c) The specification called for softwood to be Douglas fir, Western hemlock, European redwood, or Canadian spruce. Premier Builders had used deal, a far inferior softwood to those specified.

(d) Contrary to good practice, Premier Builders had not properly secured the joists to the retaining walls.

The repairs took ten weeks to complete and were carried out by Crabbe & Co. at a cost of £32,000. In addition, Mr Soole's fee was £3,200 and R.B. Ricketts charged £1,750 to redo the ornamental plastering. The piano was beyond repair. It was worth £3,000, but Mrs Priestly had to buy another at a cost of £5,000. She has lost £2,500 income from piano lessons because of the collapse of the floor. Finally, Mr Priestly's mother was not able to move in until three months after she had planned and Mr Priestly had to pay her rent over that period, a total of £4,800.

Counsel is asked to advise Mr Priestly as to liability and quantum.

18.5 Polly Partridge

Your instructing solicitors act for Polly Partridge, who is 45 years old and well known in the art world. After taking a degree in History of Art at Oxford University, Ms Partridge worked for ten years in various art galleries in France: she then returned to England, where she deals in paintings both on her own account and as agent for various collectors.

In December 2016, Ms Partridge saw advertised in the current catalogue of Quentin Quick Fine Art Ltd a drawing described as 'Drawing in pen and ink by J.A. Dessain, 1921'. Dessain was an artist with whose work Ms Partridge was familiar. After inspecting the drawing, she was satisfied as to its authenticity, and purchased it from Quick for £30,000 on 19 December 2016.

On 1 February 2022, Ms Partridge sent the drawing for valuation to Dr Robert Rawthorne of Rawthorne and Son (Fine Art Valuations) Ltd. On 3 February, Dr Rawthorne advised Ms Partridge that the drawing was not by Dessain and that it was virtually worthless. He also stated that, if the drawing had been a genuine Dessain, it would have fetched at least £72,000 at auction. Counsel may assume that Dr Rawthorne's advice is correct. At the time it was given, Ms Partridge believed that the only remedies she could have against Quick would be in case of fraud; and Quick's conduct at the time of the sale was in fact entirely innocent.

On 1 May 2022, Ms Partridge offered the drawing for sale by advertisement in art magazines as 'Drawing in pen and ink in the style of Dessain. Artist unknown. About 1920', but received no offer above £500.

On 1 June 2022, Ms Partridge consulted your instructing solicitors and was for the first time advised that the remedy of rescission might be available. Your instructing solicitors wrote to Quick stating that Ms Partridge was entitled, upon return of the drawing, to the return of the price with interest. Solicitors acting for Quick have responded by saying that it is now too late for Ms Partridge to make any claim and that, in any event, her action in advertising the drawing for sale constituted an affirmation of the contract with Quick so as to deprive her of any right to equitable relief.

Will counsel please advise Ms Partridge as to her remedies.

18.6   Dreamy Travel Ltd

Instructing solicitors act for Dreamy Travel Ltd ('the Company'). The managing director and principal shareholder is Mr Basil Dream. The Company's business consists primarily of package holidays arranged by the Company and sold to its customers online. The Company prides itself on providing a good service to its customers. Their website advertises all available holiday packages and every year an email is sent to all previous customers and to anybody who has expressed interest in the Company's holidays.

For several years, the Company has traded with Greed Hotels Ltd, whose managing director and principal shareholder is Mr Gregory Greed, and which operates several seaside hotels. Each year, the Company takes an allocation of rooms in several of Greed's hotels, and pays a fixed weekly rate for these rooms, on a full-board basis, whether or not such rooms are occupied. Of course, in this way, the Company is able to have the advantage of a much cheaper rate than would otherwise be the case. The Company then endeavours to fill these rooms with its customers.

In 2019, Mr Greed informed Mr Dream that he had acquired a valuable site at Brighton and was building a luxury hotel. On 17 December 2021, Mr Greed told Mr Dream over a lunch at the Greed Hotel, Bournemouth, that the hotel at Brighton was finished and would be available for the 2022 season, from the beginning of April 2022. He said that the hotel was in the four-star luxury category, with an Olympic-size swimming pool, two saunas, three tennis courts, two large lounges, a bar, cinema, games room, and smaller writing and television rooms. He said that the hotel was within five minutes' walk of the sea. He supplied Mr Dream with photographs, including a photograph of the swimming pool, which looked magnificent. Mr Dream was about to go on a cruise with his wife and did not go to see the hotel, as he otherwise would have done.

On Mr Dream's instructions, the Company wrote the following letter to Greed Hotels Ltd on 7 January 2022.

Dear Sirs
This is to confirm that we wish to book the following allocation from 1 April to 30 September 2022.
Greed Hotel, Brighton
36 double rooms at £500 per week
12 single rooms at £375 per week
The above prices include room, full board (two persons per double room), all usual hotel services, and to include VAT.
Yours faithfully
Dreamy Travel Ltd

Greed confirmed the booking by letter dated 14 January 2022 signed by Gregory Greed to the Company. Payment of the full price (£585,000) was duly made on 22 March, before the beginning of the season.

The Company incorporated in its brochure package holidays based on the Greed Hotel, Brighton, describing it in glowing terms in accordance with Mr Greed's description to Mr Dream, and featuring a reproduction of the photograph of the swimming pool. All the rooms were booked for the whole season and paid for in advance. The Company charged its customers £750 per week for a double room and £570 per week for a single room.

From the start of the season, the Company received a stream of complaints about the Greed Hotel, Brighton. Mr Dream went down to see for himself on 9 May. The hotel was only partly finished. The builders were still on the premises, and there was considerable noise. The swimming pool was not complete, and it was clear that the photograph supplied to Mr Dream must have been of another swimming pool. One of the saunas was not in operation, as it had not been completed. There was only one lounge. The second lounge was being used as a makeshift dining room, as the dining room was not finished. However, it was not suitable as a dining room and there was considerable congestion. The games room was not operational as there were builders' tools in it. There was no television lounge. By no stretch of the imagination could the hotel be described as in the four-star luxury class. Virtually every customer complained.

The Company was obliged to write to all its customers on 10 May. To those who had already stayed at the hotel, or were there at the time and completed their stay, it offered a 50 per cent refund of their money plus compensation for distress and inconvenience and expenses. To those who had cut short their stay, it offered a 100 per cent refund plus the same compensation. A 100 per cent refund was automatically sent to those who had heard of the difficulties and cancelled before arriving, even if this was at the last moment. Those customers who had yet to start their holidays were offered three choices: (i) a 50 per cent refund if they took the holiday up; (ii) a 100 per cent refund plus £20 for expenses if they cancelled; (iii) an equivalent holiday at no extra cost at another hotel, if possible in Brighton, otherwise elsewhere on the south coast.

The Company felt obliged to offer these generous terms in view of the volume of complaints from customers indicating that they would never book a holiday with Dreamy Travel again, and in view of some very bad press publicity which must reflect on the future goodwill of the Company.

Mr Dream was able to negotiate with Mr Greed a total cancellation of the booking from 22 July and a full refund of the money paid in respect of the remaining period (£225,000).

A total of £437,500 was paid back to customers by way of refunds, plus a further £57,500 in compensation. The rest of the money received from customers was retained, but the cost of alternative holidays for those customers was £400,000.

In order to make all the rearrangements and offers, the Company incurred postal and telephone costs of £900 and had to employ two extra temporary staff from an agency for two months, at a cost of £10,000.

Counsel is asked to advise the Company as to quantum.

18.7   Peter Boggis

Instructing solicitors act for Mr Peter Boggis, who is a partner in a firm of architects, Goodhart Boggis & Co. Mr Boggis's car, a Volvo Estate reg. no. YP17 BOG, belongs to the firm, but is exclusively used by Mr Boggis. On about 13 July 2022, he telephoned Rural Motors Ltd and booked it in for service on 20 July 2022. He spoke to the service manager, Mr Wort.

A few days later, Mr Boggis discovered that he was going to have to go abroad on business on 20 July. Therefore, when he took the car in for service on 20 July, he asked Mr Wort at the reception desk if Rural Motors could store the car for a few days until he was able to return and collect it. Mr Wort replied, 'OK, I'll store it for you, but if it's for too long, we may have to charge you something extra'. Mr Boggis agreed to this.

Mr Boggis then drove his car into the service area and was just about to leave when Mr Wort pointed out to him that there was a large quantity of high-tech video equipment in the boot. This was Mr Boggis's personal property. Mr Boggis obviously couldn't take it with him on his business trip and had no time to return to the office before setting off, so he asked Mr Wort if it would be all right to leave the equipment in the car. Mr Wort replied that it 'should be OK'. Mr Boggis accepted this remark without a second thought and left the car with the equipment inside it.

As it turned out, Mr Boggis's trip lasted longer than expected and he did not return to collect his car until 3 August. He paid for the service using a partnership credit card. He was not charged for the storage. He then went to drive his car away and noticed that the equipment was not inside it. He therefore returned to the reception desk and asked Mr Wort where it was. Mr Wort apologised and went off to have a look for it. After about ten minutes, he returned empty-handed and said that the only explanation he could give was that 'it must have been nicked'. Mr Boggis told Mr Wort that he held Rural Motors Ltd responsible for the loss, but Mr Wort replied that they were not responsible and pointed out a notice over the reception desk which said:

> Whilst Rural Motors Ltd will endeavour to take every reasonable precaution, it is regretted that no responsibility can be accepted for loss or damage to any property left inside vehicles.

Mr Wort went on to say that the equipment might have been stored somewhere and that he would have a look for it, but Mr Boggis was obliged to leave without it.

Instructing solicitors have written to Rural Motors Ltd making a formal demand for the return of the equipment, but received a reply from their solicitors to the effect that:

(a) the loss of the equipment was Mr Boggis's own responsibility since he chose to leave it in the car: the storage was free of charge and so the garage could not be held liable in any event;

(b) the garage was protected by the notice; and

(c) even if the garage was prima facie liable, Mr Boggis was contributorily negligent.

Counsel is asked to advise Mr Boggis whether he can recover the value of the equipment (£13,000) from Rural Motors Ltd.

18.8 Roger Lucas

Roger Lucas was injured on 30 June 2019, on his last day of work for Don Godfrey & Co. Ltd, before starting work as a long-distance lorry driver. His date of birth was 1 March 1991. Counsel is asked to advise on quantum.

Roger Lucas will say:

I was very severely injured in the accident, sustaining a paraplegia from which I have been told there is no hope of recovery, and my life expectancy has been reduced by about ten years. I am confined to a wheelchair. Jenny, my wife, has been a wonderful source of support. Before my accident she had two part-time jobs working as a nursing assistant at the nearby cottage hospital for five mornings a week and as a receptionist/nurse for our local family general practitioner each weekday afternoon. She has given up the receptionist job to look after me and persuaded me to take a positive attitude to my misfortune. From June 2018 to May 2021 at the suggestion of the District Rehabilitation Officer I attended a course at the York Rehabilitation Centre training to become a pharmacy assistant. I passed the end of course exam with flying colours, but unfortunately have been quite unable to get a suitable job. Our local cottage hospital has no vacancy for a pharmacy assistant. Only one assistant is employed, and she is still ten years from retiring age. Whether the hospital will still be open in ten years' time is a rather uncertain matter. The course organisers have told me that I could almost certainly get a job earning £600 per week net if I were to apply to a big city hospital. But this would entail moving to live in or close to a city, which I do not want to do. Neither does my wife, though she too would have no difficulty obtaining employment as she is a trained nurse. We are both country folk born and bred. I have been quite unable to obtain work locally and can see little prospect of ever finding a job which I can conveniently reach from home. I can drive my specially adapted car, but not for distances of more than a few miles.

The losses which I would like to claim arising from my accident are as follows:

(a) Loss of earnings. At Don Godfrey & Co. Ltd I received a net weekly wage of £600. As a long-distance lorry driver, I would have netted at least £750 per week with a weekend working bonus of £185 net every fortnight. I had never worked weekends while in Don Godfrey & Co. Ltd's employment. He had regular weekend drivers. Before I began my rehabilitation course, I received £90 per week incapacity benefit. While on the course, I was given a grant of £150 per week. I am now in receipt of £135 per week in benefits.

(b) The cost of building a ground-floor extension to 14 Peel Road, which is a three-storey cottage. My architect advises that it is quite impossible to fit disabled person's escalators to this old stone cottage, so I am confined to the ground floor. The proposal is to build an extension into the garden, which will give me as much accommodation on ground floor level as the cottage has on all three floors. Unfortunately, access for contractors is very difficult to the rear of our cottage and the cost of the extension, including professional fees, will be in the region of £180,000. My solicitor points out that I could buy a three-bedroomed bungalow on a new estate about seven miles away for £230,000, but frankly I cannot face living on a new estate. My cottage is presently worth about £240,000.

(c) £375 per week net to my wife for looking after me each afternoon and at weekends. This is what she has lost by giving up her job as a receptionist/nurse on 1 September 2019.

(d) £185 per week to my sister-in-law for looking after me in the mornings. She also comes in most weekends to give my wife a break. She has been doing this since 1 September 2019. I have not been paying anything to my sister-in-law, who is simply a housewife, but would like to do so. Professional nursing attendance for four hours a day, seven days a week, would cost £750 per week. Eight hours a day would cost £1,000 per week. It would cost another £375 a week to have a nurse on call at night.

(e) The cost of converting my car to enable me to drive it without feet controls. This was £3,000, and this expense will be repeated every, say, five years.

(f) The cost of a special battery-operated wheelchair which I find much more comfortable and versatile than the chair supplied free on the NHS, £3,500. The life of these chairs is about ten years.

(g) The cost of my lost fortnight's holiday in Portugal planned to start on 18 July 2019. The cost was £1,200 each for my wife and myself, covering flights and accommodation. The flight portion of the holiday was insured, and I received £400 from the insurance company when I had to cancel. I had unfortunately decided against insuring the whole holiday, which I could have done for an extra £20 premium.

(h) The cost of employing a professional decorator to decorate my lounge, labour charge £600 plus VAT.

18.9 James Davies

James Davies worked as a motorcycle courier until he was injured on 1 November 2018. His date of birth was 2 October 1993. Counsel is asked to advise on quantum.

James Davies will say:

I had pains in my right leg and shoulder so I went to the Accident Department of the hospital. A doctor carried out an X-ray and said that there was nothing wrong except rather severe bruising, which would heal in a few weeks if I took things easy.

I stayed off work and rested but both my knee and ankle joints remained painful. I went to my GP in February 2019, and he referred me to a Consultant, whom I saw on 1 and 15 March 2019. On the second occasion, she told me that the results of my test were not certain, but that I had potentially serious injuries to both knee and ankle joints. My leg was put in plaster for three months. In June 2019 I was then told I should exercise the joints as I had some form of rare necrosis and might have to have an arthrodesis operation to pin the joints into a fixed position. My exercises and physiotherapy treatment were not successful, however, and in January 2020 an arthrodesis was performed to both joints. As a result, I cannot now bend my right knee, nor move my right ankle.

I have had to give up motorcycling and cannot undertake any physical work. I was earning £500 per week net when I stopped work. For a year after my accident I received £100 per week in benefits, and thereafter received £80 per week until I ceased to be eligible in May 2021. I had to sell my bike and my gear. I received £2,000 for the bike and £500 for the gear, which were good prices, but I had paid £4,000 and £750, respectively, for these items originally.

Before I was injured, I used to play the saxophone with local bands for fun and to earn extra money, almost £100 per week. I was unable to earn anything from saxophone playing between the date of my accident and 1 May 2020, when I resumed playing. Between 1 May 2020 and November 2021, I earned on average £250 per week. While off work I practised a great deal and improved considerably. In November 2021, I became a professional. I now earn about £800 net per week. I travel considerably for my work now and have to use public transport, which I estimate costs me at least £1,500 per year more than the cost of going by motorcycle.

There is, however, no job security in being a professional musician. If times get hard, the work may dry up and nobody wants to employ an ex-musician. I am worried that I will find it very hard to gain alternative employment.

EXTRACT FROM MEDICAL REPORT of MR KENNETH BRAND, FRCS, OF 100 HARLEY STREET, LONDON W1:

Opinion: . . . in conclusion the trauma of the relatively minor injury to both knee and ankle joints sustained by Mr Davies on 1 November 2018 was responsible for the necrosis which so affected the joints that there was no alternative to Mr Davies's medical advisors but to carry out an arthrodesis of both these joints.

18.10 John Simms

John Simms was injured in an explosion on 1 February 2021. His date of birth was 5 March 1966. Counsel is asked to advise on quantum.

John Simms will say:

I was in St George's Hospital, Tooting, for a month. My head and neck were extremely painful and, despite physiotherapy treatment, I continue to suffer serious headaches and a lack of mobility in the neck. I have been declared unfit to drive forklift trucks. My employers took me back on 1 August 2022 as a warehouse clerk, which is a job I can manage, provided I do not have a serious headache. I get these about once a fortnight, and lesser headaches about three times a week. For about six months after the accident my sleep was regularly disturbed by headaches. I have been advised that I have a 10 per cent chance of suffering from post-traumatic epilepsy. From about six months after my accident I began to feel seriously depressed. I also found that I became very easily irritable and inconsiderate, whereas before the accident I had an easy-going, affable personality. Although I have had treatment for this condition, I feel, quite frankly, that it has been of little use. My temper has been a problem at work and I have got into trouble with the warehouse foreman. I am presently on a final warning and I am worried that I may soon lose my job.

As a forklift driver I took home £500 per week. My net earnings as a warehouse clerk are £350 per week. For 12 months after the accident, I received social security benefits of £100 per week and until I resumed work I then had £80 per week. My other losses are as follows. I am unable to do the home decorating and gardening, which I did before the accident. I estimate that this will cost me on average £1,200 per annum. During the first 12 months after my accident my sister-in-law, Mrs Watkins, came every weekday to look after me as my wife, who works as a canteen assistant, could not take time off without losing her job. I paid her £75 per week but, considering the amount of work she did, I would like to have paid her £200 per week and would wish to make a claim for the higher sum.

I am also told that my pension when I retire will be affected. At the age of 65, I would have received a pension (based on my employers' contributions) of £260 per week, but in view of my reduced earnings this is now likely to be only £225 per week, assuming I do not lose my job.

EXTRACT FROM MEDICAL REPORT of MR KENNETH BRAND, FRCS, of 100, HARLEY STREET, LONDON W1:

Mr Simms' injuries may therefore be summarised as comprising:

(a) Three-inch laceration of scalp over vertex, which has healed well with no noticeable scar.
(b) Head injury with concussion. There have been some complaints of nausea and dizziness. There is an increased risk of post-traumatic epilepsy in the order of 10 per cent. If Mr Simms is to suffer epilepsy, it could be anything up to ten years before this becomes apparent.
(c) Crush fracture of first cervical vertebra. Mr Simms has made a fair recovery from this injury, but will suffer permanently from occasional pain and aching in the neck, and from his present 20% limitation in movement.
(d) Depression, irritability. Mr Simms has been seen by Dr Bard, the eminent psychiatrist, but has not responded to treatment. Unfortunately, Dr Bard arranged for him to be admitted to the Clapham Hospital for the Mentally Ill for tests and observation, but Mr Simms was so distressed to see his fellow patients that he left immediately. The prognosis is uncertain, but there are reasonable grounds for expecting this aspect of his condition to improve over the next two to three years.
(e) There is no reduction in life expectancy, which remains about 20 years.

18.11 Richard Reshirn

Richard Reshirn was a quantity surveyor who suffered an accident on 1 November 2017. His date of birth was 20 October 1989. Counsel is asked to advise on quantum.

Richard Reshirn will say:

I lost consciousness and came to in the Clifton Royal Infirmary. I was wearing a hard hat and this probably saved my life. My spine was severely injured, however, and I am now a paraplegic, having paralysis of the lower limbs, bladder, and sexual function. I am confined to a wheelchair, with no hope of recovery. My life expectancy is reduced to about 15 years. I am prone to bladder infections, respiratory infections, and pressure sores.

After ten weeks in hospital I went to the Westport Rehabilitation Centre, where I was trained to cope as best I can with my physical difficulties, but I will always need some nursing assistance. This is at present provided by my wife Laura, who gave up her job on 1 March 2018 in order to be able to look after me. Her salary was £24,000 per annum net. However, she is feeling the strain and wants to resume her career. I will need about 35 hours of nursing care per week at a current cost of £15.00 per hour plus a home help at £75 per week.

Before my accident I was earning £50,000 gross, £35,000 net, and had excellent prospects of promotion in 2021. If I had been promoted, my salary would have been £45,000 per annum net. I had a secure job and was likely to have become a partner by the age of 40, when I could have expected substantially higher earnings, typically £80,000 per annum net. I am now unable to work except at home, because of the amount of care I need. I have been able to develop my artistic talents as an illustrator of children's books and have been earning about £15,000 per annum net from this work since November 2020.

We have no children. We had planned to have children very shortly after my accident, but this is now uncertain. It might be possible through artificial insemination, but I could not cope with looking after children, so we would either need a full-time nanny, or Laura would have to give up work. We would like to have children, but only if we can afford it. I am, however, very distressed by the thought that I will not live to see them grown up.

As a result of my accident we had to sell our three-bedroomed flat, which was on the second floor of a block, for £300,000 and buy a house so that I could live on the ground floor. This is at present a small, terraced house which we bought as a temporary measure for £250,000, but it is unsuitable in the long term, especially if we have a family. We will need to buy a three-bedroomed house with downstairs accommodation for me. This is likely to cost £450,000, and a further £50,000 in special adaptation for my needs.

18.12 Albert Corey, deceased

Albert Corey died on 17 October 2019, leaving a widow, Barbara, and two children. Albert was a fitter earning £400 net at the date of his death, with additional regular overtime. Albert consistently kept 25 per cent of his take-home pay and 65 per cent of his overtime for himself; the rest he gave to Barbara, who spent it on running the household, keeping the family, and paying rent and rates. Nothing was saved. Of the money Albert gave Barbara, 12 per cent was consistently spent by Barbara on Albert's upkeep, the rest on herself and the children, and on expenditure for the family as a whole, which has not diminished since Albert's death. Of the money Albert kept for himself, 5 per cent was consistently spent on gifts and entertainments for Barbara and the children.

Before Albert's death, Barbara worked full-time earning £350 per week net, but since his death she has had to give up full-time work so as to look after the children. She quit her job on 1 November 2019 and took up part-time work from that date initially earning £200 per week net, rising to £210 per week net on 1 September 2020, and £220 on 1 September 2021. Her salary in full-time work would have risen to £370 per week net on 1 January 2020, £385 per week net on 1 January 2021, and £395 per week net on 1 January 2022. Had Albert not died, his earnings would have risen to £425 per week net on 1 March 2020, £440 per week net on 1 March 2021, and £460 per week net on 1 March 2022. Overtime opportunities at Albert's place of work are spread evenly and fitters of Albert's seniority earned an average of £200 per month net in 2019, £215 per month net in 2020, £220 per month net in 2021, and so far in 2022, £230 per month net.

Albert used to do DIY work and repair work around the home. Barbara has so far spent £900 on workmen's bills for work Albert would have done and has done no redecoration or home improvement, some of which is now urgent and will cost £1,200. Barbara has spent more on babysitting since Albert's death: an extra £25.00 per week.

What is the total financial loss suffered by Barbara and the children in consequence of Albert's death as at 1 September 2022?

18.13 David Morgan, deceased

Counsel is instructed by Bruce & Bruce of 14a High Street, Tisborough, Northamptonshire. Your instructing solicitors are instructed by Mrs Annette Morgan, who is looking after her two grandchildren following the deaths of Mr and Mrs David Morgan. Mrs Annette Morgan has taken out letters of administration of the estates of both her son and daughter-in-law and wishes to pursue a claim on behalf of her grandchildren. Your instructing solicitors have been negotiating with the insurers of Manorborn Builders Ltd, who have indicated that they might be prepared to pay £200,000, if this is acceptable.

Would counsel please advise on quantum and in the light of that advice state whether an offer of £200,000 should be accepted.

Arnold Manor will say:

I am the managing director of Manorborn Builders Limited.

Mr Morgan was a good workman who had been with the company for many years. He had a basic pay which after deductions amounted to £21,060 per annum, and in addition he would earn overtime money during the summer months when we were busy. On average, I would expect him to work overtime on about 20 weeks of the year. He would then be given approximately £156 in cash for a week's overtime.

Annette Morgan will say:

I am the mother of David Morgan. His father died in 2018. David was born on 14 September 1994 and followed his father into the building trade, although he did so well at school, I always thought he could have done better. In June 2015, he married Daisy Johnson and they had two children: Maxine who was born on 2 May 2016, and Marcus, born on 5 September 2018. They lived in 'The Willows', which David was buying on an endowment mortgage costing £546 a month. When he died, the insurance company paid off the mortgage. David was killed at work on 5 September 2021. The funeral was on 12 September 2021 and cost £2,100, paid for by Daisy.

Unfortunately, only three weeks after David's death, Daisy had a fatal car accident. It was entirely her fault. I then moved into 'The Willows' to look after the children. I was born in 1974 and am very fit so I expect that I shall be able to look after them through school and, if appropriate, college. I have been asked about the family's living expenses before David's death. Fortunately, Daisy was a very methodical person. She kept an account of all the family's expenditure. Her books show that over the year before David died the family spent on average £120 per week on food and drink, £99 per week on council tax, gas, electricity, and general household items, £39 per week on clothing, and £69 per week on the car (which was written off in Daisy's fatal crash), travel, and entertainment. In addition, each week David put aside £20 for each of the children into an endowment policy, which would be payable when they reached the age of 18. My impression was that David spent very little on himself, not more than £65 per week in addition to the above. And if any job needed doing in the house, he would do it.

Daisy did not work after she married David, though I think she wanted to go back to her job as a solicitor's clerk when Marcus went to school in September. I enjoy looking after the children. They are very cheerful souls, but I find it difficult to manage financially. Since Daisy died, I find that it costs me about £4,900 a year to pay all the outgoings on 'The Willows', including the gas, electricity, maintenance, and so on, and the children cost at least £2,275 per annum each to feed, clothe, and take on holiday. The jobs around the home which David used to do are costing me about £975 a year. Also, as a special gift, I continue the £20 per week endowment policies which David started.

18.14 Susanna and Emma Williams, deceased

Counsel has herewith: Statement of Michael Morley.

Counsel is instructed by Gatwicks on behalf of Mr Michael Morley, the executor of the estate of his late cohabitee, Susanna Williams, who died in a tragic accident on 6 February 2020, together with their daughter, Emma. Probate of Miss Williams's estate was granted to Mr Morley out of the Brighton District Probate Registry on 28 July 2020.

Counsel is requested to advise whether it would be worthwhile bringing proceedings in respect of Emma Williams' death and on quantum.

Michael Morley of 18 Carlton Terrace, London SW1 will say:

I was born on 21 November 1992 and have since 2016 been living with Susanna Williams at the above address. We considered ourselves to have a stable relationship, but we never married. We had two children: Mark, who was born on 3 March 2015, and Emma, who was born on 12 October 2021. I am presently unemployed, having been made redundant from my job as an investment analyst at the Biological Bank on 1 November 2021.

I had been earning £195,000 per annum. I was given a severance payment of £78,000 and since then I have been unable to find a job and have had no income.

Susanna Williams was born on 14 October 1992. Throughout our relationship she worked as a commodity broker for Bowyers, Pierce, and Green. At the time of her death her remuneration package was a basic salary of £156,000 per annum plus annual bonus, which on 1 January 2022 had been £39,000. This financial year her net income would have been about £117,000 net of tax and national insurance. She had a company car, and her employers also paid her private medical insurance (BUPA) subscription of £1,300 per annum, permanent health insurance premium of £2,600 per annum, fitness club subscription of £1,300 per annum, and car running expenses up to £1,300 per annum. Our children were looked after by a full-time, live-in nanny whom we paid £250 per week plus board and lodging.

Since the tragedy, I have felt unable to continue looking for work and I now look after my son, Mark. Had Susanna lived, I expect I would have found a job by now at a salary of about £52,000 net, but at present I am just not interested in working. The nanny has left, and I have not replaced her. Susanna and I paid all our earnings when we were both working into a joint account out of which we paid all our expenses. The primary expense was our mortgages. We each had a mortgage with interest payments of £1,950 per month. Our other expenses included council tax of £1,950 each, electricity, gas, and water at about £1,950 per annum, and entertainment expenses of about £2,600 per month. Susanna dressed well and I would estimate that she spent about £9,750 per annum on clothes and accessories. Our holidays and out-of-town breaks cost about £9,750 each year.

I now go out very little, though I have bought a car to replace the car which Susanna had as part of her remuneration package. It cost me £16,000. Mark will start at St Michael's Preparatory School, Belgravia, this term. The fees are £2,600 per term and would have been paid by Susanna had she lived. I receive £19,500 per quarter from an insurance policy which Susanna took out before her death, and will continue to receive this until October 2052, when Susanna would have been 60 years old. Susanna and Emma are buried in the graveyard of their home village near Brighton. The funerals cost me £7,500 and £4,000, respectively, and I am erecting an ornamental marble tombstone suitable for a woman of Susanna's achievements at a cost of £8,275.

INDEX